Human Operators

Human Operators:
A Critical Oral History on Technology in Libraries and Archives

Edited by Melissa Morrone

Library Juice Press
Sacramento, CA

Copyright respective authors, 2017
Published by Library Juice Press in 2018

Library Juice Press
PO Box 188784
Sacramento, CA 95818

http://libraryjuicepress.com

This book is printed on acid-free paper.

Indexed by Violet Fox

Cover design by Melissa Morrone

   Cover image based on:

      The Miriam and Ira D. Wallach Division of Art, Prints and Photographs: Photography Collection, The New York Public Library. "Union Square, 14th Street and Broadway, Manhattan." New York Public Library Digital Collections.

      http://digitalcollections.nypl.org/items/510d47d9-4ef6-a3d9-e040-e00a18064a99

   Back cover image based on:

      Lionel Pincus and Princess Firyal Map Division, The New York Public Library. "Guide map to the Brooklyn and Queens parks." New York Public Library Digital Collections.

      http://digitalcollections.nypl.org/items/def19490-d2b3-012f-7e6a-58d385a7bbd0

Library of Congress Cataloging-in-Publication Data

Names: Morrone, Melissa, author.
Title: Human operators : a critical oral history on technology in libraries and archives / Melissa Morrone.
Description: Sacramento CA : Library Juice Press, 2017. | Includes bibliographical references and index.
Identifiers: LCCN 2017042561 | ISBN 9781634000321 (alk. paper)
Subjects: LCSH: Librarians--Effect of technological innovations on. | Archivists--Effect of technological innovations on. | Libraries--Information technology. | Librarians--United States--Interviews. | LCGFT: Oral histories.
Classification: LCC Z682.35.T43 M67 2017 | DDC 027.00285--dc23
LC record available at https://lccn.loc.gov/2017042561

Contents

Acknowledgments **vii**
Before **1**
Learning **11**
Connecting **99**
Building **147**
Collecting **179**
Accessing **253**
Being **303**
After **363**
People **365**
Works **377**
Index **383**

Acknowledgments

Thank you to all of the people who took their time to make this book happen, starting, of course, with the participants. Special thanks to Jenna Freedman, Jen Hoyer, and Ronica Mukerjee for encouragement and advice along the way. Thank you, Bonnie Gordon, for the Ruby code. Jing Si Feng, Abigail Miller, and, in particular, Bill Mazza offered crucial design guidance. I also want to recognize my many inspiring colleagues at Brooklyn Public Library, especially the smart, supportive, and well-dressed Info Commons team. Finally, boundless love and appreciation to my wonderful family and friends and to the various amazing communities of which I'm grateful to be a part, and without whose events, gatherings, and meetings I would have finished this book much more quickly.

Before

Back in 1984 when I was nine and we had a computer in the classroom, I was more the kid who was afraid of "breaking it" by pushing a power button than the one who was excited about programming a message to display in blinking asterisks on the screen. Since then my relationship with plugged-in technology has proceeded along a path of modest involvement—never a tinkerer, sure, but a fairly savvy end user, a tech translator at work, and an increasingly curious user of the early twenty-first century Internet. After the book that I edited and published, also through Library Juice Press, *Informed Agitation: Library and Information Skills in Social Justice Movements and Beyond*, came out a few years ago, I realized that none of the essays dealt with digital technology per se. This book is meant to fill that gap. And rather than putting together another collection of essays, I decided to do an "oral history" that would actually give voice to people on a whole spectrum of topics.

The content of this book naturally reflects my own partialities—such as a fascination with digital literacy and people's personal learning environments, an interest in free and open source software, and a desire to think through (and combat) oppressive systems including white supremacy and capitalism. Throughout, I tried to keep in mind a broad definition of "technology" and get people talking about how we humans build, control, encounter, use, and feel about it. During the interviews, I asked about the most useful pieces of technology for the participants and for their libraries' users; the overlooked aspects of technology in libraries and archives that they *wished* people were discussing; and the digital privacy and surveillance implications they saw in their work. I asked about articles and books they had written, professional activities they were known for, and projects they had been involved with. (In some cases, people's jobs have changed since the time of their interviews, and the text may preserve their then-current situation.) Usually towards the end of the interview I would invite them to talk about how they see or experience big structural oppressions and power dynamics as they affect actual people, both users and workers, through a lens of technology—race, gender, class, age or generational issues, issues related to ability, and even environmental and ecological issues—although almost invariably, at least a few of those would have already come up in the conversation.

I connected with the people in this book in a few different ways. There was a "call for participation" posted on Library Juice Press's website and over social media and email lists, including ALA's Social Responsibilities Round Table (SRRT) and the Library and Information Technology Association (LITA). A friend who had gone through the Spectrum Scholarship Program for library school students of color got the CFP forwarded to that list as well (thank you, Arpita Bose). I reached out to people I didn't know but admired from afar, and I asked friends and colleagues for recommendations. Some participants I know IRL and are in this book because I pinged them or they saw the CFP, including Jessa Lingel, Carmel Curtis, Celeste Â-Re, Elaine Harger, Jaime Taylor, and all the Interference Archive folks. I am a New Yorker but I tried hard not to make this book too New Yorky. Participants live all over the US, and there's also a tiny bit of international perspective—from Canada, Lebanon, and New Zealand. It should be obvious that this book is very much about US librarianship and archiving, and any similar project meant to shed light on these practices around the world would need to be seriously intentional about going about such a large task.

In almost all cases, interviews were conducted over Skype. I used Ecamm Call Recorder to make an audiorecording of the interviews, which I later transcribed with the help of the free version of InqScribe (thanks to a recommendation by Neil Shibata, who does the *Democracy Now!* transcripts). The interview with six Interference Archive collective members past and present took place in a public meeting room in my library. Five people were there in person, with Molly Fair joining in from her home in Virginia via Skype, and we passed around a Zoom recorder. Due to technical difficulties, John Helling's interview was conducted over email (I sent him a set of questions and he sent me back full written responses). Unrelated technical difficulties resulted in my interview with Michael Gorman taking place over two mornings a week apart.

Interviews were done from July 2016 through March 2017, with the majority taking place that summer and fall. People spoke to me from their office, their home, and, in at least one case, their (parked) car. They talked to me just before they had to catch a bus to work or back home, while they were comforting their child, as they were saying goodbye to their partner, sitting on the couch in their living room at the end of the day, between meetings, before they could make dinner after work. For my part, I was always at home at my desk, either before or after work or on a day off, and typically I was not wearing pants. Special thanks to Jessa Lingel for being the first interview, before I discovered that if I muted myself, the recording of the other person would sound a hundred times better, and before I learned that I needed to type out all of my questions in advance because it's really hard to go in with vague ideas and formulate the questions on the spot in an awkward artificial setting like a Skype interview.

Audio interviews averaged around an hour long, and what you are about to read represents only a portion of what each person said. All interviewees eventually received an audio file of their interview along with my transcript and had the opportunity to clarify points, strike out sections, and/or write in additional thoughts. Some people chose not to change anything, many made light edits, and a few did substantial rewriting. My role as editor has been to massage all the interviews into clear, conversational written English while retaining the meaning and tone of whatever participants had originally stated. While the selections are edited and in some cases elided, I have not included ellipses, brackets, or any other indicators of editing. However, I never drastically pushed around disparate parts of people's interviews into one passage. The number of "I think"s that I removed from the transcripts is incalculable; one of the endearing things about reflective people is their hesitance to come off like they're stating a universal truth, but for readability I made several thoughts stand as fact-based pronouncements. Parentheses are generally from people when they gave me written answers or transcript edits. Em dashes are mine, all mine.

Finally, I pulled together excerpts of multiple interviews where people happened to be addressing the same topic, so the rest of this book looks something like transcripts of conversations around a theme. Of course, with the exception of the Interference Archive group interview, the conversation was solely between the participant and me, and nobody was actually building on or responding to anything anyone else said. As with, say, organizing a library of books, part of making *Human Operators* involved the struggle to decide where segments of interviews should go when they addressed multiple topics but could be located in only one place. Unlike with a book collection, I couldn't assign multiple descriptors to the interview passages. So here they all are, laid out in a necessarily imperfect order of my choosing.

One question I asked everyone, at least to help put them in the mindset of the interview and just get them talking, was how they would define technology and what it meant to them. That's where we'll begin.

* * *

CECILY WALKER: I think of technology as sort of a medium. I don't necessarily think of it as a means to an end. I think it's just a way, when we're talking about electronic technologies or digital technologies or—the term that seems to have fallen out of favor in the library world now—when we're thinking about "emerging" technologies, I think these technologies not only make it easier for people to connect with one another; it doesn't level the playing field, exactly, but it just makes it so that anyone who has access to these particular tools or these particular channels—provided that they have the knowledge and/or training to make use of these tools—can carry out reaching out to other people, building communities, and just staying in contact and consuming the information that's the most relevant to them, or things that are of interest to them.

ZACHARY LOEB: I think it's really important, when you say "technology," to try to make it clear what you mean by it, and when you're talking to other people about technology it's important to try to ferret out what they mean by "technology." To give you kind of a quippish example of this, eyeglasses are technology, and so is Google Glass. And you can say that Google Glass is bad, and that doesn't mean that you also think that eyeglasses are bad. You can have problems with particular pieces of technology in particular contexts, while thinking that other pieces of technology are fine in that context, and also thinking that there are pieces of technology that are fine in some contexts and not fine in others. There's a historian of technology named Leo Marx, who once famously said that technology is "a hazardous concept," and I think that he was really right on there.

JAIME TAYLOR: If we're going to be saying things in a way that actually convey meaning to other people, when we talk about technology in libraries, we're mostly talking about computers, and mostly the Internet. But your desk phone is technology. The copy machine is technology. But that's not what we're talking about. When we're having these conversations, we're talking about computers and the Internet and coding and things like that. But as Zachary points out a lot and probably did to you, a book is a technology, and it's a really good one. It passes a lot of those tests that we talk about on LibrarianShipwreck a lot, what happens when you hit your technology with a rock? Your smartphone is smashed to bit and useless. Your book is still perfectly readable. Those questions about technology don't get asked, because we do mostly mean computers and the Internet and coding.

SARAH HOUGHTON: How I would define technology depends on who I'm talking to. If I'm talking to my boss, a city manager, or a city council member, I think I'd be very broad in my definition, because so much of what we do has some form of reliance on technology. The old definition used to be "anything with a plug." I remember people saying that all the time in the '90s. Now you can't say that. That's not accurate. Technology—it could be software, it could be hardware, it could be something that's solar-powered and it doesn't have a plug. Is a musical instrument technology? I would argue it is. In our library, it's a smaller system with two locations. We don't really have a dedicated technology budget or a technology staff person, so technology is just integrated into the work of every single staff member of every single unit. It's not really separated out as this other thing like it used to be.

MICHAEL GORMAN: My view of technology is quite simple—it is extraordinarily useful when it is a tool enabling libraries and librarians to carry out the basic function of enabling interaction with the human record in all its forms. When it goes beyond being a tool and becomes an end in itself, or something that facilitates activities which have little or nothing to do with the human record, then it loses me. Look at the early days of ISAD—the Information Science and Documentation division of the American Library Association, later the Library Information Technology Association. Documentation was a movement using technology in order to organize documents, principally the kind of things you find in special libraries, reports, and all that kind of stuff. It then mutated into library and information technology—in other words, much broader than the documentation discipline in much the same way as documentation mutated into "information science."

The activities within LITA used to deal with online catalogs, online integrated systems, digitization for the preservation of parts of the human record, etc. That gradually gave way to two preoccupations that do not seem to me to be particularly relevant to the role of the librarian. One is the actual nuts and bolts of computer science. There's nothing wrong with computer science, but I would prefer to listen to a computer scientist on the matter than a librarian who knows something about computer science. The other is technological activities which have nothing to do with the human record. I'm thinking now of things like what they call makerspaces and so on. None of these activities are malign or negative in themselves, but I just don't know what they have to do with the basic purpose of libraries.

JASON GRIFFEY: One of the things I sometimes talk about is that one of the universals for technology is that humans have always been afraid of it. There's a great story in Plato where he's bemoaning the fact that youths learning to write is going to destroy the democracy of Greece, because when you write things you no longer have to remember them, and we're going to destroy memory and no one will ever know the great oral poems of Greece anymore, and we're going to destroy the youth by letting them learn how to write and not making them memorize things. And that story of the bemoaning of new technologies has continued through history at every step. We had everything from bemoaning that radio is going to destroy live music, recorded music was going to destroy the fact that people listen to music, the movie theaters were dens of iniquity and terrible places, the telephone was going to be the end of Western civilization—every time we have any kind of new technology, from literally writing all the way up through the modern Internet, there's the moral panic and the "oh my gosh, kids, this is going to destroy our world." And that's never true. We always survive and come out, and we find amazing uses for the stuff. It's a cycle that just keeps repeating over and over and over. Somehow our culture hasn't learned from its history yet.

I think my favorite quote on that particular kind of event is from Douglas Adams, the author of *The Hitchhiker's Guide to the*

Galaxy, who said—and I'll paraphrase—"Anything that's invented between when you're twelve and twenty-five is exciting and interesting, and you can probably get a career in it. Anything that's invented before you're born is just natural and part of the way the world works and is just kind of the world. And anything that's invented after you're thirty-five is the end of the universe and terrible and should be stopped." I think libraries have some of that still in them; there's still that new technology fear. But I think it's getting better than it has been in the past.

ZACHARY LOEB: I think that libraries and librarians are often accused of being kind of backwards thinking, technologically, and I think that libraries and librarians are often accused of being harbors of technophobic killjoys or a terrible Luddism that's lurking around the corners. One thing I want to make very clear is that my experience in libraries has really not been that way at all. Frankly, I wish that libraries were a site of more critical resistance to technology. I think that a lot of libraries are really at the cutting edge of a lot technological change. I think that there are a lot of libraries and librarians that are extremely interested in the newest technologies and the newest technological changes. And I also would just say that I think that sometimes libraries and librarians seem to be so scared of being accused of being technophobic that they rush in the opposite direction.

SARAH HOUGHTON: Having been a librarian for fifteen years, and the first two thirds of that being technology-focused, when I look back to what technology was like, what it felt like, what it looked like, what the scope of it was when I started versus now—it's tremendous how fast everything has changed. That's a product of the consumer market changing as quickly as it has. I think the challenge for us in libraries has been to keep up with that radical pace of change in web services, hardware, software, what's popular, platforms, OSs, the device continuum, all of it.

And while I'm occasionally frustrated by some libraries' or library staff's pace of ability to accept change or to move forward, if I really do an honest assessment of how far all of us have come in fifteen years in terms of the types of things we can do now that we couldn't do then, I'm pretty amazed that we've managed to keep pace with the few resources we have and that we've been able to provide the level of service to our users that we have along the way, without losing our minds. I think that's pretty admirable, and personally—just as a human being outside my role as a librarian or anything—as a human being I'm so excited to see what happens next. I would love to flash forward to the day before I die to just see what that world looks like, because every day I'm seeing something that makes me feel like I'm living in the future. New technologies are coming about that just seem so out of this world to me and something that I could not have imagined twenty years ago.

So to me the future is so exciting, and I can't even imagine what's going to come next. I can't because things are happening so quickly and so rapidly that I don't think my brain can quite keep pace anymore. It used to be able to, but not anymore. I am positive about the future for technology and society in general. I think the sticky points to just be aware of and mindful of are those core ethics that libraries have tried to uphold from day one—privacy, open access to information, censorship. I think those are things that we need to pay attention to and lobby for and be at the table where there are discussions happening. I think if we just say, "Oh, yay, technology's on a great path, we don't have to pay attention anymore," that's false, but I do think that people are at this point more aware of those potential barriers and problems than used to be, and that gives me hope.

ZACHARY LOEB: One of the things that really inspired me to become a librarian was a line from Ivan Illich—"At its best, the library is the prototype of the convivial tool." I've always been really interested in the library as a kind of as a tool, as a technological system in and of itself. I think that libraries represent a really interesting and important different model of ownership, and a different way of using technology, of controlling technology, of bringing together technology. Because if you're really concerned about stuff like the waste that flows from technological products that are discarded, then libraries can serve as a really wonderful example of, what if instead of everybody in the community having their own computer—most of which are not used at all times—have a library where the community has multiple computers that are available to everybody? So then instead of everybody having to have one, you have a site where everybody can come together to use them.

I'm really interested in thinking about libraries and thinking about technology in terms of different and better ways that they could be used. One of the reasons that I'm interested in looking at libraries in terms of technology really is because I think they can serve as a model for a different way of reorganizing technological usage in society. But I'm always mindful that Illich's quote starts with the words "at its best." There are a lot of libraries that are not at their best, and there are a lot of libraries that aren't interested in going in these directions, and it's not really my place to say that libraries should.

I think that technologies as well as libraries embody certain values and certain ideas. The risky thing is that when various systems of value encounter each other sometimes one subsumes the other. My concern is that the values of libraries are often subsumed under technological values that are kind of antithetical to at least what I think are some of the core values of librarianship. But I think that libraries can be a really wonderful real-world model of what a different—more just, more equitable—world could look like. That's not to say that libraries are perfect but, to paraphrase Lewis Mumford, utopian ideas aren't destinations; they're compasses and we use them to help us navigate our course. I think that libraries, at their best, are shot through with some utopian values, and I think that we should hold fast to those.

```
related_subjects = []
related_subjects.push("computer labs")
related_subjects.push("the Mousing Around tutorial")
related_subjects.push("surveillance cameras")
related_subjects.push("digital portfolios")
related_subjects.push("Teen Tech Camp")
related_subjects.push("The National Inquirer")
related_subjects.push("the '90s")
related_subjects.push("apprenticeships")
related_subjects.push("team values")
related_subjects.push("Mashcat")
related_subjects.push("FOIA")
related_subjects.push("DuckDuckGo")
related_subjects.push("killjoys")
related_subjects.push("'the Change Monster'")
related_subjects.push("Excel")
```

Learning

Libraries are educational institutions, in addition to all of the other purposes—cultural, recreational, etc.—they serve. This first chapter highlights libraries as educational venues, and librarians and archivists as educators as well as lifelong students. I asked people about the ways that library patrons have learned to use digital technologies from staff over the last twenty years or so, whether in group classes or one-on-one at the reference desk. Digital privacy literacy is a large subset of public instruction these days, and people talked about privacy education in classes, at the reference desk, in the digital media lab, and in the schools. Librarians who work with youth explained the concept of "digital citizenship" and how they try to teach digital rights and responsibilities to their students. Information literacy and media literacy in particular, including practical program ideas, were also discussed.

I wanted to know about people's own history and learning environments, too. I asked about ideal library school curricula—for example, should everyone be taught "to code"?—and how they feel technology is best taught to librarians and archivists in graduate school as well as when they've been on the job for decades already. Among the topics that came up were conducting in-house staff trainings; learning about networks, filter bubbles, and other Internet issues; and mitigating uncritical technophilia. People shared which technologies are most useful to them in their work, and why. Finally, I asked people whose work they follow, whether that's mainstream professional channels, a colleague who has a blog or Twitter account, a library or a project that's making impressive achievements, or a thinker from any field who's been influential to them.

. . .

ZACHARY LOEB: Libraries really have a responsibility to be critical in thinking of new technology. Now, "critical" does not mean "opposing" or "rejecting," but I do think it means being critical, being seriously critical. Really considering what new technologies mean to the library. As libraries are trying to figure out how to make do with less and less money, I think that really thinking critically about technology provides them with a way of saying, is investing in this technology really going to be worth the investment of money over time that we're going to have to make in it? I think that those are questions that should be asked. I think that many libraries are asking them. I also think a lot of libraries unfortunately aren't.

When you find yourself in a society where engaging in criticism of technology gets you derided as a technophobic killjoy, I think that that says very clearly that those are the types of opinions that really need to be explored more because there the opinions that are often being frozen out. When every force in society is saying "spend more time online," maybe that's a really good time to step back and ask, "why?" Ultimately I don't think that calling somebody a "Luddite" is an argument; it's just meant as an insult. Oftentimes I find that when people hurl comments like that, it's kind of a defensive move. Whenever somebody calls somebody else a Luddite, they're really saying much more about themselves than they're actually saying about the person they just called a Luddite. And I think that one of the best and most important things that libraries do is to give people the tools to help them think. If libraries can help give people the tools to think critically about technology, I think that would be a wonderful thing.

JESSAMYN WEST: Now we're in a position where over 95 percent of Americans have some access to a free computer with free Internet at the library or school in their area. But what happened is the playing field has shifted, and so even if you have access to those things, we're seeing what I call the empowerment divide, or the inclusion divide. Okay, you've got access to this technology, but if you didn't grow up in a world with tech literacy, if you didn't have a community of tech-literate people, or if your friends aren't very tech-literate, you're not going to really know what to do with that. You're in a situation where maybe all you know about technology is what you read in the paper, which is of course completely threatened by the Internet taking away their jobs or whatever the heck the deal is. As a result, a lot of what you read about technology and the Internet in the newspaper is all kind of oogie-boogie, like, "Someone's going to steal your identity! Someone's going to steal your children! There's viruses! Everything's dangerous!" And those people are maybe not fully engaged. They don't feel included. They don't feel like the online world includes them or is for them. They're like, "Oh, it's for younger people, smarter people. Not people like me."

You look at the numbers, and you see who the people who are not online are. And you find that they're the same people who are dis-included in all sorts of other ways, right? They're poor people, they're people who don't have English as a first language, they're people of color, they're older people, they're people with disabilities. Often they're people with a combination of those things. People look at who's online and who's not online, and they look at getting online as a choice. Just a choice, like, a free choice—"do whatever you want!" But then you notice that the people who are "choosing" to not be online are the same people who are disenfranchised from every other part of our society, subtly, in some cases, and not so subtly in others. Suddenly you realize that there is an inclusion/empowerment aspect.

So part of what digital literacy education for me now is about helping people find their spot with technology. Because I'm the last person who's like, "Everybody's got to be on Twitter! What are you, an idiot?" If Twitter doesn't solve a problem for you, fine. But it's important to understand what the world of online options is like, because maybe it would solve a problem for a digitally divided person who was hesitant or uncertain or who felt that the Internet was all a bunch of nerdy white people in their late twenties complaining about their breakfast. Realistically speaking, it's so much more than that, but you have to climb over those people to find your people.

A lot of what I do in my drop-in time, and a lot of what I did with email support for Open Library when I worked there, is explaining to people, you're doing okay. It's not surprising that you're having trouble with this website. Maybe they had to apply for a job and they had to go use this jobs website. I'm a professional, and that's actually a bad website. It's surprising how far you can get just telling someone they're not wrong. This is my line; I'm like, "You're not a bad person. This is a bad website." Because people feel like when they can't do a thing, and they feel like they read in the paper, or they hear from younger people, "Everything's intuitive," they feel dumb because it's not intuitive for them, for various reasons. Because they live in digitally divided communities, they don't have anybody to tell them, "No, you're doing okay." And so a lot of tech literacy in my mind now is working on the empowerment divide, working on the inclusion divide, and helping people find their place wherever their place is so that you're not reinforcing all of the other ways in which people with hurdles get dis-included from society and society makes it like it's their problem to solve, when in point of fact honestly I think it's society's problem to solve.

ALISON MACRINA: Librarians are some of the only people who I know who have a good grasp on what real rates of digital literacy are like. I know that most of our experience is anecdotal, but we have a tremendous amount of anecdotal experience. And what that experience tells me and my colleagues is that most people don't know much of anything about using their computers. They know precisely the things that they've had to learn for precisely the tasks that they needed to get done, but anything that deviates from that is a total black box. They don't know anything about how their computer functions. They don't know even a few lines of a programming language or how to open a terminal and look at what's happening behind the scenes.

And this is because we don't have any meaningful computer education. The only free computer classes you can take are usually at the library, and—because libraries are so understaffed and underresourced—most of those classes are Microsoft Word or Excel, really basic stuff, or maybe things related to job-seeking. But there's nothing about how your computer works and how you can get the most out of it, or how you can troubleshoot if things go wrong, or anything like that.

I think digital literacy is overall pretty abysmal. The gulf between people who are self-professed technical people and people who are not is massive, and part of the problem with this that the people who are building the technology don't really understand how big that gulf is. I think they think that the people they're designing for may be two steps below where they are, when really they're like two hundred thousand steps.

CAROL BEAN: In 2000, libraries did not seem to be focused on older adults and computers and, you know, that was a mystery to me. By the mid-aughts, the library community was aware there was a big community of older adults that were trying to learn computers and use our resources. But in the early aughts, when I came on the scene and said, "So where's the relevant literature?" and it wasn't there, I think there's a couple reasons. First of all, in the mid-aughts, I got people that were digital refugees. Digital refugees are people that hid from the digital revolution. They said, "No, it's a passing fad, I'm not going to waste my time." You had a lot of that in the '90s. So I don't think there were as many older adults that were actually going to libraries.

As it got to 2000, things really were moving onto the Web in a big, big way. Not only adults but children now had email addresses, and there was AOL chat—I used to, in 1996, 1997, 1998, do AOL chat with my son who was in California rather than phone calls because we couldn't afford the calls; it was still costly for long distance. But all of this electronic communication was available, and kids were doing it, and grandparents were feeling left out. So the whole environment outside them was pushing them towards getting on computers and on the Web. Communicating with their grandkids was increasingly only via computers because they weren't writing letters. So I think we started seeing a bigger influx in the late '90s and into about the mid-2000s.

But also it was a difficult move for libraries to even get computers. That's why the Gates Foundation said, "Look, we'll come put the computers in there for you." I think it was trying to be a boot in the pants—"Here. Get started. Get moving. This is important." A lot of people—and I was probably one of them—said, "They're just trying to sell Microsoft computers." But no, I think Gates saw, "Wait a minute. This is the future, and we need to enable it, and the libraries are great places to do that."

So you get computers, but there weren't a lot of human resources available to show people what to do with these computers. There was a lag there, and part of it had to do with the fact that library schools were not focusing on the technology side at all. I started library school in '97 and graduated in '98 because I was able to go full-time, and there was one or two technology classes there. That was it. If you wanted to learn about systems, you had to go learn it on your own. Which I did, I learned a lot of it on my own. But the library schools had not caught on and were not putting graduates out there that had the capability or the knowledge. The new graduates were just as clueless as the people that had been around there for years. Yeah, they knew how to use a cataloging system on a computer because it was a one-program computer, and catalogers had used it, but the reference people didn't necessarily have to use it. So the influx of the computers was facilitated and given a big boost by the Gates Foundation, but there wasn't a concomitant commitment by library schools and even by libraries to figure out, "Okay, how are we going to teach anybody to use this?" And then resources were going online, so you start paying for these online databases but nobody's using them because your clientele doesn't know how to use computers—well, wait a minute. We've got these computers. Why aren't they using them?

Librarians probably started teaching computer classes in the late '90s, because I did see some literature on teaching Internet and things in public libraries. So it was around, but it just wasn't moving forward very fast, and I think it was a major shift that libraries weren't really focusing on. Like everybody else in their forties and older, librarians were saying, "Oh, it's going to pass, it's going to pass, it's going to pass." They really weren't grabbing this, and the library schools themselves mostly weren't giving their students the technology skills they needed to go out and face this brave new world.

Sarah Houghton: Thinking about my early days working for the Marin County Free Library when part of my role was as a technology trainer, I would teach the staff how to teach the public how to use very basic things like Yahoo! email or AOL Instant Messenger. Very basic technology literacy—how to send an email, how to attach something. Instant messaging was super new still when I started. A lot of it was a train-the-trainer model in a system like that.

Moving into teaching digital literacy in a bigger system like San Jose when I worked there, that was much broader, where it was a train-the-trainers who trained the trainers who trained the people. A much more distributed system. At that point—that was in the mid- to late 2000s—that's when really you were starting to see people talk about digital literacy as a thing. Or "transliteracy," as it was called for a while, but I never really liked that because it didn't really speak to what we were talking about. I think that at that point we had more classes being offered for the public about protecting your privacy and how to have security and safety protocols on your machines, whether it was a desktop or laptop computer, a smartphone. How to use a digital camera. And those were things that quite often the staff would have to learn first because they weren't familiar with it even yet.

CAROL BEAN: Back in the early 2000s, I was hired as a computer center manager to basically teach people to use computer resources. I was at the first computer lab for classes that they set up out at a major regional branch, and I was pretty much like everybody else—"Okay, come on in! We'll teach you how to do this stuff." And I followed all of the rubrics. I had come from a law library, so I was used to teaching people who pretty much knew how to get on the Web and use Westlaw and Lexis. I had not really encountered somebody who did not know what a mouse is. And these were the types of people we were getting. They would come in to classes and spend the first half of the class basically trying to manipulate the mouse, and I was like, this isn't working. Even the ones that knew how to use a mouse and could kind of work their way through a computer screen, they weren't following everything. They seemed to be either not getting it, or they would forget it. They would come back the next week for the same class, and it was as if they hadn't learned anything. We couldn't get beyond just teaching them how to use basic Windows, which was frustrating and it wasn't achieving our goal of getting them onto the Web and showing them the databases they had access to.

So I of course doubled down, went back and searched all the library literature, and all of it said the same thing—"This is how you teach computer classes. This is how you teach technology." It just wasn't working. And I searched pretty far and wide. I actually found a couple theses and dissertations that I was able to get my hands on and read through, which was kind of interesting. But it was so sparse. It was just like, the common knowledge is that you go in public libraries and teach the same way that you teach in a community college. You know, those are adult learners. We teach these adults in the public library the same way. Well, that really wasn't working, because our demographic was primarily people over fifty-five or sixty who had not touched a computer or had had a few lessons with their children or grandchildren or nephew or something.

I actually went to the PubMed databases, and lo and behold there was a whole body of scientific research specifically on human-computer interaction. So I got everything I could. I read it, absorbed it all. And what I was reading made a lot of sense. They basically were saying, no, because of the cognitive declines, because of the physical declines, and so on—it basically laid out all of the things, in scientific detail, that I was seeing in actual physical events. So, was there stuff out about how they handled this? Well, yes, there was. They've actually been researching teaching computers to people for a long time; it's just that the library community had never come across this literature. Nobody thought to examine it and think, oh yeah, we're putting computers in libraries, and people that haven't been on computers with some of these aging issues might actually come into the library, and we would want to include them.

I published a summary of my research, and about that same time, I think it was 2004, there was an international conference at St John's University in New York City on e-literacy. What that meant was, I wasn't the only one noticing this. So I went there, and I presented my story. I actually had collected data and had a case study. It was really interesting being at that conference. I don't think that was the first time that "e-literacy" was used, but that's the first time I saw it become popularized. At that point, everybody started talking about e-literacy. The main point of the keynote speaker was, it's almost impossible today to have literacy without e-literacy. If you don't know how to use a computer, all of the information that's on the Web, that's on computers, is of no use to you. And it was a good point. That's basically what I was doing, giving people e-literacy.

JOEL NICHOLS: I was assigned to be in the Adult/Teen reference department at our regional library at the Free Library of Philadelphia, which happened to have a computer lab on site. There was really serious demand on the public computers, and there was always a line in the morning to get in. Working that public computer reference desk was kind of a nightmare, because people would need you to do all sorts of pointing and clicking for them, and it was really labor-intensive. The way the room was set up, it was hard, because it was more a computer lab-style, so you were sort of squeezing in between people to help someone click through a form.

After I'd been there for a bit, I figured out there was this lab and that it wasn't really being used except for special events kinds of instruction. So I started doing a regular computer class. I used resources, I did the typical sort of librarian Googling around to see what other librarians had developed. There were some current existing resources that the Free Library had, and I adapted them and put it all together to do what I thought was going to be a series of courses like Computer Basics, Internet Basics, Word Processing, maybe Spreadsheets or something if we got there. And I realized quickly that even though you can teach a class on those things, and it's a convenient way to organize, you really need to learn all three of those things in tandem in order to navigate well. You can't just do Computer Basics and then go on the Internet and not really have any idea about what any of this abstract symbology means like clicking through on a link, and what's an ad, what's not an ad, that kind of thing.

In those early days I tried my best to teach those workshops, and what I found is that the same individuals kept coming back and coming back and taking basically the exact same content again and again and again. In a group class, I probably had four people, and it would quickly become one-on-one happening four at once. So I shifted from standing in front of the room clicking through explanations in PowerPoint to just a really practical "do this, do that," and I started standing behind them so I could see their screens and give them one-on-one advice as we were moving through a group exercise. I did that for a while.

The next branch where I worked also had a computer lab, and I was able to do some more of that. We also had a computer lab assistant who didn't really teach classes but was like a one-on-one help desk. No matter what anybody needed, he took them through it. He was bilingual and it was a Spanish-English branch. It was really helpful. He helped all sorts of people do all sorts of things in a really loose way. I think over time my approach changed to be entirely "meet the user where they are" and teach them some basic things, have some pre-planned activities and make sure that you're prepared with some of what's within Computer Basics and Internet 101. But, ultimately, get them on a computer, figure out what they're interested in, what information they're going to use the computer for. Sometimes people would come in with a very specific thing, like "I'm going to write a resume." "I'm going to apply to this job." Other people would say, "I want to look for my niece I haven't seen in fifteen years. I have her name and her date of birth," or something. Other people would be looking for crochet patterns. So theoretically everyone was going to learn to write a cover letter and submit it in an online form, because that was the exercise I had set up. But I tried instead to figure out where people were, what they wanted to do, if they wanted to check a bank statement, if they wanted to look around the school district's "parent 'net," and work from there to do that.

As one of the first things, I did try to always get people to register themselves an email account and to use registering for a Gmail account as their first lesson, and really sit with them and walk them through it and explain everything and use that as an opportunity to assess their existing skill and figure out what they most might need. As the years went on, people would come in with a Gmail address, but they often didn't know the password for it. We would either spend lots of time in that endless cycle of trying to verify your Google account when you have low digital literacy and don't even really get what they're asking, much less the answers to what they're asking, like what month did you first open your account in. So even when people came in with an address, we would almost always end up registering a new one, with me trying to convince them that the password had to be something that they could actually remember and/or that they could write down. I told them about Internet privacy, and I told them about the necessity of keeping their passwords private, but the reality of the people I was working with was that they actually did have to write it down on a card in their wallet or make it, like, their daughter's name and the day of the month when she was born in order to remember it next time.

CAROL BEAN: We developed the Mousing Around tutorial at the Palm Beach County Library because there was nothing else effective out there. In the '90s, Microsoft had a tutorial on how to use the mouse. I found it, and it really wasn't much good. We looked at Chris Rippel's Mouserobics, but that assumed you already knew certain things about using the mouse. It kind of raced through things and got you to games and practicing the mouse, and that was great. But it didn't start at a low enough level. So I figured, I'm going to have to do something myself. There was a library consortium in Michigan that had put together a mousing tour. I looked and I said, "That's a good start." Because they started out at, "This is a mouse. This is what a mouse does. This is how you put your fingers on the mouse." It was really at that level, which is what we needed. I asked them if I could use it and modify it, and they said, "Sure." Probably in the course of making my own tutorial, I kept at least 50 percent of what they had done.

We tried this out for about six months, and watched the users and basically noted all the mistakes. My colleague at the time, without my knowing it, took what I had done and then started building on it based on what we were seeing. In the end, I guess about four to six months later, I looked at what he had done and said, "This is it!" We took the basic idea that was in the New User Tutorial from Michigan and totally expanded it and filled it in. By the time we were done, you really couldn't recognize that anything from that original tutorial was there, but I've got to say, they were the inspiration. You know, you build on the shoulders of giants. If they had not been there, it would have been a longer road.

Then I thought, I need to share this with the larger community and see if I can get some feedback from them, because I'm seeing it in my particular setting here in the library, but maybe I'm missing something. So I sent a message out to the PUBLIB list and offered it to people saying, "Could you please try this out and send me feedback?" I did get a few suggestions, which were very helpful, but mostly what people did was say, "Can I have that? I want that." And the beauty of this is, we packaged it so that it could be used offline. All you had to do was download it. And people all over the world started emailing us saying, "Can we get this?" So it was really encouraging that we had built this, and that it was useful for everybody. I think it definitely filled a need. I even had somebody that was tasked with training the US Post Office—they were going to migrate to a computerized system with a graphical user interface, and they wanted something to teach them to use the mouse. They basically wanted to take our tutorial and modify it and use it. I said, "Fantastic, that's what it's there for." That was one of the things I pretty much insisted on, is I wanted it open source. Of course Palm Beach County holds copyright, but we finally put a README file in there with licensing terms that said, "If you're an educational or nonprofit organization using this for education, you can do whatever you want with it."

That mousing tutorial was such a big breakthrough, because it starts, "Here's a mouse. This is how you position your hand on it." The first five or six frames, you don't even use the mouse; you just press the Enter key on the keyboard to advance the frames. It starts in just a real basic, non-threatening way. It does not go fast. One of the things that I heard often enough to have it drilled in my head was, these older adults would come and say they'd taken classes here or there, and they just went too fast, they couldn't understand anything, they couldn't retain it. This was one of the clues that informed our development of the mousing tutorial and our other classes—when you get to a certain age, as the literature informed me and as I was seeing, the process is slowed down. You can become very focused, but you don't process things as quickly, and you need a lot more repetition. So those principles were the ones that we basically applied to the Mousing Around tutorial and to the classes we subsequently developed as well.

We had been seeing over 75 or 80 percent of the people come back to the same class. After we made these changes, the mousing tutorial and a progression of four or five classes kind of introducing people to a computer and to the Internet, the repeat rate went from like 80 percent down to 15 percent. So I consider that a success. My brother-in-law once told me, if you want to be noted, if you want to be a success, find a hole and fill it. I didn't go looking for this hole, but I definitely found a hole.

One of the first places we found that was adapting our tutorial were the schools in Spain. By 2005, 2006 we were noticing there were places in China that were using it. As late as 2008, 2009, I remember getting a call from somebody serving the Vietnamese community in Washington, and they wanted to know, could they translate it into Vietnamese? Of course they could. When I would get requests, the things that would astound me is the breadth of exposure the Mousing Around tutorial was getting, and how many people it was really useful for. I'm not sure how many older people are using it, but I feel fairly confident it's probably still being used on the other end of the scale, for children learning how to use the mouse. But then we come to the point where with touchscreens, how many people are going to need a mouse? So there's that.

JOEL NICHOLS: Eventually we at the Free Library established the Techmobile, as a result of funding first from the Knight Foundation and then from the federal BTOP funding in 2010, 2011-ish. We started four community hotspots that were computer labs staffed with one-on-one helpers who could teach classes but also teach any kind of flexible computer help. At the same time, we purchased this digital literacy vehicle, a bookmobile with a computer lab inside. It had eight laptops and eight iPads. We came up with a variety of plans around those and offered to come to an organization and train their staff in how to use PowerPoint and that kind of thing. But what mostly happened is that we got booked by lots of mental health facilities and other kinds of social work organizations. Organizations serving people in recovery would book us. And we ended up doing a similar thing of, "Do you have an email address? What are you interested in? Do you have a library card? How can we facilitate you learning something about this really vital technology?"

The theory of the Techmobile was that it would be equally about access to hardware and about instruction. We got bookings from agencies like the ones I mentioned, and we had a really strong partnership with the veterans' hospital here in Philadelphia. But ultimately the goal of the Techmobile was to get into neighborhoods where there wasn't access otherwise. Sometimes we would also set up outside of a library branch if the power was off, or we would set up in a park or at a festival. For many people who were on our regular route, every week or every other week we would be back at that same park for the whole afternoon, and we had a lot of repeat customers in that way. So for them I think it was more about access and less about instruction, although we did lots of one-on-one help of helping people recover their password or clicking through a particularly tricky online form.

CHAD CLARK: We recently brought in another full-time person in the New Media department at Highland Park Public Library, Juan, who's fluent in Spanish. He's been going out to some of the Family Network Centers, as they're called in Highland Park. ESL Spanish-speaking families are meeting up in churches and their kids will be in daycares on one side of the church while the parents are in other parts of the church, learning life skills. So our guy Juan will go over there with a fleet of laptops and do basic Internet search or really whatever they need. He went in there with a plan of, okay, we're going to show you how to do XYZ. But then they're like, "We really just want to know how to get on Facebook right now so we can talk to people in Mexico," or whatever.

We're really proud of what Juan's doing. That's something new that the library hasn't done in the past, especially outside the library. And when we go out into the community like this, we're of course saying, "Come on back to the library, too. Bring it back in, and then we can show you the next step," and that has happened, certainly.

CAROL BEAN: Back in 2004, after we had developed all these classes, we were kind of looking around saying, what else can we do? Well, guess what. They're coming up to the reference desk and saying,

"Can you show me how to turn my phone off?" They were all flummoxed by their phones. And I seriously looked at ways that we could teach people basic use of their phones.

ALISON MACRINA: The last library where I worked, we had a pretty well-developed computer literacy curriculum, most of it scheduled, some of it ad hoc. We had a basic Intro to the Internet class. We had Microsoft Office classes. We had, I think, one that was job-seeking. So, all the typical topics. Then we also had an HTML course that we offered that was not as regular as the others; it would run for six weeks and then we'd re-run it another six months later, or something like that. We also had a good relationship with other area libraries that offered the classes that we didn't offer, so we could do referrals pretty easily. There were other things represented, some popular programming languages like JavaScript. I started teaching some privacy and security classes, and those went up a few levels—Basic, Intermediate, and Advanced.

We also had tech appointments. You could schedule time with me or somebody else on the technology staff. Those were pretty popular. We had a hard limit on the number that you could ask for within a one- or two-month period. We had a maximum of three, just because there was so much demand and we couldn't spend all our time doing that. Like most libraries, our reference librarians spent a great deal of time doing ad hoc computer literacy, so helping people who just came up to the desk. Many of the questions at the reference desk were about using computers, whether it was somebody's personal device or whether it was the computer they were using at the library. I found with this ad hoc stuff, if I got asked about one tech thing, there were six other questions that that person was sitting on, and if I had the time they'd give them all to me.

SARAH HOUGHTON: Now, at this point, what I see our staff offering are much more need-driven, very specific need-driven or subject-driven. People wanting to learn more about how to protect their kids online. People wanting to do genealogy research. People wanting to set up a good-looking website on the cheap for their small business. And it may be a reflection of the size of the library, it may be a reflection of the community, but the types of digital literacy-style classes I'm seeing being taught where I am now does trend more toward the very specific need as opposed to these vague technology skills like "how to send an email."

I think things are just a little bit more articulated as people have gained and become more comfortable with those basic skills, and I just see that continuing as new technologies arise. Like, we're just in the process of setting up virtual reality demo labs at both of our libraries. It's a little rotating things that the schools are helping us with. I anticipate that will go back to basics. People are like, "What is this and how does it work?" And they're going to need that initial training. But as some of that technology becomes more widely used, more widespread, more comfortable, then I think you see people starting to delve into the more granular, more specific needs. That's really the evolution that I've seen happen.

John Helling: In most libraries I've worked in, the staff realizes that sometimes one-on-one reference desk interaction just isn't going to do it because the patron's need is too deep. Hence, the creation of computer classes, which are sometimes well-attended and sometimes not. The computer classes I taught in at NYPL, for example, were extremely well-attended, but we also had a huge patron base, obviously. The computer classes I taught in Bloomfield were often to three or four (very grateful!) people. I think we as a society like to think that tech is everywhere now and that everyone already knows how to use it, but I completely disagree with that. There are still lots of people who need to be taught the difference between a left and right click. I think the best approach to help patrons who have more in-depth needs than a quick reference question is to set aside time where they can come and get such help on a specific topic. Even if your class isn't well-attended, you still have an option for patrons to whom you just can't offer an hour of desk time because you have other patrons who need your help, too.

Carol Bean: In 2014, I went to an international e-literacy conference in Bosnia-Herzegovina, which was really interesting because they were talking about the same things that they had talked about ten years before, just things had progressed somewhat. They weren't talking necessarily about teaching older people, but it had come down to high schoolers and college kids and e-literacy, which wasn't necessarily how to use a computer, but how to navigate and use the information. Initially it was, if you can't use a computer, it does no good that there's all this information on there, if you can't use the tool to get to it. And I think we're moving beyond that, more to today to, okay, I can get on. How can I get to the information I need? How can I navigate on my flip phone? How can I navigate on an iPad? How can I navigate on a smartphone? And sometimes even on a computer. Because literacy is a moving target, I think there's a lot still developing and still being taught out there.

JESSA LINGEL: There is a real problem that too easily descends into ageism around keeping librarians up-to-date with rapidly changing technology. Susan Sontag had a really interesting idea in one of her journals, that later in life there should be a second round of college, where people get to pursue a new line of interest or education. It'd be interesting to think about how we could have a program that gets people who've been in their field for a while genuinely excited about a new round of education and training. Right now, I think there's a certain wariness or skepticism to job re-training, but are there programs or un/conferences that could make this revitalizing and invigorating? Maybe FOSS, free and open source software, is a way to do this, like having retraining around specific open source applications that can be integrated into existing programs.

On the one hand, I think there's a certain pragmatism to saying—however much we wish it were different—getting someone prepared for the job market is going to mean training in MS Word and PowerPoint, and my idealism about open source software shouldn't take precedence over someone who just wants an office job. On the other hand, I think there are a lot of people who get the main arguments for non-proprietary software, and the public library is or should be a natural place to go to learn more about that. I think of all the work people like Alison Macrina have been doing around teaching privacy tools in libraries; learning about open source software could be a parallel to that.

. . .

ALISON MACRINA: I hear from library users nonstop. They email me. They ask me for my home number. It's not necessarily about me; it's that they're desperate for this information. I go to libraries across the country, and I've had the same reception everywhere. I'm very fortunate that I'm in a position where I not only teach librarians these things, but often they invite me to teach their public. I'll go in and teach a class where the worst day is when maybe six people show up. But even a tiny audience is always so engaged and inquisitive, and they beg me to come back and do the same exact class over again. Most of the time, it's a much bigger group. If I teach something at a library where I live in Massachusetts, sometimes I'll have one class the first week of a month, and then I'll offer the same one the third week at the same place. Well, guaranteed for that second round, most of the people from the first class are going to come back, and they're going to bring their friends.

What I hear from them—it's a number of things. One, that they've been interested in this information for a while and they had no idea where to find it. They tell me that they've been made fun of, that they've been called paranoid for caring about these things. Even if the information that I give them is overwhelming, they're so glad to know that they're heard. There is a huge interest in these subjects in our communities, and it's largely unmet. And because of the power of media around all this and also the technology that is not privacy-enhancing, people think that they're the only ones left who care. The media says all these things about how privacy is dead and whatever, and my totally anecdotal but abundant experience says that many people feel quite differently.

And this is true for all groups. It's true for older folks, it's true for teens, it's true for immigrants. Every group that I've talked to, the only ones that I find are a little adversarial are maybe older white men, but if you make it about them personally—if you're like, "Your business secrets will get stolen"—then they care. I've met many people who have been victims of identity theft of some kind, and most of them had not recovered from it, even if it happened five years ago. I've met many people who have been victims of domestic violence or know victims of domestic violence who are trying to avoid an abusive person. One time I met somebody who had a brain injury as a child and was living in a group home where he was treated like a child. He and all the other adults in his group home had their computer use monitored, and if any one person violated the Internet policy, they would be collectively punished and have their computer privileges taken away from them.

For many people, surveillance starts at home. With privacy technology, your enemy doesn't have to be the FBI or whatever; it could be your husband or your neighbor or your classmate. Most people that I meet have these kind of more mundane concerns, and I mean mundane in the sense of everyday. But it's very real for them, and it's huge. If your partner is abusing you and trying to find out where you've moved to, or who else you might be with, that's the biggest thing in your life. And then the teens sometimes are like, "I heard about somebody who got their phone taken away by the principal and there were pictures of their girlfriend on there, and their girlfriend is seventeen and they're eighteen and now they're in trouble." That's one that comes up a lot, too.

JOEL NICHOLS: In terms of privacy and digital literacy, or privacy and the library user, I would always try to let people know, "Anything you put online could be exposed, anything might be found by somebody else," but I would also try to contextualize that in terms of, "It's highly unlikely that someone is going to do that to you, and it's highly unlikely that it's going to be personalized." That it's sort of like weather on the Internet. Like, if you have an email account, you're going to get spam every now and then, and it's not anything to be afraid of, but you need to recognize the threat and know how to deal with it. You need to have an umbrella or whatever. I would try to give people big frames of how to protect their privacy and constantly explain and remind them why signing up for an email address with Google was giving them that information, which in my mind was a necessary evil or something that was relatively benign, versus signing up for a total scam "twenty free iPads this hour" kind of Internet thing that was totally about harvesting your information for spam. There's lots to unpack there in terms of Google with ad data and all that, but I think what I most tried to impart to library users who I was teaching how to use the Internet was what the landscape looked like and what to watch out for. Just sort of be aware, but let them know that I think it was still probably safe to use their bank's website, but here's what you really had to watch out for in terms of spam that looks like it's from your bank's website but isn't. There's no real easy answer there.

CHAD CLARK: A lot of times in the digital media lab, people will end up logging in to YouTube because they're uploading something that they created in there, and they're leaving themselves logged in and they don't know it. That's something small, but significant. We help people build websites and blogs, and often enough they like to add an e-commerce component. Sometimes they're willing to give us their sensitive financial information to set up some e-commerce. We're not secretaries; we're always trying to show people how to do this themselves, and what it takes, and what they need to research. But a lot of people trust librarians, certainly. "Oh, here's my credit card, can you help me set this up?" So we try to avoid that. We've had programs showing people how to clear your cookies, and what is a secure website, what does that mean? We've had security-based programs that the public has actually asked us to do. We do certainly talk to people, and it comes up when people are posting their stuff online.

Particularly I'm remembering a woman who makes movies. She's an amateur filmmaker and she puts them up on Vimeo, and she's like, "I only want certain people to view it, I don't want it to be public, and how do I work all these tools, and what about Facebook? I want this film up on Facebook, too, but I want my profile to be very controlled." That's kind of a nightmare to untangle Facebook's privacy settings, which are always changing. But certainly we need to be responsive to those dynamics, as far as sharing things on social media, and each platform's got a different set of tools. We basically start from the assumption that once it's on the Internet, it's not private no matter what, and work our way down.

ZACHARY LOEB: I think that sometimes people talk about libraries, especially in terms of a public context, and especially in terms of younger demographics, as being a third space. There's home, and there's school, and the library can kind of be a third space where they don't need to worry about some of those other presences keeping an eye on everything they're doing. So I think that some of the problems that then pop up is that contemporary libraries wind up being filled with so many different types of technology, so many different things that don't necessarily share the same values as the librarians and the libraries. So much of contemporary Internet-connected devices rely on tracking where people are, what they're doing, what they're looking at. So much of the predictive capability of websites like Google has to do with always keeping track of what you've searched for in the past.

There's certainly a lot that libraries can do in this regard—setting the default web browser on computers to a search engine that does not track, setting up ad blockers, setting things up so that the history gets deleted regularly, and certainly encouraging information literacy, teaching information literacy, teaching people the basics of protecting their anonymity online. But a lot of these things are kind of compromises, and with some of these things, there's the balance between wanting to protect the privacy of your patrons and also then running into situations where patrons come up to you and they're confused why they're getting this weird message from Privacy Badger, which is blocking certain features of a website. You can explain to the patron that this is protect their anonymity, to protect their privacy, but they just want to disable it on that site so they can go through and look at whatever. You can set the default search engine to one that isn't tracking their searches, but then you'll still have patrons come up and ask you to set it to Google because that's the search engine they're used to using.

So it definitely is a balance, and I think it's a challenge that libraries want to protect their patrons' privacy while at the same time—patrons don't want to have their every move watched by Big Brother, but I think that a lot of patrons also don't want to have the librarians standing behind them screaming "Privacy!" at the top of their lungs. I think that they would find that troublesome, too. Lots of libraries are also prepared for those sorts of worst case scenarios, for what do we do if the police ever come in and say, "Give us this computer!" You're prepared to say, "Okay, we need a warrant, and we need all of this other official legal authorization." Libraries, especially public libraries, are also aware that there are certain laws that you just follow. So if the police come in and they do have a warrant, who do you call within the library to then deal with these things?

ALISON MACRINA: The Tor Browser is the one that's definitely more in wider deployment, because it's an easier sell. We have a few dozen libraries across the US and Canada that have put Tor on their computers. Most of them have put it on all the computers, but a few of them have just tested it out on a few, and they get some good feedback from their patrons. They offer it as a backup browser. They name it in some specific way so that people know what it is. The Tor relays, we've only had a couple of libraries do that, but both of them have received a really positive response. That takes a little bit more resources, and it's a bit more exposure. But Tor Browser is something that I think should be uncontroversial. Basically it's just a web browser that gives you a little bit more privacy. Anyone can use it, and it gets used for so many different kinds of things, so that one

I think is a bit simpler. We recommend that libraries make signs or have some other thing that acknowledges what this thing is and why it's different and "if you don't want this, you can just click on the regular Chrome browser."

Carol Bean: I used to teach a class on computer security. When we taught email classes, we would say, "Okay, this is what a scam looks like. This is what a phishing attack looks like. Don't click these links. Look, this is how you can tell if it might not be real." In our Internet classes, in our online buying classes, we used to cover that, ten years ago. And we're still there where people just trust so much, and part of it has to do with the infrastructure within a library system.

I really want library directors and managers to understand, you *will* be hacked. It's not a matter of if, it's a matter of when, and so you need to have plans and policies in place on how you're going to handle things so that when it happens, you're prepared and you don't lose everything. And you need to make this information available, you need to encourage it. We encourage people to vote. We need to encourage that same level of civic responsibility in dealing with computer security. If my computer's infected and I'm connected to the Internet or I'm sending emails—we're all connected via the Internet. If one person's infected, all of their friends can be infected as well. That is the one piece of technology that, to me, is so frustrating because people don't think about it. They really don't think about it. And it's something that's really important.

Zachary Loeb: I think that it's a good thing that so many librarians are very concerned about issues around privacy. They think that it's part of their professional responsibility to be really concerned about privacy. But to a certain extent—and here I am giving my personal curmudgeon opinion—I think that for a lot of people in the Internet age, privacy is something that people just have a weird relationship with. There's a philosopher, Helen Nissenbaum, who talks about privacy as being "contextual awareness," that we expect certain types of privacy in some places and don't expect it in others, which is why, to give kind of a crude example, some people don't consider it a privacy issue to post pictures from a wild party on Facebook, but then they consider it a privacy violation if someone outside their group of friends sees the pictures and penalizes them as a result.

So I think that privacy winds up being another one of those words—kind of like "technology"—where we say "privacy" and we think that we're all talking about the same thing, but really you say "privacy" to a room of people, and every person in that room has their own idea of what privacy means. Maybe a lot of the librarians in that room would have an idea of privacy that's really about protecting anonymity and having a responsibility to protect that anonymity, but I think that privacy may be an issue where librarians are much more concerned about it than many of their patrons. However, I would say that that's probably a good thing—I mean, it's not a good thing that the patrons aren't concerned, but I think that it can be a space where some librarians can take it as their responsibility to educate people about these things.

Mandy Henk: I think that there's a lot to be said for teaching patrons about privacy. But I also think that there's two levels to think about. One is the "I don't want my ex-boyfriend to know my email" level. Which is incredibly important, and it's absolutely something that we should be doing programming on to help people learn how to manage their digital footprint and help people figure out how to make sure that the information they want public is public. That is absolutely separate from the larger question of government surveillance, and I get concerned when we start muddying the two. As far as I know, there's pretty much nothing anyone can do. This is a ship that has sailed. But just because the ship sailed doesn't mean we shouldn't still complain about the fact that it sailed and make very clear what our understanding is of the reality of how much privacy people actually have from the government, that being very, very little to none. Especially when you throw an international layer on top of that, there's absolutely none. This is all well-established and documented, and I do think librarians have an obligation to talk about it and to be upfront with patrons about it.

Béatrice Colastin Skokan: I haven't thought about surveillance in the context of the United States because that is not the site of my own trauma. Looking back, I've been focused on the security concerns of the immigrant, and maybe not been as suspicious of what would happen here in terms of surveillance. I do worry about a culture where technological developments occur so quickly that most consumers of technology may not be aware of the impact of these developments on their lives. For instance, some of us are privileged to work within structures where we are continuously exposed to or able to learn about technology. We're empowered and know what to ask and what to look for.

ELAINE HARGER: We have surveillance cameras in the library at my school. They were installed in the 2013/14 school year because there was some mischief and damage in our computer lab one day, and the principal decided that we needed to be able to have an eye on equipment at all times. Over the course of summer 2016, more surveillance cameras were installed throughout the school in the hallways, not in the classrooms. But there's been a lot of resistance to having surveillance cameras everywhere in the building. My main concern is that having "Big Brother" keeping this eye on you all the time, in order to control the behavior of students, "works" very unevenly. In the library, after I looked at the videotapes a couple of times following minor mischief, word spread throughout the school that, "Oh, Ms. Harger, she can find out who did something." And I really haven't had any problems.

But the hallway surveillance hasn't worked at all. And there was considerable parent/guardian pushback. The concern is that kids are learning how to behave because there's somebody always watching them, not because they actually have internalized the reasons why they shouldn't push one another in the hallway or break into somebody's locker and steal their phone. But the other concern is framed in terms of the school-to-prison pipeline. Ultimately, I think surveillance is a problem for all those reasons.

. . .

MICHAEL CHERRY: Pedagogy is a critical topic that needs to be addressed when considering the future of library programs. By that I mean how we teach and design learning outcomes for programs, tech or otherwise. In terms of technology, focus has been largely on access to new technologies, such as 3D printers, laser cutters, and other tools of the maker movement. Discussion has focused largely on technology spaces as well—makerspaces, media labs, and other areas of the library where these tools can be found. However, less attention has been granted to pedagogy and the practice of teaching, or developing and facilitating learning objectives that enrich library programs. While access to new technologies may help to democratize their use, it does not teach people how technology shapes society and culture. This would require developing programs that make connections between technology and our own lives. I believe this is largely the missing component, essentially, how we develop our roles as critical educators within new library spaces and around new technologies.

Chad Clark: Librarians and educators need to demand more critical approaches to these spaces of creative growth. Whether making happens in a digital media lab or in a makerspace, the process should be treated as a vehicle for deep learning. Librarians and educators should resist stockpiling popular off-the-rack tech toys and focus on encouraging active engagement with raw materials. Sure, each year our library acquires a few shiny new things, but when we roll them out we strive to make it less about the gadget and more about engaging the learner as a whole person who fully participates. It definitely helps to get closer to the schools.

Whether it's classes or linking with the schools, just dropping the tools in the library and putting somebody part-time at a desk outside the room, just checking the people in and out—I don't think that's enough. It's going to have to go beyond that if we want it to be more than just a trend in libraries. Obviously no library wants to frustrate a patron and have them come in and say, "Lookit, here's a computer that does all kinds of stuff and here are these tools that could do so many things, but you're just going to have to figure it out." So bringing in mentors, bringing in experienced professionals that can actually talk about and instruct people on how these tools work and how they function in the real world—for lack of a better word—I think is essential.

In our lab, we have a 3D printer, like in a lot of libraries, and we work hard to build programming around our printer. We certainly allow the community to submit prints and print something and do the whole deal by themselves, but we work to bring in speakers who work in the 3D industry. We believe it's important to provide more than just the tools.

Vivian Alvarez: This is something that I'm very proud of at my branch at Chicago Public Library. It's not just about consuming media; it's about creating it. And a lot of things that are created in our space are created by the kiddos. There's a lot of reflection. We have roundtables, and while we're creating we're also talking about topics that are meaningful—critical, and what I call also transformative.

For instance, positive girl image. That is a topic that we've covered for years. If we're sketching something about costumes, and we're suddenly creating costumes that are a little too sexy, we will have a dialogue on why—what is the meaning of this? Even starting to talk about the color pink. Why are we wearing pink as girls? Why is the boy wearing blue? And so it creates a space for reflection. It creates a place for a reflection that's really not happening in many places for the children that I work with. It creates a community. And that's also tapping into the mission of the library. It's social information literacy to be reflective. It's also information literacy to work on their digital portfolios and understand that it's part of their careers. It's information literacy to work with digital media and have access to media that other branches and other communities don't. So all of that ties to the meaning of libraries. On top of it, we have workshops that tie to the meaning of libraries and books. For instance, we create book trailers. We do digital folktale stories, all based on stop motion or PowerPoint presentations. We try to choose books that, if they're not humorous, then they have to be reflective of image.

The middle school population I work with, especially girls, tend to go through a certain up and down in terms of their identity between grade levels seventh and eighth. And so these topics, especially the critical ones, become in fact critical to addressing symptoms in communities—symptoms such as early pregnancy, drugs, or gangs. And that is relatively close. It is within the immediate parameters right outside of the library, happening there. And yet the children so gravitate to this one space at the library where they feel safe and feel that they can talk to someone. I feel like if they have any opinion on books and kind of look a little bit like bookworms or geeks or something, if that's how they feel, then there's a space at the library and they belong. The library is located in an area where there are about seven different middle schools, and a lot of times children don't feel like they belong unless they kind of blend in with the cool kids, which is not necessarily gravitating towards academia or a safe pathway towards their future.

JESSICA ANNE BRATT: I feel that a lot of times kids know exactly what they want to do on a device, but they don't know that the device offers more, or that now there are these streaming platforms like Hoopla that are right at their fingertips. So I think what's promising is, once you show them the vastness of what the library can potentially offer, like we've done in OverDrive trainings—even when there are all these hiccups, or anything could go wrong and turn the experience in trying to download an e-book from fun to frustrating—it's interesting for the kids to be like, "The library has everything, and they have everything even if I want it in a movie," or, "They have it whether I want to listen to it digitally or it's presented in a print material."

So it's been awesome to kind of blow their minds with the fact that the library is this vast, amazing living organism that will provide whatever you will need it to. I think that's first and foremost. And honestly, I feel like the kids that we target and interact with have a low tier of Web understanding. They know Facebook and YouTube, but asking them, "Did you know you can do notes in e-books?" or providing them with this other option or taking it past what they're accustomed to, has been super cool to see them adapt and learn and then make it their own.

JOEL NICHOLS: Digital literacy with kids is a different ball game. This is something that I wish people would talk about, that not all kids are whiz-bangs, and that there is what people have called an "app gap" with poor children who do not have access to these devices, that kids also have to learn this whole technology. If anything, it's going to be delivered by educational technology in the classroom, and I think that it's a whole different ballgame to teach kids about digital literacy. There's really fundamental kinds of ideas you should teach them about privacy and bullying online and other things. Children's librarians do talk about it, people do talk about it, but it's often left out of the conversation around digital literacy.

ELAINE HARGER: To me, "digital citizenship" means knowing how to use information technologies in a socially responsible fashion and to think about the technologies from a sense of social responsibility. Some of the basics that are taught about digital citizenship are that users need to know how to safeguard not only their privacy, but their physical well-being. You don't go and meet up with a person that you've met via one of your social media platforms without knowing who that person is. So there's a lot of emphasis on safety, and emphasis on cyberbullying. That's a serious problem, the technology makes being a bully very easy. Being a bully through a device rather than in person, face-to-face, is kind of easy. The technology makes bullying a lot more mindless and seemingly inconsequential than being a bully in person might seem.

Digital citizenship also involves learning about copyright and plagiarism. It's so easy for kids to cut and paste information from any source and claim that it's their own, so students need to know about plagiarism and copyright and the importance of giving credit to one's sources. Those are some of the basics. Another basic is knowing that what you say and do online is potentially available and accessible forever. The silliness a kid engages in as a middle school student can turn around to bite them later on as they're becoming a college student or applying for a job or whatever. That's all kind of basic to digital citizenship.

But I think that it's important for children also to learn about their responsibilities. Part of my longstanding concern—and it comes out in the book that I've just written, *Which Side Are You On?: Seven Social Responsibility Debates in American Librarianship, 1990–2015*—is that there are so many injustices done throughout the world that we, especially here in the United States, benefit from enormously. A lot of the hardware and the software, too, comes to us through the misery of a lot of other people. People who mine the metals that the equipment relies upon, people who work in the factories, people who breathe the fumes of the plastic that encapsulates the devices when they're new. When I talk about digital citizenship with students, this is part of what we have conversations about—where do these things come from, and then where do they go to when they're disposed of? Part of the whole technological world we live in requires planned obsolescence and disposability in order for these businesses to stay in business and to keep selling stuff. What does that mean to the planet that we live on, and to the lives that a lot of people lead?

When I talk to students about that, I compare it to getting a driver's license. We ask why is it that you have to be sixteen years old before you get a driver's license? Why is it that you have to be twenty-one before you're allowed to purchase alcohol? There's a number of other ways in which we have both rights and responsibilities, and those rights and responsibilities can sometimes be age-dependent, and a lot of times not. I share part of Annie Leonard's "The Story of Electronics" and encourage students to read Cory Doctorow's graphic novel, *In Real Life*.

KAREN LEMMONS: My computer apps class at my school is a semester long. If it were left up to me, I'd love for it to be a year long, just to really emphasize and be thorough about research and resources and digital citizenship. In the past I've done some intro-level type digital citizenship, and I do talk about the Digital Citizenship Day. I hope to expand and scaffold digital citizenship skills and move it beyond just the introductory, to where the students are doing some critical thinking and higher-order thinking skills and actually see that they have an ethical responsibility to become digital citizens.

Most of them have Facebook pages and Instagram and Snapchat accounts. Most of them are vocal majors, dancers, and other types of performers. I tell them—and I know telling isn't exactly teaching it, but I say, "Look, if you want to be considered seriously as a professional, you may need to create another Facebook page, or you may need to seriously look at the Facebook page you have and start weeding out things that may not reflect you in a more professional manner." Then we do lessons where they review Facebook pages. We discuss what information should be on a Facebook page, and which Facebook page is more professional. I keep emphasizing that.

I haven't discussed a digital portfolio. Some of the teachers have asked, "Oh, Ms. Lemmons, why don't you teach a digital portfolio?" They make it sound like this is such a piece of cake to teach. I just read a book called *The Innovator's Mindset* by George Couros, and the way he talked about the digital portfolio is more than uploading some pieces of work into a portfolio. It takes a little more than that. I plan to incorporate digital portfolios later.

But, yes, I am guilty of not teaching enough information about digital citizenship and their rights and responsibilities. I will say this, though. I had the students do a pre-test with TRAILS, the Tool for Real-time Assessment of Information Literacy Skills, to assess what students already know about information literacy. Interestingly enough, most of them know about digital citizenship, about using information ethically. They know about the rights and responsibilities. Now, whether they *practice* that is a different story. But they at least know the rights and wrongs. Students need to apply the knowledge.

Jessica Anne Bratt: I noticed—and it gets said in workshops all the time—that in certain areas you have consumers of technology but you don't have creators of technology. You have kids who on a base level seem like they're not interested in learning about technology. They just want to play the game; they don't want to create it. And I feel like there's also that stigma still with girls and people of color that they just aren't interested in these specific digital literacy fields. It's amazing to me how much library employees assume that kids, just because they grow up with technology, should be able to do. For example, we had a high school intern who couldn't figure out how to attach anything on an email. And it just blew a lot of people's minds, because adults use email all the time. But kids, especially teens, don't necessarily use email or aren't necessarily concerned about learning email or what attachments are. That's just a tiny example.

There was a makerspace being built, and a few other centers in Grand Rapids that are doing technology and arts, so I thought it would be cool to be the gateway to connect to those other organizations. Not try to be the sole person that they go to, but just give kids a taste to say, hey, if you like coding, you can do a ton more here, or you can come in and see how an iPad works, or see the games, if you don't have one. Our biggest program is the Teen Tech Camp. Kids spend two weeks at the library for a half day. We do fines amnesty. We remove all barriers possible so we can get kids registered for camp. They get a Kindle checked out to them for the summer, and it's loaded with books and games. Then they come and we provide morning snacks and lunches, and they learn about robotics. We use the Lego educational software kit. They learn about the computer programming. We have high school robotics teams help the kids learn how to program. We partner with another technology arts center called WMCAT that comes in to do design thinking and how to create things for others and build that empathy and understanding, and how those skills relate to technology and addressing problems and finding solutions.

So that's our biggest program. From that, we do Teen Tech Thursdays, where the kids meet up to do robotics shops or various web design or graphic design programs. For a while we did have some typing classes. They were hit or miss, and we actually had more parents that wanted to do it than the kids. We did some film. We partnered with a few film organizations to bring in editing software and video and just show them different aspects of technology, especially along the lines of animation. There's a teen film festival held every year, so we brought in some film education classes revolving around technology. And then one-on-one instruction I do with kids is databases and all the research into learning how to find things—that Web 2.0 idea where you have this iceberg of stuff that you find on Google, but how do we get to using filters and wanting to actually wade through all this exaggerated information and be able to dissect it so you aren't spending hours trying to find one legitimate source for your paper?

MICHAEL CHERRY: In terms of database training, it's important that students recognize the difference between a keyword search using Google and what a database search is like. And you have to find ways to teach them this creatively. For instance, there are more than just articles involved in a database search. I like to show different videos that provide odd or interesting perspectives on a bigger topic, such as the ability to clone one's own pet. I'll also use a lot of current events as discussion points, in addition to primary sources like *Time* and *Newsweek*. For example, there was a high school classroom doing a report on the Cold War, and at my library we have all the older issues of *Life* magazine. So in addition to showing them ways to search for content using the databases, I also showed them articles on bomb shelters that dated back to the 1960s. Some of these articles contain pictures and instructions describing how to create a bomb shelter, which to a student these days—it's not something they can necessarily see every day. These primary sources are a way to locate students in the research and could be very unique and compelling. So I think when you're doing database training, you have to almost treat it like it's a program and provide interesting content. If you can interest students in the content, it's more likely they'll be interested in the research.

ELAINE HARGER: A number of our students come out of elementary schools knowing about searching the Internet and using Google to find information that they want. However, they don't know how to do it very efficiently. Fortunately, though, Google has devised whatever algorithms they use to fine-tune a person's search. In the past, one really did need to know something about Boolean search structures and commands in order to actually get at what you wanted. A lot of that has been automated now to the extent that Google doesn't even let you know that it has an advanced search feature, which I think is problematic, because the algorithms create a sort of wall between information and an understanding of how the technology works—kind of like magic.

I've found that increasingly many teachers are not particularly interested in having students learn the specifics about how to search the Internet effectively or how to search databases. This is unfortunate, and I think that it's due to the fact that a lot of teachers themselves are not familiar with using databases and search engines in anything but kind of a basic fashion. I've seen teachers type questions into search boxes! Of course, some of our teachers do want their students to learn about databases, digital citizenship, etc. One of the most effective techniques I've used for understanding the concept of the database, and how it's different from searching the Internet, is what I call the concept of the information iceberg. I know I picked this up from another librarian somewhere along the way, but I don't remember who. By the time children get to middle school, there's always somebody in the crowd who knows what an iceberg is and knows that maybe 80 percent of an iceberg is underneath the water; you can't see it. So in using this image, I let students know that Google will let you get to a lot of information, but that information is like the tip of the iceberg, and if you want to get to even more information that's available over the Internet, you need to search more deeply, and you need to get to databases. And I describe how that requires passwords and special access, it often requires money, sometimes it requires what I describe to them as "super duper security FBI clearances" in order to access the information. We search the World Book Online, which is one of the databases our school district makes accessible to students, so that they get a sense of there being much more information than the millions of search returns they get when they're surfing the Internet. That's one technique that I use.

Another example comes from the fact that classroom teachers often don't know the broad spectrum of resources that are available through the library for students. Being involved in the planning stage of any unit becomes essential. For instance, I worked on a poetry unit with one of our ELL classes, and the teacher wanted the kids to learn about different structures of poetry—limericks, haikus, and several others. I was able to help her identify some Internet sites that had descriptions, examples, worksheets, poetry magnet games, and whatnot that her kids could use. I also brought in books of poetry from our collection and had YouTube videos with poets reading their work. The teacher and I read and recited some poems to the kids, and the kids were performing poetry and writing it. Because I was able to work with the teacher from the very beginning of her planning, I think that the children were able to get a richer experience in this poetry unit simply because of all of the additional resources that I was able to bring into their classroom. The kids did come to the library initially, but then I went into the classroom to work with them also.

MICHAEL CHERRY: In terms of programs with schools, those types of partnerships that are more about making or project-based learning, I've done a couple partnerships with a film class at a local high school. I've partnered with this class on various stop motion animation projects. We've done different projects where students create pixilation videos and learn about the history of stop motion animation—pioneers like Willis H. O'Brien and Ray Harryhausen. I've also utilized 3D printing whereby students will design and print a stop motion character on a 3D printer, and then animate that character using stop motion software. The interesting thing about this program is that 3D printing is being utilized in stop motion films, particularly by an animation studio called Laika. They've done films like "The Boxtrolls," "Coraline," "ParaNorman," and mostly recently "Kubo and the Two Strings." They're utilizing 3D printers to create the characters in their films. So I've done something similar with students and they've learned how the film industry is utilizing rapid prototyping for the same purposes.

Another project I enjoyed was with an English class where the students were reading George Orwell's *1984*. It was right after the time that Edward Snowden disclosed the NSA PRISM program. I partnered with the teacher and we did a research project that was a digital graphic novel. We were using the software Comic Life, and the program was designed like a traditional research project where each student is assigned a particular topic. However, in this case we weren't writing a traditional thesis followed by supporting statements; we were composing a digital graphic novel. The students were given topics that related to modern surveillance, such as RFID tagging, WikiLeaks, nanotechnology, and drones. Students had to research these topics and were shown various videos that related to them. Eventually they had to compose their topic into a short graphic novel, and relate it to themes in Orwell's *1984*. In this case, students were able to use technology in a new way to complete a research project and the project allowed for a discussion about technology—things such as privacy rights and social media, Internet surveillance, and digital citizenship. All these topics are pertinent to the lives of young adults.

ELAINE HARGER: How could classroom teachers get a better grasp on databases and other online information? Well, they could take up their librarian's offer to do introductions to learn more about what's available. Classroom teachers are really overworked people. And in my experience, the younger generation of classroom teachers have more appreciation of collaborative relationships than my generation, and I think that that's largely due to the ways in which college students who have decided to become schoolteachers are educated. There's a lot of cohort work being done as they're learning to be teachers. That was never the case when I went through an educational program. So I think that there's a generational thing going on there. But every school librarian that I know, we're always offering what we can do to help teachers learn about the resources and incorporate the library into the classroom work, but so many teachers feel like they need to do everything themselves. They feel like it's just additional work to do collaborative work. Recently our district has offered professional development on "blended learning"—embedding digital technology into every lesson. As a result of conversations with one of our language arts teachers, I'll be making videos that can be used at any time by teachers and students describing our school district's online resources, how to do citations, how to use different features of our online catalog and ProQuest's advanced search features.

MICHAEL CHERRY: Literacy encompasses much more than words, and this is crucial to consider when we think about the future of libraries. Media literacy educators, people like Renee Hobbs or Frank Baker, argue that in order to be literate, you need to be able to understand how meaning is conveyed in photography, advertisements, and film, and across other media. My project with digital tabloids, which I wrote a book chapter for in Sarah McNicol's *Critical Literacy for Information Professionals*, took place at the Youth Care Center in

Evansville, Indiana. The Youth Care Center is a juvenile detention center for teenagers between the ages of twelve and seventeen. It's located right across from our central library. The tabloid project examined how the media sensationalizes stories and how to critically look at information. We did a variety of activities, and the program culminated in the creation of a digital tabloid.

For one of the activities, I took headlines from the covers of *Newsweek* and *Time* and cut them out and xeroxed them, and then I did the same with a bunch of headlines from the covers of the *Weekly World News* and the *National Enquirer*. The headlines were randomly placed in a pile. I wanted the students to separate the legitimate news sources from what we would consider the tabloids or fake news. And of course the headlines were very sensationalized from both the news journals and the tabloids. They used similar fonts and bold headlines, and it was all very sensationalized. Needless to say, the students had difficulty separating the news journals from the tabloids because the headlines all looked the same. That was one of the initial activities, and that got us thinking about how news information is conveyed—basically, is there a difference between the way that it's conveyed in *Time* magazine from the way that it's conveyed in a tabloid like the *National Inquirer*? Are these news sources using the same tactics to get our attention? If so, what are these tactics?

We also did an activity that I borrowed from Frank Baker's book. It's an interesting activity—he suggests taking images of people like celebrities and politicians and getting as many as you can find. This particularly works well with the president. The example he uses in his book is President Obama; he takes covers of Obama and has students analyze them. So you might have Obama on the cover of *Time* one week looking like he's a great leader, and then two weeks later, it's a negative depiction of him. The activity works best with a variety of covers. It's an overt example of how the media spins information that we receive.

Additionally, the females at the Youth Care Center analyzed celebrity gossip magazines like *People* and *Us Weekly*. Of course we subscribe to these at the library, so I had plenty to choose from. I collected about forty to fifty of them and laid them all out on a table to let the girls look at the covers and analyze who these magazines were targeting and what ideas they were trying to express to female readers. And we found out that there were basically three major themes—relationships, body weight/body image, and pregnancy—that forty to fifty magazine covers depicted. All of the cover headlines ended in an exclamation point as if to stress urgency. One of the incarcerated females said she did not realize how she was being bombarded by these topics so consistently by these gossip tabloids. And these are issues that a lot of studies have found teenage girls are dealing with, particularly at-risk girls, issues like teenage pregnancy and low self-esteem related to body image.

What I wanted the students to get out of that project was to be able to discern information a little more accurately. I think it was very appropriate for this demographic because they're susceptible to a lot of these things. They're at risk; they don't have the support structures in their lives to help them make good decisions about media. A lot of the time they're not doing well in a traditional classroom that may not value media literacy education. There was a sense that maybe this activity at some point will empower them to make better decisions about the world around them. Once the students understood all these tactics, we were able to use them in the creation of a digital tabloid which satirized and spoofed the news media. But it didn't do so in a way that argued all news is fake. Rather it made use of these tactics to deconstruct how popular media influence the way we think.

STACIE WILLIAMS: This idea of information literacy—certainly I don't recall worrying about that or hearing about that before the past six or seven years. Definitely wasn't a thing when I got out of college. I think that has had to do somewhat with the democratization of tech. We have this idea that a lot of people can use it. The traditional gatekeepers have been somewhat neutered. As journalism students, we sort of understood that there were very specific legitimate means of transmitting information, basically. You'd go into J school and they would essentially say, "All right, you're going to learn all this stuff. And eventually you need to be working for the Times or the Post, or your entire career will have been a joke." Which was extreme and nobody needed that kind of pressure because very few people were able to actually accomplish that. Certainly more traditional gatekeepers of media had their own issues in terms of who had been running them, who had been shaping news content, and what that meant for the stories that were being told and were not being told over time.

Okay, so we understand that those are huge issues. But those had been the traditional gatekeepers. Those were the people who essentially controlled what most of us learned over time. Technology helped democratize that. Technology jumped off, and you could have regular citizens becoming sort of citizen journalists, reporting on things that they saw every day in the neighborhood, their interactions with people. You could have people really using it for a good thing, and people really using it for a bad thing. I think it's more that people figured out how you could manipulate the technology using things like search engine optimization. That's how you can have things like—I don't know if this comes up as much anymore, but there was a website that was martinlutherking.org. I used to always use that as an example in my information literacy classes, because .org was actually a white supremacist website, but the guy who ran it had learned how to use search engine optimization to plant certain words and terminology within his website that would make it come up if you were doing a more innocent Google search on Martin Luther King, Jr. The actual website that you would want to use, or at least the one related to his estate, is the King Center. It's not his full name, but if you were a younger or unseasoned researcher, you would have clicked on martinlutherking.org and read a whole bunch of craziness before you maybe realized, hey, something seems kind of wrong, or something seems kind of off about this site. There was also this really awful anti-Semitic language on there. And that's if you're a discerning researcher. I think someone who is less discerning would have just simply consumed what was on that site and been like, oh, okay. So here was a person who had learned how to manipulate that technology to do bad things. There are content farms now that exist, and people just churning out garbage, but it's finely tuned for maximum SEO impact, so you do a Google search and the garbage is the first thing that comes up. It's challenging. It is very challenging.

. . .

JASON GRIFFEY: I actually don't have any degrees in technology. I'm not a computer science graduate or an engineer or anything like that, but I grew up right at the burgeoning of the personal computer movement and was lucky enough to fall into that as a kid. I was probably eleven or so when I somehow convinced my parents to buy me a Commodore 64. That kindled my love of technology and computers, and so I always did that. And then I had the secondary luck of being in college, my bachelor's studies, during the birth of the World Wide Web. It was right literally just as the Web exploded, '92, '93, '94, when graphic web browsing happened and the Mosaic project released the first graphic web browser, and all of that. I taught myself HTML. One of my very first jobs in technology was as webmaster in like 1995. I kind of kept that skill set sharp all the way through 2004, when I got my library degree at UNC Chapel Hill. So it kind of all came together.

STACIE WILLIAMS: Technology for me has always been a part of my career, because I really came of age on this cusp. When I first started college, I can remember there was this very clear shift. We had grown up with a computer in our home. We had an Apple IIe. This was largely because my mother was a teacher. She worked for Milwaukee public schools, and at that time, in the '80s, they'd just had a special program where teachers could take home a computer for the summer. So we started having access in the summer, and then by the time I was a senior in high school, my parents had actually just purchased a computer that we had in the house. But when I started college, that was my first time ever using email. It was a totally new concept to me. I had not used it in high school at all.

So technology, even just from the beginning of my adult life, was a very big part of my life. I started writing for publications that were starting to put more of their content on the Web. By the time I left journalism, I was working for a Crain Communication publication in Chicago. Because it was a healthcare publication, we talked about technology a lot. I can remember that the first time I ever heard the word "interoperable" was while I was working at this healthcare magazine, because the big issue at that time was electronic health records. So that was actually the first time, as a journalist, that I heard about these things that we discuss a lot in libraries, like electronic records, surveillance, privacy, encryption, and then databases—storing this information. All of these types of things, I first heard about them while writing about and editing things about healthcare.

And then from the technical standpoint, as it happened, we were beefing up our web presence at that magazine. I was one of the younger members of staff, and my editor put together a team of people who would be willing to break news on the weekends. He needed a team of an editor and somebody who was comfortable with the Web, and at that point, I had become the person who was hard-coding issues of the magazine so that they could be rendered online. I was doing all the HTML coding for that, every Friday night, and so I totally volunteered to then be that weekend person, because I was already doing it anyway. Learning how to write web headlines and about search engine optimization was actually very instructive.

I'd say the Internet really always been a part of my career in some way or another. If I hadn't been using it to create access to the content, I was using it to generate my own content. Because definitely by the time I graduated college, I was doing my research on it. I was finding out about internships to apply for. I did a considerable amount of research using my computer. So I think when I decided to transition into libraries, I was looking for something that fit the skill set that I had already been polishing in that ten years. It just allowed me to apply many of the things that I had learned.

Jessamyn West: Digital platforms are really interesting because when I went to library school, it was right when everything changed. Before library school, we didn't have the World Wide Web, and by the time I graduated library school, the World Wide Web existed. But it was new enough that we felt like we could still learn how to do it. When I was in library school, we learned how to make web pages and things like that. Because it was there, and we could learn it.

In addition, part of what I learned was kind of how to be a maker in a technology sense early, and then I kept my hand in as I moved forward. But because I lived in Seattle—I went to library school at the University of Washington—I was in a super tech-saturated community. And so for my tech community, I was low-end, because all I could do was make a web page. I couldn't code, I didn't have a job in a tech company. I worked at Speakeasy, which was an Internet service provider, doing customer support. So I had to understand how those things worked, but I wasn't a coder. I was an emailer; I was all email.

What that meant was, I was in a group of people who were often early adopters. So I got on a lot of stuff kind of early. I got on Facebook kind of early. I got on Twitter kind of early. And I had a blog super early. But I was always dragging behind the community that I was a part of in the tech community. At the same time, I was a little bit of a trailblazer in the library community, which I've always thought was funny, because I felt like the tech community kept me trying, kept me like, "Try this out! Try that out! Your blog doesn't have comments—everybody's blog has comments!" So, shit, I've got to figure out how to get comments. I went through a lot of different platforms, and because I'm one of those people who's up for it, I was always trying things to figure that out. I never thought of myself as a very techie librarian as much as I thought of myself as a very librarian-y tech person.

One of the things I found after I moved to rural Vermont was that if you were in rural Vermont and you had tech skills, "librarian" wasn't the job for you. The librarians often didn't get paid very well, didn't get to do a lot of tech work, and they were great on their own. I was better as a kind of library supporter than I was as a librarian. And that's how I've managed to do the things I've done now. As a result, the way my tech friends were for me, learning my tech chops, I could be in library communities, helping people by being supportive, by being a mentor, by being friendly, by being a woman on the Internet who isn't having a really hard time. Kind of help them learn or understand what they needed to do.

▼ ▼ ▼

MICHAEL GORMAN: I have quite strong views about what should be taught in LIS programs. I think that the role of an ideal program would be to educate librarians on all aspects of library work, to give them a solid foundation in—to use the traditional terms—cataloging, reference, reader assistance, and so forth. I also think that they should give an educational grounding—not training but an educational grounding—in the use of library technology, in library administration, library economics, and so forth. What I worry about is that, for a variety of reasons, the expectations of people going in—that is, the people who wish to work in libraries—and the expectation of people at the other end—that is, the people who wish to employ educated librarians—are being stymied by the middle of the process, where the education has drifted away from library work and into some kind of mishmash of computer science and information science, largely driven by faculty who are not rooted in libraries and in some cases have no particular use for libraries.

HANA SLEIMAN: The librarianship in Lebanon at least is in a completely different state of affairs from what's happening in the US. There are very few professional librarians there, let alone digitally literate ones. What ends up happening is complete reliance on software developers. Also there's only one library school in the country, the Lebanese University. What ends up happening is that most librarians will develop their skills on personal initiative, except the ones that are then sent to train in Europe or the US and then come back with a different skill set. But I think that the problem with the way librarianship is taught in Lebanon and in general is its overemphasis on standards and technicalities, and not enough engagement with the content of the materials and the implications of standards on the integrity of archives. Sometimes standards are prioritized over common sense, which is a problem.

ANITA COLEMAN: I was recently teaching Vocabulary Design at San Jose State University. Vocabulary design is about the creation of thesauri and indexes and abstracts, as well as standards for controlled vocabularies standards and metadata describing images. One of the broad topics that I chose to focus on was anti-racism, incidentally also a Library of Congress Subject Heading. I told the students, "Within this topic, you can explore whatever you like. You can pick your own people's group, or your own narrow topic, whatever piques your interest, and then develop a mini-vocabulary for that topic and in this way we will learn the process of vocabulary design." The class was very small and I could give the students individual attention, but the lack of interest in this kind of a practical project and the evaluation I received at the end simply stunned me! These graduate students just wanted an undergraduate-type course. They were forgetting that this was a graduate-level course, where you are required to think and learn to solve problems. Instead what they wanted was a test where they learned, "This is correct," "This is wrong," and "Yes" or "No." That's really not how the real world functions. Ultimately, when you go out to work, yes, you have to know Library of Congress Subject Headings in an academic or a public library, to some extent, and, yes, you don't need to know all of it; you don't need to memorize the actual subject headings. But I think you have to understand what the subject headings do, how they enable scholarship, especially deep scholarship.

So what would I do, how would I teach? My experience at San Jose State University only reinforced what I'd already learned about our field when I started LIS teaching while I was a doctoral student at the University of Illinois at Urbana-Champaign. Because of my successful experience with library automation and cataloging, I was invited to teach Systems Analysis and Design. The young men in the class loved it, but I had complaints from the women students—it was too technical! I also taught the Systems Analysis course as an adjunct faculty at UCLA and added Information Seeking Behaviors to my teaching repertoire. Then, as a full-time faculty at University of Arizona, my area of specialization was the Organization of Information and Digital Libraries. No matter the school, top-notch UIUC or else, I experienced similar complaints—e.g. why was I requiring knowledge of HTML and databases in a cataloging course? Most students wanted to become reference librarians, and they did not want to know structured data!

I took a seven-year break, and then when I came back, I did try again. Now, I'm just really disappointed in the quality of the students that library schools still seem to be getting, and the rush to push them out. It still is the one-year degree. People are in a hurry to get a job, and then when they get the job, I don't know how well they do or don't do. Most of the librarians that I've met in the California higher education system—UCs, Cal States, and community colleges—don't appear to be the "digerati." They act insular and territorial, and appear to disrespect library and information science education, and it's just sad. A library director warned me long ago that librarians don't value the PhD in LIS, and that I know is generally true. LIS schools prefer to hire faculty whose PhDs are in any discipline but LIS. So why should librarians think LIS has any intellectual value? It's really sad.

JAIME TAYLOR: I think that we do library school really incorrectly. I have a lot of very lengthy opinions about it, but one of the big ones is that probably library schools should look more like an apprenticeship in the trades. When you're an electrician, you learn from people, but you're also taking classes and you're working at the same time. So both the way you learn ends up being a lot more practical—you're still getting that classroom learning, but you're also immediately practicing. It also would offer a different kind of financial structure than the way library school currently works, which is really broken in that right now, unless your family is independently wealthy or you're extremely lucky and you work somewhere that helps you fund your education already, most of us come out of library school with a lot of debt in the way that you don't when you're going into a trade and apprenticing, because you're working. The financial structure of library school is completely different.

In an alternate universe where my vision of library school were enacted, I think we would find people gaining those skills more as they went through school, because they'd have to learn some of them to be doing the work that they've already started to do, and they'd know what they need to know, where their knowledge gaps are. And then because you're in school, you have the luxury—since at that point your job is also learning—to learn those things, whereas I'm sitting here now as a professional, I already go to work for forty hours a week, I don't want to then spend two to three evenings a week after I go to work all day sitting in a classroom. At least my institution does offer some tuition remission, not very much, but enough to take a couple courses at the City University of New York or something. And I kind of intend to, but, again, the thought of working full-time and also going to school—which I know a lot of people do—I just don't want to. I don't know that under the current way we conduct library school there's really space to also learn in a fundamental way, a solid way, those skills. Are we going to take out, I don't know, a cataloging class and replace it with learning JavaScript? That doesn't make sense. I don't know that there's a way to integrate that more fully without making it another year of school or something like that, which would become even more prohibitively expensive.

So I don't have an answer to that. I think that the main gist of it is that library school is broken already. I wish there were better ways that we can learn those skills on the job, but, as I said, who am I going to even learn that from? Am I going to go to school? There's no one really in the building. And then also the question of time—if I could learn that on the clock, sure, I'd take a couple hours out of my work week and do it. There's certainly an argument to be made for that, though it's not one that management usually accepts, that anything I'm doing for my job should be part of those forty hours a week I work and that includes learning things. I doubt that most of us can make the argument.

Bess Sadler: I wish we were talking about better hiring. We don't write good job ads, in my opinion. We don't create entry-level positions.

We have an apprenticeship model, but we don't recognize that fact. We, as institutions, think that whenever we need a new skill set, we need to hire someone new who already has that skill set. We should be training and promoting from within. We should be feeding back to library schools and actively helping them develop curriculum around digital repositories, scientific data management, all that kind of stuff.

Jason Griffey: Coming at technology from a nontraditional standpoint, unfortunately, is fairly common in libraries. And I say "unfortunately" only because it lends itself to being less formal than maybe we need. Technologies in libraries often do come from nontraditional backgrounds. I have met dozens, I think. Library technology people, whether they're in academic or public libraries, that have backgrounds in, like, philosophy or math—not formal computer science training—I think that comes about in a couple of ways. My take on it is that with people who know very early and move very quickly and take computer science degrees, it's very hard for libraries to compete for their skills in any sort of marketplace. If you graduate with an engineering degree, you're going to move into industry or into corporate computer science most often, because that's where the market forces drive you. You're going to make much, much more money—double, triple the salary you would in a library or non-profit setting. That's really unfortunate, because obviously there's a huge amount of value to libraries and having people there who are formally trained in computer science. And there's lot of interesting problems being solved in the library world and in the information ecosystem that aren't being solved necessarily in forward-thinking ways in the other sorts of spheres, in corporate and other worlds.

I do think that people coming into technology in libraries in other ways is maybe representative of libraries as a whole. Many people come to libraries, not necessarily as second careers, but through some other interest. You move into libraries because you're interested in helping people, in instruction. You're interested in a particular subject, in history or in genealogy or in archival studies or something, and you come to libraries as an outlet for your interests. And I think that's the path that a lot of library technologists take. I think that libraries could benefit from a bit more formal computer science structure in the way that engineers approach problems. On the other hand, I'm not quite sure how we get there. It's very hard for us to compete in that world at this point.

The technologists I happen to know, the librarians I know that are in the technology field, are some of the brightest people I've ever met. So I don't think we're suffering from a lack of talent necessarily. I do think that we have incredibly brilliant people in libraries and technology, but I think that there are instances where computer scientists and such outside of libraries look and go, "What in the world are you people doing?" Which I find amusing.

. . .

ELVIA ARROYO-RAMIREZ: Keeping abreast in the field has proven difficult especially when there can be "gaps" in your career with regard to having access to resources to stay abreast. For example, early in my career, I took employment at a small nonprofit, and while I enjoyed dedicating my labor to an independent grassroots archive, I didn't have access to paywalled scholarly literature. I didn't have a budget to go to any conferences or attend workshops either. So sometimes I feel like I'm getting late in the digital preservation and archives game, but I think my current employer has been supportive of this type of professional development, and for that I am grateful. As a processing archivist tasked with managing born-digital archives, I believe we are all trying to learn on the job, while juggling a lot of different responsibilities not related to born-digital archives. It's hard to try to gain the knowledge and expertise if you don't have a set and dedicated time blocked off in your schedule to pick it up because you're juggling other responsibilities, like processing paper-based collections in the backlog.

Practically speaking, I would recommend hiring cohorts of archivists, technicians, and librarians who will all come to a specific task together while they are learning the work culture. That way employers improve team-building and skill-sharing. I think University of Arizona does this. At Princeton, there's a good team of us who are all relatively new here, who workshop issues we come across while processing born-digital materials. Talking issues out loud, whether they be technological, ethical, or practical, has helped build team competency and skill sets. Academically speaking, I'd recommend instructors reach out to more practitioners who are grappling with the current issues in the field to guest lecture. Most students earning their MLIS with a specific focus in archives do not want to get their doctorates, they want to gain the practical experience, so getting a practitioner in the classroom to share what they are struggling with at work can be really beneficial.

MARK MATIENZO: I'm very cognizant of the fact that my career path played out the way it did because of privilege. I self-identify as Latinx, but I look very white. My father's Peruvian, my mother's American. In thinking about technology in the context of libraries, one of the things that has always been very striking to me is how for a profession that's known to be very gendered and very female, essentially how white and male the technology sector, even in libraries, really is. One of the things that we really have an obligation to do, and I find to be more of a personal calling, is to do community development to make there be a broader pool. To allow people who are like me or who are not like me see the work that I do as a viable career path. To encourage people to be curious.

I have a lot of complicated feelings about this push to encourage people to learn how to code. I think it's a little bit of a cliché now, but at least a few years ago, there was a big push in librarians learning how to code. Sure, obviously, anybody should learn how to code if they want. Anybody should also learn how to bake bread, or learn how to finish hardwood, or whatever skill that you want to talk about. That's fine. But what was fundamentally frustrating about it was it the lack of awareness that not everybody will feel comfortable doing it. Not everybody will necessarily have or even just feel like they have the time or capacity to spend time doing that additional learning. I think there's a strong class issue there as well. In order to succeed at your job, you have to be willing to spend this portion of your professional time doing something which may or may not have specific dividends for your career, at the expense of perhaps your ability to work a second job—if you have some sort of precarious employment situation—or to be able to take care of your kids. While I think there have been some great ways to address that—I've heard of colleagues at other institutions who have had things like code clubs at the workplace, where people ostensibly meet for a long coffee break and work through a problem together and learn the basics of programming together—outside of that kind of context, where you've got the capacity to do that, there's a lot of assumptions that are baked into someone's ability to have the time to do that.

ANDROMEDA YELTON: The best example I have seen of someone supporting learning of technology skills in a library workplace is Evviva Weinraub, when she was at OSU. She's at Northwestern now, but I assume she is still this kind of manager. I talked about in *Coding for Librarians* the various kind of ways that she supported professional development and budgeted time and money to ensure that her people got it. If everyone did what Evviva did, we would be great. I would love to see something like ACRL Immersion course in instruction. I would love to see something like that except for tech skills. It doesn't exist right now. I think mostly it comes down to, do you luck out with your manager? Some managers are great at making sure that people have time and money to learn new skills and to go to conferences and get relevant books or courses or whatever, and some managers aren't.

ELVIA ARROYO-RAMIREZ: When I was in graduate school in 2011, there was not much in the way of course offerings to gain the practical skill set to handle born-digital processing, accessioning, and appraising. Because I was in the archives track in my program, I had very little wiggle room to choose the courses I wanted to take outside of the track. I think the courses in the information technology track would have been as relevant to me now as a practicing archivist working with an increasing number of legacy media with born-digital content. I know now there are folks like Rhiannon Bettivia and Amelia Acker who are actively incorporating histories of information and technology, born-digital archiving, and preservation topics to their curriculum and class offerings. Rhiannon actually has her remote students download BitCurator on their machines and I think that's fantastic. I would have definitely benefitted from having more hands-on activities like that as a student.

BONNIE GORDON: For what we have at the Rockefeller Archive Center that's on storage media like floppy disks, optical disks, CDs and DVDs, hard drives—I've learned that there are a lot of other types of digital media—the way that we get those materials off is through disk imaging and other digital forensics processes. These processes help us make sure that we preserve all the bits and all of the original context, and then we usually, depending on how old the material is, keep the original but also migrate the format so that other archivists and researchers can open them and look at the files. So there are some skill sets and equipment that are needed to do this. We had all this material and it had been the digital archivist's job to image this material with the end goal of making it accessible.

But the major project that I'm working on right now is to get rid of that model and blow it up, and then have all of our processing archivists do that basic baseline preservation of digital media. Because what we had was people taking it out of the collections that they were processing and then handing it over to my department, and then we just had a backlog. In addition to our reasoning that it's not great to have a backlog, this doesn't scale, it's not sustainable, and it also, I think, enforces the idea that technology is hard and scary. When in reality, eventually there won't be "archivists" and "digital archivists"; everyone is going to be a digital archivist. So it's important to make it not scary, train people, and give people the tools that they need, which include the programs and software that they need and also the documentation and the training and just, like, emotional support in order to be able to do that.

ELVIA ARROYO-RAMIREZ: I gave a talk[1] with my coworkers about the blurred roles for traditional processing archivists and digital archivists at academic research libraries. As born-digital archives become a core part of archival processing, traditional processing archivists who lack Digital Archivist job titles face numerous challenges when meeting the processing and preservation needs of born-digital collections. And while I've talked about the type of knowledge and skills required to do this type of work, I haven't discussed institutional culture as another challenge to overcome for those who are moving towards digital archiving work. Stubborn expectations about who is responsible for the management of born-digital archives can be a barrier for practicing archivists in traditional processing roles.

On the other hand, relying on the expertise of one Digital Archivist per institution is not a sustainable practice as it can overburden and overwork those in these roles. At Princeton we have only one dedicated Digital Archivist, Jarrett Drake, who's in the University Archives division of the department of Rare Books and

---

1 Elvia Arroyo-Ramirez, Kelly Bolding, and Faith Charlton, "Moving Beyond the Lone Digital Archivist Model Through Collaboration and Living Documentation" (presentation, Code4Lib, Los Angeles, CA, March 6–9, 2017).

Special Collections. But through his help, archivists at Princeton have opened up a space for skill- and knowledge-sharing that's enabled processing archivists like myself to process the digital materials in the collections we're responsible for. One of my biggest takeaways from this model is that it helps to have a cohort of people who are more or less on the same path as you with shared goals and expectations. The University of Arizona hires cohorts of people to help build team competence, skills, and trust, and I think they're definitely onto something. At Princeton this has enabled us to share the brunt of the labor of conducting research, writing proposals, and investigating best practices in digital curation and archives that—because we're not all dedicated digital archivists—would have been extremely time-taxing to do on our own. Other archival repositories have established similar institutional models like the Rockefeller Archive Center and the University of California, Santa Barbara.

BONNIE GORDON: The Rockefeller Archive Center's digital program team values were initially created before I started, so I can't speak entirely to that, but we've changed them over time. I do know that other technology departments and other organizations, like the Digital Public Library of America, have values statements, but I know that, as a team, we think it's really important to articulate values. Because everyone has them, but it's important that they are articulated, and they really affect all decisions that you make. I think as a team we strongly believe in the values that we've come to, and this is a document that we review in our quarterly meetings and we always make sure it's up to date. And they're in a rough order of—I don't know if "importance" is the right word, but one of our first ones is "engaging and empowering users," which frames all other values. To me, that's really important. It gets to talking about training and documentation and making technology less scary. But I think that it's important to consider your users, not think that you know what's best for them. They have needs. There are a lot of reasons for that. But the best way to provide good outcomes and things that work is by listening to your users and also empowering people to do things, teaching people how to fish, teaching people that technology isn't scary.

Another thing, too, is most of the systems that we use are open source, so making sure that our colleagues know that if they don't like this feature, we can probably go into the code and change it. Which is really awesome. Teaching people how to troubleshoot, and making technology really work for them, is how it's sustainable. It's not good at all to have the technologists over *here*, and when you need to do something involving a computer, go over to this department over *there*. Not everyone will have the same skills, obviously, but I think that teaching people it's okay to fail, what else you need to do to troubleshoot, what questions to ask, is really important and makes everyone's jobs easier.

An example for me personally—this is changing, but I will say that on my team I have the least amount of coding skills now. But I've worked very closely with our accessioning team on using command-line tools, like for bagging and transferring materials to the archives. Using the command line is a little scary for some people—it's new, it looks like you could break something even though you probably can't—so I definitely work with them closely on that. That includes working with them on documentation, setting aside a day to walk through how something works, and when something goes wrong because you put something in the wrong folder, or you don't actually have the permissions and you need to change the permissions on your computer or whatever, doing that troubleshooting. I think that's super important.

MARK MATIENZO: In terms of values of usability and interoperability, a lot of those are reflected in a concrete and explicit decision to rely on open source whenever possible at DPLA. One of the more important things that we've done was when the technology team and I worked to put together a set of values for ourselves a couple of years ago. We recently released them. Part of why we waited is to see how they would hold up over time. One of these values that's important to the work that we do is really focusing on using open source whenever possible. Part of that is releasing the work that we're doing, as long as there's not some sort of restriction. I think we've successfully avoided a lot of those restrictions, but there are some cases where we're not releasing something because of security concerns or things like that. But we do really try to make the work that we do accessible under open source licenses.

We also try to be very transparent about the work we do. That's a pretty strong personal value for me as well—I really do enjoy making clear the type of work that I'm doing, to both my colleagues and my stakeholders. Probably the most important value that I bring to the work, and more broadly in terms of thinking about the community-based work I do as well, is focusing on inclusiveness. Really working to develop communities and spaces and projects where people feel comfortable contributing and asking questions, where they feel safe, where they feel empowered to participate. An initiative like DPLA is so big and so broad that I've had several conversations with people where they've said, "You know, I can't fathom being able to do your job," or "I don't know how to participate." Since I've moved on from DPLA, I've heard similar feedback at the periphery of other communities I've been involved with as well. I've heard people acknowledge things like imposter syndrome when they've been in meetings to talk about a DPLA initiative, get involved in a community initiative that is new to them, or learn something, which is unfortunate.

. . .

BECKY YOOSE: There is the joke that systems librarians and catalogers are secretly siblings. We're twins, essentially. We deal with standards, we deal with a lot of technical documentation, we look at what we did six months from now, be it a script or a cataloging record, and go, "What the hell were we thinking?" You redo the entire script or you redo the entire metadata record. It's now getting easier to have that conversation with everyone who might be on one spectrum or the other, because it's now starting to become more accepted—even when your organizational structures have this dichotomy baked into it—that you can't really do data work without some sort of computational thinking or computational knowledge. And you can't be an effective library technologist if you don't know what is in your system, if you don't know the data, if you don't know how the data is structured. You don't have to know all the cataloging metadata standards, but you have to at least know what major standards are out there, what you would expect to find, what's more common to find within metadata fields and cataloging records, and who to go to when you have questions.

There's an organization called Mashcat that focuses on getting people who are on the library technology side and people who are more traditional metadata and cataloger workers together to talk a little bit more about how their work impacts the other side of the field, as well as provide opportunities for cross-pollination in forms of workshops or other conversations on Twitter or on other places like Slack—if nothing else, provide that platform where people can ask questions in a place where they're not going to feel like they're stupid. Basically "stupid questions are welcome here." Mostly so far their efforts have been going fairly well.

    I do have to say, it is easier to have that conversation now than would have been in the past. For example, when I started in 2008 at Miami University, it was still kind of uncommon to have a person who essentially was responsible for programming and maintaining scripts to help with metadata clean-up, to help with automating cataloging, to help with automating acquisitions, to automate metadata creation for oral histories. That was still somewhat uncommon even for a mid-sized organization such as Miami. In smaller institutions, there is really no divide in many libraries, where you have your systems person also be the tech services person. So the dichotomy is not always present in libraries, and I do have to acknowledge that. There have been a lot of comments from people saying, "Well, I'm both a technologist and the metadata person, so I don't really understand why we're talking about a particular divide, because I don't see there's a divide." Well, in general librarianship, we have treated it as such. Again, it's just needing to remind people that in order to be an effective metadata and cataloger, you have to have some computational thinking in the way that you approach your work with metadata and cataloging various resources, be it physical or electronic. And to be an effective library technologist, you have to know your data that you're working with.

JASON GRIFFEY: One of the beautiful things about libraries and about librarians is that there are so many different kinds. When you say "librarian," that can mean everything from a system administrator overseeing dozens of servers and basically being head-down in Apache web logs every day, to someone who's leading children's programming, to someone who works with teens every day, to someone who's working in rare books and doing what is effectively archeology on these delicate preservation materials. And those skill sets are just insanely different. The breadth of what you can get away with and call yourself a librarian is crazy, and it's very hard to find another profession that has quite that broad a gap in skill sets. So to say, "Everybody universally, all librarians need to know HTML," or "All librarians need to code" is a difficult kind of universal statement to make.

On the other hand, I do think that there are some directions we can see that lend themselves to where I think graduates and graduate schools and new librarians should maybe spend a bit more time focusing, and that is technology. I've said this a few times in talks that I've given, but, short of a zombie apocalypse, there isn't any future in libraries that doesn't involve more technology. Short of Armageddon, we know that five years from now there will be more technology in libraries than there is now, and ten years from now it will be even more so. We're not going to go backwards. There's no future that I can imagine and, I would argue, that anybody can set out that involves a radical lessening in the amount of technology knowledge that goes into running a library.

So we need some knowledge of how tech works—it doesn't necessarily have to be coding, but understanding code and the world of communications, the Internet, how databases work, how code interacts with the information in those databases. You don't have to be able necessarily to sit down and write something from scratch; you don't need to be able to sit down at a blank terminal and pound out some Python code that will do something for your library. That's not necessary. Everyone doesn't need to be able to do that. But everyone needs to understand that that is a thing that can happen, and understand how that set of skills can impact the services that we offer. So a more universal understanding of that—and I'm biased. My background is in sciences and philosophy, so I tend to think, "There should be more logic in schools! And we should have people understanding the basic tenets of symbolic logic!" Because that's really what all coding and things are. That's not realistic; that's a bias I have from my background. But there's definitely a sense in which I would feel much more positively about the future of libraries if I knew that everybody coming out of a formal program had at least a strong solid understanding of the way that the digital world works. Code and databases and the Internet and computers and operating systems—if we had a robust understanding about how all of that works together, I think there's a lot more of a future for us.

ANDROMEDA YELTON: I think it's very difficult to answer a question of what should be taught in library schools, because they serve so many different audiences. People emerge from library schools doing such wildly different jobs that it's hard for me to say there's any one skill everyone needs, other than the skill of learning more, which I think is a quintessential library skill. We're information experts, and being able to find information on how to learn more things is really something that we ought to get. But then I don't know that I'm comfortable saying that there are specific tech skills or tech literacies everyone should have, because they're job-dependent and because they change. Even if there's something that it would be great for everyone to have now, it's not the same skill that people would all need in ten years.

So, again, it doesn't make sense for library schools to be teaching specific skills so much as it makes sense for library skills to be giving people opportunities to learn new skills and to understand the how to find that information and how it is they learn. I think the things that I happen to come across in my part of libraries, which is slanted toward academics and slanted towards metadata people and slanted towards developers—I come across a lot of copyright issues, and knowing something about how the copyright system works is important. I come across the concept of databases. I think whether or not you know SQL, that can vary, but understanding how databases work is, I think, one of those concepts that unlocks a lot of understanding of how library technology does work and can work and should work, and it lets you understand the world around you in any way. I think that the idea of structured data, the idea of the API make a big difference. But again, this is in my part of librarianship, and I'm not going to say that everyone needs to know them. I think that knowing how to learn new things, and having practice in library school learning new things specifically about technology so that you understand that you're a person who can learn that subject is way more important than any specific technologies you might learn.

JOHN HELLING: The question of what should be getting taught in library schools is always such a tricky one. There is such a huge variety of need! We in the public library arena need to know a lot about the tech that our patrons are using, like e-readers, but also very site-specific things like how the school enrollment websites work. For public libraries, what I would say is that you should never feel like you're completely prepared. You should always feel like there's something you need to know, because soon enough something will come along—3D printing, for example—that you're going to have to talk about to your patrons.

MITA WILLIAMS: I'm largely self-taught in my coding skills as I've only taken one computer science course. Mostly the learning that I've done is from books, online tutorials, and workshops given by colleagues. I can't remember who first said it, but no one is really self-taught when it comes to coding because we generally teach ourselves from documentation. So everything I've learned is largely because other people had taken the care to document how to do code.

I think that code literacy is really important, and I've personally tried to encourage others, not just librarians, but people in the community to learn more about code literacy. I've done some work teaching people enough code to handle things like open data or how to make their own maps and such. I think it's important to understand the capabilities and constraints that our tools have. The more that you understand the extent of what text can do for you or what numbers can do for you, the more capabilities you can have.

I've been thinking more and more about how we should share code like how we share recipes. There's a project I'm really fond of called IPython, which is a sort of structure that is built to encourage the sharing of code. IPython incorporates documentation and code together into something called a Notebook. You can copy someone else's Notebook, swap out the data that the code is based on then run the program and see the results. So it really challenges this idea of what a document is as it becomes a much more of a "living document." And so for librarians, I think learning about code is very useful because it allows us to change the scale of the work that we do. But more importantly, it allows us to share more of the work that we do. I think the more that we can work beyond our individual libraries and work together on projects the happier we will be. Building community and practice of sharing is really important for our profession.

BECKY YOOSE: I'm going to say right out that not everyone needs to code. That's the reality. There are some folks who might benefit from knowing how to program a small script in a particular language like Python or PHP/MySQL to help with particular duties and whatnot. But in general, the more I hear about learning to code, how everyone should learn how to code, how everyone should learn how to code this particular language—"They should know how to do Python," or "They should know how to do HTML and CSS"—"No! They should know JavaScript and jQuery"—"No! They need to know about Ruby or Ruby on Rails!" You get into these holy language wars, which I have seen play out at Code4Lib over and over and over again. It just gets tiresome.

Honestly, people need to know the basics of computational thinking. How to approach a particular workflow or situation that they can go through systematically and go, okay, so, we have this particular thing that we want to do. So you go ahead and you start breaking things out step by step, and then you start adding your conditionals. Okay, so what happens if this particular metadata record has this particular code? Well, you do a little decision tree right there. If it has Code A, then Action X needs to happen. If it has Code B, then Action Y needs to happen, else Action Z happens.

Nonetheless, I don't want to discourage anyone from learning to code. Because in technical services, where you have people who want to learn how to code, who want to delve into building their own scripts because they see the potential of creating more efficient workflows, being able to provide higher-quality work in an efficient manner so that they can go through and add more records into that particular system, or work on existing records and improve them—I've seen technical services staff wanting to learn code and getting shut down again and again because library administration, for one reason or another, believes that technology skills of that nature do not belong in a traditional technical services setting. And that is not only sad to see, not only short-sighted, it also reaffirms the class structure of librarianship, where you have some functions and some roles within librarianship that don't get that much support because people do not place value on what that particular role or that particular person does. Well, if your discovery layer doesn't have good metadata, people are not going to be able to find what they're searching for.

I want everyone to have at least a basic understanding of computational thinking, a higher level of programming language structures and concepts like conditionals, operators, how things could interact with each other in a particular program or application. Enough to at least give them some sort of grounding when they go talk to that person who *does* have that coding knowledge, who does have that technical skill, and having at least a conversation where they can have a basic level of understanding that they can follow. But they should not be discouraged, which I have seen in the past, from learning how to code. That is one thing that library administration has been very guilty about, is thinking that only certain types of library roles should only have work time and support to learning how to code.

HANA SLEIMAN: I think librarians should absolutely learn software development, but I don't think it should be part of our job. But then the reason why we need to learn them is that we're better able to assess what can and cannot be done with existing tools, as opposed to being completely dependent on expertise that is placed elsewhere, not in the library. Or even if it's in the library, IT departments and systems librarians won't be necessarily as immersed in the work that we're doing, and thus may not know what the best solution to offer is, or will propose something that is workable but not necessarily in the best interest of the project. So a knowledge, a demystifying of the digital world is absolutely important for archives. Again, it shouldn't be us—it *could* be, but it should not be us developing these softwares. But we should absolutely have the know-how to be able to assess and plan projects. We might still opt to go for existing solutions, but a knowledge of the bigger scope is extremely important.

JESSAMYN WEST: It's not that I don't think people should learn to code; it's just that I think you don't have to be a coder to be a good librarian. Librarians who code, that's helpful. Librarians who don't code, that's also helpful. But the things you need to be able to do include running and managing technology-type projects, so maybe you don't need to code, but you need to be able to spec out a thing that someone else could build. Or if somebody builds you a website, you've got to be able to look at it and determine if it meets your needs.

I think it's really hard to point to specific technologies, because obviously that kind of thing changes all the time. I am often shocked when I meet library school students—not always, and not in all schools—and realize that they have what I would consider to be a more surface approach to tech. They're a sophisticated end user, but they really don't know what's going on under the hood of an app or a website or a thing. Or—and this is, I think, the larger problem—they're incurious. I think more than you say, "Somebody needs to know how to code," or "Somebody needs to know how to make a web page," or "Somebody needs to know how to use a thing," the thing I think people really need is to be up for it, whatever that means. Job interview questions for modern-day librarians who just have to do basic stuff could be, "How do you feel about the fact that technology's changing all the time?" I feel like you can get so many people who are like, "Oh, I know, you just finally learn one thing and then you've got to learn another thing! When will it end!" And you're like, "You are not up for it."

There's nothing wrong with that from a personal perspective; that's between you and your own moral compass. But as a librarian, especially dealing with digitally divided populations—and a lot of librarians who deal with digitally divided populations may themselves be digitally divided—part of what you have to do is model a good, healthy outlook for dealing with the fact that technology changes. So you got a new interface to deal with because your browser updated, your operating system updated, Twitter updated, something changed—well, you've got to be up for it, because that's just the way the world works. And I don't mean to throw people in the deep end of the pool; I really feel like you have to hold hands with people and be like, "This is going to be all right," but it is also how it is. So I feel like a lot of what a good information professional needs to be able to do with their users is set expectations, set a tone, be able to model a healthy relationship to technology, whatever that means, and be up for it, dealing with the fact that the world changes.

This is before you even start about money, understanding how to pay for things, understanding how to hire a person. If you don't code, you should be able to figure out how to hire a coder and how to determine if they did a good job, for example. I think because so much technology does wind up being outsourced, you have to figure out how to do project management, how to run a big tech project, maybe, and that could just be a redesign of your website. But even in my town of forty-five hundred people, redesigning the website was a big deal and involved a lot of assessment and feedback, how to run a user test, that kind of thing.

I think people who are good at technology are just going to keep on keeping on, and they'll be fine. People who are bad at it—what "bad" usually means isn't that they can't learn; it usually means they've got an emotional relationship to the technology issue that is getting in their way. For instance, I don't know how to spell every word, but I'm pretty good at working with spell checkers, the red wavy underline, and having people check my work so that to the outside world, I'm a decent speller. As far as I'm concerned, it doesn't matter beyond that, whether I can intrinsically spell words in my sleep or not, what matters is if I can use the tools that are available to me to solve the problem, which is correctly spelling words so that I can be understood. And I feel like the library technology world is kind of like that. You have to present a face of competent technology use and understanding, but it doesn't mean you have to know everything. But it does mean you have to be up for it.

Cecily Walker: The things that I learned in 2004 in library school—except for the foundational things about how to structure information and make it more findable—haven't really served me in the work that I'm doing now. But sometimes I think that the things that people need to learn aren't necessarily things that can be taught in library schools. For example, most library schools aren't really equipped to do the kind of work to teach people how to write code. I remember that we had a class on how to write HTML when I was in library school, but when I look at the work that I do and the platforms that we're using now, there's no need for me to have to write HTML.

So I think teaching and focusing on specific tools, or even specific technologies, is less important than trying to encourage a spirit of exploration, a spirit of play, and the willingness to fail and not to view that failure as a drawback or a setback. One of the things that I'm looking for when I get somebody's resume, if I'm in a position to hire someone—sure, I'm looking at some basic skills or some basic understanding of technology, but what I'm really more interested in, and that comes out in the interview, is just somebody's curiosity about the world and about technology, and for them not to feel afraid of technology. To me that's more important than just about anything else. If you don't have that, you're going to be stagnated, and then you'll be afraid to grow because you'll feel like you don't know enough or aren't supported enough by your supervisors to have that area to explore.

Sarah Houghton: I think that basic programming skills should be taught in library school for sure. And I think that more intermediate and advanced classes should be available if people want to take them. I do think that a basic understanding of how to update your website or change the dimensions on an image so that it's loading quickly on your site—basic skills like that are important for every librarian to have because if they don't have those skills, it's one of their coworkers that's going to have to pitch in and do it for them. So I do think that basic level of skill is important. I don't think that every single librarian needs to learn how to use Drupal to build a website. I don't think every single librarian needs to learn how to program in a variety of twenty different languages.

I think for librarians the digital literacy comfort level needs to be the willingness to experiment and try things, and to actually turn our reference skills on ourselves and know where to research and find information about how to learn those things if you need to. I'm often blown away when librarians say, "Oh, I need to learn this thing, but I don't know what to do!" It's like, "You're a librarian! You do this for patrons every day! You just need to turn that skill on yourself!" It's this weird little mind circle that seems to exist with many of us where we don't apply our same research skills to our own work as we do for our library users every day.

I think library schools need to be teaching more of how to teach technology, not necessarily the technology itself, but how to effectively instruct one-on-one, coach, guide, teach a large classroom-style class about technology specifically, because how you teach tech is very different from how you would teach a class on other topics. Some people are scared of technology. They don't want to break it; there are a lot of hang-ups that people have about it that you still see today, regardless of age group. I think the skills of how to effectively work with someone to get past that and to get comfortable with working with the tech is more important than knowing all the ins and outs of the tech itself. And I see most library school graduates coming out now without ever having taught a class, instructed someone, or ever been given any kind of coaching or information on how to appropriately teach technology. So to me that's a big piece that would be useful, and that need isn't going to go away any time soon.

Carol Bean: I'm glad that library schools now are dealing with the technology side. When I talk to library students today, I'm just amazed at what they're being offered. That's so wonderful. I wish we'd had that. One of the things I've constantly come across in my career is I was always a translator, because I spoke the IT language, and I spoke library language. And my bosses or managers would come and talk to me just to figure out, "Carol, what's going on? They're telling me this, is that true? What do we want to do? How are we going to do this? What does this mean? What does that mean?" I think libraries and library administrators underestimate how much they really need to know about technology. They don't need to be systems librarians, but they definitely need to be more aware of the technology concepts and the technology infrastructure, just basic stuff. Library school graduates who have been coming out in the last few years—as they get to be managers, maybe we'll reach that point. I wish it wouldn't take so long, though. A big part of my career was being a translator, and I was glad to do it, but I was also kind of surprised.

. . .

JOEL NICHOLS: In terms of increasing the skill gap of librarians already out in the field, there are so many things you can do. There are so many sorts of training opportunities or webinars or online interactions. I think that, by and large, training needs to be as personal and as basic for librarians or other library staff as it can be for patrons. I don't know of any professional development workshop I've been in about technology where someone stood behind me to make sure I was clicking right. Much more common is someone with a PowerPoint walking you through whatever tech tool you're using. And I found the opposite to be the most useful when teaching patrons basic technology. You really have to be seeing what they're seeing and pointing to things on the screen and helping them move their hand and making sure that you know really what's going on. So I think shifting the mode a little bit could really help there.

A colleague of mine a few years ago did a really interesting thing. He partnered with a colleague at the Carnegie Library of Pittsburgh, the public library in Pittsburgh. We're in Pennsylvania and they're in Pennsylvania, and we share electronic resources through a state consortium. The two of them put together this fun scavenger hunt question series thing over a period of days. The library who had the most staff awarded won the competition, and then two staff members won gift cards or a Kindle or something that was a nice prize. It was a fun and a very passive program opportunity—he just put it out there as a professional development thing that was also fun, and it was a healthy competition with Pittsburgh. I think what they did was really effective technology training for current staff, because they promoted particular resources and they made it into a game.

My point is that I think there are a variety of modes of professional development that could be effective, and a lot of it depends on the size of your staff and your training apparatus. But at a very basic level, you need to show people what you mean in terms of digital literacy and make sure they understand the tools. In my experience it hasn't been just enough to post instructional videos or send someone to a webinar. You really want to have some closer interaction. In my experience at the Free Library, people maybe get it more when they have the context of the importance of digital literacy and closing the digital divide for library users. Then it becomes less about annoying patron X who you've taught the same thing like ten times, and you don't get why they don't get it, and more like, "Right, she's here because of that, and here's what she really needs, and if I can give that to her, she's going to be able to go forward. But if I keep clicking it for her, she's going to keep asking me."

JESSICA ANNE BRATT: My experience with technology and librarians is a mixed bag. I can't say it's an age or class thing, since I have some older, or veteran, librarians who are amazing at software, and younger librarians who are just like, "I have no idea what's going on right now." But then I have some veterans who are like, "I'm close to retirement, and you're asking me to do a lot right now." So staff trainings have been tricky, partially because you always have early adapters and people who get on board, and then you always have people who are like, "You're asking me to learn something different," and then being able to teach that.

I think what was the biggest learning curve for me is the fact that a lot of librarians, up until recently, never needed any type of teaching skills, or they had never truly taught. Now we're asking them to learn the skill of teaching and be able to show it in a manner that makes the person feel empowered, so they don't feel like it's a non-genuine or condescending way of learning something. That was a learning curve to how to teach, like "train the trainer" type of issues. I learned early on that I do improv a lot, or I just wing it, and it was a learning curve for me that not everyone feels comfortable winging it. A librarian ended up pulling me to the side and telling me that, whether I do video instruction or a script, I'll have to essentially use technology to teach technology. So if that means eight pages of screen shot by screen shot of how it looks—for example, we were tasked with building a summer reading game. There were all these ideas flying around, but no one had actually created a game or had any idea about it. Yet we were supposed to teach this game to our staff. So I ended up spending time on Paint and copying and pasting avatars and making it into a legit paper game, so that they could see that if we could play on a paper game, then we can make a digital game out of it.

People's understanding of technology and learning how to teach it, I always feel, is different. The success I've always had with it is, A, patience, and B, just being really, really clear, whether it's step-by-step, or, even further than hands-on training, giving people some type of visual guide that they can spend time learning how to do it themselves. Because there would also be a thing where, "Oh, we did it in training perfectly, and then when I had to do it on my own, I had no idea what was going on." So I make sure that there are roundabout ways or guides that people can learn with.

JOEL NICHOLS: I went to library school in 2007 and 2008, so although in some ways it wasn't that long ago, it feels kind of far ago in terms of web tools and the ubiquitousness of fast connections. I would say that there's some fundamental basic instruction skills that librarians should be taught—facilitation skills, presentation skills, instructional skills. Things like classroom management that could be applicable to children and/or adult classrooms, specific techniques around teaching adults and how that might differ from what some librarians might be more comfortable with, interacting with kids. I think those kinds of skills framed around "teaching is an explicit part of your job as a librarian and you're going to have to instruct" would be really helpful, even if they weren't only about digital literacy. But I think it would make a lot of sense for any public librarian to have to dig into what it means to teach basic literacy skills.

I would make Jessamyn West's book, *Without a Net*, required reading for every library school student because I think even though most of them would be apt to get it and get her argument right off, I do worry that maybe some aren't as exposed to it as quickly as they need to be, when it could also be paired with the instructional skills that I was just talking about. In that book, Jessamyn lays out really clearly what digital literacy is and what it means for a librarian, and all the different things a librarian might need to know about engaging with it. One of the things that I found inspiring when I was teaching Internet Basics, as a result of Jessamyn's book, was that she did all the theory and argumentation work around why this is important, and she did a very little bit in the latter chapters of definitions of a computer—a whole series of chapters that attempted to solve the problem that this is what you might not have gotten in library school, but this is what you should really be conversant with in order to help patrons. So when I was writing *Teaching Internet Basics*, I was totally trying to give my colleagues—people who I imagined could be my colleagues out there, and my own colleagues in my buildings—access to resources to help make it easier for them to do this kind of thing.

A lot of the people I work with are really uncomfortable with the Internet or with certain kinds of technology themselves. I would say, in my life, most librarians I've ever met are super tech-savvy, and more tech-savvy than I am. I'm constantly surprised. But there's always a significant number of people for whom that's not their focus, that's not what they're natively good at, they've never really been interested, they've never really had the access to practice. It's only recently, maybe in the last ten years, that they have had demands put on them about their use of computers and have had one in front of them every day. I'm not that familiar with the Urban Library Council's Edge initiative, but the last time I read it carefully, which was a couple iterations ago, it gave some pretty clear benchmarks around definitions of digital literacy and what a library might expect itself to do. And I think that using that kind of framework, a competency framework—at least as a map that would map out the corners of this ever-changing landscape—would be really useful.

BESS SADLER: I'm not someone who thinks that every librarian needs to be able to write code. But, I do think that every librarian should understand how the Internet works at a high abstract level. How digital surveillance works, and how to resist it. What free and open source software means. So let's say you can't write code—I do think there are concepts from software development that are super helpful in lots of other fields. For example, version control. I think librarians should be able to talk about effective version control. The other thing I would like to see taught in library schools more is concepts around spatial data. I think that's a growing area of importance that we, as a profession, have not caught up with at all. And scientific data. I want librarians to be able to talk about data management. I want them to be able to explain to patrons what is the open data movement. What is the open science movement? Why are these things important? How do you write a good data management plan for any grant that you're coming up with? Even if you don't have a grant, even if it's just your local water quality project, how do you have an effective data management plan for that? I also want libraries and librarians to be thinking about the geospatial data that we are creating constantly in our world today, and what's happening to it. Where's that going? Because for the most part, it's disappearing right now, and I think that that's a really big problem.

ALISON MACRINA: Digital literacy among librarians reflects a lot of what we librarians have seen with the public, that we as librarians don't get a good robust digital literacy curriculum in most of our schools. This is another thing that I've observed a lot first-hand, because I do so many trainings in library schools. Many people I talk to find library school to be really disappointing, and these are largely people who wanted to love it. When I went to library school, I had worked in a library already and I knew the kinds of questions that I got from people, and I knew how we could develop ourselves professionally to go further in helping these people. Those could have been things like learning some programming languages or learning in-depth some things about how our computers function, and also some basic teaching strategies. Education for adults, especially people who have for whatever reason some learning challenges.

In my library school, we learned none of those things. Instead we took, for example, literally a class on the business management technique that "30 Rock" always made fun of, Six Sigma. All these female students in class were like, "Why are we learning this when it's unlikely that we'll become managers for a couple of decades?" and the man teaching it—because of course it was a man teaching a management class—just didn't get the complaint. All these library schools love to congratulate themselves; they get awards and whatever and there's all these rankings, and those things don't mean anything in terms of what the profession itself actually needs. I try to address this need with what I teach at the Library Freedom Project. We want librarians to get at least a basic familiarity with privacy best practices and privacy tools, because libraries are community centers and have a lot of ability to influence culture.

Getting back to what library schools should do, it would be great if we had some super basics of how networks work, how are packets transmitted, where does the data go, how does network infrastructure send information and receive it. Ingrid Burrington's work on this is really great because she makes it easy to understand for even non-technical people. Just how does data move across the Internet—I think that's a really valuable thing for anyone to know, especially people in professions like ours. And along with that, how servers send information to each other, what the different Internet protocols are—like, what does it mean to use HTTP? How the Internet is structured and learning that as a way of learning how your computer works, that it's not this unknowable thing, that it's this thing that makes some very specific choices based on the commands that you give it. I'd love to see some classes for the more versatile popular newer languages like Python or Rust. I would love to see something that even gives an overview of what the different programming languages are and what they're used for and why some of them are being favored more. For example, what makes a language memory-safe, and what does that mean for security or privacy? How is a memory-unsafe language risky?

A lot of these other things will teach you about the privacy and security stuff in a tertiary way, because if you get how networks transit information, you'll get why encryption is important, because you'll see all those points along the way where you can be exploited. If you think about this in terms of librarians' values, lifelong learning obviously is a value. Well, we should do a better job at learning many different kinds of things to anticipate that.

MYRNA MORALES: I think even before we can get to digital literacy, there needs to be some kind of critical race literacy. I guess "social justice" is the catchphrase we're using these days. Right now, in library schools we have a lot of folks that are vocal, who have a justice-centered lens—but I feel like before we can even get into digital literacy, there needs to be a baseline where we're talking about whiteness, or we're talking about what lens do we bring into this work. Because information is power, and power corrupts. We have this idea of libraries being neutral and amoral, but that's because we don't necessarily self-reflect and reflect on the ways we make decisions about things.

So for me, what has been absolutely important in terms of my digital literacy skills has been the ability to question people's perspectives. I think being able to do that gives me the competence to ask questions around the black box of the data mining world. I've sat in classes where I didn't understand jack shit of what was going on around the technology and the data mining, but I will ask the questions and I will continue asking until I get a little bit, just a little bit, of the understanding. And I think that comes from functioning outside of society so that I'm constantly having to assert myself within spaces. I'm feeling hard-pressed to think about digital literacy without thinking of having some kind of social justice literacy, maybe.

. . .

ALISON MACRINA: I would love for us to focus on real issues of access in the twenty-first century, rather than make it seem like all of these kind of vague book challenges that are not at all "banned books" are the real access issues of the day. If we want to talk about censorship, we should talk about the way that Internet governance works. That the Internet is controlled by a handful of United States bureaucracies and US private companies, and that US law enforcement has the power to take down any website that it wants to at any time. Or how about the fact that US libraries that receive e-rate funding must install invasive and overbearing filters on their computers? These are just some of the real twenty-first century US challenges when it comes to censorship. It's not some parent somewhere who's like, "I think this book that's in the kids section should be in the teen section." I just don't really see that as much of an issue. What I do see is an issue is the future of the Internet. And I wish that we knew the first thing about it.

Another thing is that I wish we had some meaningful education around public records law and public records requesting. I think that FOIA is this area that we should know something about, and we don't know the first thing about it. In the digital era now, FOIAing has gotten a lot more simple. You can follow up on your request much more easily. And it has applications in libraries outside of the obvious kind of political stuff. You can use it for genealogical research. That's an amazing use of FOIA. But we librarians don't know much of anything about these things.

KAREN LEMMONS: I went to our state technology conference, and there was a video a presenter showed about how Google controls content. And I was livid. Oh my God. I was so livid. I was on this mission. I wasn't going to necessarily slander Google, but I really started scrutinizing it a little differently. I'm definitely going to share with my students that particular video, about how Google will filter your information based on your IP address, what you've been searching before, the whole nine yards. Even though this is a mathematical formula—they use algorithms and all of that—the bottom line is that they're still filtering information based on what they think you should have, based on what your previous searches were.

I remember sharing this with last year's class. I said, "You know what you need to do? Change your computer seat, number one, and then search everything. Search all over the place. Stop looking for homecoming dresses"—because you know, most of our girls would—"or prom dresses, or shoes. Start searching for far-out trips to Egypt or Saudi Arabia or Dubai. Just scramble up the searching." I did a short exercise for students to see how Google filters. I had students who sat next to each other search the same term. The students were surprised with the results. In some cases, the results were similar, but in other cases, they were different. Students had not really paid attention to the ads or results. Now they do. I told students the fact Google filters the results is scary to me. I do not like Google to make that kind of determination of what information it thinks I should have based on how I search. What information are you leaving out that would make me a more informed person?

Later, while working with a review team, I noticed that our team leader's default page was DuckDuckGo. I asked what that was, and he said, "This is a search engine that doesn't track you." And that's what it says! "DuckDuckGo: The search engine that doesn't track you." It presents the same information as Google, and it doesn't make any hints about tracking you or what they think you should have. It puts the information out there—the good, the bad, the in-between. There's another search engine that I often recommend to my students. It's Sweet Search, which definitely has a specific audience, usually K-12. So they're going to get more of the educational sources. But that's okay for them in terms of doing their research projects and things of that nature. That's good. But DuckDuckGo—yes, I'm a fan. Because at the very least, I find comfort in knowing that I'm getting all the information that's presented on the topic. I use DuckDuckGo and I like to use it at the reference desk, too, because if the patron sees my screen, they'll sometimes say, "Oh, what's that?" So that it's an opportunity to explain using DuckDuckGo as a search engine option. I mean, we already have the control issues going around now, and as teachers, we wrestle with control. But for somebody on the outside, for you to just make this determination, because I decide to research Egypt, you're just going to give me, like, travel information as opposed to some political or social information—uh uh. No. I don't think that's being talked about enough.

STACIE WILLIAMS: With information literacy, I think this whole issue of fake news, or content farms—it's become so insidious that there are highly intelligent people I know who have passed on a weird Facebook thing or whatever. Some weird link that they thought was true, and you go down to the bottom of that link and it's like, this isn't even a real thing. So I think with information literacy, we should be asking ourselves questions as we're reading a thing. Did I click on this because something about it was going to confirm something that I already thought? Did I click on this because I was trying to genuinely find out more information about something? I think in order to really fight information literacy, we have to ask ourselves, what is it that I think that I'm going to get out of this particular article at this particular time?

And be reading different things. Be understanding of different perspectives and different mindsets so that when you hear it, you can kind of tell if what you're hearing is actually coming from, at a minimum, a reputable source. I think the idea is that you're not going to agree with everything that you read. There are going to be things that you read that might be very provocative. They might even be wrong. You might read it and be like, this is not even accurate. But I think if we can ask ourselves these questions before we're reading the thing, after we're reading the thing—what do we hope to get out of this? Is this is something that's just confirming a bias that I already have, something that I already think? At least for me, that's something that helps me assess what I'm reading.

Who's writing what I'm reading? That too, because I think one of the big things to know about journalism that also affects libraries and the type of information we're using and picking up is that once everybody could have a hand in the game, journalism became less about the actual paper or magazine you were working for, and more about the actual person. The biggest names these days, they're free agents. They write for whoever, whenever, whatever. So you have to look at the person writing certain things, too—is this a person that's pushing an agenda? Is this a person who's getting paid to talk about certain things, so therefore they're going to have a certain bent or a certain agenda? I think that's very, very important to know. It's less about that old-school journalist who would just work in a spot and crank out things and eventually rise. The digital era absolutely created these sort of celebrities.

And it's kind of the same in libraries, too. There are librarians and archivists who stay on the circuit. Well, I think it's fair to ask ourselves, what do those people do? What wisdom are they imparting that's going to be ultimately helpful to whatever program we happen to be in? Are the people who are talking about a thing the absolute best people to talk about the thing? Are there other voices who we could be, or should be, listening to get that different perspective? I think technology has made these issues really complex and very gray. What we could be teaching in library schools is that sort of understanding and empathy of different views, different perspectives, and, as always, keep the focus on the user. Library schools will teach you things that you need to know to do your job, more or less. I think there's some people who might argue less. But library school's going to teach you how to do a job. Not many library schools are teaching you about how to interact with the people who are going to use what you have. The people who are going to come in and say, "Can you help me figure out how to spell this word?" The people who are going to come in and want to create a website for their small business. Or the people who are going to come in and need to use the computers, but they don't have an ID because maybe they just got out of jail. Those are actual patrons I've experienced. Library school doesn't really tell you how to help those people.

And that's really what we should be bringing it back to. That tech is just a tool. It's a cool tool, but how do you use the tech to help the guy who doesn't have the ID because he just got out of jail? How do you use the tech to help acquire different collections from underrepresented or marginalized users? How can we use the tech to leave people alone? I think that's a question that some people are now starting to ask because we've used tech to now gather so much information on people, it's understood that you could do really bad things with that much information. And some people are attempting to do bad things with big data. So how can we use the tech to keep people safe? How can we use the tech for the benefit of our users—not just for the sake of ourselves, but how can we use it for them?

ZACHARY LOEB: I think that in a period where people have very little faith in their political leaders, have very little faith in a lot of traditional sources of "progress," people are really going in on an ideology where technology will bring about progress, where technology will improve the world, where technology is making everything better, and is continually making everything better. I think part of the reason that people can go in for this belief is because they often don't see the full cost. They don't see the environmental destruction and the labor that goes into these devices, and they don't necessarily want to think too critically about the cost to themselves, to their own relationships, to their own lives. And asking these questions is a really good way to get yourself not invited to parties. Talking about this stuff is a really easy way to get people to kind of roll their eyes at you and dismiss you a technophobic killjoy, or just a killjoy.

I'm going back to my academic nerdiness on some of this. I think that there's actually a lot to be said for killjoys. This is something that I've thought about a lot in the last couple of years, in regards to the Edward Snowden revelations about surveillance. Without in any way, shape, or form wanting to take away from the important and brave things that he did and revealed, everything that he revealed—if you look at thinkers who've been dismissed as technophobic killjoys, they all said, "This is what computers are going to lead to. Computers and the Internet are going to lead to this massive surveillance state." You can go look at the work of Lewis Mumford or Jacques Ellul talking about computers. They could look at computers and say, "This is not going to be the wonderful techno-utopian landscape that people think it's going to be. These are some of the things that this technology is going to lead to." And we often don't listen to those voices. We often banish them. We dismiss them as technophobic killjoys, but then often, from hindsight, when you look back at them, you have to admit, "Well, these people had a point."

So just to conclude this by going in the full-on apocalyptic direction, one of the things that I find very concerning right now is that the killjoys right now, what they're talking about is how serious the threat and the danger of things like climate change is. And those are the people who are now being shooed off the stage and ignored and accused of being technophobic killjoys. I think that part of the issue is that we always believe that there is going to be a technological solution to the problems that have been created by our unthinking embrace of technology. Naomi Oreskes's work has been great on this topic. We always think that technology is going to solve the problem, but we don't often think enough about the problems that are going to be created by the new technologies.

This last year, while I was at NYU, I was a TA for two courses. I was working with undergrads, primarily freshman, and I wanted to get them to think about these issues. But at the same time, sometimes if you go at people with too much of the critique, they resist and they just back off. I think that a really good strategy can be to get people to ask themselves the critical questions. Give them the questions, but let them kind of work on the answers. Neil Postman has a set of six questions to ask of new technology. In some of my blog posts, I've suggested some additional questions that should be asked. I think that those questions can be a really good starting point for these discussions.

. . .

Cecily Walker: Someone mentioned to me, you know, it would be really interesting to go back and look at library-related magazines and journals, say, over the last ten years, and look at what everybody thought was going to be the next great big thing, the next disruption or whatever in libraries, and go back and look at where they failed and find out the reasons for that failure. Or to look at those things that didn't necessarily fail but were touted as the thing that's going to revolutionize library service, but it never really got off the ground. The thing that caught my interest the most was there was a period of a couple of years, from like 2008–2010, maybe going into 2011, where the job title "Emerging Technologies Librarian" was really, really hot. People were really hot to have somebody with that title in their organization because it would add a dash of hipness or cool to people's perceptions of the library. But by and large, as these sort of "emerging technologies" became so commonplace, that title has just fallen out of favor.

It would be really interesting to map out that change. Like, what influenced it? What was the thing that happened in society at large and in libraries in a smaller scale to make people's perceptions or interest in this kind of thing shift? I think it would be great to go back and try to see, where did we fall off, and where did we go wrong, and *did* we go wrong, by just saying, "You know what, this is not something that really matters." It was very cool at the time, and maybe it was just a way for us to justify our continued existence.

JAIME TAYLOR: I feel like the best thing we can do about tech stuff when everyone's like, "We must adopt the newest thing because it's the newest thing!" is to look at Second Life. No one uses that. I've literally never used it. But libraries some years ago, even when I was in library school—and I finished in 2009—were like, "Oh, Second Life, we can do so much with this! We'll do reference services and all these things!" And sure, some people use it, but no one really uses it, let's be honest. So pointing out that these things have come and gone in ways that we needn't have even paid too much attention to them in the first place, I think, is a useful tool.

MANDY HENK: So often any kind of resistance to technology gets characterized as, "You're afraid of progress," or "You're not willing to learn a new way to do your job." So people who do make serious efforts at resistance end up being attacked and marginalized. I was in a meeting once with a vendor, OCLC, and they were talking about the transition that we would have to make in our library—we were moving from one library catalog to theirs—and they referred to something that they called the "Change Monster." They had this whole graphic and everything. They really tried to frame the debate in such a way that you couldn't say anything even vaguely negative without them attacking you. Fortunately it was a meeting where they were on the phone, and there was a bunch of us sitting in a room, and we started moving our hands like little puppets every time they would say "Change Monster." Because it really serves to silence people, and it serves to make it so that any argument that you articulate, no matter how valid, no matter how sound, no matter how good it is, is completely brushed aside because the problem is *you*, and you're afraid of change. And that's something that I think we as a profession really need to be conscious of. I think we do it to our patrons sometimes, and we need to be really conscious of when we're doing that.

JIM DELROSSO: Most of the conferences I've been to have been a mix. I've gone to very few where it's like, "Oh my god, no one here is having a real discussion." I used to go to Computers in Libraries with some regularity, and while there were definitely some people there who were just talking about the latest shiny thing and making presentations that didn't have a lot of depth to them per se, one of the more interesting sessions I saw was one that Jennifer Koerber, who at the time was at the Boston Public Library, and Michael Sauers, who is currently at Do Space and was previously at the Nebraska Library Commission, did that I think they entitled "The Next Big Thing." The title of the session was very much in keeping with that sort of "what's the next big technology coming down the road, what's the next big new thing on the horizon" approach. But what they did instead was actually get everyone in the room talking about the next big project they were looking at in their library, the next thing they were going to have to tackle. And they didn't set any kind of floor on tech levels. It wasn't, "What's the next technology that's only been developed in the last three years that you're going to implement?" It was really just, "What's the next big thing that you are trying to do, and do you have any ideas about it?" It turned into a really good conversation, because in the room you've got a lot of people who are actually charged with delivering on these kinds of projects. So it ended up being a really practical, interesting conversation about that sort of thing. And those two, they wrote one of the better books[2] that I've read on library technologies a couple of years ago, which always kept that practical focus.

ANITA COLEMAN: Thoughtful understanding about change and the implications of constant change, and realistic ideas about progress, are critical self development tools. Knowledge is always changing

---

2 Jennifer Koerber and Michael Sauers, *Emerging Technologies: A Primer for Librarians.* (Lanham, MD: Rowman & Littlefield, 2015).

as new discoveries come to light and new explanations are debated, constructed, and distributed, with old ones being discarded. We have to discern what changes to implement when. This needs a clear vision as well as courage and tenacity to keep on changing one's skill set. Notice that I'm not saying "growing" but am instead using the word "changing" deliberately.

I realized this when I implemented the NOTIS Library Management System. The university had signed the contract in 1986 and three years later—I joined in September 1989—had still not implemented it. Within three months I taught myself JCL (Job Control Language) so I could work with the programmer about the problems, and we brought the system online for technical staff in the library. A few years later, I'd put aside JCL—I'd left the job but even if I was there, I wouldn't have needed it—and was working with the Unix-based Awk. In another year, I had put aside Awk and taught myself web technologies and protocols as I realized their potential for my dissertation, which was the design and development of a hypermedia journal for "information work." I was hired by a psychology professor to teach HTML, PHP, and MySQL to industrial engineering students in a Human Factors class. Students were learning to design interfaces as varied as aircraft control and power plant management.

So librarians have to keep changing our technological skill set, but the values and broad vision of a global knowledge society remain the same. We shouldn't get on every tech bandwagon or cultural shift that's heralded by the media or think-tanks, but neither can we afford to bury our head in the sand. Solution—we must read widely and frequently, and reflect individually and collectively (on listservs, Slack channels, and Twitter and IRL) as deeply and as long as it takes.

JIM DELROSSO: I've really come to believe, as someone who's usually charged with being on the lookout for new technologies for a library to adopt or to investigate or to take a look at, that technology is only ever as good as the people you have using it from a staff side. Most of the time, the best thing you can hope for out of a new technology is that it's going to remove some roadblocks that people have for doing the kind of work that they want to do. It's not going to be a revolution. If anything, the best you can hope for, and really the thing that you should shoot for, is hopefully trying to make people's lives a little easier. And that fits into that sort of "tool" definition of technology.

MANDY HENK: A lot of times there's a tendency on the part of library managers to want to Taylorize. You want to be like, "You click here, and then you click here, and then you click here." And I think that if instead we let people develop their own relationships with these instruments, these sort of tools, they have a better reaction to it. So rather than walking up to someone and saying, "No, you're getting to that window in the wrong way, you should be getting to it this way," let them get to it in the other way. People have to have relationships with their own tools that aren't mediated by others. With the ILS, if that's something you're interacting with all day, having someone standing over your shoulder telling you how to use it is not productive. So that's number one, is to respect their relationships with the technology.

And number two, I'm a huge fan of drawing diagrams and comparing it to the way things might have been in the past. I use this with students, too, because if I can show them a physical journal and say, "See how there's a bunch of articles in here? Yeah, so, this website that we're looking at is the same thing, but it's on the Internet so it's easier." It's something that I've found to be pretty effective.

So respecting people, using analogies for the actual physical world, and, number three, I think sometimes there's a tendency for us—especially if you're good at automating things, and I'm good at automating things—to want to automate things, perhaps unnecessarily. One of the examples I would use for that is, at my previous institution I was responsible for circulation. I very well could have had a completely automated overdues process that no one on my staff would have had to think about. But I made the decision to actually keep it as a mediated process so that my staff members would continue to maintain relationships with their patrons, because I thought that that was really important. So not blindly automating, and looking and asking yourself, what am I going to get with this automation? And recognizing that efficiency is not the god at least that I want to die for. I think that a lot of times with technology, it can come across that way, especially for people who may not be technologically comfortable or adept. Recognizing and acknowledging that there are things more important than getting things done efficiently is really important. So relationships are important, and making decisions that prioritize relationships as you're working with technology is perfectly valid. It doesn't have to be all-in.

Chad Clark: I think everybody works in public libraries forever, because it's such a great job. We've certainly got a segment of our staff that have been there for a long time, and something like the digital media lab is a big change for them. So there was a certain amount of explaining, "This is why we do this." Our director is very progressive and open-minded, and she as well as the management staff fully supported the lab. There were a few staff members who've been there for a long time who were kind of like, "Why does the library need this?" and "Why should we do this?" So there was a bit of explaining or selling it to them as recognizing that the library is a place of discovery and lifelong learning. It didn't take too much, in the long run. I found the best thing that worked for us was just coaxing their hobbies out of staff members who were questioning the presence of a lab. I can remember particularly this one lady who works down in cataloging who just was like, "Well, okay, digital media lab." I ended up talking to her and learning that she loves to photograph birds. She likes to do birdwatching. So we ended up getting her in the lab and helping her put together a little portfolio of her birdwatching stuff on a weblog. "Okay, I get it!" Throwing out the catch-all phrases of "why it's important" or "what it can do" doesn't really ring with people until you can latch onto something that they're connected to.

Vivian Alvarez: I feel that the leaders in my library have been very curious about the digital media movement taking place with libraries overall. When I came in I opened a conversation on, "This is a program that's relatively new, how can I work with you? And how can we work together so that we can continue working with our community as a family?" So there has been a lot of dialogue and open communication. When I came in, there were already conversations, for instance, at the ALA and in every single tangent to it, like the Public Library Association and YALSA. They've all been having conversations already about considering change, moving from being a traditional environment to being a change organism. I feel like I was pretty lucky that those conversations had already been taking place, because when I looked within educators' minds it helped that we could both come together and share what our expectations were. I also came in with a very respectful opinion of the library, because the library before I even stepped in had been built on loyalty and trust. So it was also my job to continue honing that and treasuring it just as much.

. . .

JAIME TAYLOR: I hate to say it, but one of the most useful pieces of technology that I use in my day-to-day work is Excel. I hate it, but I use it all the time, and it's so useful to me for sorting through thousands upon thousands of catalog records and sorting and extracting the information I want to see. Yeah, I hate it, but there it is. Excel is amazing, but it's also disgusting. I'm actually really bad at using Excel. There's so many things I don't know how to use. I use it in a really basic way, but there's pretty much no other way for me to dump ten thousand records out of my catalog and find what I want to find.

SARAH HOUGHTON: I don't even want to give the first answer that came to mind because that's scary. It's sad. I was going to answer that Excel is the most useful piece of technology, and that's probably true. It is definitely. Excel is the most useful piece of technology day-to-day in my role as a director because there's so much data that I need to compile and create nice-looking charts and graphs for people to see so they can digest that data more easily. But I think quite frankly the bigger answer would just be the desktop computer, because without that so much of what we do would be so difficult. That's a very bland and late '80s answer, but a good 80 percent of my work happens on this one screen on this one machine that sits on top of my desk, and without that, it would be a much harder prospect to get all that work done. Yeah, Excel and a desktop computer. That's a sad, sad combination of answers, but I think that's what I'm going to go with.

JESSA LINGEL: I wouldn't get far without a word processor. I love the Internet. I sometimes get this reputation for being a Luddite or someone who refuses to embrace new technology. But it's really not true. I'm just trying to be very careful about the technologies that I embrace. And I can be contrarian, I'll admit that. But it's also about thinking through what are the politics of this particular platform. But I love the Internet! The Internet has given me so many friends, so many relationships. Lord knows it's given me a career. But I do genuinely love the Internet, and I'm glad that it's here, and I think it's a really powerful tool.

JARRETT DRAKE: Post-it notes and pencils are the most useful pieces of technology that I, as a digital archivist, use every day. This may appear simple, if not nonsensical, but the simplicity of both a pencil and a Post-it note is the heart of their beauty. Surely, I rely on complex tools and software applications and even a forensic workstation to do my job, but the most invaluable tools in my office are my pencils and Post-it notes. If—not if, when—I make a mistake, I can either erase it or crumble up the paper and start fresh to attempt another failure. This ease of access to failure is a key ingredient to success.

MITA WILLIAMS: You know, it's funny, right now it's a tossup between answering whether the most useful piece of technology for me is my cellphone or whether it's a notebook. I use them both in essentially in the same way. For example, I take many photographs with my cellphone, largely as a memory aid or to capture something that's interesting or as a way to encourage myself to see interesting things in the world. But I also always travel with a notebook. I take a lot of notes every day, but I never really revisit them. I use them as a way to help me capture information in my memory and to force me to take a moment to reflect the moment, just like I would take a photograph. And both with the photographs and the notes, I don't necessarily go back and review them. Which I think I should.

There's a writer I'm really fond of, Clive Thompson, who wrote a book called *Smarter Than You Think*. He writes about how over the course of history people have had these commonplace books where they make notes, and how essential it is to keep notes if you're a writer or an artist or just a person who wants give yourself a moment to capture and reflect on the things that are of interest to you. And he said that it's really important to go back and review your notes. I'm currently in this mode of reflection and that's something personally that I'm trying to do, review and go back and relive what I've captured before, because if it was really important I should at least remember why.

. . .

JOEL NICHOLS: I don't necessarily think that library science monographs are going to reach a very wide audience, or that they necessarily reach everywhere they could. I think it's really important that we have lots of blogs. In terms of how to use iPads and tablets and e-books with children, the blog Little eLit, run by Cen Campbell, and the Show Me Librarian, Amy Koester—really the blog format was the perfect place because of the constant shifting nature of apps and trends in e-books. My editor or publisher would be chagrined to hear me, but blogs are always going to be more useful than my book because they're going to always be part of the conversation much more with what folks are actually doing, and they're able to adapt with the times. So I'm really appreciative of that.

Outside of that, I don't know if these even exist as such, but when I was first becoming a librarian, there seemed to be a lot of LITA white papers. QR codes is too new of a thing to actually have been one of these white papers, but something like that—or blogs, a white paper in 2007 on everything a librarian needs to know about blogs. I found those things really useful. I love how smart and forward-thinking and innovative and experimental librarians are, and I love that in many cases they are also really good at documenting and sharing those experiences. And it sort of affirms for me something that I think should be a core of librarianship, and being a librarian, that we're a "see one, do one, teach one" profession, like this stereotype in surgery or medicine that a doctor in training sees a procedure and then does the procedure and then teaches the procedure. I've found in my library career that the best way for me to really learn how to do something is to watch another librarian do it or have her teach me how to do it. I love it when librarians think of themselves as "see one, do one, teach one," because I think that we are very effective at sharing knowledge—practical, hands-on knowledge, especially in programming.

Jaime Taylor: Library Twitter is pretty strong these days. There are Mashcat chats every once in a while, things like that. There's a Slack channel, too, that has a lot of systems librarians on it. I think just hanging out with library Twitter is really great, both in a morale-boosting sense, but then also you can often go to it with a specific problem and be like, "Hey, how do I sort through catalog records using MarcEdit?" "What can I do to turn this XML thing into something I can dump into this system?" And oftentimes someone has a link to a script they wrote and you can use that instead of having to reinvent the wheel. So library Twitter, generally speaking, I think is really great.

Vivian Alvarez: I follow a lot of ALA. I'm right now a member of ALA and other family tangent branches. For instance, I have subscriptions—oh my goodness, almost twenty different subscriptions. I'm part of LLAMA, PLA, YALSA, RUSA, LITA—the list can go on and on. I'm following these journals and authors that write for the journals, and leaders, in order to have an understanding, an insight. My appreciation for libraries and the need to combine librarianship with an educational framework is my reason for pursuing my master's program. So I became a member of all of these different divisions, and I have more of a sense of what's going on in the world, not just at my branch. The couple of leaders in my branch, they're also members of some of these divisions. We get to have conversations on, "What do you think of this new approach to XYZ?" So it opens the conversation as well, more like a roundtable.

Stephanie Irvin: I try to keep an ear out as far as what's generally happening. Of course I keep up with the World Wide Web Consortium updates because that's the most important thing to me, knowing if their accessibility guidelines change and things like that. I have alerts set up regarding different things. And of course I follow what's happening with the Library of Congress and the National Library Service.

Sometimes that stuff connects. At the conference at California State University, Northridge, there debuted a newer, cheaper refreshable braille display, which is ridiculously exciting. Refreshable braille displays are used by individuals who are blind to read electronic documents on this particular device. It basically creates raised dots so they can read braille on it, to put it simply. It's a great way to privately read whatever is on your tablet, without having to use text-to-speech or anything like that. But in the past they've been cost-prohibitively expensive. That's part of the reason we don't give them to our patrons who read braille, because there just wasn't a way to make ones that are cheap. When it came out at CSUN, it barely made a blip anywhere, but it made a *huge* blip in the various circles that I fall in, just in general alerts, because that's a game-changer for our patrons. Of course, I also keep in contact with colleagues, but there's no one big thinker that I really listen to. I just try to listen to all of those around me—and my patrons, of course. That's a great way to get an idea of what's really helpful with technology, and what *would* be really helpful, and what I should definitely keep an ear out for.

Chad Clark: As far as who I'm following, I'm communicating more with our school systems teachers, specifically the STEM teachers.

I'm trying to get more of a perspective on what it's like to work with people in general on a more consistent basis, trying to involve and engage people beyond the one- or two-visit affair, which at least we found was typical at the beginning of our digital media lab. Our goal is to work with people from start to finish. Setting somebody down in front of a tool and saying, "All right, now just put your best foot forward and learn it. And I'll be out here at the desk, checking my email," is just not going to cut it. The people I follow lately are educators, working mainly in the school system, and we're talking about projects and how to accomplish more of a long-term relationship. And if I'm following people, like on Twitter—it's noise; you're following hundreds of people—but the ones I'll pinpoint are Kevin Kelly or Stewart Brand, sort of the old tech guys. Clay Shirky, people like that.

Michael Cherry: There are a variety of writers and educators that inspire me. Sylvia Libow Martinez and Gary Stager's book *Invent to Learn: Making, Tinkering, and Engineering in the Classroom* should be on every technology educator's bookshelf. It's probably the single most important book written about the maker movement for educators in the past several years. Renee Hobbs and Frank W. Baker are two significant contributors to the field of media literacy education. Renee Hobbs also contributed to the Young Adult Library Services Association's white paper "The Future of Library Services for and with Teens." Sections of the white paper discuss the importance of media literacy education today. These sections help to frame information literacy within a broader context to include many of the key points of media literacy.

Sarah Houghton: I follow as many people's work as I can ingest, but I find myself, especially as I've gotten out of the technology side of librarianship, following more and more people out of the library industry. I'm following more things having to do with technology and the whole of information access, government trends, legislative actions that could affect what we do—trying to get outside of our box of librarianship. I actually wish I had done that sooner, when I was still focusing on technology, because I think more broad thinking and more innovation comes from that, instead of all of us in our little library bubble talking at each other and saying the same things every year, hearing the same presentations at the same conferences every year. Expanding and broadening our horizons a little bit to people working in the arts, to people working with disadvantaged youth—those are the voices that we're going to learn the most from.

STACIE WILLIAMS: I really love Amelia Abreu's work on tech and care ethics. She's a UX design expert who has done work with libraries and archives, and she explores a lot the feminist ideas of care as they relate to technology and our understanding of that labor and its implications. I also follow Eira Tansey, who talks a lot about the implications of climate change on archival work and our special collection; Jessica Johnson, a digital humanist who focuses on black history and black futures; and Jarrett Drake, who's like family to me, and many of his theories on post-custodial stewardship of archives and the idea of "liberatory memory work." These are people whose ideas challenge more traditional models of library and archival work and who have very important perspectives on end users through these unique lenses. I'm fortunate enough to have engaged with most of them in person about their ideas and learn ways that I can explore or implement certain things within my own repository.

JAYCIE VOS: I follow the Oral History in the Digital Age website, which draws from people all over the place. Doug Boyd is a primary contributor to that, and I also follow Doug's work at the Nunn Center. I look at what the Samuel Proctor Oral History Program is doing, and Baylor's oral history institute, and the Center for Oral and Public History at California State University Fullerton, which Natalie Fousekis runs. I follow work at Duke—specifically the Center for Documentary Studies, which had a really great project recently with different leaders in SNCC. I follow the Southern Foodways Alliance. I'm starting to get more involved with the Society of American Archivists and hope to learn more from other archivists who handle oral history through that.

HANA SLEIMAN: We follow a lot of the work of oral historians, especially those working on women and Palestine. Sherna Gluck was one of the figures who I think was attempting to build the first online oral history archive back in the '90s. Some parts of their thought process were very essential to how we talked about this project in the early phases. And then the work of Rosemary Sayigh, Bayan al-Hout, and

Rabab Abdulhadi, and the way that they conceptualized the need for these archives. They collected them, and then they contributed to the conceptualization of the organization and archiving. So they kind of followed the whole cycle from start to finish. These are the ones that stand out.

MITA WILLIAMS: I follow a lot of people's work. Right now I'm trying to transition away from Twitter and get back into more long-form reading and long-form thinking. One person I've been following as of late whose work I really enjoy is Shannon Mattern. She's at The New School in New York City. I don't believe she's a librarian but her communication studies perspective on library technology and the larger context of technological infrastructure and social infrastructure is really quite incredible. She puts out an amazing amount of work. She makes her syllabi readily available so some of that is also on my to-read list. I guess what I'm trying to do right now is read more people who are studying technology issues but not necessarily within librarianship. I've been following Deb Chachra. She's an engineering professor from Olin College. And I've been reading Mandy Brown. She has this newsletter called "A Working Letter," and I've been really interested in some of the reading that she's been sharing about looking at new forms of utopia as a way to frame our understanding of how we should go forward into precarious future of global warming. She wrote this great newsletter about how if we keep thinking of our heroic future, we're going to set ourselves up for a tragedy. She suggests that we should think more of a comedic future where we have to improvise and scramble and make do with what we have. I find her very perceptive, and what she shares is really interesting.

Another person I want to mention, Rebecca Solnit, is my new patron saint. I just finished her book *A Paradise Built in Hell*, and I think the world of her. I'm going to do more reading of some of her older work. I think her stories of how communities have reacted in times of crisis has been some of the more life-affirming readings I've done as of late. When things are grim it's really good to have these sources that can show you the sky again.

ELAINE HARGER: I have to admit, I'm a pretty scatterbrained follower of anybody's work. Naomi Klein is one of my heroes. She seems to get it all. I also highly recommend one of the books that I encountered when researching the book that I wrote, *The Political Responsibilities of*

Everyday Bystanders by Stephen L. Esquith. It is this amazing investigation into how everyday people are the beneficiaries of extreme violence in various places in the world. His work was informed by the work of other people, too, but that was a very eye-opening book to me. Anything that Angela Davis writes resonates with me. Michelle Alexander's book, *The New Jim Crow.*

I'm very interested in and very concerned about race. In conjunction with the climate crisis that we're definitely into right now, and the way in which race is used to divide people in this country and what is happening in regard to the police brutality and killing of black people, I'm afraid that the period we're in right now is just preparing our society for getting used to the idea that some lives are expendable in order to keep other people "safe." Racism allows that to happen. And so I think that it behooves every librarian and every educator to really investigate the way in which racism is used to keep people apart and to justify levels of violence that are not justifiable. Also to investigate the whole matter of privilege. I mean, I'm white, so white privilege is what I have to recognize and be always cognizant of in any of the interactions I have with other people of any sort. I'm following discussions regarding the Black Lives Matter movement. I think that both climate change, anti-racism work, and anti-capitalist work is where I'm at right now.

CARMEL CURTIS: I'm influenced and inspired by a lot of people. All of my fellow members of XFR Collective, current and past members—I'm inspired by each of them in their work as archivists, and their work as filmmakers, and their work as activists. I'm inspired by my friends and family who work as teachers and dog walkers and doctors. This is in no particular order. I listen to "Democracy Now!" every day; Amy Goodman and Juan González I follow. I just finished reading Assata Shakur's autobiography. Assata Shakur I follow. Angela Davis. I am a supporter and follower of the comedian Tig Notaro. Also the comedians Phoebe Robinson and Jessica Williams. I follow their podcasts, "2 Dope Queens" and "Sooo Many White Guys." I am an avid, avid movie-watcher and don't even know where to begin on that list. I'm very much indebted to screenslate.com to help me stay up on all the New York movie happenings.

ALISON MACRINA: To stay up on technology, I follow a lot of people who are doing infosec and cryptography, or just writing about technology in interesting ways, like Evgeny Morozov, Matt Green, Matt Blaze, April Glaser, Kelsey Atherton, malkia cyril, Sarah Jamie Lewis, and Maciej Cegłowski of Pinboard. Then I follow a lot of people who are activists for privacy; obviously there are big organizations like ACLU and EFF, but there are a lot of individuals talking about surveillance capitalism. I follow a lot of people who are thinking about networks and things, from the cultural and social aspects, so Ingrid Burrington is obviously one of these people. Another person is Addie Wagenknecht, who started Deep Lab and is an artist who works with technology. Trevor Paglen is another artist who's thinking about networks and surveillance and all this. I try to see kind of the whole landscape of the scene—not just the precise thing that makes the computer lights turn on and off but how human beings are thinking of this.

As far as library people, I pay attention to #critlib, basically anything that's critical librarianship or radical librarianship. The radical librarians in the UK are people that I stay up with. They're cool because they're branching out to Ireland, and I think there's some folks in Scotland who are starting a Radical Librarians Collective, plus folks in Scotland who do LFP-style trainings. I'm always on the lookout for library grassroots activism of all kinds.

Celeste Â-Re: I'm looking at people who are doing work in terms of social justice and library and information science. Tiffany Veinot is a library and information science person, and she talks about the need for community-level analysis in doing research work. She draws connections between information behavior and sociology, and how we need to look more at the social component of libraries, not only in terms of information behavior but policy and practice and how to go about doing that. Another person who stands out for me is Kathleen de la Peña McCook. Paul Jaeger and Gary Burnett and their information worlds. It's all tying the social component of library and information sciences. It's not just about information retrieval; it's all social justice frameworks. I recently discovered, as I was doing my work, Tony Dunbar, who wrote his dissertation on what he called critical race information theory. That was very interesting because I kept thinking, if we're gatekeepers to knowledge and collective memory, then we've got a responsibility to keep ourselves honest and ethical and to provide and talk about those things that folks don't necessarily want to talk about in terms of archiving and bringing forward things that have been kind of not discussed in library and information science. Jarrett Drake. He does a lot of interesting work on community archiving and opening it up to community members. And of course Christine Pawley, with her initial work on race and libraries. Not only race, but race, class, all of that. She's definitely got a critical theory perspective. So I would say folks who do work in critical theory and analysis and social justice frameworks, that's who I'm looking at.

ANDREW WEISS: I'm a fan of speculative fiction. William Gibson, for example—he's obviously not a librarian, but I think it's important to be speculating on where things are going and where the future's going and how technology impacts what we do. That's of course the case for everyone, but libraries have seen a lot of change, and I think it's important to get in the habit of speculating on what could happen, since there are always unintended consequences to adopting any technology. It's important to see every side of it and not just the IT side of it, but also the philosophical side of it.

JARRETT DRAKE: I should say that I don't follow individuals' work so much as I follow their ideas. I'm an idealist. I hate shopping for clothes, or food, or anything, really, but I love shopping for ideas. It is a hobby of mine. My favorite places to shop for ideas are on Twitter, because from Twitter I may find a rough idea—such as a massive tweet stream—or I may find a refined idea—such as a link to a journal article. I am obsessed with Twitter insomuch as I am obsessed with ideas, and I love following the people I follow because they are amazing suppliers of ideas. I secretly want to be like all the people I follow on Twitter.

```
related_subjects = []
related_subjects.push("Jürgen Habermas")
related_subjects.push("IRC")
related_subjects.push("answering the phone")
related_subjects.push("hackerspaces")
related_subjects.push("the Black Panther newspaper")
related_subjects.push("jail")
related_subjects.push("gentrification")
related_subjects.push("Zuccotti Park")
related_subjects.push("SXSW")
related_subjects.push("universal design")
related_subjects.push("World Wide Web Consortium")
related_subjects.push("wifi")
related_subjects.push("Kindles in schools")
related_subjects.push("'The Web We Lost'")
```

Connecting

This chapter explores multiple dimensions of what it means to connect with one another. Interviewees meditated on meaningful Internet communication in general, from bulletin board services to Slack, and what professional online communication has looked like over the last decade or so. I asked about partnerships that some have developed with schools, community groups, and less traditional venues. People also described the ways that librarians and archivists can use their training to support social movements and activists. In "Learning," we heard about baseline tech skills that librarians and archivists should know, and in this chapter we hear more about ways to make connections and communicate effectively with technologists.

The ways that we're connected—or not—to resources and to one another online are explored as well. People discussed accessibility and what we can do to help people with (and without) disabilities. And what is the "digital divide," and how has it evolved over the last ten to fifteen years? Finally, political, corporate, and social forces that can limit our ability to connect are addressed. People talked about government censorship, Internet filtering software, and the centralization of digital platforms. I also asked how technological evolution in communication and cultural production has changed what libraries and archives can collect from communities.

• • •

JESSA LINGEL: When I think across the different communities that I've studied, a thread that you can trace through all of them is this idea of using technology to create a sense of shared space. I hesitate to use the word "space" because I think we have a lot of spatial metaphors about the Internet that aren't helpful, or are even very problematic, and I'm not just talking about the old-school "Information Superhighway" kind of space. The idea that the Internet is a space can trap us in very geographic understandings of the Internet that aren't true. But the sense of building togetherness through different forms of technology, I think, is really a thing that you can see. And so I've been thinking a lot about how those technologies changed over time.

It's difficult to convince young people that a technology like Internet relay chats, or IRCs, or BBSs, bulletin board services, really could feel like a space to people. If you sit a millennial down and put them in front of a message board and try to explain, "This really felt like a *space* to people," they sort of give you this look like, why would it feel that way? And yet, it's interesting to see that same generation of people who might be very skeptical about the capacity for community on what they consider bare bones interfaces—the same people can have these intense and extended conversations within an Instagram feed. In the Instagram comments you can have these really long conversations that go back to this very Habermas view of a third space, like a cafe where people come together and strangers talk and build a discourse.

All this is a very roundabout way of saying that I don't know if it's a technology so much as a function of technology. If I had to pick a technology to illustrate it, it would be a comment forum or a discussion board. I think those are the most important technologies in their capacity to give people an ability to build a dialogue and convene a public through that shared dialogue. That thread that I would weave through these different communities that I've studied, of trying to build a sense of place and shared togetherness, is also a thread that you can see in very different successful platforms that might look very different aesthetically or in their design. They have different ways of building this function, but they tend to end up with these discussion boards, even if they're not called that anymore. Say I'm on an Instagram photo board or even in a Pinterest profile. Users find a way to build spaces—again, I'm using that word with hesitation—for themselves to have these dialogues. I think any time we see technologies that really support community, they have that function.

BÉATRICE COLASTIN SKOKAN: The Internet has been extremely useful, because it has allowed us to be in contact with people that we would not reach otherwise. The Web and email continue to help us to establish very immediate contact with people that function outside of our immediate circles and creates alternative spaces for interactions. So much of my time is spent writing, corresponding with people by email. I think the Internet has facilitated this type of instantaneous exchange. I remember when this technology didn't exist; I'm old enough. I remember how fast the transitioning was. Technology just evolved so quickly.

JOHN HELLING: I know this is going to sound trite, but easily the most useful piece of technology for me on a daily basis is mobile email. It's so nice to be able to just respond quickly to people who need quick responses, and not have to worry about calling a meeting or returning voicemail, etc. If you use it properly—respond quickly to urgent things and slowly to everything else—then it truly is a timesaver.

JESSAMYN WEST: From a purely network connectivity perspective, I'm an email nerd. So much of what I do for a job—all those different jobs that I do—comes in and out through my inbox and gets managed through my inbox. Back in the day, I would have a paper filing cabinet and maybe a tickler file that said what I was going to do, and I'd have a whole bunch of to-do lists, and blabity blah. More and more lately, it's all finding different ways to take what's in my email and massaging that to turn it into to-do lists—things to look up, people to contact, places to get started. It's nice because even though I access it through the Web, it's essentially a text-based environment, for the most part. And I can get it from anywhere, I can interact with it from anywhere, and I can get in touch with the most people that way. So it has a high degree of utility for something that's actually using a fairly low degree of tech. That's probably what I use the most of all the things that I use, in both physical and interactive interface ways.

JIM DELROSSO: From a public service standpoint, in terms of technology, really one of the most useful things is still email. A huge number of our questions come in over email, and those come from people who are directly part of the ILR or Cornell University community. The School of Industrial Labor Relations is a New York State school. So we have a land grant mandate to serve New York State and the citizens thereof, which made the open access thing for our repository a no-brainer. But because of the unique nature of some of our collections, we'll get emails from people all over the world. That's usually the best way, especially for people who are not within traveling distance of Cornell, to get in touch with us. That being said, when we're talking about people coming in from outside of Cornell and asking us questions about our collections, we still get a number of phone calls, too.

I was hearing about the demise of email as a communication method ten years ago. I don't know if that's just passed or what, but it's been a little while since I've heard people talking about the demise of email. The phone, too, is still seeing a lot of use. I'm personally not a fan of talking on the phone, but if I'm on the ref desk and it rings, I pick it up. So it is interesting to me that two of the core technologies that I use are literally decades old. It's not like they're working in the exact same format that they used when they were founded, but they're still fundamentally decades old, and still very functional and still very key to our communication with portions of our communities. And I say "portions" because both of those do require a certain set level of technological access to utilize. Looking within New York State, and certainly within the world, we shouldn't assume that everyone's going to have Internet access, and honestly, even if they have a phone, if they don't have Internet access, they're going to have a tough time finding our phone number.

So those are two of the core technologies that come to mind if we just talk about work day-to-day. And of course that's just talking about external communities; email is the lifeblood of my communication with people within Cornell and within my organization. It's both the communication method and in many cases the primary source of documentation for all of our workflows. Every once in a while we'll have time to sit down and write something up for a wiki or something, but a lot of times, it's, "How did we handle this last time? Let me search my email."

ALISON MACRINA: The most useful piece of technology that I use daily is probably something like IRC, Internet relay chat, which is an ancient-by-today's-standards, but-not-really-that-old-in-the-greater-scheme-of-things, piece of technology. IRC is made up of many servers, and users connect to those servers to chat with each other. You can think of it as a more privacy-conscious, non-corporate version of Slack. It's fairly straightforward; anyone can set up a server and then you can just connect to that server, and there are chat rooms to chat with people. I find this very useful because the way that IRC tends to be used now is just by a bunch of geeks, and that means that it's a very good place to go to get questions answered about other technology. That to me is the most valuable, since the work that I do requires that I know a lot about a lot of different kinds of technology that is often changing, and some of those pieces of technology are very hard to use. So for me the most valuable piece of all of them is the one that can tell me the most about using each piece. It's also a good way to communicate with people synchronously when you don't work with them face-to-face. We use IRC for meetings and informal discussion at Tor Project.

MARK MATIENZO: We use Google Hangouts and other videoconferencing software for meetings, and we use Slack as an internal communication tool, and a number of other communities that I'm involved with use both Slack and IRC. Basically the technologies that you use to directly interact with people and have a conversation, some sort of real-time or quasi-real-time communication—regardless of if that's text-based or just audio-based, or video and audio—are the most useful that I use for work.

CECILY WALKER: When talking about the kind of projects that I have to manage, and also because I live with a couple of chronic illnesses and sometimes can't be at work during the day, but I still need to be able to check in with my team—the tool that's been the most invaluable to me lately is Slack. It used to be a business tool, but I know a lot people are using it as a social tool as well. It allows me to connect with my team no matter where I am and no matter what I'm doing. It allows me to transfer files. It now allows people to make video calls as well. It's made it so that even though in an organization like mine, where, based on your classification in the organization, being present is something that's paramount for your position, it's made it a little bit easier for somebody like me, who is ill and who does have to be away from work sometimes for days at a time, to still check in and to still be in the loop of what my team is doing and still be available to them. I might not necessarily have the energy to get up every day to physically go into the office, but because this technology exists, I'm still able to provide supervision and direction and to keep the social lubrication going, which is so important when you're trying to build a team when you have disparate personalities. You're not just robots in the machine; Slack allows us in a way to break down those walls that exist between us, especially if you have really introverted people that you work with. I've noticed that Slack just made it easier for me to try to break through those natural divisions that happen based on people's personality types. So, yeah, it's pretty much revolutionized how I do my job.

CARMEL CURTIS: In terms of what piece of technology is most useful for my daily work, I probably would answer this question differently depending on the day. My day today involved having to communicate with a team of people across multiple floors and sections of the United Nations, so today a technological tool that was extremely helpful was Slack. Just being able to communicate with my team, to have them be able to ask me questions and each other questions, and to be able to share information with each other while we weren't in a close enough proximity to walk over to each other's desks, was extremely helpful. There are other days where we're working close together, and Slack is something that we rely on less.

But I do think that one of the most useful tools that I use in my work is some kind of communication tool, some kind of tool that allows me to communicate with people who aren't right there. In this project that I'm doing now, that's the vendor who's digitizing our materials, or that's people in other departments at other jobs that I've had, or that's former classmates of mine to ask their advice on how they have done something. Being able to have access to other people's minds without them being right next to me is one of the pieces of technology that I rely on most.

MYRNA MORALES: What is a tech that I can't live without in the course of my work? I guess texting. The ability to have a phone and to text is really important. It's one of the ways in which we communicate, and communicate on the spot, when we're organizing protests or demonstrations for any kind of organizational work that I do with Community Change Inc. Texting becomes a really important avenue. And of course it's how Trump got his bid for presidency, because of that NationBuilder platform. NationBuilder has the capacity to harness all the potential people to vote and send out a mass text message, the same way that Roberto Lovato from Presente used to get Lou Dobbs from his position. He would just tell us all to text "Basta Dobbs!" This was in maybe 2010. So I think texting is one of the most important technologies that I've seen. You don't have to talk to anyone, and you don't necessarily have to make the effort—at least for me; I hate talking on the phone—but you can also get the information, and you can be clear and concise and get it to a large number of people.

STACIE WILLIAMS: I was just graduating college when cellphones started to become a thing. I remember kind of scoffing at them. Who even needs a cellphone? But very early on in my career as a journalist, I would sometimes be driving in my car and a source would call me back on my cellphone. One time I was on the expressway. I pulled off and into a gas station really quick, because it was a source I had a lot of trouble getting in contact with. So when he finally called back, I was like, "Man, I've got to talk now!" That was when I really started to realize the importance of the immediacy of it, the ways in which it allows us to keep in touch. I mean, you can make the argument that we're too into our phones, but it's been so useful and, I think, such a necessary part of our regular world, in terms of the technology that's firmly ensconced. There's always been the phone. There's always been the need for communication. Even before Alexander Graham Bell, we needed to be able to communicate with each other in these ways. So I think the cellphone really has been the best tool, and it was a great tool for me even before I had an actual smartphone. I was an adult as I saw the rise of cellphones become a thing in our society. Certainly the first phones didn't even have all that, but my ability to send a text or even take a muddy photo—I can't imagine what those photos would look like now, from the earlier versions. But my ability to create information and transmit that information in a portable way, I think, is probably the most important.

. . .

JESSAMYN WEST: I was an early librarian on Twitter. Now people look and they're like, "Ooh, you have a lot of Twitter followers," and I'm like, "You know, some of that is just math." You get in early, and you just get more. It's the compound interest of the social Internet, basically. And ALA Think Tank, which is a big huge group on Facebook that I'm a part of—I know the guys who run it, so they made me a moderator in case I could help. I don't actually do that much moderating, but I am kind of a high-visibility woman who hangs out there and talks to people and answers questions, and I feel like that has utility and I can help set a tone and expectations. I feel like I can help people who are newer to the profession understand the things that I think are important about it.

SARAH HOUGHTON: My digesting digital information is what initially prompted me to start blogging, because I was going through hundreds of sites and listservs and RSS feeds and looking for new tools—usually free tools that libraries could afford—new legislation to be aware of, new trends, statistics, and information we could use to make better decisions on technology changes and projects. I found that I was compiling all of this for myself and thought, well, I *am* a librarian, maybe I should share this with other people so that they don't have to go through all of this effort that I'm going through. That was really the genesis of why I did what I did, to try to save other people the time and effort that I was putting into weeding through all the useless stuff to curate the most relevant data for my work as a digital services librarian. When I look at some earlier things that I wrote, it really was nothing more than what now would be a tweet. It was, "Here's this thing. It is useful because of x reason. Yay." We had lengthier posts on things that were more weighty, but a lot of it was simply resource-sharing. At the time, there was no Twitter. Blogging was the best way to do that by far.

As Twitter came around, you saw more and more people, including myself, turn away from blogging as a platform and towards things like Twitter, Instagram, and Facebook as a way to share those resources and information. I don't find it's as easy to parse or as well curated, but it is the way things have moved and shifted. I think the other piece that fits into that idea of digital communication between librarians is just websites in general, both public websites and intranets—they used to be really hard to make, and you had to know how to program to build one. You had to know how to program just to add a line of text to a page that already existed. Now, as more accessible and easy-to-use platforms have evolved—TypePad back in the day; WordPress is the best example now—you can have library staff at any technology proficiency level adding content and sharing it either with their communities or with each other, if you have an Internet environment, or through state library association websites or ALA chapter sites or whatever. There's just so much more sharing happening now because the information is much easier to post.

I think that's the biggest change that's made me happy as both a librarian and a technologist, that the ability to share ideas and information isn't limited to those few who could actually grok the technology anymore. Now it's more accessible and open to anyone with a good idea that they wish to share. And that democratization of expertise is critical to what we do as public libraries, so it seems to have worked out very well for us so far.

Anita Coleman: I'm impressed with and admire the librarians involved in critical librarianship. I participated in a #critlib Twitter chat once. It was fantastic how empowered and connected I felt during that time. But the connection didn't last beyond the hour. Even though I tried to follow those who'd responded and build the relationship using Twitter, very few responded. So for most people technology still has clear limitations in instilling a sense of shared purpose or community.

Michael Gorman: The kind of thing that used to go on ten years ago—the blogging of insult—seems to have mutated into just using the Internet to communicate ideas. It is in principle no different from self-published journals. It probably sounds impossibly elitist in today's culture, but I am in favor of mediated communication. It seems to me that in a world where everybody has something to say and it is all treated equally, very little communication is taking place. (Trump seems to have disproved the wisdom of crowds theory.) There is a reason for the peer-review system, for all its faults. There is a reason why publishers publish some books and not others. The current forced egalitarianism about distrusting experts and all that kind of thing is reductionist at best. Amid all the vacuity, trolling, and porn, there is a stream of mediated useful communication going on. A reason to have some hope.

. . .

Anita Coleman: I'm on the board for a library here in California. This is going to sound really strange, but I think they use technology very wisely. This is a small public library. They have chosen not to join the county system. The cities in the county, as they developed, made the decision whether they would go with the county system or have their own city system, with their own public library. Most of the cities in this county have gone with the county system, and they're constantly complaining. In fact, according to my former mayor, my own city—which has gone with the county system—has received money back every year because the county can't offer all the services for which they're contracted. So the mayor and the councilmembers were always fighting over that money that is returned because then it doesn't go towards libraries; it goes off to something else. But Placentia Library, on whose Foundation Board I served, chose to stay separate, as a city library. They have strong local connections and a supportive community. They're located in City Hall along with the police and all the other city offices; the library is right there in the center of the community. I don't know whether it's because of that or because of a forward-thinking board of trustees along with a foundation and friends, but the strong community presence and strong volunteer board are impressive. It's one of the few public libraries that I know that appears to have such a solid financial base.

I believe part of it is because they have used technology wisely. They offer various kinds of Internet and Web training that their community needs. They don't go beyond that. I think they've managed their own stress level very wisely because of that. Whereas some of the other public libraries either resist every technology and don't offer any, or they go overboard and offer too much. This library, for example, offers e-books through OverDrive, and Internet training which is grant-funded. They do all the other usual after-school programs and storytelling that a public library does, in terms of children's, youth, teen, adult, and senior services. Very cutting edge, but not to the point of alienating anybody, and this is the magic formula for managing change in libraries.

MITA WILLIAMS: Our local hackerspace, Hackforge started in Windsor, Ontario, in 2013, and my participation with the group came about because of a library event. One of the things I like about the Code4Lib community is that they encourage people to host their own local unconferences, so in 2012 I helped host Code4Lib North in Windsor. I promoted it not only to the library community but on my social media, and so we had some people from the larger community show up. One of them ended up being the first president of Hackforge, and he invited me to participate in the founding of this hackerspace.

Hackforge from the beginning was largely geared as a community-focused hackerspace dedicated to the people who work with technology, or who wanted to work with technology, and it aimed to bring them together and help them support and learn from each other. To start a hackerspace you need dues-paying members, space and equipment. The thing is, you can't recruit new members without space and equipment but you can't pay for space and equipment without dues-paying members. Hackforge was very lucky because the Windsor Public Library lent us prime library space on the first floor of their Central Branch to help us get started. All the equipment we added to the space were donations from the community. Without this support we wouldn't have been able to get started. And it had other benefits. Being located in the library encouraged Hackforge to take on the ethos of what was expected from a public library. We've since moved into our own space, but that foundation of being central and accessible to everyone in the community is something that I think has really shaped us. I'm still grateful for the Windsor Public Library for letting us form there. Hackforge's being hosted at Windsor Public Library came about because we knew someone who was working there, and they were working with someone in upper administration who was very receptive. And so our work dovetailed with theirs. The Windsor Public Library has their own technology space now.

There are two things that come to mind that I've learned from that experience. First is that community partnerships are essential, and those partnerships usually take a long time to develop. Secondly, it's essential to host open events for the community so you can be seen and discovered. Also, you have to go to community events held by other organizations so that you know who they are and can better understand the work that they're doing. I guess a third lesson that I have taken away from Hackforge is that the strength of any hackerspace or makerspace really comes from its people. You can provide amazing but complicated technology that's completely inaccessible. But with creative and patient facilitation, you can make an amazing hackerspace with very simple technology.

JESSICA ANNE BRATT: The DigiBridge partnership came about when I first started working at the Grand Rapids Public Library. We had no teens in the library, and everyone in the department at the time said that teens just didn't come. We were surrounded by a few high schools, and I would look outside my window during my off-desk time and see droves of teens walking from school but never coming into the library. I really wanted to find out why that was, so I tried emails and phone calls and school visits, and there was nothing, of course. I finally called the library media services, where I was like, "Hey, is there anyone I could talk to?" They said that there was a woman who wasn't in that day, but she'd happily talk to me. To preface this, after music education, I taught at a Chicago public high school for a year before I went to grad school. So I grabbed a ton of flyers for teen programs that I'd planned, and went in to this school and said, "Hey, is whoever that I spoke to about the library media services in?" I talked to her and kind of poured out my heart and told her that I'm really passionate about getting teens into the library. "Do you guys have a teen population and if so what can I do to talk to them or spread the word?" She said that they had the same problem, and they had come to our library.

Back then the mentality was, here are the library services, and if it works for you, then use them. And if it doesn't, well, then, that's okay. That's just how it was left. So a lot of the services we provided at the time, the schools had no interest in or couldn't use. I remember asking her, "What would you want from us, and what are your needs? I will try to take that back and see what I can do." She point-blank said some of her concerns and wants and asked, "Could you write up any ideas around that?" So I went and wrote up a small paper; it was legit, not even that much, but just what we could do to partner and build up the love for the library. Then she forwarded that to the assistant superintendent. At the time, I was new; I was not even six months into my job, and I didn't know who was who. The assistant superintendent ended up calling to have a meeting with me, and so then my whole library organization freaked out because there's this new person, I didn't even know half the things we had. I remember that was the first time I'd ever met with the director—like, literally knew who that was—as she's trying to coach me through what to do when I go into the meeting.

Long story short, I was able to bring one organization to the table and then bring all of the stakeholders and the heads of my organization to the table where they could hash out what are the priorities, what are the needs, and then what could the library do to address those needs. Out of that was born an MOU; we named it, and then we came up with seven initiatives. The Teen Tech Camp was a pilot one, just to see if it would be a mutually beneficial partnership, which it was. Out of that we did digital library cards, which was really intense because we had to get lawyers, and we had to call OverDrive and the research databases so we could navigate the student IDs basically being made into digital library cards. That was a really cool, eye-opening first learning experience right off the gate. We ended up not being able to do OverDrive, partially because we don't filter materials and the schools would need content filtered. The second initiative was the full library card, so that way kids can be able to access our e-books or e-audiobooks if they so choose.

From that, we started removing all types of access and barriers to library cards, because the first thing was, hey, we have about four or five thousand students that have fines, and significant fines, so let's talk about that. We started waiving. We would go to school orientations and school open houses, and we would just waive fines left and right. And it really made an external difference about how they viewed us in the community—people are like, "My teacher talked about this!" Or people would come in with their kids and say, "We heard we could get our fines forgiven." It made a difference as well as internally, when people started realizing that we no longer had to be this stiff structure. We don't have to assume that everyone's trying to take advantage of us. We don't have to be the FBI and make sure that people are who they say that they are, like they're out to get us for whatever reason. So it was really nice to implement this change internally and externally. We started being considered by the community, like when there's a parent night, "Oh, let's invite the library," or when there's a literacy thing, "It would be really cool to have the library."

. . .

Hana Sleiman: Thinking about how librarians can support social movements—there are two different things here. There are librarians in institutions that are centers of power who could support movements through granting access. I've seen librarians go out of their way to make materials available to users who otherwise couldn't have access to it. There's this very basic level of allowing representatives or individuals from social movements into restrictive institutions that aren't necessarily sympathetic to the cause. Then there's the other level of collecting and availing materials relevant to social movements. Librarians invoke scholarly or historic value to convince institutions to digitize and organize archives that support social movements. But then there's the question of how do we ourselves archive the social movements, and can we? Outside of institutional frameworks, how do we document and preserve traces of what we're doing right now? It's kind of easier in the analog age than it is in the digital age. A lot of materials were produced in analog—posters, flyers, etc. But so much is online, and this is where digital literacy is even more important. How are librarians and archivists or people who are interested in documenting social movements able to contribute by archiving the flood of digital material? I'm not sure, but it's very important.

JEN HOYER: People react to the Interference Archive collection in so many different ways. Some of them are frustrated that it's really physical and they can't search an online catalog to find everything, but then some people are overjoyed to get their hands on things. I can think of a great example from just the other week; it was a crazy experience for me in that it exactly fulfilled a stereotype that we imagine. Two visitors came in who had just visited a gallery in Chelsea that had copies of the Black Panther newspaper all over one wall as part of an exhibition, hidden behind plexiglass. And they were amazed that they could come to Interference Archive and just flip through those papers. We realize what some of the norms are in our world with respect to interacting with this historic material, and so providing a space where people can touch it and use it the way it was intended—that, I think, is really important.

We also had some young artists and activists visit recently. They're part of an artist collective that's inviting local artists to create portraits of people of color who have been murdered by the police around the country, and then they're having these public printing parties once a month or so to just print all of these designs. They were excited to come in to Interference Archive and see this heritage of other folks doing similar things—creating material as part of social movements, as part of organizing around different issues. They were really, really excited to come in and see this collection that was a clear path to the work they were doing.

HANA SLEIMAN: In Lebanon, there's an attempt to create an archive for those disappeared in the civil war, and there's an attempt to create archives for the different urban social movements. These are often scraping for skills and software, and often are doing a lot of work with no guidance and at best having to redo and redo it. So what librarians can offer, or should be doing, is extensive outreach programs that reach out to these different groups and help them with the knowledge we already have.

Jaime Taylor: It turns out that librarians make really good jail support people because we're anal-retentively organized and intensely detail-oriented and patient, and those are most of the things you need to do good jail support. I've been working on jail support since the very, very early morning of January 1, 2012. My first day of jail support was a four a.m. to nine a.m. New Year's morning shift outside a precinct in Manhattan. I processed fifty people at a precinct, never having done it before.

In terms of working with jail support and prison support and arrests and prosecutions and things like that, technology is a real two-edged sword, because one of the things that is hard to get across to people is that the videos and photos you take and the things you say can become incriminating evidence against you or against someone else. So don't post your videos to YouTube. You're going to get someone in trouble. You're going to end up being evidence in someone's court case against them.

That said, something like Signal has become really important to jail support, because we can in a small group chatter very securely about what we're doing and what's going on in ways that have features like self-destruction, so you can set your Signal chat to not be saved. You can set it so that once you leave the group, it disappears off your phone, things like that. There still are sometimes things that we don't say over it. Maybe that's someone's full name, maybe it's something important about what happened when they were arrested. But on balance, that kind of secure—especially group—communication feature is really important, that we can have these conversations. It's not 100 percent secure, nothing is, but we're fairly sure that there are no cops reading it. Of course, I don't know how often stingrays get used in New York. We've yet to discover that; it hasn't really come up yet. So for all we know, anything that we do with our phones can be intercepted and they're all listening to every single thing we say and storing it somewhere on a server, but we don't know yet, in New York at least, how much that's being done.

JESSA LINGEL: One activist project that I'm most excited about right now involves working in a county jail here in Philadelphia. I've been working with the wardens there, and I go one day a week and I help manage the library. I work with the librarians and I run a book club. I spend a lot of time thinking about the role of technology in that space because, on the one hand, there are some really advanced technologies there—I mean, every inmate has a wristband with a barcode and their photo on it, and they have another wristband that gives them other privileges. There's all these different kinds of technologies, but then at the same times, a lot of the gates that people are opening—they're just *keys*, man, normal keys that you and I would have to open our houses.

So the range of technologies is huge. On a nitty gritty level, it can be frustrating for two reasons. Well, it's really the same reason. It can be frustrating because there's the sense that some of the corrections officers aren't super comfortable with technology, so they're not always best-equipped to make decisions about how a proposed technology might help in the jail. Let's say I want to build a library catalog in the jail. Right now they're using Excel, so they can't track circulation at all, and this is a circulating collection. When I try and say, "Hey, can we get Access? I will pay for Microsoft Access, I will pay for Filemaker Pro, I will pay for whatever system you guys want to use," and they're like, "No, no, no, we can't use that technology, we can't give the inmates that technology," you get the sense that if they were just a little bit more comfortable with technology—which I realize I'm using very broadly—they wouldn't make those snap judgements, and then I could say, "Actually, we can think of this as a form of preparing people, giving them database experience, helping them for the workforce." But it's hard to have those arguments. The other way that that gets frustrating is when you see some of the COs really struggle with different forms of technology themselves, like when I was first going through volunteer training, and it was almost painful. It's that classic generational thing; it's almost painful to watch someone so uncomfortable with technology be in charge of a technological process. I do think about technology a lot in that sense.

But that said, I think there's so many stereotypes about jail that aren't true—but then some of them are. I haven't been incarcerated, but I do go to jail every week, and the things that people are able to do and their relationship to technology and circumstances of precarity and ingenuity are just really fascinating. They're willing to compile stats on circulation through this sort of by-hand process that most librarians I know would groan at—like, why would you ever do it that way, it's so slow. But it's important to them; they really want to know how many books are moving and how many get lost.

One thing I will say about the jail is it's really fun to go back to brass tacks or bare bones librarianship. A lot of what I do in the morning volunteer shift is just reader's advisory. Someone walks in and says, "I want this book," and then you say, "Well, I don't have any James Patterson, but I have some Jodi Picoult. Would you like to read that instead?" That's funny because I haven't done work like that in a very long time, but I enjoy it.

CELESTE Â-RE: A discussion about library and information skills in anti-gentrification movements seems like it's not happening much in the US. It seems to be happening in Canada and Europe. I'm hoping, as I proceed with my dissertation, I'll find more people who are considering this. A lot of times when I bring it up, they'll say, "Oh, I never even thought about that." And it's like, first off, libraries and archives and museums are being used as the anchor for these placemaking initiatives. It seems to be the trend. And we need to be thinking about this, because we're basically coming in to do the dirty work, in my perspective. Now, maybe I'm a little jaded by that, because I feel like I had to move because of gentrification. I had to leave New York, so it might be personal. But I think we need to be thinking about that and having discussions around it. If our organizations are doing that work, how do we support those people who want to stay in place? To provide them with the resources that they need, and to find communities that have been able to resist and stay put? What are the measures used to be able to do that?

When I was at the Allied Media Conference, I did a track on creative placemaking, and one of the things that came out in the discussion was that they wanted a database of resources. They wanted to be able to go to a place to find information about issues that relate to gentrification, or find out about people who've been successful in resisting it. There's nothing that they could go to at this point. So I'm hoping I'll be able to find folks that are doing the work, and maybe we can collaborate on creating a database or a digital portal or a website to make that information important, because it's impacting people, not just in the US; it's happening all around the world, with globalization and austerity measures. It's an issue that I think librarians and archivists and curators need to really get at the forefront of.

JAIME TAYLOR: At Occupy Wall Street, in the library at the occupation, it was this strange mix of stone age and technological. If you go to Zuccotti Park, you will notice here and there little electric outlets, but they turned off the power and their lights in the pavement. So any power that was produced at Zuccotti had to be brought in. We did that by batteries and generators, and things like that. At the height of it, we were running a gas-powered generator in the middle of the library that powered lights. We had, I think, five laptops that were donated to us. We had wireless hotspots, as well as being able to charge our cellphones. That said, it wasn't like we were sitting there happily typing away at these computers. We were sometimes, but being able to actually run this generator—we actually had a series of generators. The first one, the fire department came in and took. We had a lovely community man named Sean who was our generator-runner-in-chief.

It was this real mix of the books and paper and pencils—just a lot of paper—and also these laptops that didn't have hard drives. That was a privacy thing. We got one of the laptops from my friend Eric, who kind of found it in the garbage somewhere because he's a dumpster diver and made it workable for us, and then the other four came from some tech magazine. They sent us four laptops, and they didn't have hard drives. So in order to use it, you inserted a thumb drive with the operating system on it when you turned it on, and then you'd boot up that operating system from the thumb drive. You couldn't save anything on it, so you'd have to email it to yourself or save it to Google Drive—which is a bad idea—or save it to another thumb drive, and then you'd unplug all your little drives and the thing would power down and it wouldn't have an operating system and it wouldn't have memory. Anyone who needed to write something up or check their email could use these things, but there was literally no way information could get saved on these laptops because it didn't have a hard drive. It didn't have its own operating system. Anything you were doing was gone when you unplugged from it.

We probably had the most consistent Internet in the park because we had a hotspot that we would stick in a high place in the library for a few hours until it ran out of power. But we were mostly working from cellphones. I think without smartphones, nothing would have worked. The occupation would have been an entirely different scene without smartphones. That ended up being a personal thing, you know—do you have a smartphone? Is it new enough and running a late enough version of your operating system that you can use certain things? I think that we all became much more adept at the things our smartphones could do in a few months. We all started using Twitter very heavily. We were using Celly, which people are now turning away from because there's better tools now, like Signal. But at the time, Celly was a big thing, and because there was a text interface, you could use it from a dumb phone.

At the People's Library, we kept zero circulation records on purpose. It was really an excellent merging of the practical and the philosophical. We didn't keep records because it would have been next to impossible to keep anything resembling accurate circulation records. So we didn't even try. The only possible way you would have known that someone was reading any of the books we held was to have seen them reading it.

* * *

BONNIE GORDON: I had been volunteering at Interference Archive before I got the job at the Rockefeller Archive Center. I started doing that when I was in grad school. Being involved in the cataloging working group, which is the working group that implemented CollectiveAccess, our open source catalog, taught me a lot about both library technology and helping people who aren't technologists use technology. By observing two of the technologists working on that, I learned a lot about how to talk to people about technology, and how to work with users to understand what their needs are. What a developer needs to hear to make something work the way a user expects isn't necessarily how a user will initially articulate it. Learning how to have that conversation was incredibly valuable, being in a room full of people with varying levels of expertise as well as working on a system that at the time had pretty minimal documentation. Being somewhere in the middle and seeing what technologists' expectations were, and seeing the varying assumptions and expectations of people who were less familiar with cataloging databases or other forms of technology, was so valuable, and something that I definitely use at my current job.

DANIEL KAHN GILLMOR: I think that experimentation is critically important to the decision-making process about using a tool. If you're someone who's building tools, I want to stress that making it easy to try something out really will help your tools to get adoption, and it will also help you anticipate the concrete use cases and think about what you specifically want to optimize. At some level, what I want to encourage people who are building tools to think about is, how do I make it easy to deploy for experimentation, but also how do I make it so that configurations can be made and then rolled back? That is, experimentation within the particular project. CollectiveAccess has grown some of that ability to save configurations since we started using it at Interference Archive, which is great to see. So you go in and fiddle something and say, "How does it work now? Does it work better? Oh, it does? Well, that's the configuration I want to keep." It's really nice to be able to do that knowing that it's easy to roll back. That "undo stack" at a system level is something that really lets people feel a lot more comfortable with the tools.

ALISON MACRINA: In my work with Tor, I think of myself more as a librarian because my focus is always on the broader public and how they can engage with this. Also, I don't call myself a developer because I don't write any code for Tor. There's a word for the way that I approach this, I guess, in the technology world, and that is from a usability approach. But it's more than that. It's not just making this thing usable for somebody to use on their own, but finding out what they need from it and making it make sense to them.

How do people treat me as a librarian working on Tor? They're tickled by it. I think that is the reason for some of my success; people are like, "Wait, Tor is doing *what* with libraries?" The connection is unexpected and it makes people stop and ask questions, and I think this is a great thing. Also, what's neat about the free and open source software community is that library values are values that they have, too, and they had no idea that libraries had values like privacy and open access and all this. And they're like, "Oh, this is a partnership that just makes sense. We should have this connection." So many of the developers have been super supportive of LFP from the beginning.

We librarians can help developers in a lot of ways, too. Number one—give usability feedback about tools. We should use things ourselves, and then we should tell the developers, "This doesn't make any sense," "This is broken," "This is weird," "I don't get this." We can do this by writing support tickets. We can also just get directly involved in the projects. There is so much work to do, if we have the time to volunteer. Even just by teaching people about using these tools, we are bringing so much back to the free and open source software world. I think that there's a huge untapped potential here of us working directly with developers. We have access to the public in a way that they don't.

Another thing that they can help us with is that we have some of the worst software for anything. We have these horrible contracts where we have to take the lowest bid, so we get what we paid for. Our vendor agreements don't make any sense. Our vendors don't share our values. Our ILS systems are crap; they're so unusable, and they're expensive. I really would love to see us develop a relationship with FOSS developers to a point where we can get them to make us better stuff. We can leave behind these ridiculous bloated vendors and we can create a technical environment in our libraries that makes sense for us and is actually built for us by people who understand us, and that we can reciprocate by giving back to the technologists what we know about regular people and how they use their computers. I want to see much more of that kind of relationship-building, and it's something I've been trying to work on for a while.

JESSAMYN WEST: For a couple years I went to SXSW and did talks about the digital divide and why it's important and what developers need to think about. I got some good feedback from people, and it was sort of nice, but there was an aspect where—and I've heard this with people who do diversity work, that you're at a company, maybe your company has a diversity problem, maybe you're a person of color, and you get an awful lot of attention from people being like, "Help us with this problem!" And you wind up doing a lot of unpaid "keepin' it real" discussions with people about how they can work on their diversity problem, but they're doing that instead of spending money recruiting in the right places, doing a hard assessment of why they don't have more people of color or more women working for them, or that kind of thing. I felt like my role at SXSW was getting like that, that everybody wanted to sort of talk to me for free about how they could deal with digitally divided people. Then what would wind up happening is that they'd have an idea, I'd give them a bunch of free feedback, and they would be in a state of having talked to me about it but not actually having done the things that they needed to do about it.

I feel like the people who were doing the best at working with digitally divided people are the government in some ways, or at least have been in previous administrations. You look at the work that groups like 18F have been doing, because the government really has a mandate to serve everyone. You look at things like the Social Security Administration, where you can log on and look at your benefits. In the interest of security, they tried to roll out two-factor authentication, when you have to use your phone or get a code in order to log in so that they know it's really you. It's very secure, which is great. The problem that they found at the Social Security Administration when they rolled out two-factor authentication—which I'm sure was an idea that a tech person gave them that sounded good at the time—was that Americans weren't ready. You couldn't make them have a cell phone, get a code, and type the code in; it was actually keeping people from being able to log in when you made this mandatory. And they had to find out the hard way, basically rolling it out, finding out it didn't work, and then having to roll it back in. So I think part of what actually gets the point across is insisting on a lot more user testing, and the people who are getting this built for them should be some of the people who do that. Insisting on statistics.

I feel like one of the things libraries could do as an institution nationwide is working higher up the food chain. So, like, a library in Vermont might not be able to look at an online catalog and say, "Oh, it totally meets section 508 accessibility requirements so that people who are visually disabled can use it." But the State Library sure as hell can. Some of those decisions, and the pressure that then should come down on people who sell software tools just to libraries, should be from a high enough level that people take it seriously. We've got companies who sell integrated library systems to libraries who still store passwords in plain text. That's ridiculous. That hasn't been an industry standard for fifteen, twenty years, and yet there hasn't been a large enough group of libraries to drop the hammer on this company and make them do anything different. Part of the problem is figuring out how to apply pressure in useful ways. Sometimes it's just reinforcing through feedback, through comments, through blog posts and tweets and phone calls to people. "Hey, I've got a print-disabled user and they actually can't use this thing." "Hey, I've got a user with a shaky hand and they can't click that tiny triangle that hides the privacy settings." Literally speaking your truth, which is whatever your patrons are having a challenge with. You don't have to tell people how to recode it, you don't have to fix it yourself. Give feedback to companies in, if you can, a high-profile way, and, if you can, not super embarrassing, but just, like, "Hey, we have to have *all* of our patrons use this at the library. And they all can't because you forget that people can't read tiny text or they can't click a tiny triangle."

I spent a lot of time at Open Library in meetings just reminding people that people with visual and motor skill disabilities exist, because they just don't see those people in their day-to-day life. Part of what we do in the library is remind people that these people exist and that they buy software and that they have a right to the same user experiences as people without shaky hands or as people without visual disabilities, even more cognitive disabilities that make super confusing websites even more difficult—so applying general pressure, working up the food chain of whatever your library chain of command is. I'd like to see more State Librarians demanding better software, more accessible websites, and a whole host of other things, so that companies would actually be like, "Oh, it's the state of Vermont!" and pay a little more attention instead of, "Eh, it's libraries, they don't even know good software when they see it, so why should we be listening to what they say."

STEPHANIE IRVIN: In general I wish that universal design would be discussed more. Because it's not just one thing and it doesn't specifically have to do with one piece of technology; it has to do with everything. It's basically the idea that whatever you create, regardless of what it is, try to find a way to design it so that anyone can use it. I think if we did that, we would automatically be more friendly towards our patrons. We would open up more options for groups that may not have used us in the past to interact with us and to realize that we see the importance of anyone being able to access our material. That's kind of a mindset more than just one piece of technology, but that is something that could be applied to most any technology. I don't believe in looking at something and saying,

"Oh, well, they can't use this because they have such-and-such a disability." I prefer to look at something and say, "How could this be used by someone with a disability, and what could I do to make it easier for them to use it?"

. . .

JESSAMYN WEST: Technology gives us an unprecedented ability to have economies of scale. That can be the good news. If you're the Internal Revenue Service and you want to get people's taxes paid online instead of getting pieces of paper, and you save two bucks for every American, well, that's money that America saves, regardless of how you feel about the IRS or taxes or anything else. So economies of scale can be very good. However, this same thing can turn around, and if you have a terrible interface that somebody has to interact with in order to do a thing, economies of scale can quickly become what I call economies of hassle. Whereas before you would have a hit or miss chance of talking to a good or a bad person on the telephone, you can have a website that just barely doesn't work, and you can harass a million people simultaneously with that terrible website.

I think we have to be responsible to that. I think we also need to be responsible specifically to the fact that the people we're harassing with our maybe-not-perfectly-functioning technology are the same people who have every other thing in the deck stacked against them. That's our responsibility, too. If our website is harder for a non-English speaker than an English speaker to use, and we don't have a way for them to mitigate that, if somebody with poor color vision can't use our website, and they have a hard time with other websites, if someone with a shaky hand can't get to their privacy settings—that's on us. The worst part of it is, those people—the color-blind person, the person with the shaky hand, the person who maybe doesn't have really good English—they think it's them. And that is horrible. It's because we don't have a fully functioning national conversation about technology, and too many people are passing on "computers are hard, what can you do?"

STEPHANIE IRVIN: What technology means for me are tools to help individuals live their lives in a manner that works for them, or basically tools to make their lives easier. All of my patrons are individuals with disabilities, which include those with reading disabilities or physical impairments so they can't hold or handle a book, and a lot of our patrons have visual impairments or are blind. Technology is supremely important in a lot of their lives. In particular those who are visually impaired or blind now have more tools than ever before to access online media. So the idea that you shouldn't design your website or materials for someone who is blind or visually impaired is now ridiculously outdated, because there are so many ways that they can read them using different types of screen readers or other technology. You cannot discount the importance of technology to people with disabilities. It's basically the resounding cry whenever I go to meetings for groups of individuals with disabilities, because technology is how you open up new doors for yourself.

HADASSAH DAMIEN: I very firmly believe that there's no one platform or tool that's going to address accessibility and the complexity of the many, many intersectional social issues that all the different types of humans in the world bring to their use of technology. So I think it's really important to think about analog solutions as well as digital solutions—solutions that people will use together, and solutions that people will use asynchronously in different places.

There's an argument for accessibility, but the word gets used in all these different ways. So someone might be using "accessibility" to code for talking about class, and talking about, "It's not accessible if we have things online, because some people don't have computers." That is true. But people sometimes also use "accessibility" to talk about young people, and they're like, "Well, it's accessible, because I can load it on a phone." A lot of younger users of technology are doing 70 to 80 percent of their interactions on Internet-enabled mobile devices. Sometimes people say "accessibility" and what they're actually meaning is, is it ADA-compliant? Is this a digital interface that a screen reader can use? And if your site isn't ADA-compliant, well, it's not accessible. But then sometimes people mean "accessibility" like, oh, it's digital, and people with physical mobility issues who can't get out of their houses *can* get this information, so it *is* accessible. And I think that all of these things are important and worth thinking about, but there's no one answer. There's actually not a great language to address these issues, because it's not quite specific enough yet.

Stephanie Irvin: Libraries will understand that you want to serve your public. People with disabilities may not be a large part, but they are part of your public. And you want to make it so that users can use your site. You don't necessarily have to go out of your way; it's sometimes just a matter of some very small changes in order to make things friendlier to people with disabilities. Because you don't want someone to turn away from the library because they think that they can't use your material. That's always heart-breaking. You can make something that is beautiful and is accessible for all, and then everyone can use it, and why wouldn't you want that if you're a librarian? That's exactly what we want, free access to material for all.

So just the idea of universal design is what I always try to tell people about. You don't have to sacrifice style in order to make it accessible. The World Wide Web Consortium has some great material, particularly their Web Content Accessibility Guidelines, now version 2.0. They have big mammoth checklists that look really really intimidating, but if you look at it—even as someone who doesn't know much about web design, you would see there were things that you knew how to do. Like, have decent contrast. Don't have text that goes all the way across the screen, because frankly no one likes that. And that's the great thing about making things accessible for everyone—sometimes you end up making them friendly for people without disabilities, and you don't even realize. So it helps everyone.

I would love to see more focus in general on people acknowledging that "visual media" is now not just visual. I think it's finally reaching a point where people realize that there are various forms of visual media that are now becoming accessible through different means, like when the Internet finally heard about video description, thanks to Netflix getting it on "Daredevil." That was great. But that's the sort of technology that's been coming out for a while, and sometimes you just need an awareness of it. I haven't seen too much of a cultural push towards accessible web design.

Mark Matienzo: I still think for the most part most digital library projects don't do a great job with accessibility, or when they do it's at the simplest level. There are some really interesting opportunities to strongly think about developing accessible content or accessible interfaces that change the interaction paradigms for everybody, regardless of their ability to see, hear, or have fine motor control. We have a lot of work to do in the digital library world, and just in libraries in general. A lot of people are aware that we have a lot of work to do, but a lot of that is really defining the work in the context of what you're doing. Archives in particular, I think, suffer from this even more so. I think the only reason why libraries have a slight leg up here is because it's a much larger professional community, and the community of archivists is much smaller by comparison.

STEPHANIE IRVIN: The first thing that we try to make accessible is our website, and that way people have a digital front that they can come to for information. When I started, the applications were not accessible. I wanted to make it so that our patrons could fill it out on their own time, print it off, and mail it to us without having to worry about getting someone else to write it out. We also have various other PDFs on the site that I've made accessible, and for things like our social media—Facebook is mainly what we use now, because we have a good following there—it's knowing how to make posts so that our readers can still figure out what's going on with the post, even if they don't have a specific screen reader. And the last one is a YouTube page, which is something that I added and argued for because even if our patrons are unable to see the video, they can still hear the audio and it might be helpful. Plus we have users who have a physical impairment or a reading disability, so that's why it's important to have the visual component, and captions for those that may have a hearing impairment or those, like me, who actually like to read instructions while they do something or watch something. It's very handy.

JOEL NICHOLS: Our libraries have access technology stations that are set up for people with visual impairment, but it's not every library in the system; it's just some libraries, and then staff in the moment is not necessarily equipped to then teach them digital literacy on the access device. I worked in branches where the computers were set up at tables that were so tight that someone in a wheelchair couldn't really get to them very easily, or they could only get to the one on the end, or other patrons had to shift or move so someone could actually sit in front of the computer. I think that's unforgivable in terms of making a universal experience that's open and accessible to all. We need to do a lot better than that. Our Techmobile, for instance, was wheelchair-accessible, but only through a lift in the back that by default made it very difficult to use. So I'm very conscious of that.

STEPHANIE IRVIN: In terms of professional organizations that focus on accessibility for users with disabilities, there's ALA's ASCLA. I serve on committees with them. There's a similar one with the Georgia Library Association, Library Services for Persons with Disabilities Interest Group, which I'm the former chair of. We try to provide a place for library staff to exchange ideas or anything else that might be interesting regarding serving our patrons, basically just keeping a general mindset of acknowledging that these are our patrons that might need some degree of attention that a lot of people wouldn't necessarily think of. Basically, you don't want someone coming into your library who is blind and you not knowing how to interact with them in a respectful way, so just having these groups that create that sort of awareness is fantastic. Beyond that, we try to encourage accessible web design and all of that.

In general, every state has a talking book library or is in partnership with one, but there are other groups that serve the community or specific subsections of the patrons that we serve. Like, the Lions Clubs do a lot of work with individuals who are blind. I went to a Lions Camp for the Blind recently, and it was fantastic albeit very hot. Because Georgia, and summer. Those are the main organizations that I know of that are trying to push for more inclusion in libraries, and acknowledgment of serving these groups that initially might have been dismissed because, "Oh, someone's blind, they can't read." That's so not true. There's a million ways they could read! You just might have to provide different tools for them, or need to be aware of them to guide them to them.

A question that would be neat to ask would be, "Who can I contact if I'm interested in making accessible media?" On a self-study course, look at materials from the World Wide Web Consortium. Look at their Web Content Accessibility Guidelines and use those. Aside from that, it wouldn't hurt to reach out to your talking book library to see if they have someone that might be knowledgeable, because chances are they do. If you're in Georgia, ask me, I don't mind! Sometimes it's not that hard. It's just a couple of little things that you can do to make it so that your patrons can read it. So why not do it?

ANDREW WEISS: At California State University, Northridge, with a lot of the work I'm doing for our thesis scanning project in particular, what we want to do is provide digital copies for students with disabilities. One of our main rationales for converting a thesis from its print version to a digital version was, for example, if someone was blind, it would allow the student to at least have some sort of digital reader to read out the abstracts and the full text of the work. Of course, we also have to do this within the confines of our funding model, which means that we can only do so much for the sake of accessibility, since it's very time-consuming. For example, if you're trying to make a PDF as accessible as possible, then you would need to add tags and headers to every page. Unfortunately, because we just don't have the funding, we are unable to do that. I think we're able to do as much as we can, but there are always limits, and those limits are often unclear.

STEPHANIE IRVIN: I think that there's been great strides by different tech companies, particularly Apple, to make their devices more accessible for their patrons. If you were to go to a meeting of individuals who were blind, you would find a lot of them have iPhones. That's because they can use it to contact their friends and family, or to find maps to know how to get somewhere. They can use Uber in order to travel. They can use an app like Be My Eyes to see whether or not the milk in front of them has expired, and just a magnitude of other things. Apple has built screen readers into their devices, and Android devices now have them, too. You can also find screen readers to put on something, like, say, a laptop. My laptop has one when I need to test our media, but it's great that there are more pieces of technology coming out that you can just open the box and use. Google devices have started being pretty friendly, too, but Apple always deserves a big brag for being accessible out of the box. You set up a Mac, turn it on, brand new, and leave it for a minute—it's going to start talking to you because voice over has come on, so you can use it even if you're blind.

. . .

JOHN HELLING: I went to library school thinking I'd be an academic or an archivist but immediately gravitated to public libraries when I saw how much people depended on them. Not long after I entered library school the unemployment system was changed so that you could only apply for benefits online—which I think pretty much sums up the need for access to technology for the public. In terms of volume of use, I don't think we as public librarians have done any better than the desktop PC. Trite, I know, but access to that particular piece of technology is often what stands between people and what they need. For example, when they recently opened the application process for Section 8 housing, we saw a huge influx of people who needed our technology in order to do that. We often hear secondhand that someone—the IRS, for example—just refers people to the library for things that used to be available on paper but are being phased out to cut costs. And obviously, you at least need a printed copy of your resume in order to apply for a job. Public PC usage is definitely declining as more and more people start using their own devices, but we're still providing that baseline computing technology to quite a lot of people.

SARAH HOUGHTON: I think that the most widely-used technology in our library is our wireless service. Without a wireless access point or points in a building, you cripple many of your users from being able to use their devices and participate in the digital economy. We've seen usage of our public computers decrease every year for the last three years after a good two solid decades of increase, increase, increase every year, and it's because more people are bringing their own devices and expecting connectivity wirelessly. I think that, by far, having solid wireless access is important. We're going to be upgrading to gigabit ethernet here at both of our libraries at the end of this calendar year.

CAROL BEAN: There's so many technologies associated with wifi. Sometimes we forget that cellular data, can be very expensive, especially here in the United States. I lived in Serbia for two years. As I traveled around the Balkans, a lot of the restaurants and cafes, which were everywhere, offered free wifi. Kids—I say "kids" because they were the ones primarily with the smartphones—could walk down the street going from cafe to cafe picking up the wifi. That was how they accessed the Internet, rather than use their data, which is extremely expensive for some of the kids that didn't have jobs. And we come over here, and it's not really talked about a lot, but cellular data is expensive. I think a lot of people maybe don't realize that with the libraries having wifi, that's a really great tool, probably one of the most significant tools, technology-wise.

STACIE WILLIAMS: In college, cellphone culture was definitely tied to a class issue. I went to the University of Wisconsin, Madison, for undergrad, and the first kids on campus to have the cellphones really in that kind of way were what we called "the East Coast kids." The East Coast kids tended to live in private dorms that were semi-on campus, semi-off. They were generally identified as being the more privileged of the students on campus, and you kind of had to be if your parents were paying out-of-state tuition at that level for you to come to this school in the midwest. So they were the first kids with cellphones, and I remember that was always the criticism. People would be laughing, "Oh, what are they talking about? Jeans on sale at the GAP?" All these many years later, I can be like, yeah, they probably *were* talking about jeans on sale at the GAP—but everybody does. I have used my cellphone to talk about jeans on sale at the GAP. I guess they were talking about whatever I would have simply talked about on the home phone with a friend.

But I do remember that the criticism at the time was very class-based. I guess if you're looking at it over time, it's never ceased to be class-based. Now because they want to repeal the Affordable Care Act, this lawmaker is like, "Well, people are just going to have to choose between buying an iPhone and having healthcare." It's kind of like, "Bro, anyone can have an iPhone." Also the cost of healthcare so far dwarfs the cost of an iPhone, it's just not even an apples to apples comparison. I find it interesting that as technology has advanced, it's always been tied to class issues, because, really, who can afford to be early adopters? Everybody can't; you're waiting until it trickles down and you can afford it. You're waiting until they've worked out the bugs for you to decide to get it without it being a hassle. There's always that tension there.

CAROL BEAN: I find it interesting to see how the digital divide has been redefined over the last fifteen years or so. Originally I think there was at least a hat tip to those who have Internet access and those that don't. And then it came to be the assumption that, well, everybody has Internet access; the digital divide are the ones that can use computers and the ones that can't use computers, what we call the "digital natives" versus the "digital immigrants" versus "digital refugees." I think for a while that was true. From about 2003, 2004 to maybe 2012, that was the case. I think there was a big segment of the older population—the fastest-growing segment of the population—that was getting Internet access and getting online, yet they really didn't know how to use computers, they really didn't know what they were doing, and they were so lacking what we call e-literacy. They really needed training. I think since 2012 that segment of the population has adapted and kind of found their niche of what they can use, what they're capable of, and what they like using. They've found that niche, and they're kind of there.

We're back to looking at digital access, how many people actually have access to a computer and the Internet, because we've moved to where almost everything is available online. I still am encouraged that there's a lot of things that aren't totally Internet-focused, but at the same time it's sometimes distressing. That said, I think the digital divide has come back around to the people that have access to Internet and the resources on the Web, versus those that don't. I see this as I look at the Pew Internet reports, which I follow religiously. They periodically come out and track, okay, where are we today on high-speed Internet access and how people are accessing the Internet? The most recent report I'm familiar with is the one basically showing that Latinos and immigrants and a lot of poor African Americans primarily access the Internet through their cellular phones, and not all of them have smartphones. These might be just Blackberries or flip phones. They can send and receive texts, they can get certain kinds of websites. It's an interesting development, because a lot of poor people are on the Internet, but it's very different how they're experiencing it. That, I think, is part of the digital divide and part of what we have to start looking at, what the digital divide is today.

JESSAMYN WEST: I feel that because of the way start-up culture works, at least in America now, there's a lot of money being thrown at a lot of attempts to fix the digital divide as long as those attempts to fix the digital divide can scale. What everybody wants to do is dump a lot of money into a program that will then run itself and help the digital divide. I think one of the problems with that is it's all about creating an app or a website that's going to help people learn technology, but you have people who have inabilities or unwillingness, or a combination of the two things, to using websites or apps. The website or app is not going to solve that problem. But then, again, you wind up with a lot of blame directed towards the people who are having a hard time using the website that you built to teach them to learn technology skills, and I don't feel there's a lot of after-the-fact assessment of a lot of these attempts, because start-up culture, right? You just throw money at it, and then later you hope you have some numbers that come out the other side that make it look like it helped. Realistically, what helps people is a lot of one-on-one or small-group or community-based or friend-based assistance and mentorship, that kind of thing. But for some reason, even though there's other hard-to-serve populations in other issue areas, it's like, "Why can't you solve racism with a website?" "Why can't you solve institutionalized poverty with a website?" "Why can't you solve the healthcare crisis with a website?"

The hardest people to serve, for various reasons, are very hard to serve. I feel like late-stage capitalism really believes that what we should get is something that works for 90 percent of the people, and then we're really mostly there. Because if you're Coca-Cola, and you can sell your product to 90 percent of the people, you're fine. You don't have to care about the other 10 percent of the people. But realistically, with the digital divide, if what you're really trying to do is handle that problem—and this is why I work with public libraries, because I find this problem interesting. You've got to give a shit, not only about that 10 percent, but you've got to make that 10 percent your problem, and that's challenging. It's resource-intensive, it's labor-intensive, and it's super frustrating. I think you get a lot more attempts to work on it now in 2016 than you did maybe ten or fifteen years ago, but I find that there's a blinders aspect to a lot of these attempts, because everybody wants to solve the digital divide with an app or a website, and there are some specific reasons prima facie why that doesn't actually work.

JIM DELROSSO: I have a noted and notable distaste for the kind of faddism that tends to show up a lot in the library world. I spent a lot of years going to some of the at least nominally techier kinds of library conferences, and the notion that if you get the right app, if you get the right program, it's going to revolutionize everything, was always very prevalent. It never seemed to actually relate to most people's library experiences, whether it was because the stuff being promoted was beyond the ability of those libraries to afford it, or it was just the sort of thing people embrace without seeing how it's going to connect with their communities. Of course, nobody would ever describe themselves as being fad-oriented. But that lack of connection to community is something that did jump out at me, where people would be like, "We'll adopt this app, and it will make all of these things easier." Well, only if people use it. Only if people can afford to use it. And those discussions were not as much a part of the overall conversation as they should be.

JESSAMYN WEST: As far as what technology is useful to the people in the library and the people who I work with—most of whom come from what I would consider sort of the other end of the digital divide—a good network is the thing. A lot of the people that I see who have technology questions and problems are coming from a house or an apartment with iffy connectivity to begin with, and one of the things that you learn about apps and devices and websites in 2016 is that many of them are created with the easy presumption that of course you're going to have a good network connection all the time. I live in an apartment that has decent cellular reception, and I've got a broadband connection that maybe isn't even broadband anymore, because they've redefined broadband and I've stayed in one place. For the people that I work with in rural no-place, an always-on fast connection is really the thing that enables them to do everything else. I know it's kind of like saying, "What's the most important thing in your library?" and being like, "Literacy!" But realistically, for people who haven't had that always-on connection and have dealt with the completely frustrating experience of apps and software and websites that just presume you have that—they assume you can be online all the time; they assume you can have a steady connection while you upload a thing, download a thing, update your software, do all the stuff—having a 100MB connection like we do in my public library really is a game-changer for a lot of people relative to what they have at home. Only then, when they've got that always-on connection, can they understand what in god's name is the utility of something like Instagram or Twitter, which just seems bizarre to people who have to dial up and get their messages from the Internet. To be fair, we don't have *that* many people doing things like dial-up, but we don't have zero.

So, always-on network—most important thing. And then the second thing, what we find people are really into are community builders like Facebook, obviously. But not Facebook per se, but these little Facebook groups. Everyone in town has someplace they like to do and buy and sell things. There's a lot of localized Facebook groups that are just for that. We have a mailing list called Front Porch Forum. It's kind of like Nextdoor, which is this larger thing that most people have heard of. Front Porch Forum is in Vermont, and it's literally a once-a-day mailing list of what's up with your neighbors. People can make little posts. It's like you got a mini-Craiglist delivered to your inbox. I see tons and tons of my neighbors who won't be on a mailing list, who won't get on a website, who barely use Facebook, but they can send an email, and the email goes to the mailing list, and then it goes to other people, and then they can find a plumber, sell their thing, find out who's got eggs, find the missing dog. It's interesting to me that it gets a kind of uptake, because we hear all the time, "Oh, email, nobody uses that anymore," except people totally do. The people who don't use email are the people who are yammering on Twitter about everything, but realistically speaking, in smaller communities, email is one of the ways, digitally, that people stay in touch, besides all the in-person ways that they also stay in touch.

Sarah Houghton: In terms of technology access with the public, the most important thing I can say is that the digital divide is still very much alive, and that is not a thing to be happy about. The ability of many of our residents throughout the country to access even basic Internet service in their homes is lacking, either due to their location in a rural community or a socioeconomically disadvantaged community, or the fact that they themselves do not have the money to pay for an expensive monthly broadband connection to the Internet. Many of the people in the more rural parts of the county that I live in—even though it is a wealthy county—only have access to satellite access to the Internet. That's why the library's higher-speed access has become more and more critical as time goes on, and the data we're accessing becomes bigger and has more bits and bytes and needs more time to download. People don't want to wait seven hours for the TV episode they want to watch to download onto their computer.

I am hoping that this is something that's going to change, but I think that the socioeconomic and the rural-urban differentiations in terms of technology access and basic literacy are very real, and it's something that many people forget and that gets overlooked in conference presentations and books and discussions. Many of the people having those discussions are coming from communities or libraries of privilege—a large urban system, for example, and not a rural community. Because that rural community can't afford to send its library staff member to that conference to attend, much less present. So I think there are a lot of voices that are silenced because they're not at the table having conversations about the very basic technology needs that still exist, and so many other pieces of diversity fit into that—I mean, race, class, age, socioeconomic status, you name it. I would love to see that end in my lifetime, but I'm at least happy to see it slowly, slowly getting better partially as libraries are able to fill the gap and also partially as mobile technology becomes more affordable and gives people access through mobile networks to something that is at least approximating a full digital experience.

JOHN HELLING: In general, I think when most people hear the word "poverty" they immediately picture urban areas. Obviously, urban areas experience poverty, often very concentrated poverty, but there is also a large instance of poverty in rural areas that is less visible because it's so much more spread out and people are much less mobile in those areas. In Bloomfield—and I'm sure in rural libraries across the nation—we were the only place that people could go. There were parts of our service district where high speed Internet wasn't even available for purchase because the cable and phone companies had decided it wasn't worth the investment to run the lines out there. If one of our patrons needed to apply for unemployment, how exactly is this possible without the library providing access to a computer and the Internet? And this is in Indiana, a forty-five-minute drive to Bloomington, home of a major research institution. On the scale of American rurality we weren't that high—not nearly as high as areas in the western US, for example. It's vital that these libraries keep their doors open, which is simply becoming less and less possible to do in a vacuum. If you aren't collaborating, if you aren't creating partnerships that help support your mission, then you're slowly dying, and you're also failing your patrons.

STEPHANIE IRVIN: People with disabilities tend to have a much higher rate of unemployment, particularly those who are blind. I found statistics that go as high as 30 percent of people who are blind are unemployed. So basically class affects a lot of our patrons, because a lot of our patrons are more likely to not make as much as the average Joe, I suppose. That's part of the reason we provide free talking book player to all of our patrons, because that way someone has a basic device—and I say "basic"; they're pretty nice, I mean, they actually outlast my iPhone by like four times at least—and that way people have something so they can read their material. If they want to get an iPad or an Android device or something to read their books, they can elect to do so, but it's not obligatory. There's no part of our program that you have to pay for at its basic level. If you want the device and the app, fine, use it. If you can't afford it, that's all right, we'll still have you in books forever. If you break the player—that's pretty impressive; they're very sturdy—we'll get you a new one. If you break one of the cartridges for the books, we'll get you a new one. So we do try to have at a basic level the equalizer of everyone gets free reading material and a player. There's no cost involved for it. Everything else is just extra.

You'll sometimes see some of our patrons that want to get jobs or otherwise navigate outside the house, and that's where it's great if they can have an iPhone or an Android device, but that is daunting for a lot of people because they're very expensive. That's why we got so excited when Google started putting TalkBack on their Android phones. We were so happy, because then there's a screen reader on a significantly cheaper phone that my patrons could use. It's very exciting. I'm all about having yet another way that my patrons can get out to do whatever they want to do. It's not everyone who's going to have the tools. There are some groups that help with that, in particular VA hospitals. Sometimes our vets can get free technology from their counselor. That's nice when they have an equalizer there, but not everyone's going to have that available for them. So that's the main thing that you see, people that want something beyond our basic services but who may not be able to get it because they can't afford it.

The only other thing that somewhat comes into play is the idea of age, because kids get free material in their school, but once they graduate it's kind of a "you're on your own" sort of thing. And then on the opposite side of it, a lot of our patrons are older. A lot of us lose our vision over time. There's this idea that people who are older are not good with technology, or have problems with it or don't want to learn it. That may be true of some people, but that's true of people of all ages. One of those things that I try to do when I visit various places is to understand that regardless of the age of whoever's in front of me, their age is not indicative of their technological expertise. I think that's a very healthy mindset for you to have, because you may encounter the young person that doesn't have a phone for whatever reason, isn't tech-savvy, and you may encounter the veteran that has more pieces of technology than I have personally. You just never know.

. . .

ELAINE HARGER: Halfway through the 2014/15 school year, Amazon gave our school almost twelve hundred Kindle HD7s, one for every student. First, it's important to know that the school that I work at serves a full spectrum of students from all demographics—economic, racial, ethnic, linguistic. We're one of the most diverse middle schools in Seattle, and we have five academic programs. The school that I work at and the high school to which many of our students go are racially and economically segregated internally due to academic tracking here in Seattle.

What I discovered about giving a device to every student in my particular situation was that those students in the upper academic tracks who came from families that had purchased devices for their children, and who knew about the academic use of such devices, were able to immediately begin using their Kindles to access articles that a few of their teachers had made into PDFs and loaded onto the Kindles instead of photocopying. So that cohort of students was able to actually use the device academically immediately. The other students in what at that time was called our General Education program, plus the English language learners and special education students, were so excited to get these devices. I mean, everybody was excited to get their Kindles. But for the most part, the devices were so new to the kids, and what they were most excited about were some of the games that had been put onto them. All the teachers engaged in conversations about what kind of applications we wanted on the Kindles, and there were some educational games put on them. As it turned out, it was the games that captured students' attention most. What was discovered in the classroom is that the Kindles started to become more of a distraction in the General Ed classes than a helpful device. Teachers became very disgruntled.

If I had to do it over again, I would have the devices checked out to the classes, not to the individual students. The rollout of all of these Kindles to over eleven hundred kids happened so fast that few of the teachers actually had any idea of how they might want to use them. The teachers didn't have an opportunity; they had no time to plan any lessons or really think about how they would want to teach the kids how to use them, or to even, in some cases, learn how to use them. I don't think any of us even anticipated that the devices would become more of a distraction to the children. A child would be sitting in class and they'd hide their Kindle under their desk so that they could be playing with it rather than doing what they were supposed to. It's kind of how kids use their cellphones sometimes. In any event, if I had to do it over again, I would do the rollout much more slowly and make sure that all of the teachers had an opportunity to figure out how they might want to use them, and maybe not give the devices to each student immediately, without basically any instruction. When we did the rollout, I did a digital citizenship lesson with all the kids, but everything was just way too hurried.

KAREN LEMMONS: At the beginning of the netbook project at our school, we were given like twenty-two carts with thirty netbooks each. All the teachers were excited. "Yeah! They can take netbooks home!" The fine print was the netbooks that the students were taking home were to come from the carts assigned to the teachers. Teachers said, "Well, wait a minute. If a student takes one home, then how are we going to have a class set of netbooks for our class?" I said, "I don't know." So now these teachers were a little bit annoyed, because they're thinking, "Okay, we've got netbooks that we can't actually use in the classroom. Students can do it for all kinds of projects and assignments. But now we've got to take from *our* cart in order for them to be able to take one home?" That created a whole interesting scenario. As it turned out, some of the teachers decided, "You know what, I don't want the netbook cart. Somebody else can use it." The end result was I would distribute netbooks to students from those carts that teachers weren't using. Students do use the netbook for homework assignments as well as in-class assignments and projects. But we also had some updated labs so teachers who don't use netbooks can take their students to the computer labs and they can do projects in there as well.

JESSICA ANNE BRATT: We did an e-reader project through DigiBridge with the schools, which at the time was called the Nook Project. There was this fear that by the time kids go to college, if the textbooks all go online, would kids know how to download them? Would they know how to put them on an e-reader? Would they know all these things that—I feel—when the technology comes out, you have to figure out. There were some skills that they felt that the kids wouldn't necessarily pick up intuitively. And then there was also an issue that you had some schools that were able to get the funds to have these amazing iPads and Chromebooks and whatever the technology was at the time, and then you have other schools that aren't given anything. We really wanted to target those populations that just don't have anything. We bought like fifty Nooks and loaded them with content and distributed them with classes. I remember there was a reporter there, and that was the first time I ever got sideswiped with a question, where I think I had my mouth hanging open, because the woman was like, "You know, it's so good that the library's now supporting the schools. What are your feelings that in this other really ritzy area, they were able to give their kids a one-to-one ratio of iPad to kid, while you guys have these black and white Nooks?" And I was like, "I don't even know what to say right now."

But we do this Nook celebration—or now it's "e-reader" since we've moved to Kindles, because we've gotten grants and things like that. Kids get Kindles, and they're loaded with a whole bunch of reading materials. Teachers across the city at four or five schools get them for their seventh and eighth grades. They read the same book and then do a whole bunch of projects. The book last year was *A Long Walk to Water*, and then they invited "lost boys" from the Sudan to talk about it. At last year's celebration, it was really adorable to see my director cry because the kids at this one particular school that has been struggling for years got the Kindles, and then the kids decided they wanted to do a "pay it forward." So they raised money so that the library could buy more Kindles so more kids could have them. It's really thoughtful and heartfelt.

From there, we do research and database trainings system wide at the schools, which was to promote the digital library cards as well. The school couldn't afford the subscriptions to databases, and so we're making sure that the kids have access to research materials, especially since some of their school libraries don't have the necessary supporting materials for what the curriculum requires.

VIVIAN ALVAREZ: I wish we had the budget to talk more about technology. Some branches don't have the modern technology. I come in with my Windows 10 experience, not Windows 7. And Windows 7 is the operating system in some branches. So I kind of feel like the conversation sometimes cannot really take place because the budget hasn't supported the infrastructure for it. When I say, "Hey, we're going to put this in the cloud storage," some people don't have an idea. They haven't had the training. It reminds me a little bit of my mom when I tell her, "You can totally send this in a text message," and she goes, "What? I know I have a cellphone; I just don't know how to do it." I feel like the staff also needs that support. They need that professional development, so that they can understand how technology is evolving.

I wish we could talk more about digital books—for instance, if we talk about them, that particular conversation takes place more in another part of Chicago Public Library than it would at my branch. At my branch, we're just delivering the service. We're not necessarily decision-makers there. But the professional development training would help for them to chime in and help with those decisions. I kind of feel like we haven't really been modern enough—because those are economics—in order to have conversations that I can have at, for instance, in my program, at YOUmedia. At YOUmedia, even though we're in the same branch, we have a different budget that's supporting the program. Our budget enables us to have conversations about the new iPad, or the new tablet, or the new this or that. Now, that's different from talking about circulation and cataloging, but what we can agree on is that when I turn on my laptop, and they turn on their computer, while we both have a PC, mine is definitely cutting-edge. And it shouldn't be that way.

* * *

JASON GRIFFEY: What I've tended to work on over the last few years is near-future technology stuff. It's like the burgeoning edge of technology and where I think tech is going to be in five to ten years. The thing I'm focused on the most right now, mostly due to some of the research and policy work I've been doing at the Berkman Klein Center for Internet & Society, is the combination of censorship and access and how those two things are still far more prevalent than they should be in libraries. I feel really strongly about open access to information, and the censorship that is involved in certain parts of the world bothers me a great deal. A lack of access to connectivity in rural America and the lack of infrastructure and the amount of work that needs to be done in that is something that I would love to have more ongoing conversations about.

As we walk through those two topics in my head, I also think a lot about the kind of upcoming new tech that attempts to answer some of that question. That gets to everything from security and privacy and things like Tor and the technologies that underlie the need for secure communication on the 'net, and the next-generation 'net that's happening. Most of the writing that I've done over the last six months or so has been about the decentralized Web. I've been lucky enough to be part of a couple of really wonderful events revolving around the decentralized Web and how some of the new technology in that area is being built with the anti-censorship, encrypted technologies at the base level of them. So it's a big conglomeration of interests and things that I think are important, but it all comes back to access to information and the barriers that people find, whether those are technological barriers like censorship or physical barriers like lack of access to robust connectivity. All of those are things I think we should be talking about more and that are ultimately going to be very, very important over the next five years or so.

KAREN LEMMONS: Let's talk about privacy and the blocking of certain websites. Until recently, we could not access or had limited access to YouTube, Facebook, and Twitter. Very frustrating. We are educators. You—meaning the IT Department—know my IP address; I know you know my IP because this is networked. You know this is coming from a teacher's computer. As an educator, I'm going to use these social media tools for education purposes and lessons. Now we are able to access YouTube, Facebook and, sometimes Twitter. I remember they blocked one site, ThingLink. It's a different way to present information where you have an image and then you can add links and video to it so that it becomes a source of visual information. Love it. They blocked it. I immediately contacted our IT person and explained the purpose of ThingLink. It's just another way of presenting information in a visual format. They did unblock that. So we've had that issue.

SARAH HOUGHTON: I've been studying Internet filters since 2007. The technology itself has not improved, and it's not gotten any better than about 80 percent success rate for any higher end filtering technology that you look at in terms of filtering out text content successfully, which is the only thing that's required by CIPA. In terms of image and video content, you're looking at less than 50 percent efficacy in making the right decision if something is okay or not okay. Software hasn't improved, and it's not even vendor-specific; they all just suck in different ways. The cheaper-end software, which tends to be what rural and socioeconomically disadvantaged communities implement, have even less accuracy than that.

Filters, I believe, create a mental barrier for people. People behave differently when they know they're being watched. They will not look for topics that they think will somehow be traced back to them. So I have grave concerns based on personal experience and all the studies I've done on the long-term impact of filtering of any kind, whether it's at a national level, as it's done in countries like Australia, or at a very specific library or school level, as it's done in many parts of the United States. I do not and have not ever worked at a library that filters because I believe so strongly against the use and implementation of filters in a public library setting. I think that it puts library users who rely on us for Internet access at a distinct disadvantage to be competent participants in the digital economy. They're seeing a subset of the Internet. They're not able to see things that they should, because things are falsely blocked. I have a real problem with that. I do not believe that's our role as the public library. I think school libraries are in a distinctly different and more complicated situation than we are, and I can understand the hard place that they find themselves in.

But I don't see Internet filters having changed in almost ten years. The technology is not improving, and I don't see it improving any time soon. More and more libraries are turning away from putting filters in place in order to obtain e-rate funding as they realize the negative impact it has on their users' ability to get information, and also the negative budgetary impact it has. Yes, you get, let's say, $40,000 in e-rate funding for doing so, but you're spending usually one and a half to two times that in software costs, licensing, hardware, staff time in order to implement and maintain those filters in place. So it's a net loss.

The last thing I'll say—because I could talk about this for ten hours—is that I think it gives people a false sense of security, particularly parents. If they feel that a particular computer is filtered or has somewhat limited access, I believe they have this false sense that they could put their child down at that computer and that the child won't see anything untoward or that they wouldn't approve of. Given that 80 percent accuracy rate of filtering text and the 50 percent accuracy rate of filtering any kind of images or video, that's problematic. It's giving those parents a false sense of what they can expect from that piece of technology in a library. And I think that's a disservice to the community as well, in that the parents are trusting us to keep their kids safe, and we say, "Yes, look, here, this computer will keep your kid safe," and the reality is that that computer will never do that because that an AI software cannot do that with the technology that currently exists. So I look forward to the day when libraries do not have filters at all. I look forward to the day when progressive nations can look at a position where they will not filter their users' access to the Web, and that we have a more free exchange of information, as is the mission of every public library.

. . .

BÉATRICE COLASTIN SKOKAN: We have more digital content as part of the archives. Here at the University of Miami, we felt the need to adjust our collecting activities to capture much content that was not in traditional paper format. It was primarily through a human rights lens, or through grassroots organizations, that I first became aware of the need to move beyond our paper-based training. I'm interested in documenting grassroots organizations in South Florida, and at some point, I realized that a lot of these organizations were active on social media and the Web because it's cheaper and faster than producing and delivering time-sensitive information on paper. Other colleagues who were also documenting Latin America and the Caribbean realized that many human rights issues were being addressed through those mechanisms, and if we didn't develop a way to track these electronic content, we were going to miss key information.

We ultimately adopted the software Archive-It, which can crawl websites. We collect the websites of collections that are already included as analog collections or within the scope of our collection development interests. This approach seems to provide a more comprehensive collection development plan that captures the increasing and often complementary content that is created for the Web. We can't capture all of the social media and that is frustrating. We're concerned about all this ephemeral information that isn't produced for paper but lives on social media.

DANIEL KAHN GILLMOR: There's a lot of material that's created today that's created digital. It's thrown up, like a Facebook event. Facebook themselves might have archives of it, but nobody's going to ever see it or even be able to get it out of Facebook. Whereas somebody made a poster in 1965, and we still have that poster. Even if they didn't make it on archival-quality acid-free paper or whatever, that thing still exists, and we can experience it as humans with the same kind of machinery—our eyeballs—that you would have experienced it with in '65. I don't know what kind of digital documents were even available in '65. There were some, actually, but it would be a very complicated process to read them today. And I don't know if, in another fifty years, the documents that we think of as being trivially accessible and permanent will actually still be there. But I think the things that are printed will. I mean, I don't think our online catalog will be working in fifty years. As someone who maintains technological systems, I know they don't stay up unless someone's pouring their time into them. The paper is still there.

BÉATRICE COLASTIN SKOKAN: Based on my experience and the prevalence of social media, I really wish there was a concerted effort to find an efficient way to capture information from these sources. For instance, I don't know of any software that can crawl Facebook or manage tweets from the grassroots organization whose archives we house. It is so easy to feel overwhelmed by the amount of information. I can't help but wonder if perspectives that may be questioning established norms are filtered out by the very structure of the information gathering process, and if some of the creative intellectual output is taking place in other platforms that we have a hard time keeping up with. I feel like the general public is experimenting with different modes of expression through technology, and I don't know that we're capturing all of it. I know that's daunting, but I wish we wouldn't get too comfortable, and challenge ourselves to look at options that may lie outside of our field.

MANDY HENK: Censorship is one of the things that I think it's very easy for people to discount. But I actually think that the more that we consolidate information into very few hands—and we have certainly done that to a great degree, or we have allowed that to happen under our watch—I think that we really do risk cases of information disappearing. I don't think that that's an overblown thing. I don't think it's an absurd thing to worry about, and I think that as we look as the US becomes more and more unstable and you have a greater chance through every election cycle of someone who is completely off the rails becoming elected, we need to work more and more to build structures in place that will make sure that information is in hands that are trustworthy, but also that it's in multiple hands. The idea that an information resource can be owned and should only be held by one body who has a legal right to it, is a pretty dangerous idea.

CELESTE Â-RE: When I was at the Digital Blackness conference, Mark Anthony Neal touched on something that I often think about. It's wonderful that people are tweeting, blogging, and using social media as a space to be heard and to organize, but who owns the servers, the content delivery systems? That's an important question to address. How do we create and operate such an infrastructure? Is there a model? Could we pool resources and server networks to form a cooperative? This country is faced with a political absurdity in which anything could happen. What if we couldn't access the Internet because it was in opposition to the current administration or some other preposterous reasoning? What if we couldn't access Google or use social media? We don't own it, the hardware, the infrastructure. That's a discussion that gets subverted. I'm interested in knowing more about what people are doing. The Freedom Tower that was set up in Zuccotti Park during Occupy. The digital justice work Allied Media Projects sponsors. The mesh networks built in Detroit and in Red Hook—we've got know what people are doing to work around corporate media organizations to stay linked and communicate. There are folks in the margins, at the intersections of race, class, gender and able-bodiedness, doing this work.

JESSA LINGEL: We are actually getting to a point where we're starting—not to see any sort of equality in terms of race, class, and privilege on the Internet or in digital technologies, but I do think we're really starting to see a multiplicity of Internet use that makes for at least a more complicated picture. I think Black Twitter is so important and powerful in this way because it really represents, hey, there is a group of people using Twitter in a way that matters to them and their community, and it's totally fine if other people don't understand how that works. When you see that there's Twitter and Black Twitter, and it's on the same platform, you realize people carve out these ways of using a technology that reflects their needs and their ethics and their values. When that happens in such a public way, it makes it possible to realize, oh right, there's Black Twitter. And if you start to realize the way that Black Twitter is its own thing with its own set of practices, you similarly realize, oh, we shouldn't be making fun of how "old people" use Facebook. They have a totally legitimate way of using Facebook for their interest, the same way that teens use Facebook for their interest. And then suddenly you start to see this proliferation of all these different practices and ways of using digital technologies. I think that is a really good first step, because once you step away from this sort of monolithic, single-use mentality of "this is how you use this platform" to "these are all the ways you can use these platforms," and one is not inherently or innately better than the other, that's a much more just way of treating technology.

That's a little rosy. There are still huge barriers in terms of who has access to technology and who doesn't. I've just drawn this picture of, "Isn't it great, some people are using Twitter like this and some people are using Twitter like that?" but the fact that, for example, women are using Twitter for certain forms of social support doesn't mean that they're not harassed online in ways that most men never experience. It's not like the fact that people are carving out these spaces and communities for themselves means that they're somehow protected completely from other forms of harassment and violence. I think that's really disturbing.

But I do want to hold on to a sense that we're better off than before when we were more inclined to treat the Internet as if it had these sort of monolithic uses. Which has not always been that way, right? When the Internet was being played with and messed around with in the way that Anil Dash was talking about in "The Web We Lost," in the way Kevin Driscoll talks about when he does the history of BBS, or Finn Brunton talks about when he does the history of spam—there is a lot of experimentation and play in the '90s and then you saw sort of a lockdown in the 2000s. My hope is that we do start to see more experimentation and play now.

```
related_subjects = []
related_subjects.push("Linux")
related_subjects.push("'the walled garden'")
related_subjects.push("MySpace")
related_subjects.push("Domain of One's Own")
related_subjects.push("J. Edgar Hoover")
related_subjects.push("LibreOffice")
related_subjects.push("Archivematica")
related_subjects.push("ePADD")
related_subjects.push("the bounty model")
related_subjects.push("bicycling")
related_subjects.push("Code for America")
related_subjects.push("bananas")
related_subjects.push("Photoshop")
related_subjects.push("clothes")
related_subjects.push("unmakerspaces")
```

Building

Free and open source software represents both invisible digital infrastructure and a politicized movement to support community control over tools. In this chapter, people talked about the promise, practicalities, and limitations of open source software in libraries and archives—from ILSs to digital assets systems to word processing programs on public computers. I also asked about open data initiatives in municipalities and how libraries and librarians can engage with them.

Makerspaces and digital media labs are other areas where we see "building" in public and school libraries. People talked about 3D printing, robotics, and video production as well as more analog creative activities, while considering how these resources can be offered with more of a pedagogical rather than a consumerist approach.

. . .

BESS SADLER: When I was in university, I was a women's studies major maintaining the science fiction and feminism sections of the university bookstore, and figuring out how to get them a website, and figuring out how to maintain their inventory system. That was what kind of got me into technology. Oh yeah, and pirating Books in Print for Internationalist Books, this great bookstore in my hometown, Chapel Hill, North Carolina. Getting them a CD-ROM drive. That was high-tech stuff at the time. And getting them the old copies of Books in Print that other people were stealing, because it was a very expensive publication that other people were throwing away, the out-of-date ones. Then around that time, in the mid-'90s, I heard about open source software. It would have been at Internationalist Books. So I was finding that I really liked technology, and it felt to me like there was this tremendous promise in the idea of open source software, the idea that people could work together to build something tangible to solve problems. That appealed to me tremendously. Linux was still relatively new and pretty hard to use. And, wow, I spent a lot of time installing Linux on computers that other people were throwing away. And just loving it. That was what I did for fun.

JESSAMYN WEST: I think we're seeing open source browsers like Firefox becoming just what people use. I feel a little weird about the open source office software market, because OpenOffice and LibreOffice were right in there for a while, but now hosted solutions like Google Docs are becoming more ubiquitous because people don't have to carry them around. On the one hand, I'm like, "Yay! It's easier!" But on the other hand I'm like, "Ugh, Google." They don't even pretend to not be evil anymore. I feel weird about sending our patrons there. On the other hand, it's the easiest solution, so I feel weird not giving people that opportunity.

The cool thing that's happening is we're seeing more middleware companies helping smaller organizations solve these problems for themselves, with kind of pooled money—almost a mutual aid approach, to be honest, which makes me very happy. On the other hand, the response from industry is, "Yeah, but don't you want all your stuff in the cloud?" Almost by nature of how it works, the cloud is just someone else's computer, right? But it's a thousand other computers that all act like one computer on the Internet. That's kind of a thing that isn't quite as available to some of the open source alternatives, and so as a result there is still a little bit of a wrestling match for that.

One of the other things we haven't seen a lot of traction with is, what does open source social media look like? The code that a lot of the big social media platforms are on—nobody knows how a lot of it works, and some of it works is not necessarily in the best interest of the people who are using it. On the other hand, part of what makes social media appealing is that all your friends are there, so when you try to launch an open source social network, how are you going to have it be the place where all your friends are? Slack is an interesting productivity tool that people really like. Basically what Slack is is kind of a reimagining of IRC, which is an old-school open source chat platform that worked on everything. So we're seeing people skimming and proprietizing things that used to be code that belonged to everybody. One of the reasons I like email is because it really runs on top of open source code, even though the front end isn't necessarily. But a lot of the transactions that get my email from me to you happen along pathways where I know what's actually happening, and I can because I can go look at the code. That's not as true for some of the other things that I would like to do online, which is slightly too bad, although I don't know if that's what I was expecting. And the shift from the open Web to apps—same kind of thing.

One of the things about tech literacy is, if you've got a question with a website, ultimately you can look at the source of that website and see how it was built, see what it's doing, see who the website is talking to. Not as much with JavaScript loaded on everything, but you've got hope. And you can build your own website if you want to. Apps are a little bit harder to do, and sometimes impossible to take apart. The sort of "walled garden" that people talk about with regards to iPhones and that kind of thing is a real hurdle for users understanding code. Which isn't to say that it's necessarily a bad thing, but it is one more thing that gets in the way of the open Web, which gets in the way of people fully understanding the tools that they're using. I feel the same way about on-board computers in cars. It's kind of nice to understand what your car is doing, and as we saw with the giant, ridiculous, oh-my-god-those-people Volkswagen lawsuit, you can make your code in your car's computer do a bunch of things that people don't necessarily know is happening. It would be nice if there was a checks and balances system for that, not because I could necessarily read the code in my Volkswagen car and know what it was up to, but that *somebody* could. I believe as computers take over more and more of the world—not in a creepy way, but just Internet of Things way—access to the code that is running those things that are helping us run our lives is going to become more important, not less.

JESSA LINGEL: Sometimes I feel like our collective imaginations fail us in terms of what the Internet could be, how it could be otherwise. There have been moments in the history of Internet development where users were either required or encouraged to make the

Internet fit their needs. Think about the Internet of the mid-'90s when you had to have some basic HTML skills in order to create a blog. Now everything is embedded and bootstrapped. That's great because it means more people can blog more confidently, but you had to have some familiarity with inserting hyperlinks, or with making lists. And even that familiarity with markup, I think, was an important way of realizing that there isn't one Internet; there are many Internets. You can change how something looks in your screen, which I think is actually a really important way of chipping away at this black box mentality that the Internet is made by a bunch of dudes in Silicon Valley and the rest of us have to take what's given to us. We've had different moments in Internet history where you can look at a much more classical, a much more experimental, a much more DIY approach to code or platforms that we're using being encouraged for everyday users. I think that's really actively and deliberately stripped out of dominant platforms like Facebook, where you cannot change your own interface the way you could on MySpace. We're told that's to protect a sense of safety, or that it prevents harassment. But I think that's a paradigm that's not innate to the Internet, and that means that we can also take it away.

If we had a sense of how people can shape their own experiences of Internet use rather than taking what comes down from Mark Zuckerberg or Jeff Bezos, then we could have more creative experiences of Internet interactions. I really do think there was a sense of playfulness that can be recreated. That to me is much more exciting than thinking about the latest killer app, or how smartphones can make us more efficient workers, which are the two dominant paradigms of what technological innovation means. And that's just so sad. We're all using the Internet every day, and the best we could come up with is Pokémon Go?

MITA WILLIAMS: One project that comes to mind as something that's not being discussed enough is the Domain of One's Own project, although it's not really library technology but education technology. The Domain of One's Own project comes from the University of Mary Washington. It's an educational technology project that gives students server space so that they can create whatever they would like on it, whether for a professional portfolio or of their personal interests. In doing so, it gives the students an opportunity to build the skills to create a space for themselves outside of Facebook or

LinkedIn, or a course management system. I think those sort of projects are worth looking at and supporting if we want to have an alternative to Facebook and Twitter, which increasingly act in ways that are not in our best interests.

In terms of library technology, I think that libraries haven't realized the full potential that come with making use of a LibraryBox, the open source digital file distribution tool. For example, a LibraryBox could allow us to provide copies of e-books or texts to our community in a way that's fairly easy and not restrictive, while maintaining their privacy. Unfortunately, it seems the Library Box is still regarded largely as an individual's plaything. It would super interesting if libraries considered adding libraryboxes into their existing infrastructure.

Daniel Kahn Gillmor: When you host stuff on somebody else's machine, they ultimately will have access to that data. I know that Interference Archive hosts a lot of material about social movements, and social movements have a history of being criminalized and pursued. I would assume that there are researchers coming into the Archive who are interested in these social movements, and probably sympathetic to them. And the idea of building a system that collects metadata about what people's interests are that could then suddenly be turned over without even our say, or even potentially without our knowledge—that did not sit well with me. If someone's researching the Black Panthers, and somebody comes along—you know, we get the next J. Edgar Hoover who decides that the Black Panthers are a menace, and all of a sudden they're interested. I don't know what kinds of metadata gathering are going to happen, but metadata gathering is happening at scale right now, and it's going to get even worse. So the more that you have physical control over your infrastructure, the more you can at least be aware of intrusions like that, or of requests for that kind of access.

Drew Gordon: To illustrate that Interference Archive's catalog is hosted ourselves, I think it's helpful to say we have our own server on an iMac that's posted up on the wall near the ceiling. It sounds like you do have a lot of autonomy with that, but it's an interesting dynamic where, if it goes down—and I really actually like these moments, because it's kind of fun—you put the message out there and all of a sudden everyone's like, "Okay, the server's down!" and people are responding like crazy.

Bess Sadler: What I really wanted to do was open source software in libraries. It just seemed to me like it was such an obvious place for possibility. Around 2005, what we called OPACs were just really terrible. There's been a lot written about how terrible they were. One of the first halfway decent ones was developed at NC State with the help of this company called Endeca. It was pretty nice. But it was also outrageously expensive. We knew, at the University of Virginia, there was no way that we were going to be able to afford to do that. At the same time, Bethany Nowviskie was working for Jerry McGann's group there in the library doing digital humanities work, and they had this interface called Collex. I thought it was pretty cool, and I thought, what if we took that and turned it into an open source software project and just indexed MARC records into it? I thought that would be a lot better than what we had. And it really took off. Initially I thought that maybe this would just be a research paper that I could publish, but as soon as we started doing user testing with it, people started asking us, "Well, when is this going to be the real library catalog?" So that was an interesting grassroots effort around convincing the library administration that this was a good idea, and figuring out how we were going to support this and coming up with a model for collaboration with other institutions. The big breakthrough was when Stanford decided that they were going to adopt Blacklight. They did, and that was awesome.

Jason Griffey: In most libraries, the move to open source is made difficult because of the reluctance or inability to cultivate in-house technical expertise. Overall, an open source infrastructure for libraries would be better, more flexible, and ultimately far more powerful and useful for patrons. It would even, in most cases, be more affordable on a purely economic level, but it can be expensive organizationally and a hard sell to boards and others that control budgets, because the value is indistinct and distant as opposed to the more immediate impacts of outsourcing.

Bess Sadler: Open source ILSs that I know about include Evergreen and Koha. There are other ones out there, too; those are the two I know the most about, and both of those communities seem really great to me, but I mostly know about them from the outside. I'm much more familiar with places that have implemented open source discovery layers. One challenge is that commercial software companies have marketing budgets, and I think that it would behoove librarians to know how to advocate for open source solutions in the face of the fact that your library director and your IT director are probably getting lobbied by people with money to throw around and really slick marketing materials. We don't have that. We have conference presentations and journal articles and blog posts, but just what we could do for free. Some libraries feel that they don't have the local expertise to support open source software, and so they want to buy it from a vendor. That's the number one argument I hear against open source in libraries.

So my answer to that, typically, is—here are vendors from whom you can buy open source solutions, and, in my experience, you're going to be spending money either way. The question is, are you spending that money to build up the skill sets of your local staff, or are you spending that money on software licenses and paying the marketing budgets and much smaller staff that are going to be supporting a commercial product?

Jaime Taylor: There seem to be two kinds of libraries that are well-positioned to take advantage of open source solutions, whether that's an ILS or a digital assets manager—either the really small ones or the really big ones. Unfortunately my institution is kind of in the middle, where we have a lot of records but we don't have a lot of staff. We're not a university, so we don't have piles of grant money and government funds and things like that. The open source ILS that I hear the most about is Koha. The thing about something like Koha, or a digital assets manager like Islandora, is that instead of paying for the software or the program, a lot of them now are more on the model of software-as-a-service, so you're actually paying for subscriptions to web-based stuff, which I'm a little ambivalent about. Instead of paying to buy this finished product, you end up putting your money more into people, because you need to hire developers.

So if we were going to have an open source catalog instead of Aleph, say—I'm the only person in the entire department, and there's maybe a total of a half-person elsewhere in the building combined between several other people's spare time who works on our catalogs in this way—I couldn't run Koha. I don't have the development background and skills. So instead of paying for software, you end up paying for staff, and you need a particular kind of staff. You can't just hire any librarian and be like, "Look, you know how to catalog, you'll figure it out." You need developers, because they're going to be the ones that customize it for you, keep it running, install updates, and things like that. Currently you can get a lot of that from having one IT person and making the software provider help you with it. If there kind of is no software provider—not that there are no software providers for open source systems, but not in the same way that you have a support system with some of these for-profit companies—you end up needing to hire people. And librarians know that it's hard to hold on to those people, and it's hard to make the argument for people. For some reason it's a lot easier to argue to your administration and whoever's writing the checks that you need to buy a thing, rather than hire people. The other side of that is maybe you have people in your budget this year, but in five years, you might get a budget cut and then you don't have that person. So when your open source catalog breaks, there's no one to fix it. Whereas for some reason administration finds it a compelling argument to shell out tens of thousands of dollars to pay for a software subscription in a way that they're unwilling to shell out for people to do work.

When we at my library went through a very lengthy process in the last couple years to pick a new digital assets management system to replace one that's no longer being developed by the software provider, we looked at a couple open source ones, and figured that the sticker price on the open source one is less, but you're going to end up needing to pay for staff forever. Whereas the sticker price on the proprietary one is higher, but you get a lot more in terms of getting set-up, having help with migration from your old system, and things like that. There were other reasons, too—the features it offered and the interoperability with our other existing systems. Your other problem with these weird homegrown things is that you're less sure they're going to interoperate with the rest of your systems and catalog ecosystem. But one of the things was that we would definitely need to hire a couple of people, and developers aren't cheap. They're more expensive than librarians, which is unfortunate, but that's the truth. So we went with a proprietary system.

JOHN HELLING: I think contributing to the development of open and non-proprietary tools is a very high bar, even though I would love to get there as a profession. We just have so many calls on our time and are facing constant pressures to "do more with less." I think the big libraries have an opportunity to truly lead the way there—like with New York Public Library's e-book product, SimplyE. Even after development and implementation, using an open source product means you are more or less on your own for ongoing support, and a lot of libraries simply don't have the capacity for that. Falling short of that though, I think there is much to be done. I would encourage everyone to be aware of the tools that are out there and to consider them as potential solutions. You should identify problems and then work toward solutions—not vice versa. It doesn't have to be as big as an ILS. What options are there for your public PCs? Your makerspace? What do your patrons want to see available in your library?

JESSICA ANNE BRATT: Our software decisions are all through our IS department and our director. Honestly, I feel it usually comes down to budget issues. Even if we know our patrons want Microsoft Word, or they complain because we don't have Microsoft Word, it really doesn't matter because it's going to come down to money and licensing and things like that. We do trials of different software that's already built, and most of the time our IS department is like, "Well, we can build something better, and much cheaper." Which has its own pros and cons. When we were looking into computer reservation and print management systems, our IS said, "We're going to build it." So they built systems, but on an operating system of Ubuntu. That was interesting because half the library freaked out that our patrons would not be able to adapt—you're asking them to go to Windows to learn a full operating system software, and then they're not necessarily going to be able to work it correctly. And our IS department was like, "Well, you know, that's on frontline staff."

From there, they put in LibreOffice, which is the Libre word processing and spreadsheet program, and GIMP, which is the open source graphic design program like Adobe Photoshop. It has its plusses and minuses. Mostly we staff have moved to using Google Docs for all the things. Due to our shared network, usually I still use Google Docs and download the file as whatever it needs to be and throw it up there, but some librarians do choose to use the LibreOffice software. It's been a mixed bag with our patrons. Especially when they come in with USB drives already with the .docx, they're very much formatted with Microsoft, and then when they load it, if Libre can't read specific formats or they don't have that function, there's not much we can do. And that can be frustrating at times, to essentially say, "I can help you format it, but it might not look as pretty as however you had it designed in Microsoft Word."

CARMEL CURTIS: The field of audiovisual archiving has a number of open source tools—QCTools, MediaConch, Fixity, VRecord, DataAccessioner, Archivematica, Webrecorder, and the Cable Bible, just to name a few—that are used to facilitate various steps of the process of archiving, preserving, and providing access to audiovisual materials. This is not my area of expertise, but I think that there is a lot of potential there, and I would like to encourage people to participate. One of the reasons why I feel the field of audiovisual archiving is so encouraging of open source tools is because of the risks involved with using proprietary software, of having to be dependent on a company who is closed, whether that's a proprietary file format, digital assets management system in which you're storing your data and metadata, or storage system. There are risks involved when a corporation is in control. The Association of Moving Image Archivists has been doing a Hack Day at the beginning of their annual conference in which participants will work on a different technological need of the community. Then they create a goal for the day, or for the conference, or sometimes for longer than that, and members of AMIA and the community at large will then contribute to these goals that are centered around developing some technology that will assist in audiovisual preservation and access.

ELVIA ARROYO-RAMIREZ: For the most part, the digital archiving and curation community is very collaborative and embracing a lot of open source software and tool development. The BitCurator environment—ISO native install on a Linux machine—has been great in facilitating our local workflow for accessioning and ingest of born-digital assets. What I really like about BitCurator is that it comes equipped with open source tools to help build a local workflow, and it allows for a number of different processes like disk imaging and analysis to be broken down into digestible steps. The tools in the BitCurator suite we currently use at Princeton are ClamTK for virus scanning, Guymager for disk imaging, and bulk_extractor and fiwalk for disk analysis and extraction, among others. BitCurator has been a really exciting suite of tools to learn and use. Its user community is very active and a model of responsiveness and adaptability to its users and their needs.

ePADD, an open source tool to extract and manage email content, is another emerging tool developed by LAM developers at Stanford University. It's still in one of its early releases, but my colleagues and I were involved in the call-out to the user community to develop an author lexicon to filter email messages based on the terms in the lexicon. I really like that ePADD developers reached out to their primary user base to ask for input and feedback, which I think makes open source tools the most successful. LAM professionals can support open and non-proprietary tools by using them, testing them, submitting tickets on their GitHub repos, and engaging with developers about the current issues in the community and how to best use development time. Libraries can help the development community by providing resources and support to their development staff.

HANA SLEIMAN: I think part of the rationale of projects like the Palestinian Oral History Archive is making more tools available in Arabic—or making more tools available to respond to whatever challenges, whether it's language or medium. In an ideal world, we would have liked to develop our own program, but what often happens in the bureaucracy of libraries, especially academic libraries, is that there are many different departments. We have wishes and needs and dreams, and the IT department has fifteen other departments asking for software. If librarians and archivists were actually empowered, both with skills and also with infrastructure to develop solutions when needed, we could be better placed to not compromise on a tool that is not totally perfect. That would be a much more productive process in terms of identifying needs and responding to them in ways that offer longer lasting solutions to both our problems, and that would allow us to give back to the community.

That said, there's a lot that's free and open source, and whenever we can, we prefer to use that. Part of our decision to use the Oral History Metadata Synchronizer is because it is A, free, and B, will be open source. The rationale had always been once it's released, then we can do all of these developments and adaptations to our needs. This is obviously a longer lasting project; it's going to acquire and index more collections. But the awareness of the importance to do that is there.

BONNIE GORDON: Because I work primarily with born-digital materials and digital preservation, I work more closely with the digital preservation system Archivematica than in ArchivesSpace. But the Rockefeller Archive Center is an ArchivesSpace member. We're actively involved in the ArchivesSpace community and are on committees and involved in that development. We find open source to be really important because that's how we build a profession. That's how we provide the broadest access, by helping folks who have fewer resources. It benefits us, too when other people use open source. So participating in this community and really contributing to the profession is important to us.

Archivematica uses the bounty model of open source, which means an organization will fund a feature and then everyone can use that feature. Like, instead of hand-typing all our rights information for digital objects, we want to be able to upload a .csv. My organization will fund that, and then everyone else can use that functionality. We've funded a fair amount of features in Archivematica. We're funding one right now that's a pretty small thing, but it'll automate something that takes a lot of time, a lot of copying and pasting, and it's exciting because it'll help us. But I think that making these systems easier to use and more efficient, and helping other institutions implement digital preservation systems and provide access to their materials is really important. I'm not a developer, at all, so the ways that I try to contribute to these communities and systems are largely related to improving documentation. I feel like a lot of complaints I've heard about free and open source software is that the documentation is not great, and I think it's important to be able to contribute that. Luckily, I have time at my job, and it's considered important to do.

ANDROMEDA YELTON: In terms of particular use cases for coding in libraries, a lot of my students have been catalogers or other people who deal with metadata who find themselves needing to do bulk editing processes on data. Or they have a lot of data where they need to make a simple, repetitive transformation—changing all of the file extensions, or finding all of the titles that match a certain parameter and doing something with them. Those are the sort of things that are incredibly time-consuming and error-prone to do by hand, but that computers are very good at. I also encounter a lot of people, unfortunately, who are using coding to hack around the inadequacies of library software. They're finding ways to modify the appearance or the interfaces or the usability of their ILS or other library software, because library services to patrons are mediated through technological interfaces so much these days. People are writing code to make that library service better, because often the out-of-the-box version from vendors is actually not all that good, unfortunately.

Then occasionally you see really large-scale specialized work, like the DPLA and like what's gone on at New York Public Library, where people are using significant coding skills to be imaginative about what we can do with the data we have and give the public new ways of exploring it and using it. I think that's wonderful, but that's also not how an average workaday librarian could use software, because that's a whole other level of skill. I think average, everyday librarians are using it to make their workflows or their patron-facing services more efficient or more usable in small but awesome ways.

BONNIE GORDON: Right now, I'm learning Ruby on Rails. As part of this project where I'm training some of our processing archivists on imaging and viewing born-digital materials, I'm building a little digital media inventorying application. We have all of these floppy disks and CDs and whatnot, and the way we had been inventorying them was by taking really detailed inventories in a Microsoft Access database, which obviously could not integrate with any of our systems. That was also contributing to the backlog, in that it was taking a long time because we were recording and manually copying so much information. So, in order to have a more efficient system, I'm learning Ruby on Rails to build this app. The idea is that we're going to be recording minimal information and be able to use ArchivesSpace's API and grab minimal information directly—the folder title, the collection name, that kind of thing. That way we can really harness the power of the awesome open source systems that we use. Another goal of this system is to apply minimal processing principles to legacy media. When it comes to born-digital, there's a tendency to record everything with really detailed item-level description. But I believe that you can apply the same principles and techniques that you've been using with all sorts of other materials as a processing archivist or accessioning archivist or whatever.

MITA WILLIAMS: When we talk about open municipal government data, we're really talking about the idea that if the government produces data, that data should be readily available to residents because the data is theirs, and it's part of where they live. In Canada, we have a different context for open data than in the US. In the United States, by and large, you guys have much more open data because you're under the ethos that if the government has already paid for producing the data, it should be readily available to everyone for free. Whereas in Canada, we've followed the Crown copyright model, which is that that data should be available on a cost-recovery basis. There is speculation that most of those cost-recovery activities don't recoup a significant amount of money at all and in doing so restrict a lot of the potential of what that data could do for other organizations and other people.

Mapping is a great example. Our city makes maps for the work of managing and planning the city. They have raw GIS information of the city and they make some of this mapping data readily available to the community. This, to me, is an essential service because no one in the city itself, as an individual, has the capacity to map the city themselves. So by providing the raw geographical information data to all, the city releases the potential for anyone to take that map data if they have the technical understanding to handle that information and create their own maps. For example, there are activists in our community who are fighting a recent decision to place a future hospital outside of the core of city and out by the airport. They're able to take these maps and use them in their activism to say, "This other location is better than that one because it serves more elderly people who rely on public transportation," and challenge some of the stated reasons for the location decision with data, because they have those skills.

It's important to note a couple things. First, by making data readily available it doesn't necessarily level the playing field between, say, organizations and regular community members, because not everyone has the technical capabilities to handle that information. So I think there's a huge role for libraries to expand our work in data literacy, or to do the hard work of taking the raw data and putting it into formats that make it easier for people to make use of it. I think public libraries could play a role in this work in particular, because they're a trusted central representation of the city.

Joel Nichols: I don't know a ton about open data, honestly, but we do have a fairly robust municipal open data project in Philadelphia, where all sorts of agencies and city departments have put data up and people have made things with it. They've made really cool maps, they've made interesting visualizations, they've done really interesting analyses, they've built some web tools. It's the role of the public library to be a laboratory where people are interacting with the open data with knowledgeable librarians who really know what's going on in terms of the city agencies and the data. If the library had a creation lab where people were explicitly being trained to use open data to solve their neighborhood problems—that's the utopian vision that's really cool. I think, as it is now, it's still in the domain of developers and really engaged folks who are making cool things that some of us see and understand but aren't necessarily very accessible to most people who live in Philadelphia, say.

I am very interested in thinking about what kinds of data the library could offer up in terms of open data. We have a bike-sharing service that a lot of cities have nowadays. There are stops all over the city, and they released all their ride data. There are stops outside of the central library and also outside one of our neighborhood libraries, so I pulled all the trips that left from those places and tried to look at their duration. I think there might be some really interesting ways to let the library release this information we know at the library about our people's behavior and be in conversation with some of these other open or municipal data sets.

One way that I could see it happening, most immediately, is with our work on getting some smart turnstiles. They're like fancy door-counter things that would help us figure out not only the raw count of how many people came in the library in a day, but exactly what time of day they came in, and how long they stayed in the library. This is the sort of thing that we really just don't know. In our libraries we get a visitor count for every location at the end of the month. We're going to pilot the turnstiles in one or two locations. I'm really looking forward being able to see the busiest days of the month and the busiest times of day. So far we're able to look at that data only in terms of circulation and computer use, but I know from working in a branch that not everybody is there to use the computer or check out a book. For the first time, other than through observation or anecdote, we'll have some real information about how many people are coming to the library, when they're coming to the library, how long they're staying in the library, that kind of thing. I'm pretty excited about that. And I could imagine maybe offering that up as a data set, which might be kind of interesting, especially if people could make it talk to some of the open data from SEPTA, our transportation authority. I'd love to have someone build a web tool about library traffic and bus line traffic, to whatever extent that might be available. Maybe it would make sense to align the bus schedule with the library opening hours, or align library programming with heavier usage on the bus line or something. I just think there's probably a lot of super interesting stuff, and that would be the tip of the iceberg.

SARAH HOUGHTON: Open data fits very well with the mission of any type of library. We've seen the Code for America movement really take off quickly here in the US, and many US libraries jumped on board to participate in that. I know several cities—Chattanooga's one—where the library is really the sponsor of the Code for America brigade locally and helps with the projects. Here in Marin County, we're a cosponsor. I was one of the cofounders of our local Code for America brigade, Code for Marin, and I do think that libraries are in this lovely position of having the data expertise to work toward open government data. I also think we as government institutions—public libraries as part of government entities—are in a unique position to be able to describe to the public and hopefully make less difficult to understand what government data exists and why government might be a little wary of releasing data publicly en masse, and also translating between the technologists and the government officials about why open data is a benefit and it isn't something to be afraid of.

I think that libraries could really do more for the open data movement than we're currently doing systemically, but I'm very heartened by the small chapters and small movements that people in specific cities or other areas have done. Ideally, Code for America itself would have been something that libraries would have done, because it makes perfect sense—taking data that's already there and making it accessible and transparent to the communities that pay for that data to be created in the first place. And that is the role of the public library. To increase public access to data and locally created data is even more of an argument in that regard. So I'd love to see libraries on the whole do more toward that movement, but I think we're off to a good start.

JASON GRIFFEY: The public library in Chattanooga played a huge role in both working towards the kind of robust bandwidth capabilities they have and sharing out that information to the world. The academic library was kind of insulated by the university, whereas the public library worked directly with the municipal Internet provider in Chattanooga that does that work, EPB. Because they're part of the municipality, because the city is all involved in that, the public library had direct connections with it. They were able to go directly to them. I think at the time the head of IT, the assistant director and head of all the digital stuff, was Nate Hill. He has since moved on; he's now head of the METRO consortium in New York. But at the time, the kind of work that he and his team were doing inside the city to try and work with the city on all of these fronts for sharing bandwidth and such was huge. They were also talking once the Google Fiber story started to unfold in Kansas City and other municipalities in the US were beginning to see the Google Fiber experiment happen. Chattanooga became a place where those places came to understand what that level of bandwidth would mean and what sort of changes they might see. The public library became very much an ambassador for that with the other libraries and the other cities that were seeing this new thing happening. So I think the library has a core role in those sorts of city-led municipal activities.

BESS SADLER: One of the things that I've been working on the last few years has been GeoBlacklight and GeoHydra and GeoCommons, which are part of the Hydra ecosystem. All of these are taking our existing software stack and expanding it to be able to handle spatial data. Geospatial data is data about the surface of the earth. It's often also called GIS data. Libraries have a lot of this data. Frequently it's not well-described or cataloged. Often it's not really even in the inventory. The ability to manage GIS data is, I believe, one of the next big problems that libraries are going to need to tackle.

For example, a lot of government data that used to be produced on paper maps is now GIS data. I remember working at the Scholars' Lab at the University of Virginia, and someone came in who was following Congressional districts and how those Congressional districts and voting precincts had been drawn over the years. We could give them all of that data until a certain point. As long as paper maps had been produced for the voting districts, we had them in the archive; we could produce those. But at some point, whatever local government agency started instead drawing the maps on the computer. And then at that point, there was no preservation strategy for what those voting precincts were. To this day, this is the way that most government agencies are doing things. When they need to produce a map, even if it's something that they reproduce every year—like what are our current school district lines? what are our current voting districts? where is our current water infrastructure?—they just save over the old copy. They might put the new copy up on the website, but then at that point, the old copy disappears. We don't have a preservation strategy in place for that. We don't have a collection policy in place for that. And we don't have the technology infrastructure to allow us to create those collections.

So what I and a really wonderful team of developers—I'm definitely not trying to take credit for a lot of work that's being done by a lot of people who are not me—are doing is starting by building the technological infrastructure, so that we at least can manage geospatial data, discover it, describe it, share it between institutions. And then there also needs to be a discussion among the institutions about how we're collecting this data. How do we update our agreements with local government agencies so that we're not only getting a copy of printed reports but also of any GIS data that they're producing? I've been talking about political data, but the GIS data also goes into the realm of climate change, environmental scans, public health data. There's so much out there being produced by scientists, government agencies, NGOs. It's vital. It allows you to ask longitudinal questions, for example about climate change or environmental change. But unless we're collecting it and describing it and sharing it and preserving it, it's just disappearing.

MITA WILLIAMS: I have a mapping-related collaboration that I think is a good example of bringing together the community through librarian skills. The Leddy Library at the University of Windsor has an excellent data librarian and mapping support, so the mapping work that I've largely been doing is through Hackforge. It's been very gratifying because I've been able to help community groups by teaching them mapping skills and then see how they have applied this work for their own activism. I'm part of an organization called Bike Windsor Essex that wants to encourage more cycling in the area. In order to make the case to the City of Windsor that there's a lot of uncounted cyclists who already make use of our particularly flat terrain, I approached a cycling company called Strava and asked if we could buy a data set of anonymized use data from Strava app users in Windsor. Not only did they agree, they also allowed us to make the data set readily available to the community. We used the data as an exercise to show what routes cyclists were taking in the city, and also we used it in a workshop to teach developers and software enthusiasts in the city how to handle mapping data.

Now that more and more people have a mobile phone, there's a greater demand to add a spatial component to available information. Using web-based mapping tools that can work on the mobile Web is very different from the traditional GIS mapping tool that libraries traditionally supported. This shift from GIS to open mapping tools for the Web is a really interesting transition that's happening right now, and I've been able to help out with that.

. . .

Elaine Harger: In the fall of 2016 I posted a statement as part of a brief conversation that took place on the Progressive Librarians Guild listserv about makerspaces, which I consider a bit of a fad. One thing that's important to keep in mind is that K-12 education is a huge market. Businesses make a lot of money selling stuff to schools. As an educator, after you've been in the system for a few years, you begin to see the cycle of "new" ideas about how children learn best being offered. There's like a four-year cycle of all of these things. You barely get used to a new curriculum, new techniques, new methods of teaching, and then something newer comes along.

Then there's another cycle in which some of the old stuff is brought back out as new. As for makerspaces, every school library that I've worked in has always had spaces for kids to make things, whether it's paper and pencils and markers, glue, blocks, puzzles, etc. What is new about makerspaces is that there's a lot of technological gadgets that are being marketed and sold to schools and public libraries. Devices that have batteries in them that you can poke into pieces of fruit and watch an electrical current do something or other. There was one that I saw during a training that involved a banana, and all I could think about was that it was a big waste of a perfectly good piece of fruit that they were doing this makerspace activity with.

Essentially, my take on the whole makerspace phenomena is that there are people who want to sell things, they have to generate a "need" and make educational claims justifying purchases, and so this idea of makerspaces in libraries has come up. People are jumping on the bandwagon and creating makerspaces, moving books out of the library in order to make way for these other activities. A lot of the activities are worthwhile. I absolutely think that students should be able to engage in activities where they experiment with electronics and chemicals, but in schools that happens in the science classroom. In a public library, of course, there is no science classroom, and so, yes, there might be very important learning that's taking place there. But in a school, those kinds of activities take place under the supervision of a teacher who is conducting lessons so that the children can learn the concepts that the devices are designed to demonstrate. About makerspaces, I can say with certainty that I'm not going to be bringing any bananas and electrical currents into my library. We've got kids who are homeless, and kids who have to go to the food bank. I'm not going to be wasting any fruit in my library in order to have a makerspace. But that said, I made a "Makerspace!" sign last year, with our art supplies during National Poetry Month. The featured activity was to compose book spine poems and make little collage things that we hung up in the library with students' book spine poems. It was all pretty low-tech.

Understand that I'm not the only librarian I know who is skeptical about makerspaces, because we've all had kids doing stuff in our libraries. Twenty years ago I had kids learning how to knit in the library. But the makerspace phenom is just something that's packaged and being sold, and people are being made to feel like if they're not on board they're behind the curve. A lot of us have put together makerspaces that are kind of low-tech in the school libraries. But there are a number of librarians, my colleagues in the middle schools in Seattle, who are really excited about these things, too. So I try not to be, as they say, a Debbie Downer too much, but I've been around too long to know that there's a marketing and consumer society aspect to this that is being largely ignored.

JESSICA ANNE BRATT: In my experience at least, kids don't have the creativity. They're used to, "This is what I do to figure it out to build something cool." So we try to structure the Teen Tech Camp around the idea of potentially what robotics could be used for, both good and bad. We always have them watch a documentary from the BBC that's basically why aren't robots ruling the world, which talks about how they have to be programmed for every different scenario and we're not there yet with our technology for them to be able to physically replace us. Not to say that there aren't robots that do dangerous jobs that humans used to do. There's that element where they get to see what is considered a robot, and yeah, there are these really cool robots that they can now send in to places, whether it's engineering robots and things like that, and then there's the fact that you can work on a military base and design robots that destroy human lives.

So there's definitely that. I always feel that we never have enough time to actually get that far. We only have enough time to spark the curiosity and create a space where they can be engaged and find some type of creativity, or what that looks like, or understanding that they don't necessarily need a guide or rules to build something that functions.

KAREN LEMMONS: We had a science teacher who was a robotics coach. Well, he retired, and his partner, who works at the school, started looking for someone else. He asked almost the entire staff, especially the science and math teachers, whether or not they would be the robotics coach. All of them said no. So he goes back to administration, to my principal. He mentions that he could not find anyone who could help him on this robotics. My principal said, "Oh, did you ask Ms. Lemmons?" I happened to be in the office at that time. I'm like, oh my God. And he said, "Ms. Lemmons!" I was like, "Oh no! What are you asking me?" He said, "We've got a good robotics team. We need a coach who's actually a teacher in the school"—because he's not; he's a mentor. I said, "Okay. What does this involve? What *is* this?"

That first year was definitely a trial, a baptism by fire, all of that. I learned that this robotics was a little bit different from what I had envisioned it to be. We have a team. In January of each year, there is a kickoff where we see what the robot is supposed to do. Points are given for each task. At the competitions, teams form alliances and compete against each other to score the most points. The first year, I had a lot of seniors. That was a good team. They had worked together since they were sophomores. That first competition was recycling. Our robot was supposed to be able to pick up noodles, recycling cans, and gray totes, and move these items from one part of this field to another. We had six weeks to build this robot. Six weeks. After six weeks, we had to bag the robot. We couldn't touch it until the week of our competition. So we spent a lot of time, about three to four evenings a week and Saturdays, figuring out the design of the robot and what we wanted it to do so we could score the most points. We were also responsible for programming and wiring the robot.

When I went to my first robotics competition, I saw firsthand the excitement and the energy. It was just a phenomenal experience. It left me speechless and breathless, because I also had this thought—"We had to build a robot to do *what*?" I was the adult and had to be present, but the key thing was that the students were the ones that had to problem-solve and figure out how this robot was going to do these tasks. They had to use time management skills, communication skills, teamwork—you name it, they had to employ all of those skills to build this robot. So that first year was pretty cool. Recycling, that was right up my alley. I was like, "Okay, we've got that!"

In 2016—oh, they kicked it up a notch beyond belief. I was concerned because all of my seniors from 2015 graduated and we had to rebuild the team. We had a combination of freshmen, sophomores, and maybe one senior. This competition was castles. We had so many different terrains. There were moats, towers, some kind of low wall, a high wall, an uneven terrain that the robot had to cross to capture the castle. That competition was something else. But our team made it to the quarter-finals, and that was cool.

Now into my third year, I'm feeling a little better about robotics. It is a lot of work, especially during that six-week intense robot-building period. But just to see the kids come up with the design—they work out the programming, they work out the electrical, they work out all of the technical and mechanical details. And then to see that robot work and move around and do what it's supposed to do is an awesome thing. I'm the team's support. I handle the administrative work and logistics. I don't teach any robotics skills, even though we do go to quite a few pre-season robotics workshops where we learn about CAD/CAM design and other different types of skills that would certainly help us in terms of building our robot. I would say that collaboration between educators and librarians would be necessary for educators and librarians to move to the pedagogy aspect of these activities. Both the educators and librarians can list the essential skills our students need, then develop unit/lesson plans and activities that teach and reinforce these skills.

The robotics project is certainly about collaboration, communication, and teamwork. Students do learn some technical skills as well. I had a student who is heavily into animation. He just lives by animation. But I will tell you, he became an excellent programmer. He was top-notch. I had another student who was a music major. She played the violin. She was an excellent programmer. So while their comfort zone is the arts, when they learned programming, it took them out of there and taught them a new skill. It's expanding their skill sets and broadening their horizons. In addition, the students learn how to work with people who are different than they are or just have a different mindset and work ethic. But they all work together. The communication was a little rough at first, but they kind of gelled toward the end, which was a cool thing. They learned communication is essential in order for them to work as a team and build a robot.

Michael Cherry: According to the National Association of Manufacturers, the state of Indiana has the largest percentage of workers employed in the manufacturing sector when compared to any other state. You could witness this firsthand in Evansville's local economy. We have a Toyota plant right up the road that builds cars which are largely built with the help of robots. We have different plastics industries such as Berry Plastics and SABIC and hospitals like St. Mary's Medical Center. A lot of these industries are influenced by technologies such as robotics and 3D printing. So we try to make students really aware of this in our classes. Toyota Manufacturing of Indiana has supported some of these programs through grant support, and we'll show students examples of how these industries are using different types of robots or 3D printing technology. I think it's important because it's not just about showing them how to use a piece of technology; it's also about demonstrating to students how it relates to their own lives, perhaps their future. We look at other industries outside of Evansville too, companies like Boston Dynamics and Festo. These companies are doing some really interesting things with robots and biomimicry.

In terms of advice for other libraries, I would say that manufacturing is an industry that is changing. What we used to consider traditional manufacturing is now becoming more influenced by coding and different types of technology, such as robotics and additive manufacturing. I would suggest that librarians look at these tech industries and see where they are in their local economy. Robotics is more than just automation; it's aerospace, it's a variety of other disciplines. I know a lot of libraries have media dispensers where they dispense videos and you can check them out with your library card. That machine is a robot, too. We used to have a Media Bank at our central library, and when it would dispense the DVD it would say, "The robot is dispensing your DVD." So it's something to consider. Robotics is shaping a lot of different industries and it's worth investigating where that's happening in your local community.

CHAD CLARK: There are a few ways people use our digital media lab. I'd say the number one use is conversion, mostly home movies. They're taking pieces of film and transferring it into a digital format. We get a lot of home movies, VHS tapes. We're also getting second and third generation materials like 8 mm that's been transferred in the '80s to VHS and now they want to digitize it. So the number one activity in the lab is certainly conversion, but I do believe there's some creation behind that, too, because often people are looking to edit or narrate the story in their own way. Maybe the typical archivist is used to not touching a piece of content, trying to preserve its original form as much as possible, but I get so many patrons coming in with different clips and pieces of media that they want to craft their own narrative behind, whether it's a family history or an event in their life. They want to take things out and add titles, subtitles, data like that to it.

After that activity, photos. People love to work with their own photos, whether it's touching them up or just playing around with them. Photoshop is huge. I think just the name attracts people to the lab, like, "I want to *Photoshop* this." They use it as a verb, just because they've heard it, and it's a good gateway to the lab—"Well, did you know there's also this, and that, and you could also do this…"

After that we get into more eccentric stuff. We do have the ability to record audio. We get people—mainly, I've noticed, the twenty-somethings and high schoolers—doing audio projects. We've got a few podcasts that have been coming out of our lab. Kickstarters, actually, too; Kickstarters are starting to come around. We probably get one a month. I've got a girl just this week, she's like a sophomore in high school, and she's got a business centered around drones. She made a Kickstarter campaign, and she's coming in and using our cameras and filming and editing her sales pitch. So that's starting to take off. We have a 3D scanner. People are afraid of that, but we're starting to introduce it. We're trying to get people used to it. It's finicky; I can't blame them.

JOHN HELLING: I think the best public library makerspace in the country is at the Johnson County Library in Kansas. I would point everyone to learn from them as an example of how to execute that type of space. I think the team there is producing the best mix of planned and exploratory programming I've seen, and I also think they're doing the best job of demonstrating their relevance to the general public, not just teens. And they're doing it with a team that is made up of people with and without backgrounds in public libraries. I think that balance of outside and inside perspective has served them extremely well.

CHAD CLARK: We've done a few things with the content that people have produced in our digital media lab. Two summers ago we did something, a part of a larger program called "the 90-Second Newbery." Newbery is a children's award and they select books each year. So we challenge the kids to take their favorite Newbery book and condense it into a 90-second story on film. Some of the kids did claymation or stop motion. Some kids just filmed in their backyard. So we did that, and it went well. We shared their films on social media, with their permission, of course. We had a little film fest where we screened the films in our main adult services area of the library, made popcorn, had a red carpet.

We did a podcast. We've had adults make some podcasts, and we've helped them to share theirs on iTunes, SoundCloud, and YouTube. We had a kids' podcasting club over the summer that went really well, but we didn't end up sharing any of those. We were prepared to, with their permission, but it never even got as far as asking the parents because none of the kids who participated felt comfortable sharing their podcast online. I think in that case, we just made CDs for each of the kids.

We've had instances where people have recovered or brought in material that they wanted digitized, mainly 35 mm slides and old photos that had ended up in books. I recall a lady whose father was in World War II somewhere in the Philippines and had a couple hundred amazing photos. We helped her digitize them, and they ended up in a book. We've had small projects where we've done green screen things based around events, like "Star Wars Day"—"Come into the green screen and take your picture in the Death Star." And then those kinds of things are shared all over the place, all over social media.

MICHAEL CHERRY: Regarding the labor force, we stress the fact that there are jobs in these fields. When we look at animation, we're looking at the industry as a whole, like, how do animators create these films? Well, there are lighting technicians, voice actors, writers, animators, and directors. It's a huge business with a variety of different positions. With robotics, it's connecting it to the local businesses and saying, "You may have an opportunity to do this at some point someday." So it's about letting them know that there are job opportunities in the real world that relate to these learning experiences. That a Lego robot isn't just a toy; it's a tool for learning. You're learning how to iterate a design and solve a problem.

CHAD CLARK: When we first seriously started looking at STEM programming in 2013, we found that at first—and still today—we do get more boys than girls among the younger crowd. We try to balance it without imposing our will, I guess. For instance, we're starting a robotics team, and we can only have ten kids on the team. We had a meeting just this weekend, and I had forty-five kids show up. Counter to what you might think at a library, that we accept everybody—not in this case, we can only let ten of you in. So in this case, we're going to say, "Okay, we're going to draw randomly ten people," but we'll split it. We'll put all the girls in one pile and all the boys in the other pile, and we're going to draw fair like that. Actually I get to do that later today when I go into work.

Anyway, we've continued to do more STEM programming, and we find that, yes, boys have been showing up more than girls, but we're working to steer that. Last summer we brought in a group of girls, Girls Driving for a Difference. This organization was a group of undergrads from Stanford going through the IDEO program, and they're driving across the country in a bus. They came to our library and served about twenty girls, just girls, between the ages of ten and fifteen or something like that, and they worked on design challenges. So we have brought in specific girl-targeted speakers and programs to help boost our programs, as far as the boy-girl ratio goes, and I will say, it has grown. I think the more comfortable we make the environment, the more open we are, the more aware of the influence we can have on people—it is getting better. I'll hear from active parents who are certainly aware of this. "My girl is the only one at school into this. Why is that?" Well, I don't know why, but I can certainly try.

MICHAEL CHERRY: It's also important to reach out to audiences who may not have access to these technologies. I think that's a huge responsibility for librarians serving their communities. For example, working with at-risk students who may not have access to these technologies at home or in school, or designing STEM programs for female students. We've partnered with an organization called Girls in Bloom, which hosts a one-day event where girls learn a variety of STEM skills. We've partnered with this organization for several years and taught robotics workshops at the event. So it's trying to find these underserved communities, and providing access to new technologies, but also going beyond the access—it's not just about the tool; it's about making those connections to the world around us.

VIVIAN ALVAREZ: On an average day at YOUmedia at my branch, let's say yesterday, kids show up to the programs and start working on their homework. We help them with any inquiries that they have with their homework, so that from there we can work on the activities we have planned for the day. The goal is for them to build their digital portfolios. How they do it can be very different, because there's a variety of interests. For instance, I had one student who preferred to do a sketch. Right now we have a theme of DIY Halloween costume fashion design, and she decided to do a sketch first. After working on it with pencil, she transferred the image to a simplified virtual image using an app in Adobe. The iPad captured the silhouette of her sketch and converted it into something very simple and usable for her portfolio, and it gave her a different view of the sketch compared to how she envisioned it in the first place. Another student wanted to use actual Photoshop to work on designing a virtual image of her face that she already had. She wanted to use the virtual canvas to work on that illustration.

It's a drop-in center; not everyone is at the same pace every single day. So there were a couple of kids who were absent two days before, when there had been a couple of different activities. One of them was a recorded narrative of a film that they just watched, "Middle School: The Worst Years of My Life." It's a very humorous and adorable film. That was part of this portfolio, the reflection part, and also to listen to themselves recorded—this for the purposes of public speaking in the theater or organizing their thoughts and so forth. And then I had one more student who was working with beads. The children and their families in the community that I'm in like to work a lot with their hands, and they have a huge appreciation for analog activities. So this student started beading a design that is very geometric and also very simple. It kind of looks like Minecraft, except that it's a flat image. After creating that costume-based design, she asked if she could make a sticky note installation of it onto the window. Now, because each bead can practically represent a sticky note or a Post-it on our windows, it's actually very easy to transfer it from a small product to something that we can celebrate at the library and have installed on our own.

So it's a makerspace, but it's a makerspace in not just the media part, but also the part that gets to the media part, if that makes any sense. It is a makerspace where we can start from sketching, and then build from there to use the digital resources in order to learn how to use digital tools to do what we still do with our hands. And to learn about what's out there in terms of technology.

. . .

ELAINE HARGER: There is one other technology that I take every opportunity to include in the library—agriculture! I am very involved in our school garden and work closely with science teachers and our community partner, Green Plate Special, to have students learn about what I consider the most important twenty-first century skill we can pass on to our children—namely those technical skills and a mindset that recognizes how climate change will impact global food systems. Food sovereignty will become centrally important in the lives of people. Every fall, I have students in the library for a seed-saving activity that I teach. I love watching them open up the dried-up scarlet runner bean pods and seeing their eyes light up when they discover the treasure inside of this gorgeous, mottled purple-and-black bean. In the spring they plant their beans with Green Plate Special. So, the library is a place for pencils, digital devices, books, and beans. Technologies all!

KAREN LEMMONS: For makerspaces, one of the ideas that I have is actually in connection with an initiative called Future Project that's in our school. Future Project helps students "unleash the passion, power, purpose, and possibility." There's a lovely young lady, Bri, who's our Dream Director, and I told her about a project that I think would be good for our school. The project is to take clothes that students discard and end up in a landfill and do something creative with them, either repurpose them to make some new clothes, or create some wearable art, or create a wall hanging or some kind of fiber art. I have this thing about recycling. I'm not, like, 100 percent there with the total recycling, but I'm there enough to know that we need to do some things to really reduce, reuse, and recycle. Bri and I just have to work out the logistics and perhaps create a makerspace for that.

I went to this makerspace training, and I recognize that makerspaces can be very low-end—the recycling of t-shirts to make cute little bags—to the high-end kind of technology stuff. I guess I wanted to focus mainly on the low-end until we were able to go into the high-end. For my comfort level, I want to start low-end, and then also I wanted to try to keep in mind the type of students we have and what activities would attract them. I figure all our students wear clothes, and maybe they have something old that they can repurpose into something else and that might generate some new ideas, or that feeling of "Ooh, I made this myself!" And then the other aspect was that perhaps if they make things well enough, they could perhaps sell them and make a little money, so they could become little entrepreneurs. So that's the direction I'm headed.

JESSA LINGEL: I wish people were talking about environment consequence of how we treat technology more. I wish people talked about the production process of these technologies. When I worked at a food coop in Brooklyn, I thought it was such a great experience because it helps you see a little bit of where food comes from. You don't have to farm, you just have to work at a food coop and suddenly you see—even food getting off the truck, you're like, well, this is a part of the process that I never really thought about before. I think it would be great to have more conversations about where these technologies come from and how they're built and how they're made. A lot of the conversations that I've seen around makerspaces, I just worry it's too much an echo of perpetuating this tinkerer in the garage mentality rather than a different set of questions that we could be asking, which isn't about hey, what can we design that's going to be this whole product we could sell, and more about, how did these products come to be?

Amelia Acker, who was at the University of Pittsburgh but is now at the University of Texas at Austin, taught an archives class at Pitt that involved disassembling technology. She would bring all these pieces of technology, like tablets and phones, into the classroom and have her students dismantle them. She talked about what a powerful experience it was for a lot of these students to unpack—literally unpack—these technologies and see what they're made of and think about how you could rewire them. I think that that partly goes back to what I'm saying about the environmental consequences, but it's also giving people a new way of thinking about technology. So maybe unmakerspaces would be what I would like to see people talking about.

CECILY WALKER: One thing that I've been really interested in is the idea of makerspaces in libraries. In these makerspaces that we've created, we're assuming a certain level of comfort with whatever our makerspace is focused on. For example, here at Vancouver Public Library, our makerspace isn't a makerspace, it's a "Digital Creation Space." But that Digital Creation Space—even though we offer programs and courses, and we offer tutorials for anybody who wants to understand, at a very basic level, how some of these tools and technologies work, like how you can use our video camera and our green screen to create a movie, and how they get that thing on YouTube—one of the places where we're really falling short is to help people get a deeper understanding of that technology. Like, what's at the back end to make this work? If people are interested in computers and digital technology, have them understand and be able to identify and work with the nuts and bolts of the things that they're working with. Maybe have a PC or a video camera or some other server, just, like, cut in half so that people could see a cross-section of what's actually inside, so that they don't understand things at just the most basic surface level.

I think it would be really interesting for us to go back and think about how we are using makerspaces, and how makerspaces as an idea—no matter what our good intentions are—might be fostering exclusion. Because we're creating something that's either very high-tech or requires a specific sort of skills that, if you don't have that skill or knowledge, might then make you think that this library is not a place for you, or that this particular makerspace has nothing for you. And therefore the door that we like to believe is so wide open for people starts to slam shut a little bit by little bit, with every new fantastic idea that we create. How can we ensure that that door remains wide open, and that everybody, regardless of their level of proficiency, feels like it's a space where they can not only feel welcome, but where they can actually walk away with a skill or even a hobby that furthers their knowledge, that helps them learn how to learn and how to produce something that maybe they didn't think was even possible?

```
related_subjects = []
related_subjects.push("Hollerith cards")
related_subjects.push("Universal Bibliographic Control")
related_subjects.push("Blacklight")
related_subjects.push("sheet music")
related_subjects.push("the Chafee Amendment")
related_subjects.push("Open Library")
related_subjects.push("neoliberalism")
related_subjects.push("pixels")
related_subjects.push("the Nakba")
related_subjects.push("public housing")
related_subjects.push("Oral History Metadata Synchronizer")
related_subjects.push("Sing Sing")
related_subjects.push("plumbers")
related_subjects.push("Hydra")
related_subjects.push("datalization of culture")
```

Collecting

Collecting, classifying, describing, and storing materials are core functions of libraries and archives. This chapter covers a lot of ground, from the card catalog to e-books to oral histories. We start on the ILS level and then go into specific formats in the collection. I asked people about their views of library e-book lending, especially considering privacy concerns, digital rights management, and the complexity of proprietary hardware and software. People also talked about online journal subscriptions, demand-driven acquisition, and open educational resources. I asked about the movement for open access, both among librarians and college and university faculty, and how technological as well as philosophical changes have affected open access in the last decade or so. The history and composition of a couple of individual digital repositories—DigitalCommons@ILR and DLIST—are described here.

This chapter also extensively explores oral histories and community digital archives, including the Haitian Diaspora Oral History Project, the Southern Oral History Program, and the Palestinian Oral History Archive. Archivists talked about trust-building in communities and the particular needs of audiovisual materials, whether or not born-digital—processing them, preserving them, and promoting their use. Solid collaborative approaches and technological choices also came up in a discussion of successful (and less so) models for large-scale digitization projects such as the Digital Public Library of America, Google Books, and HathiTrust.

Michael Gorman: The first technology with which I was involved in was in the 1950s. The public library in which I worked pioneered a circulation system called photo-charging. This succeeded what was known as the Browne system, where there was a little ticket in every book and the user had a library reader's ticket, and when you took a book out you took the ticket out of the book, put it with the reader's card, and filed it. Photo-charging was a means of recording on microfilm the name of the borrower and the name of the item borrowed. This was backed up by a card sorting system in which the cards were notched and you inserted a kind of needle, and the ones that met the criteria dropped off and those that didn't stayed on the needle. It was later mechanized using Hollerith cards.

Early on, I came to realize that the pursuit of efficient library economy was dependent on machines. Take the cards in the card catalog. In those early days the cards were hand-written, then typed, and then printed centrally. The card catalog became history, and that ushered in wholly new technologies. When I started work in libraries, we had manual circulation systems, serial control systems, catalogs, and other systems. Over the years these became mechanized and ultimately digitized. This affected the nature of library work in so many ways.

I think what has happened is that the concept of technology as a tool has metamorphosed into the technology becoming the dominant factor. In other words, for some people, technology is no longer a means of getting from A to B but one of the Bs you want to get to. For example, the idea of an online catalog has given way to an all-inclusive kind of thing that is in itself part of the human record, seen as some kind of good in itself, rather than a means to an end.

Elaine Harger: One day, at an auction fundraiser, I received a bag that had a picture of an old card catalog drawer with a caption that said, "Never forget." I still don't know quite how to interpret that. Is it a sentimental, nostalgic caption, or is it a warning? "Don't ever forget how lucky you are that you don't have to file cards in the card catalog anymore." So, to answer the question of which piece of technology I appreciate most for my work—it is the online catalog. I have had the experience in my professional life of actually filing cards in a card catalog, and that's a very tedious, onerous, time-consuming task. The catalog for the library—all of the software, hardware, and infrastructure that it depends upon in order for my students to access the holdings, the collections, the resources in my library—is invaluable. I have the deepest appreciation for that bit of technology.

MICHAEL GORMAN: Automated and later digital catalogs had been a great improvement, for two reasons. I worked in very large libraries. The library of University of Illinois in Urbana-Champaign is the largest library in the world that is nowhere near a big city. One of the self-evident facts is that at a certain size, card catalogs cease to work. Sending somebody to a catalog containing millions of cards is basically telling them to get lost. Not only that, but even the best card catalogs were records of what you owned or believed you owned. What automated and then digitized catalogs made possible was the realization of large current union catalogs and a step towards the cataloging ideal of Universal Bibliographic Control. In other words, theoretically, a user anywhere would have access to records of every part of the human record. That is both a conceptual and a practical change of enormous magnitude.

MANDY HENK: I'm going to be a very boring and pedantic and sort of traditional librarian here, and talk about the library catalog and indexes. The ability to use search terms, to use searching, especially structured searching, to locate a piece of information that you need—it's absolutely miraculous. I have people who I support who predate all of that, so they learned how to do research when people were literally putting together book indexes. Of course there were people doing that indexing, and they would have to come up here to the library, look through those indexes, go to the shelf, find what they need, read it here—because we didn't have photocopiers yet—take notes on it, and then proceed back to their office, where I imagine they were using a typewriter. So they would have to trudge back to their offices with the notes that they had taken in the library, and then write things out either on a typewriter or by hand.

The transformation that we've seen with information technology—Jesse Shera used to call it "the library problem," and I think this was common terminology back in the previous century, but the fact is that we've solved that, technologically; anything that anyone would ever want very well could be available to them electronically. We've erected legal barriers that prevent people from accessing it, but the technological barriers have been mastered. And I think that that is one of the most amazing things that human beings have ever done. I just wish it hadn't come at such a cost. I wish we hadn't chosen to erect barriers.

BECKY YOOSE: The most useful technology for patrons, the one that tends to get the most attention, at least on my end when something goes horribly wrong or if they want to change something—that's usually why I hear from patrons—is the library catalog. That is still the gateway to library resources. That's where the work with metadata and cataloging is invaluable, because your catalog is as good as the metadata that is in it. If you have garbage metadata and your patrons are trying to find something on a particular topic, or do a known item search, or do a subject search—if your metadata is not going to be able to support that search, then they can't find that item.

If your library catalog can also facilitate, for example, Schema.org, that makes things more discoverable on the general Web, like Google. While people do use Google a lot as their first place, sometimes your library catalog can facilitate that type of discovery on that level. I'm watching that particular functionality with various catalogs as we go along, because there are a few that already have Schema.org implemented for every record. I'm right now watching BiblioCommons work their way through their implementation of Schema.org within their discovery layer. Honestly I can't wait to see what happens, because that will be really awesome if a patron searches Google and they find something that's within the Seattle Public Library catalog. Of course they would have to have location services turned on with their search to be able to find something from our particular catalog, and that of course has some privacy implications to it. There always is when you're dealing with Google searches and location services and whatnot.

But I would say I know a lot of people do not like the library catalog, and they have very valid points. Library catalogs are pretty basic. They don't search very well, depending on which product you have. At the same time, it's what we have. It's what we have to give to our users, to say, hey, these are the resources that we have. Be it a traditional library catalog or a discovery layer or a federated search, that is still essentially the gateway to what have. And that's what makes it one of the very important tools for library patrons.

JONATHAN HARWELL: Probably the most significant technology in my work, and for our patrons, would be the discovery layer. Before we had discovery, a lot of patrons found it very difficult to go to a list of over a hundred databases and choose a place to search. There were brands that maybe did not say anything to them in terms of content, and there was some figuring out they had to do just to a do a basic search instead of going to a single search box like they were accustomed to online—in Google, for example. Now that we have services like Summon and Primo and EDS, where they can go and search virtually all of our content, including our library catalog, that just makes more sense to most of our patrons, and that makes it easier for them to find the information they need.

Bess Sadler: Blacklight is a discovery layer. If you hearken back to 2005, you had this software system in libraries, the integrated library system. The idea was that a vendor was going to sell you a system for managing all of your ordering, all of your business processes—basically an inventory control system—and then kind of tacked on to that was this ability for users to search the collection. But honestly, the interface that they were creating was terrible, and the libraries didn't have a lot of leverage to get a better one, because you're probably not going to migrate all of your back end business processes just to get a better user interface. It's just too expensive.

So the thinking at the time was, what if we could decouple the discovery interface from the inventory control system? That would give us a lot more control over what people are seeing, and libraries themselves could have a much larger role to play in the design. I'm really interested in libraries controlling their own search algorithms. When we talk about a search algorithm, we're asking the question, what is significant and what is relevant? Well, when you're talking about allowing people to do research, those are very loaded questions. Putting the ability to ask those questions as close as possible into the hands of the user—it's still mediated, I get that, but it's a lot better than having a single answer that was provided to you by a commercial vendor. So Blacklight is an open source discovery layer. You can use it for your physical collections, you can use it for your digital collections. People at this point use it very widely around the world, for all kinds of things.

Alison Macrina: Library technology is such a shitshow. I wish that people would stop acting like this is just our reality and we have to deal with it. We have to put up with these terrible applications that no one likes and no one can use. I remember the last library I worked for, we were picking a new ILS, and everyone hated them all. I wish that people at the administrative level would be more honest about this. I wish that we had a totally different relationship to our vendors. Maybe that's the thing, the one thing that I would want to focus on. We venerate these vendors, we don't want to say anything against them, we don't want to have an honest conversation with them about why what they're giving us sucks. We tiptoe around all this stuff because we're afraid that if we complain, it's going to get taken away from us. I get why that is—we have no money and no one makes us anything nice, and we have this collective inferiority complex among our profession. And what's that resulted in is getting all these pieces of technology that don't really work and make our patrons less likely to use us. Even thinking about the way that our websites work, the way that our discovery tools work, it's impossible to have meaningful searches on library catalogs unless you know the exact thing you're looking for. We can do better. We've just kind of resigned ourselves to this. Not only have we resigned ourselves to it, but I don't even think we've fully acknowledged that this is all a problem.

JAIME TAYLOR: Library software and cataloging software and things like that are kind of a mess. It's really bad. It's bad for everyone except the people who we have to pay lots of money to make the software. It's this strange mix of really old stuff and then new stuff that doesn't often make a lot of sense. The catalog software that I work with the most, Aleph, is twenty years old in its basic components. The institution I work for has had this software for ten years, and even looking at it as a cataloger—forget as an end user—if you aren't a certain age, it doesn't look like computers to you. Like, the Save icon when you're making a catalog record in this software is not even a floppy disk that someone under twenty-five might not really recognize, because they've never used one; it's a filing cabinet. So it's that kind of thing, where there are parts of it that are really old, both in how it looks and feels but then also in how it works.

The problem really lies in the fact that libraries are, for the most part, not parts of businesses—like, we don't generate our own money, we're not in the market in the same way that a for-profit entity would be. Our funds are limited. And therefore we can't really push our software providers as well as other service providers like scholarly publishing to do things, because we can't threaten them with money in the way that you can in the for-profit marketplace. The flip side has to do with competition between these catalog creators, the ILSs, as at least some of them are known—Aleph is one of them in that it provides the catalog, it provides circulation, it provides ILL if you use it, and things like that. Relatively speaking, there are very few companies that make these huge bits of software, because my guess is that ultimately the market is limited. Libraries have only so much money. At this point there are a couple open source ones like Koha, and then there's three for-profit companies including Ex Libris that make these giant complex software systems.

There's a great chart that Marshall Breeding puts out every year showing this flow chart timeline of the merging and creation of these library catalog provider companies. If you look at the beginning of it, in the '60s there's a couple companies as the MARC record idea—instead of cataloging on cards—happens. Through the '70s and the '80s and the early '90s, the number of these companies proliferates for a certain amount of time. They start as just a couple, and as it becomes a market, the number of companies making this software grows. Then there's a point where you can see, all of a sudden, all these diverse companies that gave libraries a choice to figure out what they needed and what company might provide those needs better for them in particular versus some other kind of library—there's a point at which the number of companies shrinks, and now there's like three, as well as a couple open source options. Some of them maybe go out of business, but a lot of them just get bought up and gobbled up by a couple different companies, of which Ex Libris is one. That's where we get our software. And even Ex Libris itself was just bought less than a year ago by ProQuest.

So now there's not only this lack of competition and innovation between people who are providing similar services and kinds of software, but there's this question of companies like ProQuest and Ex Libris merging with each other, where ProQuest is a provider of content, and Ex Libris is a provider of the database structure. Can we trust ProQuest as the owner of Ex Libris? Right now there's no evidence that they're doing anything malicious, but can you trust that for infinity, basically, will Ex Libris's search engines and databases always be content-neutral? Will they always treat the content that is provided by their parent company, ProQuest, the same as content coming from other places when you search somewhere? That's kind of the question now, when a couple of these mergers have only recently happened. Yes, it seems like everything's really fair right now, the search engines are content-neutral, but in ten years is that going to be the case, when there really is a financial incentive for these very large companies—some of which are owned by finance corporations, not by themselves; owned by investment companies ultimately, sometimes, as Ex Libris has been in the past—are they always going to be content-neutral? Will you always be able to trust them to not favor their own content and therefore drive the search traffic and scholarly output through their own material?

That's kind of where we stand now. Those are the two things that are the problem, this really old-style software and this larger question of the financial side of it and the problems we have where capitalism interacts with nonprofits in this way, because most libraries are non-profits or government entities. We end up with this software that's really insufficient for our needs, that was hard to use when it was new and that's what computers looked like. But now you've got a new librarian who might be twenty-four years old now. I'm thirty-two and I can at least remember that the computer programs I used in elementary school looked and felt and functioned like my catalog. Like, you can't scroll through drop-down menus in this program. So it functions in a way that I can at least recognize, but if you're a new librarian who's twenty-four years old, it doesn't even make sense to you. You've literally never seen anything that looks like this, and this is what's running my catalog, Harvard's catalog—really important institutions just have this dinosaur software.

MICHAEL GORMAN: We used technology very effectively, in my view, to work toward the idea of Universal Bibliographic Control. The idea was that every part of the human record would be cataloged and made retrievable. That ideal has been vitiated by the search engine dynamic, by IT people who do not understand the value of cataloging, by libraries that have either very small, now, or no cataloging departments, and by libraries in which the catalog is just a Google-like grab bag of keyword searching. We were so near to achieving Universal Bibliographic Control. Nowadays, if you look at even a prestigious institution like the British Library, their catalog is virtually as useless as a vast card catalog. It's okay if you just want a couple of things that may or may not be relevant and you sift through them.

This disaster has been caused by three factors. One is the stupidity of library administrations who, in the words of Wilde, know the cost of everything and the value of nothing and have abolished cataloging departments. Second is the incursion of IT departments, people who know nothing about information retrieval other than by search engines. Third, the acquiescence of the public who have become so Googlized that all they expect from any search is just a pile of stuff to sift through, rather than meeting the objectives of the catalog as set out in the nineteenth century by Cutter. Cataloging is the area of such small amount of expertise as I have, and I could weep to see its state today.

KAREN LEMMONS: My most useful technology right now is called OPALS, Open-source Automated Library System. Let me tell you why I'm such a big fan of that particular library system. We had one before, at my second elementary school. It had some limitations, and it was very difficult for students to access. Students wouldn't be able to search books or anything because the system was not user-friendly. We kept it because it was inexpensive to the district. When some other library management system companies came to me and asked me about trying to get Detroit on board, I'd say, "Okay" and give them the name of our district supervisor at the time. Of course after she reviewed it all, she found that these library management systems were too expensive, so we remained with that inexpensive company.

Well, that company went out of business and left me without a library management system. I had to manually check out books. I didn't even bother cataloging. Cataloging was just out of the question, because there was no way for me to link, to barcode, none of that. So when I started receiving a grant from the Daughters of the American Revolution, I had to figure out way to get a library management system—because I was getting these books, and I wanted them to get to the students. The Daughters of the American Revolution had a literacy project to help students read classics and other books. Through the radio station we have in our building, in which the Daughters of the American Revolution participates in fundraisers, they found out that there was a library in the school. We connected, and they said, "We want to spend $1000 to purchase books for the library." I was ecstatic. I have not had a library budget for a while because of Detroit Public schools' financial issues. We are a Title I school, and Title I funds are allocated for the academic/core courses. I gave my book list to the Daughters of the American Revolution for them to purchase.

And I just *had* to have a library management system. I remembered a conference call that I had with OPALS and another person in IT. I fell in love with their library management system, with the ease and flow of use. They had pathfinders, they had all of this good stuff that I wanted to use. So I bit the bullet. I called them and asked if they remember me from that conference call. They did. I pleaded with them. I said, "Look. I have these books. They need to be cataloged. I want to get these books to the students. I do not have a library management system. And I need your help. I need your support. I know you have a thirty-day trial. I'm willing to try that, and let's see where we can go from there." And they received me with open arms, and they have allowed me to be their pilot, so to speak, because they're also trying to get into the Detroit Public schools. So we have a nice working relationship. It is so effortless how I can just create records, download records from different sources, link books with OPALS. I can pull up records. I can create all sorts of information for the staff. So, yeah. That's my technology that I love.

Before I begged OPALS, I did talk to my principal. My principal is very supportive of what I do. I always include her in any communication I have with them. She's known me long enough to know that I'm not going to do anything that's going to reflect badly on the school. Everything that I'm trying to do is definitely for the good of the school and ultimately for the good of the students. So there's a level of trust that we've established over the years where she knows that I'm just going to do what's right for the school and ultimately what's right for the students. She gives me a little freedom, but if I get out there too far, she'll pull me in.

BESS SADLER: Convincing decision-makers. I've done a lot of that. Often it's about figuring out what their concerns are. It depends on where you're starting. Are you talking to someone who's never heard the term "open source" and thinks that it's off the wall? Start by advocating to use Firefox on the library browsers instead of Internet Explorer, or something like that, and have good arguments about protecting patron privacy and resisting spyware. Are you talking about someone whose heart is in the right place but doesn't really have much experience with technology? Reassure them that there are active support communities, and get familiar with those active support communities. I mean, the big challenge around open source is that you are doing it for yourself. You're not doing *everything* for yourself; there are lots of people who could help you and depending on the product in question, there are people that you can pay to help you and that you can have support contracts for. The open source community is very diverse, too. I mean, if we're talking about Evergreen ILS, that is an enterprise-scale solution. Yeah, it's open source, but it's also supported by a well-funded, well-run company, the same way—frankly, *better* than a lot of the larger commercial ILS systems on the market. That's a really different thing from implementing Blacklight; you probably would need someone on staff who's able to index the content themselves. So that does have staffing implications, but I would say they're worthwhile.

The ability to respond to what the users want to find in your collection and how they want to find it, how they want to search it—okay, so here's some examples. At the University of Virginia, when we were trying to convince the administration that Blacklight was a good idea, we had some experimental interfaces set up, and I worked a lot with our music librarian, Erin Mayhood, to help improve the user experience for music students. She was really outspoken about the fact that the music collection was not well-served by our current discovery interface. For example, we had a huge collection of sheet music, and one of the most frequent reference questions was, "Can you help me find some sheet music? I play guitar, my friend plays violin, we want to do a duet together. Show me all of the sheet music that has a guitar and a violin." Even though our catalogers had gone to the trouble of cataloging all of the instruments that were used for all of that sheet music collection, you couldn't search by that field, because the commercial ILS vendor did not deem that one of the fields that was significant in someone's search results. So there was no way to discover that information.

One of the first things that we did was start indexing that. But even better, we said, you know, the search needs of the music scholars are really different from the search needs of the more mainstream users of the library collection. When someone from the music department searches for "Beethoven," they're more likely to be searching for something written *by* Beethoven. When an everyday user is searching for "Beethoven," they're more likely to be searching for something *about* Beethoven. Through our user studies, we found that different communities just had really different expectations for what relevancy meant.

Some of the other things that we've really been able to fix for our users that I don't think would have been addressed otherwise were searching in native scripts, when you have content that is not in Roman character sets. Naomi Dushay at Stanford did outstanding work that has been pushed back to the Solr community—that's the underlying search engine that Blacklight uses—around searching for Chinese, Japanese, and Korean. A problem like that is important to the users who want to use it, but it's not a large enough population that it's really commercially interesting to a lot of commercial companies. So open source allows us to solve the problems that we think are important, not just the problems that can make money.

JOHN HELLING: When I took over as Library Director at the Bloomfield-Eastern Greene County Public Library, the decision had already been made to move from SIRSI to Koha. At the time, the library was part of a now-defunct consortium that shared a catalog to reduce costs. Almost immediately after we made that transition, we became aware that the State Library had decided to pull back the funding it had previously given to the consortium's parent group, INCOLSA, which was effectively a death knell. The library had to decide whether we were going to go out and buy a new ILS or join the brand new consortium, sponsored by the State Library, that was using Evergreen. Simultaneous to all this was a new law being talked about in Indiana that was going to put a cap on property tax collection—our main source of revenue.

So for us, moving to Evergreen was almost a necessity, from my point of view. We had to give up some things, such as local control of our fine levels, which went from five cents per day to twenty-five cents per day on books. We also had to be okay with the possibility of "outside" patrons putting holds on our books and taking them outside of the library district, both of which were sources of wariness for lots of people. But our most recent annual bill from SIRSI was north of $150,000, which was the consortial rate, and this was from a total budget of around $500,000. Evergreen required us to give up local control of some things, but the cost savings were immediate and substantial. Also, some of the drawbacks, like sending books out of our district, actually worked both ways. Our patrons now had access to all of those other collections, too. It was absolutely a learning experience for both staff and patrons, but at the end of the day it was net-positive, I believe. We made the transition in 2009 or so, and the library is still a member.

JESSAMYN WEST: I feel like what we've seen in the last maybe five years with open source software in libraries, especially with ILSs, is the rise of service companies. My little library, forty-five hundred people, three and a half full-time employees—not necessarily the best candidate for an open source ILS because one of the things about open source, people say, "free like kittens." You have to do a lot of work to keep it going, and that work isn't always straightforward and easy for a non-techie. But what we've done in Vermont is have an informal consortium called the Green Mountain Library Consortium, so not a big state consortium. And we've got ninety-plus libraries that all chip in together to share an ILS that's open source. We use Koha, and I think we use ByWater, which is a company that will help you install and do support and help you do upgrades and stuff through your ILS. So it doesn't wind up having to be the job of libraries, but they can pool their money and get the economy of scale you would get from having software that you pay for, but there just becomes this sort of middleman person who can help you with the sort of support thing.

. . .

MITA WILLIAMS: I think librarianship still has to go through a real reckoning about e-books. I'm still a little dismayed about how librarianship transitioned so quickly to largely proprietary server systems. Essentially what we did was outsource the ability to handle our own e-book collections. I remember reading a blog post from a public librarian who wrote that a gentleman wanted to donate his e-book to the library but they couldn't because the e-book platform was from a private company, and they had no mechanism to include his e-book in their collection. The technical constraints that we've built in to our own systems are really disconcerting. I also recognize that digital rights management software has placed additional constraints on us. I think some years from now we're going to realize the magnitude of the error of buying so many collections that had digital rights management software, because unfortunately as soon as a company goes under or decides that it's not worth maintaining their licensing server, they can pull the plug on the DRM server, and all of a sudden our access to those books essentially disappears.

I have a Kindle DX, which I used to use quite a bit because it allowed me to read long PDF documents on a large screen without glare. I used to be able to upload PDFs directly from my computer to my Kindle, but recently Amazon disabled that functionality. Any technology that can have functionality disabled by a second or third party is troubling. One the reasons why I'm interested in software such as IPython notebook is because you're encouraged to make a personal copy of the text. So even if the original disappears, you will still have your own copy. Libraries still have lot to answer for. How do we keep local copies of e-books? How do we deal with all these different formats? How do we decide when an online work like a web page is not a work in progress but is a final work like a book. There's a lot of work still to do.

JONATHAN HARWELL: In terms of e-books, the main innovation that has helped us more than anything else in the past several years would be demand-driven acquisition. At our library we do demand-driven acquisition through YPB for the platforms of ProQuest—formerly ebrary—and EBSCO. This is giving us a way to really do data-driven collection development. It lets us get automatic batches of e-books added to our collection on a weekly basis; whether we've already paid for those e-books or not is invisible to the patron. They would simply go to our discovery layer and see these e-books and access them free of charge unless they hit a certain usage trigger, in which case we would then pay for the book. This has been a real benefit to us. It also helps us to do manual demand-driven acquisition. So as a collection development librarian, if I'm receiving request from a faculty member to buy a $400 book, it's much easier for me to do that as a DDA option, to say, yes, we'll add this to the collection, but we're only going to pay for it if someone is going to use it. That's much more justifiable with a library budget. This helps us actually grow our collection exponentially while also stretching our budget further, which is a huge help. And at the same time, it really opens up more content to the patrons.

JESSAMYN WEST: I really think that the shift to leasing, not buying, and the shift to more and more digital content that libraries are shifting more of their budgets to, is actually this giant land grab that is essentially taking public money and sticking it in the pockets of private corporations. Then the library winds up not owning anything, and

I feel like that's a problem. There's nothing inherently wrong with e-books or digital content necessarily. But I do think there's something a little sketchy about the model where you lease content and don't buy it. You're spending more and more money on access to databases and e-books that you don't own, and I really think it winds up just shifting money that should be staying in the community. If the library buys the book, the book stays in the library; that community owns a thing. But if the library leases access to a database and then they don't pay for that anymore, that money has just gone out the window and doesn't stay in the community. I really think we need to have a more sophisticated conversation about that kind of thing and find better ways that businesses can still get paid—I'm not anti-business—but libraries can still own community content, not just pay for accessing it. I don't think that's a real responsible thing to do with the public money that you've been entrusted with, to say nothing about the exorbitant, completely ridiculous cost of a lot of access to journals, databases, and that kind of thing.

I really think we need to, number one, find better models. Number two, start telling the people who are giving us the contracts for the stuff that we are paying for that these contracts suck and we need better ones. We need to come at it from a better bargaining perspective in order to be able to do that. In addition, I just think more and more open access accomplishments should get shouted from the rooftops to larger populations. I know in small public libraryland where I am, they kind of know about Public Library of Science, but the whole idea of open access and self-archiving and having access to your own digital content—even if you're not an academic—is a useful conversation for libraries to be having with their patrons and with their populations.

JOEL NICHOLS: In my experience working in the branch libraries, maybe once a week or once every other week, a patron might come in with their e-reader and be like, "I don't know how to use this, I don't get it, I don't know what's wrong." And I'd do this typical, "Let's sit down and I'll walk you through it. Bring your password and your this and your that." A lot of times we would end up in the same place, trying to access a library e-book. As with someone with a lost Google password, they'd have to download an app or register something. For a while you had to do this authentication with Adobe Reader on e-readers that was really complicated, and frankly even though I had resources that our electronic resources coordinator had put together, I didn't really feel like I was that skilled to do it. I felt like I was just troubleshooting the best that I could, but I wasn't always successful in getting people's e-readers to work. I think there are probably vast amounts of library users who are using e-books, but I don't necessarily see them in the library with that kind of problem. I will say the problem I was just describing was fairly infrequent, but I also think that has to do with penetration of e-readers in the neighborhoods where I was working.

The other thing that I see with e-readers in life in general—at work but also in my private life—is that lots of people who, when they hear that I'm a librarian, sort of guiltily say, "Oh, I read on my Kindle, I don't go to the library anymore." So sometimes I'll say, "You can get library books on the Kindle," and they'll say, "Yeah, of course I do that sometimes." But frankly, the whole way that OverDrive has this monopoly on library e-books, and the way you use the OverDrive app and the library website and it's not seamless, and the library doesn't own the book—you get this sort of third party interference in a way that doesn't necessarily enhance the customer service of how easy it is to access an e-book. I see a lot of people using e-books and being really enthusiastic about them; I read some of them myself, but I've got to say that I find it a lot easier, and other people tell me that they find it a lot easier, just to buy an e-book than to get one from the library.

One thing that I don't see that's very promising is e-books in browsers, reading a whole book totally offline. Long ago in the library catalog, way before we had OverDrive e-books for download, there were always research books and resources that you could read in the browser. For most kinds of books that people want to read—actually read the whole thing, not just skim a chapter—I don't see that as being a very effective way of delivering them, particularly if people are only having a half an hour or an hour on the computer session in the library. I don't know, maybe if the library were lending tablets or had somewhere you could sit in a chair and spend more time with a book in a browser, but otherwise that strikes me as a dead end.

ANDROMEDA YELTON: E-books chiefly fill me with despair. They're so messy in terms of legal status and DRM and negotiation. The fact that our aggregators are the ones performing the negotiations with all the content providers, and that dictates what libraries can do but doesn't necessarily give libraries the scope to do things well, and the fact that libraries don't necessarily have the tech skill in themselves to build better interfaces—it fills me with despair. That said, New York Public Library is doing great things with e-books these days. Their Library Simplified platform is looking at how you take all these different electronic content streams from different places and give patrons one unified straightforward interface. They're working with access to e-books across the digital divide, getting e-books into the hands of kids from districts that don't have a lot of money. Many of these people do have smartphones or some sort of access to the technology that would let you read them, but not necessarily the content itself. So New York Public Library is doing some great work. And I think that now that we have a shiny new Librarian of Congress, there's a leadership potential there that may reshape what possibilities are available to us.

SARAH HOUGHTON: I do not see anything positive or hopeful in library e-book lending. I see things going down the same negative path they've been going down from the beginning, which is more and more restrictive licenses, although more publishers are at least willing to license to libraries. They're still doing so at an exorbitant rate without any justification for that increased cost. I think that the streaming models of e-books—looking at Hoopla as a model—is an interesting one, but not an easy one for libraries to work with. We just launched Hoopla today, in fact, and it's scary for me because it's budgetarily unpredictable since it's a cost-per-use model, which is the only way that they say that they can offer a streaming service with multiple simultaneous users on any title. It creates unpredictability. As a library director, I can say, well, we're going to allocate $10,000 towards this, but we could run out of that in six months and then have to shut the service down and have people be pretty angry.

So to me there is no good e-book lending model. I don't understand why, other than capitalistic greed, we are in a world where libraries are not getting the same fair use copyright exemptions and the same bulk discount pricing from e-book publishers that we've had all along. How things magically changed to our and our communities' detriment with the advent of digital information is forever a thorn in my side and something I continue to campaign toward changing. I see it having long-term repercussions on our ability to act as a digital repository for our communities and to cost-effectively provide services to our communities, and I'm very concerned about the sustainability of pretty much every digital content model for libraries that's out there right now. And as someone with that very firm ethical viewpoint, I have to balance that against my responsibilities as a library director to provide those services and the types of content that our community demands, which is increasingly digital content.

I feel like I'm straddling this very thin line of trying to keep our users happy with content but also knowing that I'm in some ways violating my core ethics with every contract that I sign. Working hard to change the terms of those contracts and to change the underlying law that governs copyright and governs libraries' access to digital content is the only way, I think, that I rationalize keeping those two things going at the same time.

ANITA COLEMAN: I love e-book formats. I love their distribution. I think it's very promising, because one of the things I've learned with my own e-books is that people discover them later and reread them, so that to me is wonderful. I know you do it with the print, but I think we're moving into this economy where it's not so much about ownership as it is about access. I think initially libraries were struggling with e-books, but for libraries to help people, librarians should embrace both independent publishing as well as e-books. Libraries have had trouble figuring out the costs because, previously, once you bought the book you got the book; you owned the book as long as you kept it in the library, no matter how many times people checked it out. This has changed with e-books. We need creative, empathic, and thoughtful minds on the problem of e-books in libraries.

But in general, I'm really excited by e-books and by independent publishing. Independent publishing has not been tapped enough in libraries, and it needs to be leveraged much, much more. Some of the big ARL libraries—University of Michigan Library is one of them—have become publishers themselves. Collaboration with publishing houses or university presses, as in UM's particular case, is very good and innovative.

JONATHAN HARWELL: In terms of ecological issues, one thing that has encouraged me is that our environmental studies faculty who are very active book requesters also tell me that they're perfectly fine with e-books for the books that they request for purchase for the library. I actually keep a spreadsheet of which format different faculty members prefer across campus. The environmental studies faculty are very cool with e-books, which means less paper produced, which is great for the environment, of course, as well.

STEPHANIE IRVIN: At Georgia Libraries for Accessible Statewide Services, we do not have the green cases that came in the mail in the '90s anymore; those were cassettes. Prior to those we had records, if you can believe that. We actually shipped out record players to patrons, and they could listen to their records that way. The players were very heavy. I'm kind of impressed that people with disabilities would want to lug them around, and thankfully they've gotten better and better since then. We went from that to cassettes, and now we're actually on our digital talking book players. They're much lighter, and they use a cartridge. Although if you look at it, a cartridge is basically a jump drive that has a plastic casing on it to make it easier to handle and put in the front of the player, and generally just to give you something more to grab onto. Plus there's braille writing on the top and large print and some other handy stuff. So people can just pop it in the front of the player, hit play, and they're good to go.

We also have an app called BARD Mobile for people to download books, and it's very friendly. The public libraries are aware of OverDrive for downloading e-books, which has multiple steps to check out, and the books have DRM on them and expire within X amount of days. Because our materials are created to be used only by a specific group of individuals, that is, those with print disabilities—reading, physical, and visual disabilities—they can log into the app once and after that they can just go for it and download whatever books they want. The books stay on their device as long as people would like them, basically. Which is great, because it gives a lot of flexibility for those who need more time with their book. It makes me very happy. You can't really move the files around to other devices, which is a little bit unfriendly, but they do make it so that the app can be put on multiple devices. I do have patrons that will listen to it on their iPad and their iPhone, or on multiple devices and use books that way, and you can have a lot of those out at once. There is a little bit of protection on them, but they're a little bit easier to use, in my experience, than buying media through other sources like Amazon or getting them from a public library. Again, I think it's because it's something that's meant for a particular group of people, and that was just an understanding when they designed it the way that they designed it. So that's most of how we get our materials now.

As far as visual components, we tend to not to have much of that. I did create a YouTube page because YouTube is considered to be generally accessible as far as creating videos go, as long as you put captions on them—and it has to be real captions, not the auto-generated ones. Those are terrible. We do use that component but we don't put books there, because it's a big long thing regarding the Chafee Amendment and the rights that we have to change books into different formats. Basically what the Chafee Amendment says is that a material can be made into a format for individuals with disabilities; it just has to be used by people with that particular disability. I'm very loosely paraphrasing. It's worth looking up, but that's essentially what it is. That's what gives the Library of Congress's National Library Service for the Blind and Physically Handicapped permission to take the latest Patterson, record it, and then make it available to people with disabilities without having to pay for it in any regard. The reason they get away with it is because it's meant specifically for this group of people with disabilities that otherwise may not be able to access that type of material. That is basically what allows talking book and braille libraries to operate.

It's also worth pointing out that there have been publishers that have been ridiculously friendly with us. And I say "ridiculously" in the most positive way. They've basically been agreeable with the National Library Service and give them their files for audiobooks in order to make them available in these platforms for people with disabilities, so that one of my patrons can be listening to the same audiobook as the person that buys the commercial audiobook version. I think it's a fantastically friendly thing for these publishers to do.

JESSAMYN WEST: Open Library is a project of the Internet Archive, which is a huge free culture filing cabinet of digital stuff. Open Library was a project started by Aaron Swartz quite some time ago, and the idea was a web page for every book. "Every book" doesn't just mean Alice in Wonderland; every book means every edition of Alice in Wonderland, all the time. And there's a page for every edition. That expanded to be, hey, we've got digital versions of books, let's make them available. That expanded to, hey, we can scan a bunch of books and then receive digital versions. They got a lot of grant money, scanned some books, and built a sexy website, and then they started pushing the envelope, which is my favorite part of the whole thing.

Theoretically—well, realistically—you're a library, you buy a book, you can lend that book out all the time. Print book, it's legal. Legal, legal, legal. It's enshrined in copyright law that you're able to do that. Let's say you took that book and scanned it, and then you put the book in a box and didn't circulate it, and you had a digital copy and you lent it—only one copy at a time; you don't make a thousand copies—is that legal or is that not legal? Right now that's in an interesting gray area. What the Internet Archive decided was, we think it's a good idea and we're going to try it. So Open Library lends a bunch of e-books that are technically in copyright but, realistically, most of them—not all but most—nobody cares about. They might be orphan works. They're definitely older works; a lot of them are, like, romances from fifteen, twenty years ago; family histories from the 1950s; kids' books from the '90s—a big collection. They have a quarter of a million books that they lend digital copies of, worldwide. Anybody can borrow the books. They use Adobe digital rights management to keep one copy at a time circulating. Now, they're automatically scanned and automatically OCRed, so you can borrow a PDF, you can borrow an EPUB, or you can just read it on screen in kind of a flippy book format.

It's pretty exciting. When Open Library started eight years ago, there really weren't other people doing what they were doing. Since then, libraries have gotten in the e-book market, which has been kind of awesome, and everybody was like, "E-books! They're going to put print books out of business!" And then over time, I feel like society in America has kind of reached an equilibrium. The latest Pew report said, "You know, there's really only 6 percent of Americans who are e-book-only readers." A lot of people still read print. A lot of people read a combination of both. E-books aren't killing print books; they're just occupying a niche that is useful and helpful for people. And then you see New York Public Library, who came out with an e-book reader called SimplyE. One of the things we learned at Open Library is digital rights management is a pain in the ass. It's awful and everyone hates it. But, if you want to be a library where you're lending a book and you're not just giving away a thousand copies of a book, that's kind of what you've got to do. So, New York Public Library developed this thing called SimplyE. Basically, you log in with your New York Public Library card, and it does all the hand-shakey stuff on the back end so that you don't have to log into Amazon, log into OverDrive, log into 3M, log into whatever.

I really think that's the future of libraries plus e-books. Because the problem is right now we're in this uncertain time where it's like the Wild West. Everybody wants the market share. Everybody wants to get you come in to their store to buy—because a digital book is the freaking same no matter where you buy it, honestly. And I think it's an opportunity for libraries to be like, "Come here and you don't have to worry about where your book comes from. You just come get it here. We have your book, and the experience doesn't suck because we have this e-book reader that isn't terrible and was developed by geniuses at New York Public Library." Everyone hates Adobe and the licenses costs money, so the Internet Archive technically loses money on Open Library—although realistically I don't know how the numbers work and don't have to, but licenses for DRM cost money. SimplyE can theoretically make that work. You may have to pay money on the back end, it's unclear—you'd see me waving my hands here if we were looking at each other.

I feel like there's a future in which digital books become much more of a reality to more people, because the interface finally gets to the point where it's not the impediment to people accessing content, but it's actually the draw. I know that there are some websites that I use more than other websites that do the same thing, because I like interacting with that website better. I'm optimistic that it's going to just get to the point where you can get the format you want without being super tech-savvy, on the device you want, and the technology will handle itself because smart people code it on the back end, not expecting you to have to do the hurdles on the front end.

* * *

ANITA COLEMAN: When we look at scholarship, we see that libraries have some standard professionals, developed over time, such as the library liaisons and the collection development specialists. Technology can make the work of these professionals to be more transparent as well as reach a larger audience. When you're a collection development specialist in a university library, or even in a community college library where the resources are more limited, a lot of times what happens is that not everybody gives input into the collection development process. Previously, when we didn't have a digital tool like web surveys, we depended often on personal relationships or the librarian connecting with the department or the faculty in charge to get broader input. We also often did needs analyses and other kinds of studies to assess and evaluate.

That kind of relationship and evaluation still is there, but it can now be scaled to a larger group much more easily by using emails, electronic surveys, and even social media. For example, new acquisitions lists can be hyperlinked to the online catalog and highlighted if it is by a librarian or faculty member. Many universities and colleges have a database of their faculty's areas of interests and expertise that can be juxtaposed and used as appropriate.

We are living now in what I would call the Information Glut Age. This has been growing on us, but we now have more information than we can deal with, just like we produce more food than we can eat. And so libraries have to be very careful in how much information they collect, what kinds of information is collected, and what is done with that information. Tying this back to the relationships and the conversations, this means we must learn individual information needs and use technology to deepen the relationship and the conversation. We now have a lot of different ways to do this, whereas before we had fewer choices.

JONATHAN HARWELL: I worked with a colleague, Geoff Timms, to develop an open source system for library subscription reviews, the Ongoing Automated Review System. Geoff actually did the programming, all the coding on it, by himself. Essentially, we strategized about how to make the serials review process more streamlined and more viable for libraries, because there wasn't a tool in place for libraries to do this. Everyone was trying to invent their own wheels when they were faced with large budget cuts and had to do serials cancelation projects. It usually involves long lists and spreadsheets, basically creating a process out of thin air, and it's very time-consuming, especially at larger libraries. And it's also tricky because there are not many easy ways to identify the journals that you really don't need. We can rely on usage statistics and faculty feedback to some extent, but we wanted a way to bring all of that together, along with impact factor ratings.

So this system actually allows us to collate those recommendations from faculty, usage statistics, and the impact factor to arrive at a formula that would give us a list of journals to consider for cancelation. Of course, this is not the final decision, but it's a decision point for the librarians to look at. And if you're at a large library with a lot of individual subscriptions like I was before, it was a huge help for me, because the alternative was spending months and months on it—as I had already done one year on a cancelation project, just using spreadsheets. This was a way to feed all of this into an open source product that anyone can adapt and use to produce a list of journals that would be good candidates for cancelation, basically the low-hanging fruit that would not make much of an impact if we canceled them.

MITA WILLIAMS: I know that the challenge for a lot of libraries is knowing what our readers want from us, and so I think demand-driven acquisition is something worth exploring. However, I think that this form of collection development has to be balanced because I've heard "demand-driven acquisitions" be described as "assignment-driven acquisitions." It's not a terrible thing to listen to our users—especially listen to the people who make use of our collections—so I think demand-driven acquisition is worth investigating, but I think its results need monitoring and compensating.

JONATHAN HARWELL: The access model of providing some form of DDA for articles from serials is something we're still talking about. We've got an article we've published on this topic, which sprang from a Charleston Conference presentation that I did with Jim Bunnelle from Lewis & Clark College in 2014. We saw a bit of interest not only from librarians but also from vendors on making this happen. It's something vendors are talking about, but it's very complex because of course you have some vendors who are serial distributors, some vendors who provide discovery layers, and some are also book and serials publishers. Even with a single publisher, the book side and the serial side of the house don't always talk to each other and strategize together.

So there are a lot of moving pieces to this, but if we could get together to an industry standard and make it happen for serial content just like we did for books some years back, it would again be a huge benefit to the library patrons. Currently we're relying on subscriptions, which are an all-or-nothing proposition; interlibrary loan, which goes to one patron at a time; or pay-per-view, which again goes to one patron at a time and again is not perpetual access. If we had a way to add articles to our library collection for perpetual access, this would open up the possibilities. It would let patrons actually access things through our discovery platform, and we would be doing micropayments for those articles as we go. This could be an option to supplement the large number of subscriptions we already have. For example, perhaps there's a very expensive physics journal or medical journal that we would not be able to subscribe to but that would get use on our campus. This would be a way for us to not only get that publisher some revenue, which they would never see through interlibrary loan, but it would also provide instant access as opposed to the patron waiting for an interlibrary loan from that journal. So that's where we see some benefits for that model.

With e-book interlibrary loan, we do see some vendors—for example, Springer—who are more open to that. But that's still a small portion of the market. We're talking about publishers in some cases who are resistant to doing DRM-free e-books. I remember around 2000, I was at a library conference and mentioned the possibility of ILL for e-books, and people looked at me like I was nuts. The presenter said, "Why would anybody ever want to interlibrary loan an e-book? That's preposterous!" But we're seeing more movement in that direction now. It would provide one more avenue for patrons to access a book from another library without a physical book being shipped across time and space, by taking advantage of the technologies that are already there.

ELAINE HARGER: Recently there was a discussion about *Progressive Librarian*, the journal that I'm an editor of and have helped with my colleagues in publishing for the last twenty-six years. We've been told on several occasions over the course of several years that we could save a lot of money if we abandoned our print journal and just published what we want online. We would save both in printing costs and in mailing costs. And that is true, that's absolutely true. However, this digital "age" that we're in is not a very old one. In my own professional life, I've gone from the card catalog to the smartphone. I've seen, personally, all of these changes, and I've been a librarian for thirty years. That's not very long. But I also have some knowledge about how people can get drawn into supporting things and becoming used to them and then being charged ever and ever increasing rates in order to access it.

One of my hesitancies in publishing *Progressive Librarian* only in an online format has two components. One, I don't know that digital forms of information are going to be able to outlast paper. If you ask me which I think is going to be more permanent, paper or electronics, I would definitely say paper. Anything online is completely subject to either electrical lines, or in some cases you have to have satellite transmissions. There has to be electricity and air conditioning to those "clouds" that they call the air-conditioned cement buildings located where real estate and electricity is cheap. Our access to anything online is so dependent on such a highly sophisticated system that can be controlled either by the government or by corporations. We could begin to be charged more and more for our access to what we now take for granted as being free. Right now we're talking for free over Skype. Well, Skype might turn around and say, "We want to charge you ten cents for ten minutes to use our services." They could do that easily. And we might pay, or we might not pay.

So there is, for me, a considerable amount of uncertainty as to the stability of this technology that we have access to. I can easily see only rich people being able to access it at some point in time, and all the rest of us—we're out of luck. Also, we're keeping *Progressive Librarian* in print because there's something about the tactile nature of a book and the ease with which it can be scanned. I've read articles online; I wish I could say I'd read a whole book online or even on my Kindle, but it bothers my eyes too much. But you can scan through the pages of a book much more easily than you can the pages of an e-book. There's also neurological research recently that suggests that people retain more information when their brain is engaged with print than it does with electronic. Not only is there a higher retention rate, but a person's attention span is greater with print than with online information.

So I think for all three of those reasons, speaking as an editor of a journal, I'm going to stick with whatever it takes to maintain the journal in print. But we also turn each issue into a PDF and post it online, so it's open access, too, although we wait to post three months after the print version comes out. But as soon as we publish every issue, the PDFs automatically get sent to EBSCO and Wilson and they're in the major library databases. So this particular journal is—I don't know if you'd officially call it open access, but if it's not triple-star open access, it's double-star open access, and in print.

MANDY HENK: I think we don't talk enough about the relationship between political economy and technology. At least the argument that I would make is that as this technology developed, sort of parasitic capitalistic forces that had previously been fairly tame took advantage of the technology to essentially take over the commons. So what had previously been a large commons of print resources that were shared fairly freely all of a sudden became taken over by companies who then erected barriers to their use. I actually talk about this in the second-to-last chapter of my book. I think that the use of technology by largely economic actors to control access to information is something that we don't talk about enough, and something that we seem to be very nervous about confronting. And I would say that this really does go beyond looking at full-text stuff, all the way into looking at our library catalogs. If we have five companies that are making 90 percent of our library catalogs, we've given them an enormous amount of power in our lives, and we've given them an enormous amount of power over our collection. Paying attention to this, talking about it, and not being really afraid to engage assertively by saying, "I don't think that this is a healthy system," is something I would like to see us doing more.

. . .

JIM DELROSSO: Open access is a model of access in which the cost is not put on the end user or reader. That's a very specific way of putting it, because it's not a business model. It doesn't assume that all information wants to be free and we can also freely deliver all information without cost. But it says that under open access, the cost for producing and disseminating that piece of information is not put on the end user. It's not put on the reader or the library who purchases it. In fact, it obviates purchase by the library; it moves the cost to a different place. From a practical standpoint, that means no paywalls and no subscription fees in most cases, unless it's a voluntary kind of thing. So open access really focuses on removing prices and paywalls from the delivery side of things.

Gold open access is about material that's delivered in that way right from the beginning, so it usually centers around gold open access journals. The stuff that's published in these journals is never behind a paywall; it's always freely available on the Internet. And of course "on the Internet" assumes a certain amount of technological infrastructure for people to actually take advantage of it.

Green open access is what I tend to do for more of my day-to-day. It usually centers around making material available on the Internet through institutional or disciplinary repositories. It's not material that was necessarily originally published open access. So you get a lot of authors putting their postprints of published articles into a green open access repository, or getting permission from a non-gold open access publisher to put the final version into this green open access repository. Rather than being centered around journals, green open access is centered around repositories. At some point, someone needs to pay the fees for the software that puts the material up, for the storage, for the Internet access of all of the people who actually need to make it work, etc. But that's just not passed along to the reader.

ANITA COLEMAN: DLIST, the Digital Library of Information Science and Technology, was founded in 2002. The idea actually came out of an independent study I supervised by a student, Mark. The University of Arizona in the late 1990s had been criticized and, in fact, threatened with loss of accreditation because neither cataloging nor classification was being offered to their LIS students and yet these students were going to become ALA-accredited librarians. I was hired to primarily teach cataloging and classification but my background in information technology, with practical library automation experience implementing systems, databases, and electronic resources, along with my digital library research on the Alexandria Digital Library—one of the first National Science Foundation digital libraries funded—was very much welcomed. Mark took the Organization of Information course with me and became fascinated because I required the students to learn markup languages as one of the information standards that librarians needed to know. At that time, very few people were talking about cataloging as metadata or as descriptive markup.

Mark was intrigued, and he came to me and talked about an independent study. One of the issues he researched at my request was open access. As a practicing librarian I had seen a disconnect between the library faculty and librarians in the field. I wanted to connect practicing librarians with faculty and students, and in the process of connecting the documentary outputs of practice with research and teaching, to also give everybody valuable technology skills, for example through self-archiving. And then there was the journals crisis, the serials pricing issue libraries face. I had realized one aspect of it for myself when an article I had written was included as a reading for my course. The librarian informed me that the library would have to pay. I had written the article, refereed other articles for that journal, and edited a special issue, all for no payment. It just did not seem correct or fair that the library would now have to pay for my class to use my article.

So that's how the open access repository in library and information science was started. It had as its goals getting faculty to self-archive their research, but it also had the grand idea of librarians putting things that they were creating—such as subject guides and bibliographies—into the archive. We wanted all these different kinds of documents, as well as student portfolios, collected in the repository so that we could create a very robust information resource economy that would showcase our field and also not cost libraries quite so much. Nowadays, there are different movements—open access repositories, open education resources, open platforms for showcasing code and creative work, and so much more. DLIST was an innovative experiment in wanting to bring into one place all of the different types and formats of documents being created in order to give the small community—there are fewer than fifty MLS-accredited schools in the US—global visibility and showcase the work that library school faculty and doctoral students were doing as worthwhile, not just something esoteric, and also that it was intrinsically connected to the librarian community, which is far larger than library schools in the US.

Paul Bracke, now Director of Libraries at Gonzaga University, served as first voluntary DLIST Project Manager and took on the hosting of DLIST as part of his job as Systems Librarian in the Health Sciences Library at the University of Arizona. This was very bold of him when the whole campus and administration were all so afraid of open access and reluctant to come alongside. Kristen Eschenfelder and Marija Dalbello, both untenured young profs like myself, came alongside as co-conspirators. When I set up the global DLIST Editorial Team, they emerged as DLIST leaders.

JONATHAN HARWELL: At Rollins College, we have an institutional repository, and so we rely on publishers who allow our campus authors to deposit versions of their articles in our repository to make them open access to the public. As academics or members of public libraries, perhaps, we have access to certain types of information, but there's a large swath of information that's still behind paywalls. Not every library can provide everything, of course, so there's always a pocket of information that people would have to either use interlibrary loan or pay themselves to access. So it's important for us as mediators with the publishers and vendors to provide ways for the public to access information. This might be information about their own medical problems, or any number of things that people would want to find out about. And it's not just the general public outside of academia, of course. Sometimes we have professors who are between jobs or retired, independent researchers, or our own recent graduates—people who still have a need for research sources but might not have the library that can support them.

JESSA LINGEL: I don't know how much activists—to the extent that you could use that word so broadly—are super angry that they can't access a particular article, but I do feel that when they encounter a paywall it is a very crystallizing representation of how much academia retains knowledge for itself and doesn't make it available for a broader group of people. And we do that in terms of how we write. We're taught to write for a certain community that doesn't usually include people who don't have graduate degrees, which is crazy. So we're taught to write exclusively, and then a lot of times our institutions are set up exclusively so that you can't even go into a building if you don't have an ID card. And then even on top of that, let's say an activist wants to read an article by Virginia Eubanks but they can't because it's behind a paywall. What reasonable person wouldn't encounter that and think, good lord, these academics are not really interested in sharing knowledge, because it definitely doesn't feel like they're sharing knowledge in that moment.

CELESTE Â-RE: I say yes to copyleft! There's more discourse, discussions on listservs and in the literature. I think people are becoming more aware. I'm going to license my dissertation using Creative Commons. It's an option now; it hasn't always been. I think Creative Commons and open sourcing level the playing field.

Andrew Weiss: Open access is definitely becoming more mainstream. I don't think it's reached critical mass yet, but it's certainly growing. Obviously one of the issues is economics and the problem of paying way too much for single journal titles, essentially the unsustainable model that we're experiencing. I think repositories and gold open access publishers have a model that can counterbalance that strange model that we're currently forced to deal with. But I think at the same time, the traditional publishers know their place within the scholarly life cycle. They're sort of the only game in town in some cases, or certain journals are the ones that faculty members have to publish in. So I think the solutions have to come from various sides. It can't just be we're attacking the publishing industry because they're evil. They certainly provide a lot of good. But at the same time, the fact that they're requiring faculty members or scholars to sign over copyright to them in perpetuity is really the crux of the problem. Not reimbursing authors or peer reviewers also makes the publishers look a little less benevolent.

I think it's just, again, the economic model has gotten a little bit skewed. The publishers are very much making their money off of scarcity, and unfortunately that's at odds with the point of scholarly communication and academic publishing. The point was to get your ideas disseminated as quickly and easily as possible. But when you have very high restrictions in terms of price or just in terms of the authentication of getting into the databases—all of those barriers really are kind of contrary to the spirit of the whole thing. I think we've made a lot of progress over the last ten years, but a lot more has to happen before it can really become a viable model that's able to even exist on equal footing with traditional publishing. I think right now, even though more people are adopting it, it's seen as almost a fringe-y type of thing. As more institutions accept or embrace it, then it becomes a lot more legitimized. We're not quite there yet, but it's almost there.

Mandy Henk: I really think that the entire scholarly communication system as it currently exists has to be replaced with a system that is based in open access. At the moment, market forces are really behaving in sort of a parasitic way on top of the system, and we have to pry them away from the impact that they're having on us. So what I would like to see is a system that is based on open access with libraries really serving the role that publishers have served in terms of providing infrastructure. In the past this might have been print-based; now I think that we need to do it with an electronic infrastructure, and one that's supportive of the natural environment and has as little an impact as possible.

When you're looking at things like energy use, you're looking at things like dangerous minerals that are mined in order to support all of this wonderful technology. What we need to do is work to build a technology that is substantially safer for the natural environment. I believe that it's not something that the library community can do alone. We need to partner with the tech community to push that project forward.

What I do see happening is the development of open access, but I also see a co-option of the open access movement on the part of the usual commercial players. At the same time, when you see things like the sort of research archives that we're maintaining for our lecturers and a lot of times our post-grads, too, that's being converted into a tool for administrative control, which worries me. I think it's probably less developed inside of the US than it is especially in the UK, for example. I think that the overall neoliberal project to radically transform the university is far more advanced outside of the US. I know US folks might be dubious on that one. But I promise you it is actually more advanced outside of the US.

STACIE WILLIAMS: I think the open access movement, while critical, is still being hampered by the role that publishing plays in the promotion and tenure process. University models are still very closely following models of ownership that trickle down, so there's very little means to push back against or deincentivize the idea of forcing university libraries and staff to pay to access their own work. University libraries or librarians can only push so hard, but our budgets are finite and we're forced to choose in ways that we'd rather not about what we will have access to. There would have to be a complete top-down decision to not only no longer pay these exorbitant prices for journals *and* to no longer tie promotion and tenure to being published in such journals. And it will take transparency from larger institutions to tell what they are paying for access to journal bundles or e-licenses for content.

ANITA COLEMAN: I worked with faculty friends to encourage them to self-archive by explaining the benefits of an open access archive. I contacted tech-savvy faculty who had already uploaded and linked to their papers from their personal web page to give us permissions to put them into DLIST. Then, we experimented with crawlers and harvesters to get the articles automatically from their personal web pages and put it into the repository. We also used a number of other strategies to grow DLIST and you can read more about them in the articles I've written.

Jonathan Harwell: Our campus actually passed an open access policy in 2010, a couple of years before I came here. The policy basically encourages faculty to deposit versions of our scholarly publications in our institutional repository if at all possible. And we actively seek participation. Every year we look at a list of publications—our digital archivist is the main person responsible for this—and as liaisons we encourage those faculty who have not deposited their publications to do so. This has grown quite a bit; we see a lot of participation. I've been at places where there's been not much enthusiasm from some faculty because maybe they don't see the benefits of open access, or they don't see the benefits of archiving their research in an institutional repository. Sometimes they think, "Oh, anyone who needs access to this information already has it because they're an academic." There are a lot of assumptions there. But we try to make sure that we're not only archiving these resources for future reference, but that we're also making them accessible to the public, which is important to us.

Anita Coleman: In the last decade or so, I've been very pleased to hear about the laws that are being passed. States are now legislating open access for publicly funded research. University of Arizona, University of California, and University of Illinois at Urbana-Champaign—which are where I've been—are public institutions. We get taxpayer money for the research we do as faculty. And yet, at University of Arizona, when I pointed out the imperatives and ethics of our research and our work, I just remember being told that as an untenured faculty, open access projects and language like that would get me into trouble. It angered me, the injustice. Because to me, what is the whole idea of getting tenure? Tenure is supposed to protect you. I'd already been tenured once and so, yes, I can understand as a new faculty going through promotion and tenure, again, I should be afraid. But the integrity, the ability to take the moral high ground, as a public servant, researcher, and faculty is absolutely key, too, if education is indeed enlightenment. I felt we had to strive to make our research—research we were able to do because of public funding—open.

It's been absolutely great for me to hear now that in some states, like in California where I am now, there is actually a law that requires all publicly funded research to be open access. Its been a long time coming, but it has come. State universities *have* to maintain open access repositories for faculty research. The sad part is, what I'm seeing, though, is how this is now getting subverted. I am absolutely thrilled to see that digital scholarship and scholarly communication jobs are on the rise. That is awesome. A lot of universities are trying to implement and promote institutional repositories and OA with libraries often taking the leading stewardship role. So that's very gratifying to know that what I did with DLIST was truly ahead of the times. Open access has clearly brought visibility to the profession and, dare I say, more prestige and status as well. Equally importantly, it has also grown the profession; scholarly communication is now recognized as a librarian expertise and it has brought in very different kinds of jobs to academic libraries and librarians—Copyright /Intellectual Property Librarian, Scholarly Communication Librarian, Institutional Repository Librarian, to name just a few.

The subversions that I see happening, I believe, are caused by the proliferation of institutional repositories where librarians or some other person or group of people will put the papers for you into the repository. As an aside, disciplinary repositories would have been better for scholarly communication, but librarians and library organization put their weight behind IR. Scholarly information behaviors are not changed, and it doesn't enable more use of the materials. Uncitedness, that is, how most scholarship is never read or cited, continues unabated—which is a needless waste! On the other side, librarian workloads have increased. Even in every institution that has its own IR manager, a lot of the publicly funded research doesn't get put into the open access repositories. Way too much information is being produced, and the strategies to put them into IRs fall far short of what they can be. So they stay unseen.

IR librarians require good old fashioned technical skills and cataloging. Most reference librarians in the US really don't want to do this kind of information organization work. They don't have the temperament or the skills for coding and scripting repetitive markup, metadata, and similar "grunt" tasks. So the repositories don't get populated as much as they can be. The profession is also not investigating enough into crawlers and harvesters. I believe we should be integrating those technologies. Instead, OA aggregators such as Academic.edu, ResearchGate, and Google Scholar are thriving, and even faculty seem to prefer them to their own IRs. These companies appear to be doing the crawler and harvester work. More importantly they are actively reaching out to scholars to get their works, providing use and citation statistics far more proactively and attractively than many IRs can do.

MITA WILLIAMS: There are so many different ways to look at open access, but in many ways we're still grappling with this idea that online distribution is fundamentally different from paper distribution—making copies is not a very difficult thing to do, and text is no longer scarce. I like to believe that open access reinforces the idea that the most important thing about publishing is the work that supports the text. You still need to have peer review, and you still need to have people dedicating time to create and edit works of text that have gone through the process of proper research, regardless of what platform you choose.

That being said, there are still a lot of questions about how the work of publications should be paid. Should they be paid by the author? Should they be paid by the library? Or should they be sponsored by a funding organization? I think the philosophical component that has been affected by open access is in the question that each discipline needs to now ask itself—how public should they be? Is there a public-facing side to their scholarship? I've found that the disciplines that are really interested in open access either have strong public components, such as public history or public health, or they have a strong social justice component. If you're doing research about a community, that community deserves access so that at least they can read about themselves and what's being written about them.

JIM DELROSSO: I don't know that this is a change, but there is definitely a lot of focus on the pragmatic. I see certain people within libraries talking about open access and the functional side of things and the "how does this actually work" side of it. I see a lot of librarians talking about making sure that we're not kept out of the conversation—as there are some open access advocates who don't really talk about libraries—and how vital a part we're really going to be of this. And within academic libraries, I see a lot of talk about putting our money where our mouth is and making sure that we're doing these things for open access. We're trying to publish in open access journals when we can. We want that what we put forth is good scholarly communication practice and that we're living it, too, as opposed to just telling our faculty or other authors we interact with, "Hey, this is what you should do," and then when it comes time for us to do it, saying, "Whoa, that's way too scary. I can't be negotiating with a publisher." I'm seeing more push—"No, we really need to put our money where our mouth is and live and operate in the way that we're recommending that other people do."

ANDROMEDA YELTON: I think open access is thoroughly on the side of the angels. A thing that we struggle with in libraries is the big picture. Libraries are very focused on their patrons and their community, which is great, except that it sometimes means we don't build that capacity to work together to address the really high-level issues that express our values or determine what kinds of options we have, what kind of ecosystem we're living in. I think open access is a great example of a place where there's a lot of great work being done. I wish there were more organization and consensus around that, because that's the kind of society we want to live in.

The copyright clause of the US Constitution says that Congress has the authority to establish copyright for limited terms to promote the progress of science and the useful arts. It doesn't say that the point of copyright is to make money for creators. It says the point is to promote the progress of science and the useful arts. That embodies a central tension between making sure that creators do get paid, so that they have the ability to keep creating, but also making sure that the works that they make are available to people so they can learn from them and remix them. Both of those things are how we make progress in art and in knowledge. I think today, the system is slanted very heavily toward the creators-making-money end of that bargain, because quite frankly those are the people who can afford the really good lawyers and who can buy congresspeople. And it's slanted against the consumption side, the ability to consume and remix, and thereby be inspired to create more stuff. I think libraries and open access are one of the thumbs on the scale in the direction of the other half of how copyright promotes progress. Open access is a great thing and we should have more of it.

I think the problems are not technological, to be clear. Open access is easy to do with technology. That's why people are freaked out about copying. Even since the Napster days, it's why people are freaked out. Digital technology makes copying and open access very easy. Preservation is hard, but short-term access is easy. But the big problems are not technological; they're legal and political. They're policy problems. They're contract problems. I think people come to expect open access more because they're used to being able to get so many digital things freely and instantly. But that doesn't necessarily extend to critiquing their own role in knowledge production. Faculty don't necessarily expect their papers to be open access just because the Internet has an infinite supply of cat pictures for them.

Probably the technological changes that are most interesting to me around open access lately are the ones about web archiving and preservation. It's people realizing that just because you can have an infrastructure to deliver content instantly doesn't mean that content will still be around in a decade or a century. Those problems are really hard. You look at the Internet Archive, or LOCKSS, or Perma.cc, or Documenting the Now—there's a lot of really interesting work going on in terms of how do we preserve this stuff so access to it stays open long-term.

JIM DELROSSO: From what I've seen and what I'm experiencing, both as a repository manager and as someone who is increasingly advising faculty within my institution about open access and related scholarly communication questions, one of the biggest things is the attempt to co-opt open access and its principles by the same scholarly publishers who created the conditions that necessitated the creation of the open access movement. I think they're calling themselves "legacy publishers" these days—Elsevier, Taylor & Francis, Sage, and the like—and they're creating open access or hybrid open access journals where they say, "Yeah, we're going to put this stuff out, and it's going to be made available to people." Or they're saying they have green open access policies—"Oh yes, if you sign up for this, you'll be able to put your material in our repository."

What's been very interesting about that, and the reason I use the term "co-opting," is that in many ways they haven't actually changed their underlying profit-seeking and rent-seeking policies.

For example, for hybrid journals—which refers to a journal that has some material that's not open access and some material that authors have paid more to release as open access—from a practical standpoint, there's no real prorating of subscription costs for libraries. If there's a hybrid journal out there, libraries still have to subscribe to it, but authors are also paying money for some material to be open access. So it's double-dipping. We had a rep from a publisher come to our campus a few months ago and ask us to not use the term "double-dipping" because it wasn't, and they said they *did* prorate the costs for hybrid journals. I was very interested, but then it came out that they only prorate the costs for basically single subscriptions. Anything that was part of the so-called "big deals," which publishers are frequently forcing on libraries who have limited budgets—which is all libraries, basically—none of those "big deals" were prorated. So they could say, "Oh, don't call it 'double-dipping,' because we're prorating these prices," but they're prorating the prices that almost no one pays and not the prices that just about everyone pays.

On a similar note, I've been seeing more and more author agreements that tell authors, "You get to keep copyright. So when we post this, it'll be 'copyright by the authors.'" And that's a very big change. When I initially saw this, I'm like, wow, okay that's actually a real change. But I was seeing it from the outside. When I actually started looking at some of these agreements, they no longer said you transfer copyright to the publisher. What it says is, you keep copyright. But you transfer *these* rights exclusively and in perpetuity to the publisher. And the rights that the author grants exclusively and in perpetuity to the publisher are all of the rights that are legally associated with copyright. I had to shake my head and give them some credit for that. Basically they're de facto claiming copyright, because they get all the rights that are associated with copyright through this contract that trumps copyright, but saying copyright stays with you. So they give up nothing in terms of their ability to use and control that research and that article, but they still get to say on the front of the article, "copyright held by the authors." It's good press without giving anything up.

Another thing that I've seen a number of times is authors paying a lot of money for something to be open access. And indeed if you go to the journal website, yes, anyone with an Internet connection can download that. They don't need a library subscription, and they don't need to pay a thirty dollar charge to see an article, but the author still doesn't get any control over that. I've had authors come to me and say, "Hey, I want to just put this in the repository and I know I can because it's open access." I look at the agreement that they signed and say, "It's open access, but you can't do this. The publisher still owns it, and they say that you're not allowed to do this, even though you paid several thousand dollars for open access."

That's the thing, some of these fees are thousands of dollars. There have been studies showing that the fees for the big publishers for their open access are in fact higher than the smaller open access journals that are being run independently or by organizations that are not traditional scholarly publishers. It's just more money. That same publisher rep who came in and talked to us also assured us that their APCs, the prices they charged authors for open access, were about the average for scholarly publishing. And I was like, yo, I know how averages work. I know how numbers work. You're the biggest player in an oligopoly. There's less than half a dozen of you who really control all of this, and you're the biggest one. So yes, your fees probably are around the average, because you set the average, and that's how numbers work.

JONATHAN HARWELL: One of the main differences that we're seeing in the last few years is more of an emphasis on open educational resources, instructional materials—what might be called textbooks—that are used in courses instead of expensive textbooks. We've been seeing so much exponential rise in textbook costs from year to year that sometimes we see textbooks costing $400 for one course, and maybe that textbook's online component expires in a year or two. For example, someone takes Spanish 101 now and takes 102 in a couple of years; maybe they have to get the textbook again. We're seeing more awareness on the part of faculty, as well as of course the students, but people are realizing that there are changes we need to make in that marketplace of textbooks.

What we've done locally is instituted an internal grant for open educational resources. We're basically sponsoring a faculty member every year on working open educational resources into one of their courses, whether they're creating those OERs themselves or identifying some that have already been created and adopting them for their courses. The librarians and instructional design technologists here are prepared to help them identify or create those, and the college is funding their needs toward that project. We also invest in organizations working to provide open access. We've done detailed work at Rollins on analyzing the various initiatives and selecting which ones to fund, including Knowledge Unlatched and the Lever Press. And I contribute time as a section editor for the Open Library of Humanities.

ANDREW WEISS: One thing that I think needs to be looked at more carefully is the state of copyright and how technology is impacting it. Especially as an academic librarian, I think fair use is essential for us. We need to be able to make sure that fair use remains strong and robust so that we can use a lot of material to make new material. I think one of the problems that's come out is that some content providers, in particular owners of film and streaming media, have come down hard on those who were using streaming video. It definitely confuses a lot of faculty here on what they can and can't use. I wish there were more discussion on technology and fair use, and how libraries and academics can use fair use more robustly than they have been because of fear of litigation.

JOEL NICHOLS: With copyright, when people would ask me why they couldn't copy a YouTube video onto their flash drive, I would explain file formats and we don't have the software that would help you do that, blah blah blah. And I sometimes might say, "And that file just isn't hanging out there for free use." People would come in and say, "I know you can get music, show me how to do that," and I'd say, "You have to go on these file-sharing websites that are not on the up-side of the law, and you can't really guarantee what's going on there, what risks you might open yourself up to." But I would also tell them, "Everybody does it, and lots of people do it." So I always felt like that was kind of difficult to negotiate, quite honestly.

VIVIAN ALVAREZ: A child may not want a beautiful image that was just created—an illustration, a photograph—shared with the public in its splendor of magnificent pixels. But the goal is still to share it. So we decrease the quality of the image, and then we share it with the public. We compress it from being an image that's probably 32MB to maybe something that makes it to 1MB or below. We're definitely below 1MB, because at that point, it's not very desirable for other people to get a hold of and keep it. They'll probably move on to another image.

Something like this did come up four or five years ago, when I was doing my thesis research. There was a student who took a beautiful photo and edited it in Photoshop. Very talented kiddo. She shared it on Facebook. Then she searched this photo two years later and found out that it was actually on the cover of a stranger's CD album. She contacted the person to demand that her photo be taken down, but he didn't agree with her and said the photo belonged to him. And she had actually created the photo herself—not only because the other staff saw it, but because, while her entire body was not part of the image, her hands and other body parts were there in a very abstract form. So, lesson learned was that if we really wanted to share something, other than just putting a watermark on it, we should reduce the quality of the image to something that cannot really be used out there. Therefore we can still share our ideas, but they cannot be necessarily outright stolen.

DREW GORDON: Something came up for me while Interference Archive got a poster donation from Inkworks Press. We had the actual physical posters, and, fortunately for us, they also had this digital assets management system with all the metadata for the posters in it. I did some of the work on that, and the big question that came up for me was I wanted them to send us some images from the catalog so we didn't have to take pictures of these posters ourselves. Lincoln from Inkworks Press was kind of hesitant to send anything too large. And I started thinking about it. I went to their site, and this pop-up comes up when you go to any of the posters, like, "You cannot reproduce this." Somebody worked really hard on this—these are posters from movements over forty, fifty years, really amazing artwork—and he doesn't want people just lifting it and using it for their own purposes, kind of bypassing giving credit and that kind of thing. It made me think about that aspect of not going above creators' heads and creating these super high-res images of the things that they've created, because it might be used in a way to undermine the work that they did.

But it also made me think of the ways that you could create all these high-res images of all this print media and all these zines, and anybody can access from around the world. That is a virtuous approach, but you also kind of want to entice people to come in and actually take a look at the actual objects. So there's this balance you have to strike between displaying what you have but also having people come in and see what the actual thing is.

JEN HOYER: I spent a lot of time reading about copyright and metadata, and then we had some terrific conversations at Interference Archive about that as a working group. A lot of the debate about the copyrightability of metadata falls into discussions of whether or not it is intellectual or creative work, in which case it would be copyrightable. I definitely believe that creation of metadata requires intellectual labor and is creative, but we believe this creative work should be shared and so we gave the metadata in our catalog a CC-0 / public domain license.

· · ·

BÉATRICE COLASTIN SKOKAN: As the Manuscripts Librarian at the University of Miami, I curate over four hundred collections that are part of the archives. I teach classes, develop collections, and am also engaged in special projects that are of particular interest to me because I want to document the cultural contributions of communities in South Florida that are peripheral to our corpus of material but nevertheless a presence in the community. For instance, people from the Caribbean and Latin America are discussed in various political, educational, and economic contexts, but do they have true agency over their own cultural representation? The same can be said of communities from the African diaspora in general—all these people that make meaningful contributions to our history but for some reason are not making it in our document series.

Part of my work as the outreach librarian is to go out to cultural events specifically, and try to engage with people and explain what archivists do and why this work matters. Individuals and groups will donate their papers or archives as a result of these conversations. I love to have public events as a platform for discussing the content of the archives. We're having one this Wednesday on affordable housing. That's what I do. Originally I wasn't sure what the outreach component of my job was going to be, because it wasn't well-defined; I think I was the first person to be in that position in my department.

Community engagement and documenting all these different voices through projects like oral histories has become my favorite part of my job. It can be challenging to get the paper trails that are traditionally associated with archives because the immigrant experience, for instance, is so transient, and people don't necessarily keep all this paper when they are not yet rooted in communities. Miami's economically challenging housing market only aggravates this sense of uprootedness. The lives of new immigrants and the poor can be so uncertain and focused on immediate survival. I wanted to find another way to capture their stories that I thought were meaningful, and that's what led me to oral histories.

JAYCIE VOS: The Southern Oral History Program was founded at the University of North Carolina at Chapel Hill in 1973 by Jacquelyn Dowd Hall. She's a historian who focuses on women's history and labor history, and later in her career she did a lot of really great work around the civil rights movement. She led the program for nearly forty years, and it's primarily operated by historians. She had a lot of students working with her over the years, and they were very involved with the research. The students have conducted thousands of interviews, and some even wrote the book *Like a Family* with her. The SOHP started out really trying to document stories of people who were often left out of the books about Southern history. Some of Jacquelyn's first projects included women activists throughout the South and people who worked in textile mills in North Carolina. She was really trying to get the everyday person's perspective on a lot of really big changes throughout the South, like industrialization and its later decline.

The program has grown significantly over the years. We have undergraduate interns now at the University of North Carolina who work on oral history projects. These interns focus a lot on university history right now, documenting different groups like student activists. The interns currently work with a group called the Black Pioneers who are the first generation of African American students to come through UNC. We have graduate students in different departments like History and Anthropology who run a lot of the interview projects and also help with workshops and different outreach efforts.

The SOHP works with the community in different ways, and it's changed a lot over time. Sometimes we're consulted by groups in the area who want to document their own stories. We might give workshops to community groups, or teach them about various online platforms so they can conduct and share their own oral histories. We also work with K-12 teachers in the area to try to make our interviews more accessible to their students.

For example, we had a focus group a couple of years ago where we brought in teachers from all over the state to see if they would want to use our materials, and how, and what we could do to make it easier for them and their students. Based on the feedback that we've gotten from that focus group and then a number of other meetings over the last couple of years, we built this online map of North Carolina where there are different audio clips from interviews. We curated playlists with short clips from interviews, because the teachers don't have enough time to listen to a two-hour interview and find the most interesting or meaningful segments. Right now the map has clips about desegregation in North Carolina. The clips are laid out on this map so students can say, "Oh, I've been to Charlotte," and see there are five different clips that take place in and around Charlotte. Or they can say, "I went to this high school!" and here's a clip that's from Carrboro High School. It's helping them to see where history was taking place and that it was happening all around them, in places where they've been and that they're familiar with. It's just an easier access point for them. We're going to add more clips around different themes or topics, like we're going to do one with different women leaders and activists throughout the state, and a playlist about World War II and people in North Carolina.

HANA SLEIMAN: The Palestinian Oral History Archive started on the fiftieth anniversary of the 1948 Nakba. There was a call to collect the testimonies of the first generation of Palestinians who experienced it. There were substantive efforts in Syria, Lebanon, Palestine, Amman, and other places to record interviews with the first generation. The Lebanon component of that was led by two organizations, the Arab Resource Center for Popular Arts, Al Jana, and the Nakba Archive. In both cases, they organized workshops and consultations on oral history as a medium. Most importantly, they consulted with experts in the field such as Rabab Abdulhadi and Rosemary Sayigh, who have historically done oral history work with the Palestinian communities, in order to develop the questionnaire for oral history, which was very important. The questionnaire covered the late Mandate Palestine up through the early days of Lebanon. Then each of these two organizations went on separately recording interviews. They basically went town to town, door to door. They asked around about who was above a certain age and had experienced the Nakba or pre-1948 Palestine. Each organization trained interviewers, and these people went out. Al Jana was working in the early '90s, whereas the Nakba Archive was working in the late '90s and early 2000s. Collectively, they recorded over eight hundred interviews, roughly four hundred each. Some of them are overlapping, so some person might have been interviewed in the '90s by Al Jana and again in the 2000s by Nakba Archive.

The interviews are interesting in the sense that they cover all twelve Palestinian refugee camps in Lebanon, in addition to major Palestinian cities. They made a conscious effort to focus on women's testimonies, because for the Nakba that presents a whole different experience. Whereas most men were away from their families, either imprisoned or fighting, it was the women who were walking along with the families to the camps and places of refuge. They also cover a wide geography in pre-'48 Palestine. Naturally most of the Palestinian communities in Lebanon came from northern Palestine, so from within that community, there's a very wide representation of the different cities and villages, and there was a focus on villager refugee women specifically.

These were collected and kept in the original organizations' offices and homes, because Nakba Archive doesn't have an office. Then there was a realization that tape as a medium, if not stored properly, is at the risk of being corrupted or lost, so they were for the longest time attempting to digitize the material. The Nakba Archive digitized it once, but the quality—it wasn't standards-compliant. Eventually they came to the Issam Fares Institute at the American University of Beirut, the Palestinian Camps Program, and asked if they could partner up with them to fund the digitization. At that point AUB applied to the Heinrich Boell Foundation, who gave the initial funds to digitize the collection. That took place in 2012; the material was previously digitized in different formats, and here's where the AUB Library came in. The library recommended formats for digitization that were compliant with international standards. After the digitization took place, the project was dormant for a while, until it was reactivated in 2013 by being moved to the library. The Archives & Special Collections department at AUB took over the material, and that's when we started to build the project.

This is where we started to discuss decisions, such as, do we transcribe or do we not transcribe? Transcription allows for browsing of the material much easier than having to listen a two-hour interview; researchers can just quickly skim and see if there are any useful keywords and then go listen to the interview. We decided not to transcribe, to preserve the orality of the material, because we chose not to reduce it to written form. It is oral material whose integrity needs to be preserved. So this is where the digital component came in, really. Using the Oral History Metadata Synchronizer was a way around transcription, because it allows us to segment and describe portions of the interview, thus rendering them searchable and accessible down to short segments, and thus addressing what transcription offered, which is the ability to browse and retrieve and search.

But to go back to the story of the project, these kinds of decisions and debates were taking place the first year. We built an advisory board of scholars, librarians, and oral historians who helped us through the thought process. We had the support of different Library departments—systems, IT, cataloging, research and development, etc. We ended up using amended Library of Congress subject headings. We saw the need to adapt them to the subject at hand because they were made for written material and not necessarily reflective of the micro experience of Nakba and refuge as our interviewees articulated it. So over the first year we were making these decisions, and the second year was really the building year where we developed the list of keywords and subject headings that we were going to use building an existing tool, and then cataloging and indexing began.

JAYCIE VOS: Another project at UNC that really involves the community is called New Roots. It's an oral history project, led by Dr. Hannah Gill of the Latino Migration Project, that documents Latino migration to North Carolina—migration, integration, and settlement of individuals from all over Central and South America and the Caribbean to North Carolina. We got an NEH grant for this project and built a bilingual digital archive and information system, so all the interviews are presented in both English and Spanish. The people running this project are very involved in different community groups that provide services for Latina immigrants or are cultural hubs for Latino migrants, like ESL classes. We work with migrants to document their stories but also, by making the digital archive available in both English and Spanish, we're trying to make the interviews much more accessible to the people who have been interviewed, and to their families and their communities. We're also doing a K-12 initiative with New Roots where we're making lesson plans for teachers who can integrate these interviews into the classroom, whether it's a Spanish class or a North Carolina history or politics and policy type of class.

HANA SLEIMAN: The Palestinian Oral History Archive is still being built. The material hasn't been put up online, so it hasn't been made accessible to the public. But what we have been doing is receiving digital requests. The families of the interviewees are always asking for their parents' or grandparents' interviews. This often happens when the interviewee passes away; the family then asks for a copy, which we provide. In most of these cases, family members were provided a copy back when the interview was recorded. We've had a few researcher requests who wanted to look at mental health issues with Palestinian refugee communities, or culture and identity, or the urban history of a specific village. In these cases, we give them access to the digital copy of the tapes, but it's not yet indexed or cataloged. And we go old-school—we have a list of the interviewees and the villages they came from and their age and gender, and we just give access to that medium. A few of the interviews have been used in commemorations with the anniversary of the Nakba.

BÉATRICE COLASTIN SKOKAN: My first oral history initiative was the Haitian Diaspora Oral History Project. The project was part of a grant that we received to support our larger Collaborative Archive from the African Diaspora initiative. The CAAD started because local institutions in South Florida wanted to document and provide easy access to content about the African diaspora experience and realized that researchers needed a common platform to be able to do that research. On the CAAD website you can pull information from participating institutions. All the members that are part of that group are listed, so the search results will point you to the institution that has the materials that you need. CAAD received a grant that allowed it to fund projects that supported this resource building originating from the surrounding community. I supervised the implementation of the project and coordinated the recording of the oral histories. We worked with a graduate student to conduct an initial twenty oral histories with individuals from the Haitian diaspora, primarily artists and activists. If you are looking at immigrant life, and specifically at illegal immigrants, you're going to find them in certain places. We found them within organizations where people are advocating for immigrant rights. That's why we ended up focusing on those groups, and also because there is a really expansive artistic community in Miami, and the graduate student that happened to be involved in the project was a music student. He thought it would be great to document these Haitian artists and especially musicians that just travel through Miami for cultural events or when they're headed to performances in other places. If you interview them before and after a concert, such as "Big Night in Little Haiti," you can talk to people that you would not normally be able to get in touch with. It was great!

Our Caribbean Diaspora project was made possible thanks to another grant from the Florida Division of Cultural Affairs. This second set of interviews is essentially a continuation of the Haitian Diaspora Project. I wanted to expand it beyond the Haitian community to capture the perspectives of other Caribbean communities that are living in South Florida. We looked at the Caribbean basin because there are many people from Columbia, Nicaragua, and Venezuela living in Florida in addition to the islands of Cuba, the Dominican Republic, Jamaica, and Puerto Rico; I wanted to capture stories from all these communities. In the case of the Caribbean Diaspora collection, we included leaders with difference specialties who were impactful as artists, activists, journalists, lawyers, and academics who were wrestling with the complex issues of immigration.

In the case of our Warmamas-StoryCorps oral history interviews, Patricia Sowers, one of the co-founders and director of the organization, contacted Special Collections because Warmamas was doing a project with StoryCorps for their Military Voices Initiative. StoryCorps coordinates the recordings with a local organizations such as Warmamas and deposits the interviews at the Library of Congress. StoryCorps usually partners with a local repository so that the local community has access to the full recordings regionally since the full interviews are not available online. Patricia Sowers from Warmamas asked if the University of Miami Libraries would serve as the local repository. The library agreed. The Warmamas-StoryCorps project focused on interviewing the mothers of individuals who had been deployed to Afghanistan and Iraq. In collaboration with StoryCorps and Warmamas, I coordinated two days of interviewing in the library. We had a concluding reception for interviewees and their families, and we now house the original recordings. Warmamas continues to record family members—not just mothers of people who were deployed—and they are depositing those interviews with the University of Miami Richter Library.

JAYCIE VOS: I think there is an oral history craze. A lot of it has to do with StoryCorps. Part of it is also that people use the term "oral history" very broadly, and sometimes they use it in ways that I wouldn't necessarily. But I think just having that language be sort of a buzzword helps to get the word out that oral history exists and is useful in a ton of scenarios. It's really just making people more aware—"Oh, this a thing. This is a way that I can get information."

The Oral History Program at UNC started as part of the History Department, and so we're really coming at it from a more historiography perspective. That's what we do, but I also think that it's great that people imagine it in different ways. I certainly don't think there's one right or wrong way. I think the more attention that it gets, in whatever format, the better, because people are realizing this is a great way to learn something and a great way to track a story over time. I encourage its use, even if it's not how I would define it.

. . .

BÉATRICE COLASTIN SKOKAN: The question of structural oppression and power dynamics is an interesting one. When I decided to work on a documentation project on affordable housing in collaboration with our campus office of Civic and Community Engagement, I was confronted with structural issues of income disparity and race that posed challenges to the inclusion of stories that originate from people who experience economic strife. I don't know at what point of the large story to begin. We wanted to include the stories of the Scott Carver residents who were victims of a public housing scandal in Miami. There was corruption from subsidized housing builders, and hundreds of people ended up with no homes. By working with the Office of Civic and Community Engagement, we sought to record oral histories in addition to the collection of whatever documents residents were willing to donate to create an archives.

These people—who had been in such a precarious situation, not knowing if they were going to have homes to live in—weren't carrying extensive documents with them. That's why recording became so important. These residents of subsidized housing were not part of the culture of structured information that is at the core of the university. If we wanted to include their stories, there would have to be the oral history component, because they carried the stories within them. The residents-turned-advocates-of-affordable-housing wanted those experiences to become part of historical records, but they didn't necessarily have a paper trail to illustrate the experience. Here was a group who had experienced transient spaces that required a certain detachment from the accumulation of mementos for the sake of survival.

I remember when we were trying to plan joint events with the community's history committee to document what had happened to them ten years earlier. The houses were finally built, but they wanted to memorialize neighbors and friends who had died, the many people they lost touch with, and the ones that survived and moved into the newly built homes. The residents wanted to document this experience, and they said, "Well, we don't know anything about how you do that. Can somebody teach us?" We organized an evening of workshops of the basic care of documents and photographs, and they took notes. I have never had people ask me for several copies of archival finding aids. Members of the historical committee wanted to see what we had done with similar grassroots organizations. They wanted agency over their own narrative.

I was impressed by this community of people who had in the past ten years been able to advocate for themselves, to slowly but successfully navigate the complicated map of affordable housing so they could survive. Now they wanted to embark on this new project to take care of themselves and document their own history. In the context where individuals experience housing insecurity, the oral history recordings proved to be a great tool to capture that experience. These interviews were recorded at the reunion party that the Scott Carver neighbors organized. Conversations that surfaced during the event also revealed that much visual content around the experience was housed on individual smartphones and social media. We had no way to track down all the different creators of that content, and I knew that more gaps were already part of this incomplete story.

JAYCIE VOS: For me, oral history at the Southern Oral History Program from the beginning has been a method or a form to push against some of these structures and to give people power where they haven't always been given it. For us that's certainly been in the form of gender and in race. It's such a democratic format because anyone with a recorder can conduct an interview. I think people who have not been in positions of power are really able to recognize that their stories also matter because of oral history, or that they can make them matter through oral history. That's where I see a lot of those different structures being pushed, or questioned, or really grappled with.

I've heard other people talk about cases where interviewees have been suspicious of oral history programs, where somebody might be really skeptical when the academic comes in and wants to interview them, and then—what happens? They just take that interview and then it goes out of the community and into the library. But by having everything available online, I think that also makes people feel a lot less hesitant to give their interviews, because then it's actually accessible to them and can still be part of the community. The interview is not just going into a library where you have to feel comfortable going into that space to even use it in the first place. Because that sort of barrier is broken down with the Internet, I think people are more willing to share.

Of course, other people are worried about their interviews being online, and not everyone has the Internet, so it's certainly not a perfect solution. But I do think that the accessibility we now have because of the Internet can help spread around power beyond the academy.

Carmel Curtis: The XFR Collective's mission statement is, "XFR Collective is a non-profit organization that partners with artists, activists, individuals, and groups to lower the barriers to preserving at-risk audiovisual media—especially unseen, unheard, or marginalized works—by providing low-cost digitization services and fostering a community of support for archiving and access through education, research, and cultural engagement." That's the text on our website, and that pretty much does capture what we do. But we are a group of volunteers. Most of us have a background in audiovisual archiving, but not only that. There are filmmakers. There are librarians. We are a group of volunteers who do work around this centralized mission—to digitize the analog media of those from marginalized communities, those whose works might not necessarily be acquired by an archive or a repository but whose voices are nonetheless obviously important. Our work is about shifting priorities and moving those who might be on the margin to the center.

For the most part, everything that we digitize we make public on the Internet Archive, which is a pretty important part of our model. The reasoning behind this is twofold. One, we are not a repository; we don't have the infrastructure to store and maintain the digital files of works we transfer. And two, we don't want the work we transfer to just go back into the closet or onto the shelf—we want this media to be seen. Also, we have been increasing the number of educational and cultural engagement activities that we do. We've been teaching a number of workshops around audiovisual archiving, not only of analog media. We've been working with people who are making media now and looking for some guidance, or to begin a conversation with someone else around managing digital media. This past year we've also done a number of free community screenings where we'll show a number of works that we've digitized in the past.

XFR Collective started as an exhibit at the New Museum in New York City in 2013 called XFR STN. It was started by an amazing group of people from the New Museum and a group called Collaborative Projects Inc., Colab, as well as a member, Alan Moore, of the Monday/Wednesday/Friday Video Club, and some audiovisual archivists also. The project was proposed to the New Museum to have this station where artists, primarily, could sign up for appointments to have their old media digitized, and the public could come and watch this process. It was this amazing exhibition where a lot of hard work was done and then also, as part of the exhibition, you could go and watch the process of digitizing audiovisual materials. Once this exhibit closed, a couple of people who were involved in that, including Andrea Callard, who's still a member—she's a filmmaker based out of New York—and a few other XFR STN members—Julia Kim, Kristin MacDonough, Rebecca Fraimow—decided to keep the XFR STN going. So they turned XFR STN into XFR Collective. It's now a 501(c)(3) and has morphed into this group that is what we are now.

I think that there is something really radical and amazing about XFR Collective in that we are volunteers. We do this for no money. But there's also something extremely reproducible about XFR Collective. We are a group of people who meet weekly and decide on the projects that we're going to work on collaboratively. Doing this work to digitize analog media as well as to teach or provide people with resources on how to manage their own personal digital collections of media is really important and also, again, really reproducible, and something that there's a huge need for. There are some groups that are have similar community-based models, such as MIPoPS (Moving Image Preservation of Puget Sound) out of Washington state, MARMIA (Mid-Atlantic Regional Moving Image Archive), and CAW (Community Archiving Workshop). Currently XFR Collective exists primarily in New York. However, we do have extended members who are around the world—in D.C., in Chicago, in Chile.

JARRETT DRAKE: I've been involved in a community-based archive that is addressing police violence in Cleveland, Ohio. I think of that archive sort of as a practical output of the research that I did on police records in New Orleans. It just so happened that, I think, three days before my article[1] was published, Eric Garner was killed in New York, and then three weeks later, Mike Brown was killed in Ferguson. So when the article was published, it got immediately relevant. Like, immediately. And it's remained immediately relevant.

The project in Cleveland really came out of a lot of different things, but for me personally, my interest was in the ways that states enact violence on citizens, especially on black citizens, and trying to uncover what, if any, role the archive can play in rectifying or remedying or repairing some of that harm that the state is causing. We, the professionally trained archivists—whatever that means, "information professionals"—reached out to people in Cleveland because of the annual meeting of the Society of American Archivists in 2015 that was scheduled to take place there. A few of us who were planning to attend the annual meeting said that we wanted to do exactly what I just said, to put our skills, our knowledge as archivists, to service as it pertains to police violence, especially police violence that impacts black and brown communities and poor communities. We got together over the Internet, mostly as strangers, and set out some ideas. We reached out through a local archivist to people in Cleveland. We first explained to them what archivists do—because no one knows what archivists do—and that we had recently learned of one particularly flagrant case in Cleveland. We said that we were not going to come to this city where police are literally killing black

---

1 Jarrett Drake, "Insurgent Citizens: The Manufacture of Police Records in Post-Katrina New Orleans and Its Implications for Human Rights," *Archival Science* 14 (2014): 365–380, doi: 10.1007/s10502-014-9224-2.

people in the streets with impunity. We weren't going to come here and ignore that and act like we're indifferent. The lives of those people who were killed—those lives matter, the lives of their family members matter. So we reached out to them, and they said, okay, we do have some different tasks that we could use an archivist skill set for.

There are community members from Cleveland who are still involved in this. There are professionally trained information professionals, librarians and archivists, involved in this still, and it's a project that a lot of people have heard about. We're trying to contain and develop the archive. Unfortunately, violence from the state doesn't appear to be going anywhere, but hopefully the archive can be a source of restoration, of reparation, of reconciliation as we hope for a better day tomorrow.

CELESTE Â-RE: Last year I attended the Digital Blackness conference and met people who worked on a police brutality digital archive. I want to get more involved with digital community archiving projects. Before I got into the PhD program, I had ideas about hosting a site for culture workers, activist librarians, and archivists to write or send photos and podcasts. A space for folks to brainstorm ideas and collaborate on digital community archiving projects. Sites like *A People's Archive of Police Violence* in Cleveland, Documenting Ferguson, Baltimore Uprising, and #NoDAPL Archive document what corporate media doesn't cover. I'd like my relationship with Allied Media Projects to continue to evolve, it's a wonderful organization and space for doing that kind of work.

JARRETT DRAKE: We did basically everything regarding the Cleveland project on the Internet, on Twitter. When I sent out a tweet saying, "Hey, we should do something in Cleveland, since we're going there for this very white conference," a lot of people were like, "Yeah, I want to be involved in this." That project had, honestly, probably close to seventy-five volunteers. I haven't even met over half of them, wouldn't know them if I walked past them on the street. Either they helped set up the technology of the archive, they recorded some stories in Cleveland, they transcribed some stories that we recorded in Cleveland—all of these different things people did, and there were at least twice as many people who wanted to help out but there was nothing else for them to do. So I was really, really refreshed by how many people wanted to help out. We raised funds for this archive; that came from the archivist community. We raised our goal of $1000 in like five hours, on the Internet, on Twitter. That's the power that I think doing the project has had, to bring together a lot of different people.

But it's unclear to me, amongst the sea of archivists, whether we are a large body of water or small bodies. I think it goes back and forth. Some people tend to say maybe it's generational. I think that's too basic of an explanation. Number one, I think that's ageist. It's ageist to say that, oh, because people are older, they'll be less likely to be interested in something like this or in these kinds of ideas. It also falsely assumes that people who are closer in age to me would necessarily be in support of this, and we've just seen this not to be the case.

STACIE WILLIAMS: Documenting the Now was something really brought about by technology. I love using social media. Twitter is my favorite. An archivist I respect very much, Jarrett Drake, started talking on Twitter about the possibility of pulling something together like this. He generated quite a bit of interest from some other archivists like myself who understand that the histories that get told is very much like the newspaper. Our collecting policies and the manner in which we write finding aids, those things all sort of—I guess *conspire* is a good word. They conspire to leave other people's stories untold, leave other people's histories untold. I think that there's a lot of us who understand that, and this particular story seemed like a really important one to tell.

And from my standpoint, I felt even more strongly about it because I know what I know about journalism and how those media narratives are shaped. Every single time a black person had been killed by the police, there was a rush by media to sort of paint this black person as being bad or being evil or really just being imperfect as the justification for the shooting. Somebody's going to write, "Well, Mike Brown was no angel," and you would read that and think, "Well, yeah, this guy maybe stole some cigarettes from the store, so he totally deserved to get shot." I mean, it's a really dangerous and irresponsible and reductive line of thinking. But the media perpetrates that by going with that as the template. In their rush to understand what's happening, they will look for any little thing to possibly say, "Here's the justification. We're letting you make up your mind, but we're saying this person wasn't perfect."

So you have that, and I understood that very much. But around the time that this also started getting a lot of attention nationally, I had just had my first son—I have two boys—so I think I also was taking this idea of police violence really, really personally and seriously, just thinking about my children. So I was interested in the project from that standpoint. It's generally the part that does not get talked about. I think many of the people who have experienced police violence or police harassment feel like nobody even wants to hear their stories. They feel like nobody will believe their stories. They've been given the message that their experiences aren't important and that justice will never come of it. So I think this project was really just about allowing people to tell their stories and allowing them to feel like, hey, my experiences are important. The things that I've experienced are important.

CARMEL CURTIS: The people whose works we've transferred and the groups with whom we've done workshops have been really varied. XFR Collective did an installation at the MIX Queer Experimental Film Festival in 2015. We set up a small station where we provided digitization services free for MIX attendees who signed up for appointments to transfer miniDVs and VHS tapes. The things that we transferred through this were amazing. They were people's home movies and experimental films, but all from a queer history. Because we were in this queer community space, the people who were attending this were all queer community members, and the works that we were able to transfer shared that history. We did a workshop with the Asian American Oral History Collective. We worked with them to listen to their projects and lay some foundation around basic principles for digital preservation such as metadata and file naming conventions and folder structures and storage. Then we encouraged them to brainstorm how these foundational principles can be applied to each of their unique individual projects.

We did another workshop with the Oral History Summer School, where we're working with them to recover and restore and create a plan moving forward for their hard drives. They had a number of hard drives where they store their oral histories, and they'd been actually doing all the things—they had beautiful file naming conventions and had been backing things up and migrating the files from hard drive to hard drive over the years. But they were concerned about creating a master drive with the most authentic version of all of their works. So we worked with them to recover some of the old hard drives, and we're creating a plan for moving forward.

Some of the other works that we've digitized have been community television programs from New York from the '80s. They've been footage from protests of Amadou Diallo's shooting that came from WITNESS. We worked with Visual AIDS and transferred a number of tapes from parades and protests and meetings. And so many other things that I'm not thinking of right now.

* * *

BÉATRICE COLASTIN SKOKAN: Our oral history recordings are digital records curated ultimately by the library's digital department. The recordings are available to the public from the library's website. Transcriptions are so costly that we are not able to provide them as an alternative access point to the content. Digital preservation is crucial to long term access. Each interviewee receives a copy of their interview, but the originals reside on the server and long term preservation is planned through the library's participation in the Academic Preservation Trust. The oral histories have been identified as needing that additional care and preservation because of their unique format.

JAYCIE VOS: One of the most useful pieces of technology that I use is CONTENTdm. That's the content management system that's put out by OCLC, and it's where I keep all the digital oral history objects and metadata records for every oral history in our collection. It helps me manage the local controlled vocabularies that we use. The CONTENTdm database is the main online access portal to our oral histories. We have a couple different ones, but the entire collection is in CONTENTdm, whereas we use other platforms like Omeka for special projects that highlight a smaller selection of the collection. CONTENTdm is not without its flaws, but it serves an important purpose for the Southern Oral History Program, and it's what I use pretty much every single day.

HANA SLEIMAN: The most useful technology I've used in my work for digital collections, for sure, is the Oral History Metadata Synchronizer. The software is developed by the University of Kentucky's Nunn Center for Oral History. It's a free online tool that allows archives to catalog oral history interviews in Dublin CORE-compatible metadata that's developed specifically for oral histories, and then it allows us to segment the interview into time sections and tag every section. In addition to the overall archiving of the interview, we create an index for the interview segments, which could be a few minutes or a half-hour long. Segments could give it a title, subject heading, keywords, GPS coordinates. We don't choose all of it, but that all is available. It also allows us to use authority lists for keywords and subject headings. A feature we don't use but I guess is useful for English material is that when you upload the transcript, you can sync the audio with the transcript. It autosyncs for English material. That feature isn't available for Arabic in terms of the voice recognition portion. But it's definitely been transformative in the way that we organize these oral histories.

JAYCIE VOS: I wish people talked more about how to do video oral history well. People talk about it, but I think there's a small number of people leading the discussion, and I wish that more people were figuring out how to do it. Those people have done amazing work, but it's hard to imagine how to do video oral history really well at a small institution. Oral history programs that are in big institutions with a lot of support, both financially and where people have expertise, can of course do great video oral history. But how do people who are doing their own community projects or maybe working at a really small institution and don't have the support—how do they do that well? The storage piece alone requires so many resources. I want to see more small-scale people really tackling that and doing a good job and serving as models. I think a lot of bigger institutions are serving as models, but that model can't be duplicated everywhere.

CARMEL CURTIS: Audiovisual materials in audiovisual archives, or archives that have audiovisual materials have, in my experience, a set of unique issues that revolve around both the preservation of these materials as well as providing access to these materials. With audiovisual files, because of their sheer size, the management of these materials becomes complicated in a way that's different than a text file, for example. From everything to doing quality control, QC, on an audiovisual file, to storing the audiovisual file, to sharing the audiovisual file—because of the size of it, there's different concerns or things that have to be considered to treat it properly or to figure out where the problem is, if there's a problem. It's one thing for an institution to be able to manage audiovisual materials that are quite large, but then you think about individuals who have personal collections, whether that's someone taking videos on their phone or whether that's an artist who has footage that's used for a production, or whether that's a student experimenting, or whatever the reason that one records digital video is. The prospect of caring for those audiovisual materials as an individual can seem really overwhelming, again, in no small part because of the large size of these files.

CELESTE Â-RE: Every audio format is housed in the collections at the federal research library where I work—cylinders, wire recordings, 78s, 45s. I'm currently cataloging cassettes and CDs. The division grapples with RDA and BibFrame standards for audio recordings because it's not a neat fit for the various formats and works in the holdings. We use an assembly line approach to processing at my job. SOP, standard operating procedure rules. We follow the workflow like a script.

There's so much audio material that needs to be processed. Collections in attics, basements, closets—and now computers, tablets, and mobile devices. How do we determine what's significant? What formats, what genres? It's all personal and political to me. Some people think about European classical music or jazz, America's classical music—"we've got to collect, catalog, and archive it all." What about mix tapes? They should be archived as well, but then that gets to be difficult in terms of copyright. If you're mashing something up, Creative Commons works. We're still trying to figure it out. Pop Up Archive makes audio archiving more accessible. I haven't used it, but I hear good things about it. For the collections that I work with, researchers get permission to use esoteric audio for soundtracks in documentary films or theatrical productions and archived interviews as secondary sources for books they're writing, or they access our database for sources to include in discographies.

. . .

CARMEL CURTIS: For my thesis in New York University's Moving Image Archiving and Preservation graduate program, I researched what access to audiovisual materials has looked like historically and currently to people who are incarcerated in the United States. I looked at the history of both prison libraries as well as prison education and recreational programs, doing primary research to look at any evidence of movies that were shown in prisons.

Actually Sing Sing, in New York, showed a ton of movies in the '30s. They did these screenings because there were so many people incarcerated in Sing Sing, and it was not built for as many people as were there. Disease was spreading very quickly, and there weren't enough guards to monitor the extreme number of people who were crammed into the space. So prison officials were like, "Oh, we can put them into the chapel, project a movie, and air will be able to circulate better, and fewer guards will be able to watch more people." Sing Sing showed a lot of films, and a lot of film distribution companies would sometimes send their films to Sing Sing before they premiered to get feedback, because it was a controlled audience.

Anyway, I also sent surveys out to people who are currently and formerly incarcerated, to people who currently and have in the recent past worked in prison libraries, and people who are currently and have in the recent past worked in some kind of prison educational or recreational program. I asked a series of questions about what their audiovisual collections looked like, if they were librarians, or what their consumption of A/V materials was, if they were someone who was or is incarcerated. Then I asked specifically of the librarians what, in their opinion, are obstacles. Of course, no surprise, it was primarily funding and space that were the biggest obstacles to being able to maintain audiovisual collections.

But the vast majority of the close to fifty people who participated in the survey—it seemed to me from this extremely preliminary research that there is so much potential for archives to be able to provide access to their audiovisual collections to people who are incarcerated. A/V archivists often have these collections and are looking for wider audiences. How many millions of people are incarcerated in the United States? Being able to connect archival collections to prisons—I think there's so much potential to increase access and for people to engage in these archival collections in ways that are not happening right now. At least, you know, until we can abolish all prisons.

JAYCIE VOS: Through our podcast, the SOHP aims to teach others in the field about oral history methodology, but it also highlights different interviews from our collection, both current projects that we're working on but also going deeper in to the archives. One of my colleagues, Seth Kotch, at UNC likes to say, "The dirty little secret about oral history is no one actually listens to the interviews." I think we've really tried to make that not true in the past few years by putting an emphasis on the audio, doing things like the podcasts, and having these different clip playlists where the audio is much more accessible. This way we're going into the collection and saying, "Here's this amazing interview from the '80s about some sort of university history or labor movement in the South, and it's still relevant and still really interesting to people today, but you might not have listened to it because it's so deep in the archives." So we'll bring it up to the surface. We'll put it in a podcast and connect it to what we're doing now, or to a current event that's happening in North Carolina or on a national scale. That's the bigger goal, to show people that this really matters, and history didn't just happen in a little box isolated from everything else. These things are all connected, and it still has a lot of relevance today, and you can still learn from it. So the podcast is a way of putting that at the forefront of what we do.

I've been really happy with it so far. It's available in iTunes and on SoundCloud, and we always try to promote it on social media. We've gotten a lot of really good responses from people at the Oral History Association and other people that we know, through various professional organizations. But also just around our campus, I think a lot of different students like to listen to it.

BÉATRICE COLASTIN SKOKAN: A number of our faculty and students have interest in the Caribbean and Latin America and regularly visit Special Collections for classes. Our oral history recordings are additional resource that students can use. The oral history interviews also serve as models for students. For instance, students that are part of the University of Miami Libraries undergraduate research scholars program have models to emulate for future projects. A number of classes or research groups have included people who are interested in oral histories, and through these projects, the library has developed guidelines and protocols for conducting oral histories.

Why are the oral histories so interesting to the general population? I'm not sure. There must be something about multimedia that captures people's attention. It's a resource that they understand and can point to. The oral history format is also a source of affirmation since the University is interested in other perspectives that stand outside the scholarly framework. Participants are usually eager to share the experience with their family, friends, colleagues, and their larger virtual community.

In collaboration with the Richter Library's Communications team I coordinated a closing event for the Caribbean Diaspora Oral History Project. The Communications team suggested a Facebook Live component. We wanted a format that was more dynamic than the video recording of the event and decided to incorporate Facebook Live. The library's communications team interviewed guests that were at the event, asking them why this was a significant project. This added an interactive component to the month-long social media campaign that they ran for Caribbean Heritage Month, which coincided with the completion of our project. The social media campaign included scheduled postings on Instagram, Twitter, and Facebook featuring each of the interviewees with a significant quote. It was so successful. I don't know ultimately what these numbers mean, but there were around five hundred views on average. Our social media activity just expanded. One labor rights activist interviewee had two thousand views. I feel like the format itself helped to enhance outreach work about the collections and the type of current and relevant topics we were trying to document. The multimedia format enhanced our ability for community engagement.

JAYCIE VOS: We've used podcasts in a couple of different ways. My colleague Rachel Seidman has really spearheaded our podcasting efforts. Before the SOHP realized that we wanted to make our own podcast, we started out by having students make audio documentaries, using that format as a pedagogical tool. We worked with students in a couple of different classes who would be either doing oral history interviews or a lot of research that drew heavily on oral history interviews. So there was this great audio content that they were either working closely with or creating themselves. Instead of having them write big term papers, they would make an audio doc or a podcast as a group. They were working with each other and using their brains in different ways, because they were processing the information differently since they were integrating so much of the actual audio into their work. The students would basically talk about whatever their big research questions were, and then they would integrate actual audio into the podcast and explain, "This really meaningful thing happened, and you can hear it right here on this interview." In doing so, they're also discussing a lot of the process.

It was cool because instead of just writing a paper, the podcast format allowed them to break it down and show some of their ah-ha moments. By having the audio available, you can present that in a much more clear way. They were doing that for a while, and we started to realize, these are really good. They're really engaging, and it's cool to hear more about the process instead of just reading a final paper. It was a lot more dynamic. We were putting the podcasts on SoundCloud and then sharing them on social media and on our website, and people seemed to be really interested in them.

I think after we realized how successful they were as pedagogical tools for our students, we wanted to take the reins and do it ourselves. It was both because it seemed like it would be really fun to do, and I think we wanted to grapple with some more complicated and in-depth problems or questions that the students didn't always have enough time or depth of knowledge to get to. So we decided to put out our own podcast, and I think we use it both as a way to explore research questions and to teach others in the field about oral history methodology. We often have a "tip jar" section of the podcast where we'll ask, there's some unique problem to oral history, how do you deal with it? We had a funny one recently that was, what do you do when there are pets? During the interview somebody has a cat or a dog in the room, and what happens when the animals become really distracting? Maybe the cat will be knocking over the recorder or something. So we'll talk about things like that in the podcast. That was one of our summer episodes, so it was a little more light-hearted.

CARMEL CURTIS: The potential for use of audiovisual materials is the same as any other kind of digital file. It can be of course used for research, entertainment, etc. For me personally, I'm in this because of an extreme connection that I feel specifically to the power of moving images. When I think about audiovisual archives, or audiovisual materials not only in an institutional archive but also in someone's personal collections, and making those accessible, I think it opens up so many possibilities not only for sharing information or histories about the creators of these materials but sharing narratives or creative processes or documentation with a wider audience. There's a greater potential to build or find a connection to something if we have a wider pool of moving image examples to look at. There's greater potential for social change if we have a greater pool of examples of previous fights for justice.

. . .

JIM DELROSSO: One of the repositories that I manage, DigitalCommons@ILR, which serves the ILR School at Cornell University, has a broad range of material on there. We have over 70 percent of the faculty from ILR represented in DC@ILR. But actually, most of our material is not published by the faculty, or even from within the centers and institutes at the ILR School. We've gone out and aggressively pursued third-party material that is of interest to the scholarly communities that the ILR School serves. We have thousands of federal documents, Congressional Research Service reports, materials from the Bureau of Labor Statistics and other federal agencies, and things from a couple of state agencies like the New York State Public Employment Relations Board that are of interest to our community and that we go out and get. Within New York State, that's through partnerships with the organizations, because New York State material is copyrighted. With the federal government, almost all the material put out by any federal agency is not held under copyright. So we can just go get that, and we do that because access to government material online is ephemeral. You have an administration change and a whole lot of stuff can go away, as we have seen.

Our Key Workplace Documents collection, which collects CRS and similar reports, has a thousand items in there. We also have around ten thousand collective bargaining agreements in DC@ILR. Most of those are from the New York State Public Employment Relations Board. A smaller section is from the Bureau of Labor Statistics, Department of Labor, and our archival collections, the Kheel Center archives. We digitize a lot of material for them. The New York State Public Employment Relations Board set-up is very interesting, because we're actually the official digital storehouse for New York State PERB contracts. If you go to the New York State PERB site where they have their contracts listed and click on any of those links, you come to our repository. We are the folks who put that material up, and, I can say because of a years-long research process that Aliqae Geraci and I worked on[2], that's actually a really rare set-up. The collection we provide of public sector CBAs in New York State is almost unique in its completeness and thoroughness and the amount of public access that we provide. So DC@ILR is a really interesting case.

We see worldwide use. Several years ago I actually ran a voluntary user survey that I put up on the site and made accessible from a couple of locations. I let people answer as much as they wanted to answer. I started with kind of basic "why are you using it" questions, and then if they wanted to they could provide more information. I left it up on the site for a year and got over two hundred responses. Again, all of it was voluntary, so I was really happy to get as many responses as I did. One of the most interesting questions was occupation—"What do you do for a living?" Knowing the ILR community, I let people check multiple boxes, because I know a ton of people who are extension faculty and also lawyers and occasionally arbitrators and occasionally union reps. We saw some really interesting things. We did see that core of, "I'm a faculty member," "I'm a graduate student," "I'm an undergraduate student," the users that academic institutional repositories expect. But then we saw "plumbers," "teachers," "union reps," "HR professionals"—workers, in a lot of cases, who were just coming in and looking for contracts, looking for workplace information, looking for something. The most common answer for why they were there was they had a question that they were researching and thought we had the answer. And frequently we did.

There was this really nice half-parabola when I graphed the answers to, "Do you come here daily, weekly, monthly, or yearly or less?" There was this glorious curve—I'm making a gesture with my hand that you cannot see—from the vast majority of people saying that they come yearly or less. We did have a core group of people saying they were there every day, which was amazing because I don't think *I'm* there every day. But there were people who were like, "I come here yearly or less. I had one question, and this was what was answered." Again, because this was self-selecting, these were the people who took the time to fill out the survey. I imagine that the

---

2   Aliqae Geraci and Jim DelRosso, "To Collect and Preserve: The State of State-Level CBA Collections in the U.S.," *Labor Studies Journal* (2017), doi: 10.1177/0160449X17703485.

slope of that curve would be even steeper in reality, to account for all the people who came for one thing and didn't bother answering the survey questions.

We're coming up on about four years since we closed that survey, and I would really like to run it again, or something similar, to see if I could do some comparisons. It was amazing, just seeing that there were people who were not linked to libraries, who were not linked to academia, who just were on the Internet and researching something about their working conditions, and they found us and found us useful. That was really powerful to me.

ANDREW WEISS: I'm finding that these days there are these new systems coming out called current research information systems, or CRIS systems, that help to aggregate a lot of the information related to your institution. I find these are becoming really very interesting and helpful. Right now we're sort of a guinea pig with this company called 1Science. They have a product called oaFoldr, which is very similar to other types of platforms like Symplectic Elements in that it's aggregating all of this information related to CSUN and CSUN faculty publications and gathering it into one bucket, so to speak, so we can then pick and choose what we would want to have pushed into our repository. I'm finding that kind of tool is a godsend for us because what we've done in the past is just look at a faculty member's CV and then try to find that citation online to get a version of that somewhere online, and then to put that into the repository. This is automating that workflow. So that's very promising.

Related, then, is the issue of linked data and being able to have unique identifiers for all kinds of faculty publications, as well as datasets, as well as unique identifiers for faculty members specifically. We're looking into using ORCID ID numbers and adding that to our metadata for the institutional repository, to make a gathering of accurate information easier for us.

JIM DELROSSO: I consider most search engine optimization to be rainmaking. You get people to say, "Oh, you do this, and your numbers will go up." If your numbers go up, they say, "Hey, I made it rain!" And if your numbers don't go up, they say, "Well, you need to pay us a little more. We need to do a further consultation." I say this because Google does not make its algorithms public, and they're constantly updating them, and so to have someone say, "We can stay on top of this," it's a little surprising to me. I do think there are some places out there that have an evergreen take on search engine optimization where they just focus on, "Look, you just need to be describing this well, and setting up solid linkages among your material." I think there is some legitimate SEO that focuses basically on accurate description, and public-facing description, and setting up the right connections among the material you have, and making sure that people know about your stuff.

And I make that list very specifically because libraries have been doing that with our material for a long time. We don't do specific SEO beyond making sure that we have solid descriptive metadata for everything that we have in our repository, and making sure that as much of that descriptive metadata is public-facing. There's a really interesting discussion that I had last year because one of the founders of Google Scholar was saying that repositories shouldn't use cover pages because they're just identical and don't have the right date; they don't have a publication date, they have a generation date on it, and they don't have descriptive metadata and that throws off search engines. And I thought, that's a really good point, but the cover pages we use don't do that. Our cover pages pull descriptive metadata like the publication date and put that out front, so it's actually very helpful. But in terms of SEO, I may be somewhat old-fashioned, but if we're putting the right metadata up there—and libraries can be pretty darn good at metadata—that seems to be getting people to find our stuff.

ANDREW WEISS: To be honest, I think our users don't really care where our things are, where we keep our digital collections, or where we keep our faculty open access publications, or even where the databases are. They don't really care where that is; they're looking for a particular thing, and all they want to know is where it is. They just want to get it. So that's been one major source of conversation between me and other digital librarians here at CSUN—how do we eliminate the appearance of the silo? And how do we make the finding of the information a lot more streamlined? I think users appreciate that way more than they would appreciate a brand new sleek-looking repository. I don't think they really care about the repository itself; they just care about what's in it and how to get it as smoothly as possible. Something like a link resolver or any kind of search engine that's searching across all of these various different types of containers would be most useful to them. As long as it's easy to use, that's what the users care about most, I think.

BESS SADLER: Hydra came out of the repository software side of things. In addition to a library's collection or inventory of physical collections, many libraries have digital repositories. The digital repository that we were running at the University of Virginia at the time was called Fedora. Fedora itself was a pretty decent piece of software—open source—but it was very difficult to use. It was an inventory control system. It was pretty good at assigning unique identifiers and ensuring that what you put into the system was going to be the same thing you got out of it. But our ability to really present the content of our digital library to users in a compelling way wasn't there yet. And there were some people who thought that the cost of every institution developing their own interface for Fedora from scratch—which is what was happening at the time—just wasn't scalable, and that what we really needed was a collaborative open source project around it. Some folks from Stanford and some from UVA and some from the University of Hull decided that that was what they wanted to do. They didn't know how they were going to do it yet.

The way I got involved in the Hydra project—at that point, it was just an idea that they were going to do this, and they asked me to come demo Blacklight. I did, and that was kind of the first piece of software that the Hydra project adopted. There was something called active_fedora, which was a library for interfacing with Fedora, and Blacklight, the discovery system for the stuff that was in your Fedora repository. That was the core of what became the Hydra project.

At this point, the Hydra project is what we call a software ecosystem. The idea is that it's not a single piece of software that you can install out of the box; it's a bunch of software components that you can put together to build the repository solution that's right for your institution. Also, what we often say about Hydra is that it's more of a community than it is a single piece of software. Really the most important thing about the Hydra project is that you have a group of people who are committed to solving a problem together, and they've agreed on a methodology for doing it. *That's* the crucial bit. We happen to be doing it with this set of software right now, but in ten years, the software's going to change. Technology moves on. The important part is, do we have the culture and traditions and ability to work together to solve whatever new problem is going to come up?

Michael Gorman: I think that the Google Books project was a massive misapplication of resources. If they had taken that money, or even a fraction of that money, and used it to digitize and make available unique resources—archives, special collections of all kinds, things that are extremely rare or only as one copy in one place—the world would be a far happier place. They started off with the idea that they were going to make every book available to everybody, when in fact almost all books were available to anybody anyway through interlibrary loan. It was an answer in search of a problem, when access to unique items is a real problem. There were side benefits, like textual analysis and that kind of thing, which is of interest to a few scholars and probably very useful to them, but the fact is that the clear majority of scholarly resources have very low potential of actual readership. I have always regarded the rationale for the existence of huge libraries like that of the University of Illinois as to collect, preserve, and make accessible the kind of things that very few people want, and to make them available through interlibrary loan. It is a fantasy to think that vast digitized collections of text are going to create a readership and a scholarly interest where one did not exist before.

The other thing I'm very concerned about is that Google is a gigantic, ruthless, and amoral advertising company posing as some kind of hippie commune, doing no evil and so forth. Google has a business dynamic that causes them to do things to make money and for no other reason. Nothing is eternal. The idea that this gigantic database is going to be out there forever, freely accessible to everybody, is, in my view, a myth. I would lay better odds on materials being available over the centuries kept in large libraries than I would in them being digitized and kept in a commercial entity's database.

Andrew Weiss: The main area that I'm studying right now is what my research partner Ryan James and I are calling "massive digital libraries." We're looking at digital libraries such as Google Books, HathiTrust, Internet Archive, and now the Digital Public Library of America. In Europe there's Europeana, and in France they have Gallica. Of course here in California, we have the California Digital Library. There's the Texas Digital Library. There's also the National Digital Library of Theses and Dissertations, an aggregation of apparently several million ETDs. The typical digital library these days, or the local digital collection, is still at a manageable scale—a few thousand to maybe tens of thousands of items. But something like Google Books has—they claim—thirty million books, though there's no way to verify that. That concerns me. HathiTrust is better. I believe they have about fourteen million titles in their collection, and it seems like it's verifiable. So that's a good thing. They approach it very much as a library, whereas Google seems to approach it just as a way to digitize something.

The author Siva Vaidhyanathan talks about the "googlization of libraries." I think that's very much a concern. I know that as systems get bigger and bigger, you need artificial intelligence or some kind of program to parse what you have. I think sometimes being able to get at the veracity of what's in the collection, or what's truly there, can be problematic if it's beyond your abilities to really examine it. That's been an issue with Google Books in particular. The other ones—Internet Archive, HathiTrust, Digital Public Library of America—may have looked at Google and seen all the problems with it, and I think they've done a good job of trying to ameliorate some of those issues, to amend some of the problems that exist with Google.

But then when you look at the actual content—the issue of mass digitization and mass scanning of millions of volumes—you get to issues of quality control. Sometimes the digital version is worse than the print version. And this is something that my research has shown. I looked at a tiny sample of Japanese language books and found just horrible scanning problems. In almost all of the ones I sampled, I found a problem with scanning. Either the scanning itself was poorly done and it was blurry, or pages were ripped or folded over and you couldn't see the whole item. There was bleed-through because the paper itself is not really meant to be scanned with light, and you see the other side of the page. The page itself is so thin; it's a different type of paper. Japanese books, for example, at least in the old style, are bound with very different types of materials, which made it harder for them to scan. They just didn't take that into account. Whole books were scanned upside down, pages were upside down. Then also when we looked at the metadata records for a lot of these books, there were errors.

So that's concerning. If people are talking about replacing the library with something like that, then I think there's a problem.

What we have already with our digital libraries as done by librarians and libraries tend to be a little more better-produced, whereas I think Google is just taking the approach of "let's scan everything, and we're not going to worry about issues of quality-control. We're not going to worry about issues of metadata." In fact when we tried to talk to Google about the problems, they were interested in our data set, but they weren't really interested in talking about what we were doing, or explaining where the problems are coming from. That kind of opaqueness and lack of transparency is also a problem.

Currently I'm getting into doing some research on big data, and I see massive digital libraries really as contributing to that whole movement of big data and the concept that everything is becoming datalized—the datalization of culture, so everything can be digitized and put into some sort of quantifiable piece of data. I think the assumptions about that are perhaps faulty. Maybe not everything can be sussed out through data. Maybe it's not only about computation, which is what a lot of people in computer science seem to be advocating, that computation is the way of the future and sciences that can't go through that process of computation in order to get at results will fall by the wayside, compared to other types of sciences. I think there are a lot of issues at stake when you have a mass aggregation of data and you're not quite sure whether there's accuracy in that data.

MICHAEL GORMAN: I am not at all against digitization. What I am in favor of is widespread digitization of unique materials, because I think that aids in preservation, particularly if it's done by non-profit concerns to benefit scholars indefinitely. Another thing that has always bothered me is the question of digital government documents. The move is from paper materials housed in depositories and made available by law to anybody—remember, we have paid for and own those government documents—to documents being held in huge government-controlled databases. I am very concerned about the government's ability to manipulate government information that is only available in digital form. We have already seen evidence of that in web pages being taken down. I just simply do not trust any government, especially not the current regime, to preserve all government information as it is and keep it freely available to the people who have already paid for it. Digitization is not inherently good or bad. It is cost-effective and highly beneficial when it is done to make unique materials readily available on a non-commercial basis.

Andrew Weiss: HathiTrust, the Digital Public Library of America, Internet Archive—I think they've done fantastic work. They've been really good at trying to maintain a lot of the traditions that grew up from the print-based library world and translating that into the digital world. Nowadays when you do a search on the Internet, you end up with very random things, and you can kind of lose touch with the context. And I think context in data is essential. You can't have useful data without a context. HathiTrust and the other ones I just mentioned have done a good job of maintaining that with pretty robust metadata. I know that they have partnerships with libraries and other library institutions, universities across the country. They do a really good job of partnering.

HathiTrust has a great program for copyright clearance; they check to make sure that the books they've scanned are definitively in the public domain or definitively not. That's been another issue that I've noticed with Google, that there are items that could be released and visible that really are in the public domain, and they just haven't done the legwork to ensure that it's accessible. I think those successful partnerships have very clear visions of what a library was, and what a library will be.

I'm very impressed with how far the Digital Public Library of America has grown. They're partnering with public library institutions in particular, and I think that's really valuable as well. I know that the Google Books project and HathiTrust grew more from the academic libraries, and you can see that when you look at some of the coverage of the collections. There are gaps, because they were meant to be for an academic audience versus working with a public library audience. I'm very impressed with the way the DPLA set up hubs for various institutions so that they can gather digital collections in their regions and then provide those to the overall collection. There are really good examples out there of what can be done well.

Mark Matienzo: In terms of successful collaborations on digital library projects, especially large-scale ones, what I've found is there really needs to be a degree of humility across the board. Part of that is there's a very clear history in the context of the digital library world that large, well-funded, elite institutions have been the ones who've been operating in this space the longest. That said, I think there's a lot of opportunity for smaller, less well-resourced institutions that have not had the structural conditions to allow them to participate in something like even a state-wide collaboration. There's really an opportunity to rethink the way that we do collaboration. Because of this history of digital library projects being situated in elite, well-funded institutions, there is a pretty serious lack of humility. There's an assumption that a relatively small group of folks has the answers for the whole community, for every potential situation that could arise. And I don't really think that's the case.

There's a lot of opportunity right now to rethink that and reconsider our obligations—like, what does it mean to develop a large-scale project? Is volume or extensiveness the goal, or is improving the inclusivity of a project the more important goal? Part of the issue that we've run into in our early days at DPLA is that it was more the former, that the metric of success was purely in terms of numbers. And I think we're at a place where we're really starting to reevaluate that and rethink the types of relationships that we need to have to develop a new conception of success for DPLA.

```
related_subjects = []
related_subjects.push("subpoenas")
related_subjects.push("SHA-256")
related_subjects.push("Schoology")
related_subjects.push("refrigerators")
related_subjects.push("HTTPS")
related_subjects.push("retro gaming forums")
related_subjects.push("BitCurator")
related_subjects.push("anarchists")
related_subjects.push("'TSA Lite'")
related_subjects.push("South Florida transportation")
related_subjects.push("memorial quilts")
related_subjects.push("the Irish Republican Army")
related_subjects.push("zines")
related_subjects.push("kanji")
related_subjects.push("CollectiveAccess")
related_subjects.push("the Fifth Law of Library Science")
```

Accessing

While privacy and security issues have already come up in talk of other topics, this chapter opens with a grounding discussion of general privacy values in libraries and archives, plus the risks that come from the ease of findability of online information, the Internet of Things, and the additional surveillance that tends to happen in special collections. The theme of trust-building and consent continues, especially as it relates to privacy in oral histories and other community digital collections.

People discussed metadata, multilingual collections, and other questions of language and terminology and accessibility. I asked how people make collections accessible to a wide range of users with varied linguistic and cultural backgrounds, and how to be responsive to communities' own desired representations. This chapter also focuses on Interference Archive, the all-volunteer "archive from below" that was established in 2011 in Brooklyn, NY. Members recounted the decision-making for their catalog's software, as well as their processes for determining how to describe and make their collection accessible.

. . .

MICHAEL GORMAN: I've always been very interested in the idea of libraries and privacy. We have always cherished the values of equal access to information, intellectual freedom, and so on. In a world in which people's privacy is invaded, those values are endangered. I have always been in favor of having systems that only kept aggregated statistics, for example. It's possibly convenient for the library to know everything, every website that people have visited or every piece of material they have used. It is certainly not good for the individual. I do not think they should disclose user information, certainly not to anyone without a warrant. I am very much against the PATRIOT Act and many of its provisions as they affect libraries.

Then there is surveillance. Scott McNealy, a co-founder of Sun Microsystems, wrote that privacy is dead, get over it. One of the malign effects of technology is that our privacy is constantly being invaded. One of the features of London is that there are surveillance cameras everywhere, which helps when it comes to crime, but I do not like walking around being observed by somebody far away. I particularly do not like commercial surveillance. Amazon and Google know far more about the average citizen than the government does. I think these developments are Orwellian and Kafkaesque.

Jason Griffey: In 2014, the Knight Foundation held a grant challenge round for library technology, and a project that I'm leading was one of the winners. It's called Measure the Future, and the idea is that we're building sensors that will allow libraries to see what's going on inside the rooms of their building. You have basically a web camera-based sensor. It doesn't videorecord, it doesn't take pictures; it's just watching the area and analyzing movement. It tracks the hot spots in a room, so you can see very quickly which spaces are and aren't being used. You can get pathways through rooms and see how people move around, and how people sit, and where people hang out and where they don't. The idea was to be able to give people a more robust understanding of the building itself, in the same way that we have a really robust understanding of how people use our websites. We have Google Analytics or some other analytics package that we use on our website; we know which links people click on and how long they were on the page and where they went after they left our page. We don't have anything like that for our buildings, and our buildings are one of our most expensive resources. One of the things that we have that separates us from a lot of other services is our physical spaces in our communities, and it bothered me that we weren't able to understand how those were being used in more fully-featured ways.

All of our code is going to be open source. People can use it free of charge; they can download it and implement it themselves as much as they'd like. We're using inexpensive hardware, so you can purchase hardware with the code on it. The idea is that libraries can see how their spaces are being used and determine if that's how we want them to be used. They can put a sensor in a room and see that, as a matter of fact, the corner where we have these chairs is never ever used—why do people never sit there? And then they can make changes and try to improve the experience for their patrons in their spaces. I'm really excited about that project. I think that's an underappreciated bit of what libraries do, and right now there's not any kind of service that is really built for libraries that allows us to do that sort of thing.

JESSICA ANNE BRATT: We always joke about Big Brother. It's very interesting just what technology can do as a staff person. For example, Security can time you when you've gone into and out of a building. On our phones, there's a button—it's grayed out on anyone lower than upper management—but essentially if they wanted to listen in to your phone calls, they could. They could also read your emails, things like that. It's just been very interesting to see what is all possible with the technology.

CELESTE Â-RE: One thing that concerns me is workplace surveillance. How many of us see "This is the property of" on our work computer? Or have tuned out the security cameras at the job? It's Huxleyan to me. I would love to hear what other people in the field think about surveillance on the job. I would like to know people's counter-surveillance solutions.

SARAH HOUGHTON: I've come across a lot of privacy issues in my work. I think that the data that libraries choose to share with vendors through authentication systems or backdoor access to their patron database is something that we need to pay a lot more attention to. ALA recently came out with privacy guidelines,[1] kind of best practices for libraries for protecting your users' data and interacting with vendors. I'm heading up a group that's going to be coming up with practical implementation plans for what that means, because

---

[1] "Library Privacy Guidelines," American Library Association, http://www.ala.org/advocacy/privacy/guidelines.

standards are all well and good, but unless you have a practical sense of what to do with that standard, that's not going to help 99 percent of the librarians out there.

I think how our data interacts with vendor data is essential. I think that reading the fine print of contracts and ensuring what level of data our vendors need and only giving them the minimum possible required is critical to protecting user privacy. I think that teaching our clientele about privacy issues is a key role for libraries, and one that many libraries have not really stepped up into yet. I'd like to see more of us doing that on a regular basis. I do think that's a unique skill set and knowledge base that we have in our community, and that we're in a good position to teach that to people.

Other kinds of privacy concerns I've seen arise have to do with law enforcement requests for patron data when they come in without a subpoena or a warrant and want us to hand over user data. I had another city's police department contact me recently wanting me to look up a particular library card number. The card had been found at the scene of a crime. I said, "I would be happy to do that with a subpoena or a warrant," and they were not real pleased with that. Nor did they come back with a subpoena or a warrant. And that's like the sixth or seventh time that's happened in my career. I get very frustrated with libraries who say, "Oh, well, law enforcement came and asked, so we just gave it to them." Well, check your privacy policy first. Check the ALA Bill of Rights. Check what we're supposed to do ethically. Asking for a subpoena or warrant isn't ridiculous, and it's something that law enforcement should be able to provide if they do have a legitimate need for the data that our database can provide them with. I see the kind of lax enforcement of privacy policies in libraries as something that's slipped as the PATRIOT Act gets further and further away from us in our distant memory. I think that the people who are responsible for that data and the people who have access to it need to be better trained in how to protect it, and how to ensure that we're not having a substitute staff member getting bullied by a police detective to hand over patron data. It's hard, because we do have so many people that do have access that you have to ensure that that kind of training and that kind of standard is upheld across the board.

Andromeda Yelton: A couple years ago people realized that Adobe was collecting a huge amount of information when it was used as the DRM server for their e-books. They realized it was actually sending back to Adobe information about what page of the book the person is reading, what time are they reading that page—which, for a profession that claims to care about protecting people's right to read and not spying on what people read, is literally the opposite of that. We were sending that information across the Internet to goodness knows who. Password security is often terrible. Lots of library catalogs, ILSs, store passwords in clear text. They don't encrypt them, which means any number of people could have access to people's passwords, and then if they reuse them on other systems—like their bank, for instance—people can log in.

I think a lot of librarians don't realize how insecure wifi is, even password-protected wifi. Anyone on your wifi network can spy on what anyone else on your wifi network is doing, and it's actually pretty easy. So unless those web connections that they're making are encrypted—unless they're HTTPS connections—anyone can see what you're doing. That means library websites need to be HTTPS. Since we claim to care about protecting people's right to browse and read without being spied on, we've got to secure those connections.

I think there's been some great work with libraries and Tor—like, Alison Macrina of the Library Freedom Project got a library up in New Hampshire to run a Tor node so that people can browse the Web without being surveilled. Our values of privacy and intellectual freedom really depend on a technical infrastructure that lets us actually live out that values commitment and not just say we care about it. We often are not looking at that values commitment in how we implement our technology.

BECKY YOOSE: Dealing with the privacy and surveillance implications is basically my position at Seattle Public Library at the moment. To give you a little bit of context, SPL is currently building a data warehouse of particular pieces of information that we use for reporting and longitudinal analysis, to better assess programs and services so we can spend taxpayer funds more efficiently—making sure that we're getting the money's worth of the programs and services that we're working on, essentially. This includes patron data. Now, there are a *whole* lot of risks when you're working with patron data, including a lot with security and privacy. At SPL, we've gone ahead and figured out how to strip not only the personally identifiable information of a particular person in the database—for example, birth dates, full address, name—we've come up with a unique patron de-identified

ID, where we've taken some parts of the patron's information and put it through SHA-256 with a salt, basically hashing it to a point where we have a unique ID but that particular patron cannot be reverse-identified, unless you can crack our hashing algorithm and break into our ILS and then break into the data warehouse and make a connection of all three.

The second part of personally identifiable information is any actions that could be tied to a particular patron. So, for example, if we want to track what gets checked out, we have to make sure that no patron's personally identifiable information gets attached to that particular title. One thing we can do is not store the title within the system. Well, what happens when people are asking what titles are popular within particular branches? We just have to make sure that patron information is not tied to item counts and such, making sure that we scrub all personally identifiable information that could identify that person, or the activities that person does, while at the same time being able to have that ability to do the longitudinal analysis to see what services and programs people are using that need more funding, continued funding, restructuring, whatnot.

At this point, security in librarianship and privacy of the patron is a tricky conversation to have, especially when you have libraries who are under pressure or at least have initiatives to do more evidence-based practices, more analysis, more data-driven practice. And when you have libraries who cannot create such a warehouse like SPL has, you have third-party vendors who'd be more than willing to take all your data and then munge it for you. The problem with that is that you relinquish control of your patron data as soon as you hand it over to a third party. That for me is a huge concern nowadays, especially with public, and academic, libraries who have signed on with various customer relations management systems. At the same time, we have to realize that not all libraries are going to have the ability to build an in-house warehouse where they can control the privacy settings and what gets tracked and what doesn't get tracked. To that end, what we need to do as a community at large—and there has been some work done by IFLA and ALA and other library organizations, but it needs to be a more concerted effort—is to make sure that these third-party vendors are adhering to the same level of ethical standards of treating our library patron data that the way that the library does in-house.

Vivian Alvarez: Because there's a lot of photography taking place at our library, we have a photo consent form that we ask all children's parents to sign. But if they want to decline, that's fine. There are different angles of taking photos, and we can take photos of hands, for instance. But the children and the families are informed, both in English and Spanish, because the parents are mostly Spanish-speakers. This branch in particular has a lot of loyalty from the community, so a lot of families walking in to the branch automatically feel that they can trust the staff. We haven't had any tension when it comes to photography or the accumulation of the portfolios or photos with other staff members for the purpose of sharing on social media. That hasn't come up, but I think it's because we have a very strong relationship with the families. In fact, it almost feels like we're all family. That is particularly special to that branch—but if we didn't have it, I could see that there would be some apprehension most likely from the parents, since we're working with the little ones and of course we have to be very protective of them.

Elaine Harger: I've put warning signs on library computers saying to be careful what you do because somebody is watching. The school district works very hard, from what I can tell, to be sure that student information does not get out and is not accessible except internally to the school district and to the people who should have access. There's all kinds of firewalls and passwords and whatnot. Student use of machines can be monitored, and I let students know that.

One of the first things that I do in the school year with the incoming sixth grade students—they all come to the library to get their usernames and passwords to access the computers at school. There's an agreement that they all have to sign, which is in technological jargon that a lot of them can't quite understand or have the patience to read and try to struggle through, but I translate it for them and let them know that there's appropriate uses and inappropriate uses of the technology. If they use any of the equipment inappropriately it is not difficult for anyone to find out, and there can be consequences to that.

More and more, there are educational applications that teachers are excited about using in the classroom. There's the Blended Learning professional development in which we were introduced to a number of new technological tools that can be used to take surveys in class, or to have students create videos or games and work on projects. We were talking about using videos for instruction, so instead of me standing up in front of a class delivering the same digital citizenship lesson like a couple of years ago, kids can access that information via a video at whatever level they might need it at. So we were doing a lot of that, and some of it is very exciting to use, but—and teachers are very conscious of this—there's always the need to keep student work private and secure. So some of the things that are available online, some teachers are hesitant to use. But that said, the school district has purchased a program called Schoology, a Facebook-like system where students can upload their work, teachers can post assignments, readings, and videos, and all of that is protected within the school district so that only students, staff, and parents can access the content. Access requires usernames and passwords.

JONATHAN HARWELL: We try to make sure that our own tools in the library are not collecting and preserving too much personal information about people. Within the library, we strive to not archive records of patron borrowing history over a long period of time. We of course need current circulation history, but we don't want to be keeping permanent records of what people are checking out, for example. There are some vendors who insist on patrons creating their own accounts to access the content in their platforms, and this is something we try to discourage with the vendors. Some of them are pretty stuck on this model. But even the ones who are requiring patrons to do that, we're also encouraging them to not gather too much information about our patrons. A simple login should be sufficient. Some of them tend to want a little more data when they sign up for an account, but we try to discourage that. Most of those vendors are just using a simple login and password to create an account, and usually that's just a free account for more bells and whistles within that platform.

CECILY WALKER: British Columbia, where Vancouver Public Library is located, has some of the most stringent privacy regulations around identifying information on the Internet and what kinds of patron information we're allowed to share, especially with companies that have their servers housed in the United States. Long story short, we can't do it. That's actually been a blessing and a curse. It's been a blessing because whenever we're about to start a project, we know what our constraints are up front.

I don't really do anything with licensing with vendors, but we had an experience with one particular vendor that was trying to sell us a product where they were building an authentication gateway where some identifying patron information was going to be stored. There are a lot of other library systems in our geographic area that were offering this particular product way before we were, and it took us so long because we kept going back and forth with this vendor for close to two years to get them to change their authentication so that we wouldn't have to worry about them storing identifying patron information, and we could offer the service to our patrons.

MANDY HENK: Privacy and surveillance concerns aren't a thing here in New Zealand in the same way they are in the US. So I'm going to have to talk about the US perspective, because the New Zealand perspective is sort of like—literally this isn't a thing here, as far as I can tell. In the US—and I think this applies throughout the US—as we've made the transition from traditional catalogs that we were self-hosting at our own institutions, or perhaps at the consortial level, to having these systems be hosted in the cloud at the vendor level, one of my grave concerns remains that it is much easier now for government now to get information. Whether it's subpoenas or warrants or other sorts of requests they might be making, we've given up our power to even know about these.

I think that that's a very grave mistake. I mean, let's think for a moment about what happens when President Trump controls the FBI. That's a horrifying thought. The rights we were willing to give up—both legislatively, if you think in terms of the PATRIOT Act, but also very practically in terms of day-to-day, who has physical control over this information—are going to come back and hurt us considerably in the future. They're not going to hurt all of us; they're going to hurt some small percentage of us. But I think those people matter, too, and all along we should have been aggressively advocating for those people's safety and privacy. But we didn't. I think now we've sort of passed a point where we'll be able to resolve anything and roll it back.

JESSAMYN WEST: We saw a lot of companies who wanted to be in the information business making a lot of sneery, shitty comments to libraries like, "Users don't care about their privacy. Why do *you* care about users' privacy?" You can answer that in kind of a hand-wavy, "Well, it's just a social good, it's a value" way, but I also think in America especially, we're being asked to tolerate a much higher degree of lack of privacy and lack of ownership of our own personal information than in other countries. Our privacy laws are significantly laxer than they are in Europe, and Americans are just used to all their shit getting hacked and winding up on the Internet and having to deal with it in various ways. Some of this is the Internet, some of it is our banks—looking at chip and PIN credit card transactions and how it's so much more secure, but we didn't get it for a long time because it cost extra money, and fuck it.

In a lot of ways, libraries are standing up for privacy and companies are really trying hard to dismantle your privacy. Even if companies are saying they want to keep your stuff private, they kind of have an inability to because of bad software, bad technology, or just it's really hard to have big computers on the Internet that have tantalizing information inside of them and make sure no one in the world can have access to that. I mean, we've seen the government fall down on it, we've seen corporations fall down on it. Not like every library is perfect—and really I think a lot of it is just who wants to break into your library—but at least you say, "This is a thing that we value."

You also have the notion of the surveillance state and the idea that the politics around the computers that are running our lives are confusing, complicated, I'm not sure who to talk to. Like, self-driving cars—I have concerns about those from a safety perspective, and I have concerns about them from a "I can't look at the code" perspective. But I also have concerns about them from a "once I use a self-driving car, the company who makes the software that runs my self-driving car knows everywhere I'm going and everywhere I've been" perspective. Right now I don't happen to have an E-ZPass, and so where I go is only as known as the traffic cams that pick me up, which up in Vermont is not that many.

I feel like I should state for the record, I freaking love computers, so I don't mean to be like, "Oh my god, it's the end of everything, computers are destroying everything." But thinking about the more we have computers that know where they are, and the more we use computers that know where they are to do the things we need to do, the more our motions and activities and actions and who we're interacting with and a bunch of other triangulated stuff becomes available to be known by—and that's kind of a dot-dot-dot, but, you know, by the highest bidder.

JESSA LINGEL: I believe that the Internet of things is already here. It's just a matter of what is going to get that label and what is not. I think it is so depressing that the Internet of things is usually described in terms of the kitchen. The Samsung refrigerator commercial that's out right now has a guy who's at the grocery store, and, oh god, he can't remember what his wife told him to get! So he'd better look at his phone, which can talk to his refrigerator, and then he gets home and his wife is so happy that he remembered tartar sauce. Well, that is a really boring vision of what the Internet of things is, first of all. That is the same vision that in 1969 Honeywell Computers had of its Honeywell kitchen computing, the tagline of which is, "If only she can cook as well as Honeywell can compute." This is a very boring vision, a very white middle-class vision of what the Internet of things is.

But really the Internet of things is already here in terms of when a college student has to swipe her ID card as a way of completing attendance for class and then uses that same ID card to buy food and get into her dorm room, and then all of her online activity can be monitored by a professor like me. I can see how much time she spends on her online courses—not just mine, but other courses. So the Internet of things is already there. The Internet of things is already here in terms of probation. Probation technologies, when someone wears an ankle monitor—some of those ankle monitors are just about location but others are about measuring alcohol use. That is a form of the Internet of things.

So the Internet of things is already here, it's just what technologies get called Internet of things and which don't. Phil Howard has a book called *Pax Technica*. He has this really wonderful argument at the end where he says the Internet of things is coming, it's already here, it's going to be gathering all this data about us all of the time, we should be able to access our own data within these webs of data gathering and surveillance, and there's nothing about technologic infrastructure that can't make this stream of data two ways. I don't think it's super likely to happen, but it could happen. I think that that would be a really powerful example of people having access to their own data. Just walking around and knowing which movements were resulting in data being gathered about you and which weren't, I think would be a really great first step in terms of having some sense of agency, or retaining some sense of control over your own data. I don't think it's possible that that data won't be gathered. Those infrastructures are already here and there are very powerful actors who are invested in getting that data. But I do think it's possible to demand that those infrastructures involve more legibility and more means of contesting how much data they gather.

. . .

ANDREW WEISS: Someone had requested a student's thesis through interlibrary loan, before it was digitized. Unfortunately that person was living in South America, I believe Brazil, and we just don't send out books through interlibrary loan through the international mail. We made a suggestion that perhaps we could digitize it and send them the digital copy, as long as the author was okay with it. We contacted the author, and the author was on board. And so we scanned it, put it into ScholarWorks, and sent a copy to the person who requested it through interlibrary loan. Then eventually, for some reason, this thesis became popular. I don't know how it happened, but apparently now when someone does a Google search for the subject—"The Planets" by Gustav Holst—this thesis now appears as one of the top two or three links in a search for "Gustav Holst," which is a fairly common search, I would think, among people who like classical music. Now, when I check the stats, I've seen that this thesis has been downloaded almost five thousand times. It's been recently cited in a journal, and it was actually not a journal related to musicology at all; it was related more to the impact of music on psychiatry.

So it's very, very interesting for me to see that. There's no way to know sometimes who is going to find a piece of information useful, so that's been a good lesson, just to see the wide net that's cast whenever something is digitized and put online.

JARRETT DRAKE: People are intimate with their digital information in a way that they perhaps were not as intimate with analog information. But I think people's assumptions are the reverse. I think that our lives, for better and for worse, are more documented than they were in an exclusively analog world. Our lives are more documented in Gmail. They're more documented in Twitter. They're more documented in Flickr, and all of these different platforms that people use to store their information. That's not necessarily a better life, but it's a more documented life, that's for sure.

What that means for me as a digital archivist is that when I get records from organizations, the ability to predict where you might encounter private or privileged information is hard to do. I was recently processing a collection that contained born-digital emails, and the creator of these emails—the person who donated them to the university archives—sent an email to a person that they didn't know, a person at an agency with which they had a business reason to be in contact. This person sent their Social Security Number over email. To me that's a classic example of digital records being more intimate with people, because they can do it so easily. "Oh, I'll put all these details in it." Whereas I don't imagine that fifty years ago someone corresponding with a stranger would say, "Here's my Social Security Number." I was processing a collection earlier today that had a folder full of recommendation letters for students and colleagues, and people write very candidly about people that they're recommending.

The end of it is that our lives are much more documented, and that imposes a whole host of challenges on the people who are processing these records, because they have a responsibility, I believe, to the people who have created and donated the records. Those persons have privacy rights, even if they don't realize that they do. But so do the people reflected in those records, who did not consent, in a way, to be surveilled by the archive. They had no opportunity to exercise agency in their reflection in the archive, and in this digital age where, in my repository, if a born-digital collection is open, we make it accessible through the finding aid to the general public. You don't have to come to Princeton, New Jersey, to visit Princeton University's archives to see the born-digital materials; they're connected directly through the finding aid. So that's a different level of exposure and potential privacy concerns that have to be taken into consideration.

CARMEL CURTIS: Privacy concerns are really important. One of the aspects that is central to XFR Collective in how it exists right now is making the videos we transfer available on the Internet Archive. We are upfront about that from the beginning, that we really encourage people to have their stuff on the Internet Archive. That being said, we totally understand the many reasons why you might not want your videos available there. When we did our installation at the MIX Queer Experimental Film Festival, it came up more than it has in other spaces. In this queer community space, issues of privacy came up more than we had been used to in other spaces, perhaps not surprisingly. We do treat everything on a case-by-case basis. We will not ever put something on Internet Archive if someone says, "Hey, I don't want that public for XYZ reasons." And that's okay.

However, it's something that we're trying to continuously think about, because even in situations where we have been given consent to post these videos on the Internet Archive—protest video, for example, where someone else is in the background or featured who may not want this video publicly available. We are working through these issues as they come up, with an understanding that we're listening. We don't want to have something on the Internet Archive that's going to make someone uncomfortable or unsafe or not feel good about the way that they're represented. We're trying to have that conversation from the beginning as much as possible, so asking the content creators—the people who are coming to us—questions around privacy, asking if they think there's any reason why this video should not be available online, not only for their own sake but for the sake of the other people in the videos. We're trying to engage them in these conversations from the beginning more and more, not only in terms of privacy protection, but also in terms of metadata and how these videos are described and tagged and cataloged on the Internet Archive.

BÉATRICE COLASTIN SKOKAN: Part of the conversations that I have to have with activist groups is that content donated to the library is open to the general public. As part of trust-building, I do let them know what it means to participate and give their content over. I feel like that's an important conversation for me to have with them so that there is trust between us. I wanted people that were conducting these oral histories to know that their interviews were going to be available online, which meant that anybody could see it. In our distinctive collections—the Cuban Heritage Collection and Special Collections—we have to think of the connections that people still have with their countries of origin. If there are oppressive regimes still in place, what does a Web-accessible interview mean for the individual who will be telling a story? It's very important to discuss the ramifications of public disclosure of information in the United States for family or friends that may still be vulnerable to retaliation overseas. Usually there's a desire for that information to be shared so others will know the story from another perspective. There is a desire for "truth telling." In most cases privacy hasn't been an obstacle to access.

HANA SLEIMAN: With oral histories, people are telling their stories, and often very politically sensitive stories that involve resistance and imprisonment. Security concerns were definitely very high up there, and one of the first discussions we had for the Palestinian Oral History Archive. Also relevant was whether or not to use digital tools such as GPS coordinates. We have the option of plugging in GPS coordinates for the interview, but do we want to provide a map where all these refugees and freedom fighters came from and went? Do we want such a substantive tool to be publicly accessible? And the decision was no. Not that we don't have GPS coordinates; the information is there, people can retrieve it, but it's about making clear connections that have surveillance implications.

Then there's the issue of consent. For 90 percent, I think, of the interviews, we have been given consent to use and make the interview available. But that was maybe before the digital age. It's kind of a different game when they have children and grandchildren, and this is an ongoing conflict. So there's the issue of how to make individual decisions about interviews. Although we have permission to put them up online, we might decide not to, for whatever reason. And this is absolutely a human decision. This is based on the judgement of the indexer and what they hear in the interview, and whether they think it's safe and appropriate to put that online.

JAYCIE VOS: We do some sensitive material screening before our interviews go online, and as long as they're not restricted, they're completely open to research. We recently developed sensitive materials guidelines that we share with students, collaborators, and others who conduct interviews that go into the SOHP collection so that they can make informed decisions about whether to restrict access to an interview. We try to leave the decision to restrict an interview up to the interviewee, the interviewer, or the person running the oral history project as much as possible. We can offer guidance, but we generally want to give these individuals the power to make their own decision. We try to explain to the interviewees beforehand, "This is going to be online, this is what our database looks like, this is an example of what your interview will look like when it's online." They sign the release form after the interview has been conducted, so if they don't want to discuss something, they know that they don't have to. Whenever we transcribe interviews, we also send a transcript to the interviewee so they can make edits before it goes into the collection.

For interviews with restricted use and access—whether the person just wanted it closed for five years, or whatever that might be—we normally create the interview record with the most basic information, like when the interview took place, without actually putting the audio or transcript online. But a lot of what we do with regard to privacy comes beforehand. We try to make our interviewees really, really aware how public the database is, because it is completely open to anyone that has the Internet.

MARK MATIENZO: While there are some very loud voices who speak out for user privacy in the context of libraries and archives, I feel like there's often a potential mismatch when it comes to operating in a digital context. I think we take a lot for granted. Part of my concern is that while librarians have this fundamental value of patron privacy, it has not always been clear until somewhat recently how to really examine how to achieve that in a digital context. I think the Library Freedom Project has done a lot of very valuable work.

In our context at DPLA, one of the things that we try to do is to elevate the standard. Not in an unattainable way, but in a way that allows—really encourages—institutions like our partners or the hubs that we work with, or vendors, to believe that the work we're doing should be taken seriously. By our having higher standards, or a higher expectation, it allows us to essentially be able to encourage everybody to reach to attain those standards. We had to make some hard decisions about how we want to gather data about usage for DPLA. We have a grant where we really want to be able to track usage of DPLA in part to show the value of our work and things like the curation activity or our API. We also want to be able to demonstrate how a hub's materials are being used and reused. But we fundamentally want to do that in a way that's not invasive, that does not threaten the privacy of the users. We've decided very clearly that we want to demonstrate our commitment to privacy.

There is a lot of work. I don't think we're solving the privacy problem just by using HTTPS. I think it's a good start, but we have a lot more to do. For the most part, implementing HTTPS was pretty easy for us, but there was one wrinkle. We only aggregate metadata from our hubs. One of the things that we require in the metadata is a link to an image. What that ends up looking like, especially when you start to present something through the DPLA front end, is an external link, or in the browser, it's an image that gets loaded from an external source. One problem is just that there's a mixed content issue, that if somebody is looking at our page over HTTPS and there's a thumbnail that's served just over HTTP, it wouldn't get loaded. The other is that even if this external server is serving this image over HTTPS, we're still fundamentally leaking information about the user looking at the content potentially through DPLA. We ended up mitigating that by putting up a simple thumbnail proxy server. It was important for us to demonstrate that if we're going to do this, we have to do this conclusively. If somebody looks at the metadata that we aggregate and they have a concern because they see this external link in the metadata, we can explain to them at least how this gets mitigated in the front end.

JIM DELROSSO: When we were moving some of our collections from behind previously existing paywalls to the public repositories, one of the things that was said was, "Well, the reason we set up registration is so that we can find out information on these people and what they're reading." And I said, "We won't do that." We don't do that. I take that very seriously.

But it's also had me asking—belatedly, if I'm going to be frank—hard questions about our use of Google Analytics. Google collects a lot of information, and Google can tell us where people are accessing this from. They can nail it down to, they're accessing this material from a given institution, or a given city. A lot of people I work with find that very useful, and I understand why, but it also gives me pause, because that's still pulling a lot of information about our users. It's a path I'm very leery of going any further down than we already have, and I'm not necessarily super psyched about where we're standing on that path, to continue the metaphor.

Dorothea Salo, who works and teaches at the University of Wisconsin, has written amazing things about repositories and is just an awesome person. If you can ever see her talk, I recommend it.

I've gotten to know her through a couple of our professional organizations. She started a great conversation on Twitter[2] that was, if we're not willing to use this data that we're collecting about individuals on an individual basis, is it any better for us to use it on these groups as a whole? My thought was, saying that aggregation does not obviate privacy is probably a pretty good starting point, if nothing else. But really we're getting to the point, especially with something like Google Analytics—which is a very powerful and useful tool, and I use it, and I get a lot out of it—of asking whether we should be using something that's collecting information on individuals, even if we're trying not to examine them as individuals. We're still potentially putting our users in the path of Google's data collection, and we need to acknowledge that and make some decisions around it. I'm still doing it, and I'll be doing it tomorrow, and at the end of the month when I pull stats and look for global reach of our repositories, I'll be pulling that out of Google Analytics. That's a decision I'm making as a professional, and as an employee, and as a worker. But it's definitely something that gives me pause.

As we get more things like, "Let us tell you which companies are using your material, let us tell you what universities are using your material," I see people's faces light up within my organization about being able to access this. It's definitely worrisome, because that's getting really close to individual users; there's no way you can put that material together without collecting information about individual users. Obviously we want to be able to meet people's needs, but we need to be more thoughtful about the balance points we're choosing. When I was putting together our user survey, I wanted to make sure it was as anonymous as possible. I did not ask people for any personally identifying information beyond occupation, and I made everything voluntary. But then we can't let the allure of those big data dumps and those visualizations mask the real questions about privacy that come up when we're collecting this kind of data on an open access repository, or anything, really. I don't have a solid answer yet, but it's definitely something that give me pause and that I think a lot about.

---

2   https://twitter.com/LibSkrat/status/765233708391538688

Bonnie Gordon: I think that we often take for granted the fact that the software and digital forensics tools that we use, for the most part, come from the law enforcement community. I mean, it's forensics. There are some things that we use that come from the retro gamer community. Particularly the 3 ½" floppy disk thing that we use, the KryoFlux, its primary audience are people that are super into Atari and have a bunch of 3 ½" or 5 ¼" floppy disks that they really want to get these games from, like, 1983 off of and play them. There are bunch of forums, and I've definitely looked through retro gaming forums for troubleshooting disk imaging some of our older media. But a lot of the software is designed for either detectives or for lawyers doing discovery, so there are a lot of implications of that.

At the Rockefeller Archive Center, we do have policies related to not viewing deleted files, and that kind of thing. And because the archives that I work for primarily deals with organizational records, there is a fair amount of filtering before things get to us. There's records management policies and that kind of thing. But I think there's a really big tension when it comes to providing access, and the expectations around providing access, and the ideas around what privacy do you expect and also who is saying that their materials can't be put online.

Jarrett Drake: Princeton is a charter member of the BitCurator Consortium. BitCurator is a project that began a few years ago and was started by the School of Information and Library Science at the University of North Carolina-Chapel Hill and the Maryland Institute for Technology in the Humanities. MITH and UNCSILS put together a grant proposal to the Mellon Foundation to develop an open source operating system that would be designed for libraries, archives, and museums to process born-digital archival materials. This software has gained a lot of usage. There are many universities now who are members of the consortium. BitCurator is the Ubuntu operating system. It's really a bundling service as much as it is anything else.

One of the reasons why we were really attracted to BitCurator is its ability to screen for personally identifiable information, or PII. There's a tool in BitCurator known as Bulk Extractor. Bulk Extractor basically searches along the file system for certain patterns of data. You can tell it to look for a sequence of three digits, dash, two digits, dash, four digits. By default it actually looks for that pattern. You can tell it to look for sixteen digits in a row for a credit card number. You can tell it to look for date of birth information, look for any sort of location or GPS information that may be embedded within the images. You can tell it to look for an email address. It's very powerful.

Tomorrow I have a meeting for the digital curation program, and a big topic will be coming up with a list of keywords and regular expressions that we want to feed into Bulk Extractor to identify certain kinds of information that should be private and possibly not even be taken into the archive, into our preservation area. One example being, "search for any file or folder with the word 'recommendation' in it." It's not to automatically throw out each and every file or folder that has recommendation, right? Because there are different kinds of recommendations. The recommendations we think of in the employment or education world pertain to a person who's seeking a new job or a new position in the school as a student, and so your professors or your colleagues write recommendation letters for you. Those are the kinds of the things we want to know about, because those are the kinds of the things we wouldn't collect, not the least because that is a violation of the student's FERPA. And it's something that people are not even cognizant that they have within their hard drive of fifteen thousand files, a folder full of recommendation letters. So that's one example of a tool in BitCurator that looks for that kind of information that can alert archivists to those potential concerns, and from there they would make a decision about what to do.

Celeste Â-Re: I process donated acquisitions made up of manuscripts, audio recordings, and floppy discs and have to inform supervising archivists about removing items in collections—a signed check, a letter from a physician, documents with Social Security numbers. When we come across these types of documents we can't leave them out in the open at our workstations if we walk away or have to go to the bathroom; we have to lock them away. When we're finished processing newly acquired collections, we destroy personally identifying information. It's something we're mindful of because if someone is going through an electronic finding aid, they could conceivably piece information together to create an identity. It's a bit disconcerting because the profession is geared toward making information available but, we also have to be mindful that materials can be used in ways that they weren't intended.

At my job, we have annual security awareness training. And people need to be more vigilant about their day-to-day personal digital privacy. I try to just use my cellphone when I'm mobile; that's why it's called a *mobile* phone.

. . .

HANA SLEIMAN: Working with mostly refugee archives, I know that a lot of our work and material is restrictive to the communities we're archiving, whether it's because of digital literacy or access to the Internet altogether, in some communities. Or because of the physical—the walls around campus and the inability for non-members to visit and use the material. But I have to say that, short of secondary sources in databases, most users, they want to very much to do it the old-school way. They come, and they see. Even though a lot of this material is online—we might then point them to public computers where they can easily browse this—most of my experience as an archivist has been with analog material, not digital materials that are already accessible.

JAIME TAYLOR: I think most researchers at the Center for Jewish History—since we are a special collection rather than a public library—have some idea that we're keeping records, and for the most part, especially if you're a scholar, your research is eventually going to be public. But we do have a lot of archival collections, not from recent political figures, but early twentieth century anarchists and things like that—basically anyone who a hundred years ago the government would have hated. So it's entirely possible that we have people coming to our library to do research on early twentieth century communists and anarchists, and maybe if that's the main gist of their research, they don't want those records kept. But there is literally no way you can come into our building and see that material without leaving a big paper trail. That's a problem for me. Our reference staff doesn't seem to have a problem with it, which is weird, but I have a problem with that. And there's not really anything to do about that, because I'm not at a decision-making capacity.

STACIE WILLIAMS: Working in archives, depending on where you're at, you do sort of get used to this idea that you're being videotaped on a closed circuit camera, as they tend to do for what they say are security purposes. I'm not trying to undermine that. I lived in Lexington, Kentucky, and worked at a small liberal arts college that had actually a really horrifying theft where they assaulted the archivist. So I'm not trying to make light of the fact that you might need that security, and the fact that there were cameras helped lead to the capture of those kids who were stealing stuff. So I get it. I do get it. And I know people who have experienced the need for that level of protection. But there's some places where there's already this expectation that you have a loss of privacy, right? You're going in; you're just a researcher doing your thing, and there's a camera trained on you because there's already the implication that you are going to do something wrong.

ELVIA ARROYO-RAMIREZ: Most physical spaces at academic repositories that archivists use to provide access to archival materials can be, by design and culture, uninviting and unwelcoming to anyone not affiliated with that academic institution or without a stated research purpose. Some places deny patron requests who don't have one or both of these. Why do patrons need to have a reason to request archival materials at academic libraries? In a sense, granting or denying access based on a patron's supplied reason is a form of surveillance, because access is granted based on the information about their purpose to be there. They need to state an objective, the objective needs to be known and approved of. The physical space patrons have to sit in tends to be heavily surveilled. Cameras may be recording them, reading room staff need to have their eyes on them at all times, etc. What happens to that surveillance video after the patron leaves? Have staff come up with a retention policy that stipulates how long these videos are kept on a server at the university? Who has access to that video and how are they using it? Even before patrons arrive at the reading room, some repositories require patrons to register and supply their government names, their government forms of identification, etc. There are a lot of liberties taken that encroach on privacy for the sake of security.

JARRETT DRAKE: I am very, very concerned at the normalcy with which special collections, libraries, and archives collect, store, and retain data about patrons who use their collections. I'm really troubled by this. Special collections, libraries, archives have become willing servants of surveillance, and it disturbs me to no end. Places that I have worked or visited as a researcher have increasingly taken on surveillance methods and practices that police and military folks use. There are some special collections and archives that not only require photo identification—which is racist, and it's classist, and it's ageist. That's what the practice is; it doesn't matter to me that the argument that gets regurgitated is that it helps keep the materials safe. That's not what it's about, as much as voter ID is not about preventing voter fraud. It's about excluding people.

So we already have these racist, these classist, and these ageist methods of requiring photo identification in our field, but to take it even further, there are places that photograph their researchers when they come in to use their materials. They photograph them, and they store the photograph with the records that they keep about the records that they request and use. I didn't know it had gotten that bad. There's a lot of writing about the archive as a metaphor for prison. There's an article by Eric Ketelaar called "Archival Temples, Archival Prisons," where he's talking about the panopticon of the archive, of constantly being watched while you're in the reading room. It's a great article. There are others that are written by people not in the archival field, one of them being *The Allure of the Archives* by Arlette Farge. I love that book.

But to me, it's like, let's just start a patron registration, or as I like to call it, "TSA Lite." It's absurd, and it's troubling. The technologies are there where we can do it easier. We can get your photograph very quickly. We can pull all this data together. We have mountains of big data. To me, the biggest issue with any sort of surveillance that you have happening, people are like, "Well, if you're a legitimate researcher, you shouldn't be worried about having your photograph taken and stored indefinitely in some space. If you're doing the right thing, it shouldn't matter." This sort of tired, hackneyed argument that we hear—it's really not even about that. With any sort of surveillance, number one, there's just the right for people to be free from oppression, to be free of being forced to be photographed to use a historical document. How can we on one hand claim that we want the widest access possible for the most people possible when we're making policies that actually discourage people from doing things? But it's always the secondary usage of that data. It's always about the abuse of that data. So if a library is saying, "We're keeping it for ourselves, it helps us if something gets stolen, we can go back and figure out all the different people who used it, and XYZ," what about the abuses that will happen? It's not a matter of "if"; we know that people abuse their authority when they get the right to surveil people. We know that governments use it to target people. There's been a lot about the PATRIOT Act in libraries and how that's impacted it.

So my contention is, special collections, libraries, and archives should stop gathering data that will further expose our patrons to more surveillance. And I think that the trend is going in the opposite direction. More special collections in libraries and more archives are trying to gather even more personal information from people to just keep in all of these systems. They don't really have a plan for anonymizing the data, they don't have a plan for purging the data, they just have a plan for gathering data. My question is, when you're doing all this gathering, who are you doing the gathering for? Video cameras, other kids of surveillance—in some of these archives, it's like going into a prison. And I've gone into enough prisons to know what it's like. We've got to grapple with why the experience of going to the prison, or through airport security, is so similar to the experience of going to the archive. Just stopping to ask why is a thing that many in our field just don't want any parts of. There's safety in a false sense of security.

BONNIE GORDON: When I think about a lot of these issues, it tends to be in terms of access, pretty broadly. Access in description, remote access, the user experience in the reading room. I think that for someone who is a digital archivist or has the word "digital" in her title, there are places for advocacy. There are implications to providing access to born-digital material in particular, and this kind of gets to the problem of being precious with born-digital, or any non-traditional format. People get really nervous around born-digital records and how easily they can be disseminated. Even though it's technologically easy to just put everything online so anyone can see it, that makes people really nervous. So sometimes there are more barriers. In general, there are a lot of conversations around providing access to born-digital materials, but the conversation is really about how to limit access to born-digital material. Like, how to set up a virtual reading room, or how to lock things down on the computer. That has surveillance implications, which is related to racism and classism and the geographical location of where a research is—can they physically get to the reading room? Will there be consequences if it's logged that they visited this virtual reading room and saw this material?

Obviously, on the other hand, putting everything online is not the solution. But I personally would like to see a more critical conversation around providing access to born-digital materials, as opposed to uncritically talking about setting up a virtual reading room, and really think about what data we're collecting and what the implications of that are. I think this also gets to why, personally and as a department, articulating our values is really important, because that's how you can create a better world or whatever, to articulate whether you value providing broad and equitable access, and what does that mean? As opposed to having these conversations where values are not clearly articulated, and then you start to see instances when providing access means restricting access.

MARK MATIENZO: There's an existing professional practice in archives that at least at its surface makes sense, which is that to use materials on an in-person basis, you have to register. That means you must be willing to provide information about yourself, contact information and so forth. The thing that I'm concerned about is that that paradigm seems to exist also when you move into the digital space, so thinking about providing access to either digitized or born-digital content in archives.

Now, there may be some very strong motivations to do so, which are often reflected by the deeds of gift that have been signed. Some of those are, I think, legitimate when there are privacy issues in the materials that are being made available, case files or things like that. But I think the process of registration and storing additional information about patrons, in the context of archives, is going to quickly become unsustainable and essentially lead to a case where there might be a very serious privacy breach. While there might be legitimate concerns about how to understand how materials are being used when there are materials that have significant privacy concerns of their own, I honestly think some of this is not just a technical problem. Part of this is also an issue with the archival practice and not being able to push back on potential donors to think through the implications of restrictions on those materials that require that kind of registration.

JAYCIE VOS: I think we operate from a place of compassion and genuine curiosity. There's a real sense that everyone who works for the Southern Oral History Program believes in their hearts that it's important to document stories about people who aren't always in positions of power, or who haven't always had their stories told or captured or portrayed in particularly meaningful ways. Some of that, I think, is just our nature as professionals. We deeply care about these stories and want them preserved, and that alone goes a long way. But we also really try to listen to our interviewees and the communities we work with, and hear their concerns and what they might want from us.

We'll give workshops to community groups. Maybe it's more empowering for us to give them the tools to record their own histories themselves rather than, from our position of power as people at a university, go into the communities and ask them all the questions and then take that and put it back into the archive. Sometimes it's more meaningful to give them the tools to actually do the interviews themselves. They can interview each other, and we can teach them about different platforms that they might use, like Omeka or something that's free and pretty easy out of the box. Or they can set up their own space. The Southern Historical Collection (SHC), in Wilson Library at UNC, is a leader in this approach to archiving. The director, Bryan Giemza, is very passionate about community-driven archiving. We've been taking some cues from them as well at the SOHP.

The SHC has been traveling around the South and doing what I described, but on a bigger scale. They've been doing some assessment and appraisal in different towns where there might be a city hall that has a lot of serious water damage or doesn't have great storage facilities. The SHC has been going in to say, "These are the records that you should be keeping, this is what we would recommend storage-wise," like having a preservation plan or climate controlled storage. But the SHC isn't always taking the materials from these towns with them for the archive, because the archivists at the SHC realized it's so important to have these materials stay in that specific community. They're just giving them the tools to actually maintain their archives and build up their own institutional repositories.

I deeply admire the work that Bryan and the others are doing at the SHC, where they're not trying to just take other people's stories but are helping other people recognize that what they have is meaningful, and showing them ways that they can preserve that. The SHC and the SOHP have different public programming events that we try to invite community members to as much as possible, and when we can, we try to make them the stars of it. For New Roots, we had a big event to launch the bilingual archive and information system when it went live. We invited a ton of interviewees in the area and their families; they were recognized and honored at this event. So I think by putting the emphasis on the people and not as much on us as an institution, that makes them feel that they can trust us and that we really respect and appreciate them. It really matters to us that they feel like they can be part of this important thing, and they can tell their own story.

BÉATRICE COLASTIN SKOKAN: Trust-building is essential to approaching communities and recording their stories. Membership in the community does not guarantee trust. What was interesting about our music student who was the interviewer for the Haitian Diaspora project was that he was *not* part of the community, but he had such a genuine interest that was appealing to interviewees who had a similar passion for a subject. He had educated himself so well that when he connected with members of these communities, who feel like they're peripheral, they were willing to start a dialogue. We would often hear the phrase, "We are *honored*." I've heard it repeatedly, and it always surprises me that people would use that word. They said, "We are honored that the university would be interested in our papers, in our stories." Trust-building is crucial, especially for people who don't feel like their stories matter.

I provide a clear description of the project and let them know that recordings will be open to the public. I tell them the truth. First of all, I'm not expecting people to make a trip to the University of Miami. I would have to explain to you why that's significant, because the university happens to be located in a wealthy neighborhood. Public transportation in Miami is not like in New York, for instance; it's nothing close to that. Public transportation in South Florida is in its infancy, so you have to really drive to go anywhere. You have to decide that you're going to go to certain communities if you want to connect. I could just come every day to work and stay here, but I would be completely disconnected from the larger South Florida community. I go out to community events. These events usually take place after work and not within the nine to five framework. I am Haitian-American. I think that must count for something, especially within the Caribbean community or the African diaspora community. In addition to English, I speak French, Haitian Creole, and Spanish—because I live here, and Spanish is so predominant. I explain what I do, and I explain why it's important to include multiple perspectives to the larger historical narrative.

These multiple and nonlinear conversations with potential storytellers are ongoing. You can have a conversation with somebody once, and they don't deposit their records. They don't come to an oral history until a year or even a few years later, but you're building a relationship. You listen a lot. You are essentially inviting them to reveal components of their being. The archivist can arrange visits to the physical space where the stories will be housed and to other events that the library is hosting that may be of interest to interviewees. You're explaining the paperwork that's connected to an oral history. You're also giving them a chance to decide that they don't want to continue. That's how the trust is built; people have to have time to know you. For the professional, one has to come to understand that this type of work may require individuals who are able and willing to settle in one geographical place and make it their own. There has to be a lot of deference, knowledge, and humility to build that trust. Storytelling and meaningful exchanges require such a context.

CARMEL CURTIS: One thing that could be talked about more in the world of libraries and archives and tech is intersectional identities and how that impacts what is archived, how it's described, how it's accessed, and who it's accessed by. It's definitely something that we as a field could think about more, and that technology could be used to help facilitate that conversation about the potential. I think that one of the reasons why I became interested in movies and audiovisual moving image materials in the first place, and then, soon after, in the field of archiving moving images, was because of resentment, or disappointment, or frustration of not being able to see people like me and hear stories like mine on the screen. And wanting to work with communities that I am a part of to make those stories accessible and heard louder.

CECILY WALKER: With respect to the kind of collections that we deal with in the Digital Services department, some of them—not that they're politically sensitive, but they carry a lot of emotional weight. For example, one of the projects that we're working on is digitizing the panels of a memorial quilt that commemorates the lives and memories of women from one of Vancouver's poorest areas who were murdered. One of the things that I learned as a result of a blog post that Tara Robertson, another librarian in the Vancouver area, had written regarding the digitization of the *On Our Backs* lesbian sex zine that had been published in the '90s was that sometimes people have incidents that happen at a particular part of their lives, and when those incidents may not be looked upon favorably by people who aren't members of that community or by their family members, there are lots of implications for making this information widely available without getting permission.

After reading that, one of the things that we had to think of as a team, or that I had to take back to my manager to have a conversation with the library directors and the Chief Librarian about, was how can we continue to feature these items in our collection when there is so much pain and trauma involved with some of these memories? Maybe there are family members who don't want this association for their loved ones to be widely available on the Internet. Some of the women who are commemorated in this quilt had been sex workers. Some of them had been drug users. There's a lot of baggage from friends and family members that goes along with that. So after reading Tara's blog post and talking to my team, and in going back to the community, we said, "You know, we know that we want people to remember as much of these women as we possibly can, but what if we run into somebody who just doesn't want their loved one's name attached to this at all in our collection?"

What we came up with as a team, and working in partnership with our community partners, was that if there were any quilts that were available in our collection that had any kind of identifying information, whether it be a photograph, somebody's name, or just part of somebody's name, we would remove them from the collection. And the last little bit is that we've been working with our community partners to find friends and family members and get their permission to add these items to our collection and make them available on the Internet. It's slowed down the process dramatically, but we feel it's vitally important, because ultimately these are not our stories to tell. I feel like we have a tremendous responsibility and duty of care to make sure that by putting this information out there, we're not causing additional harm.

So those are the kinds of things that I take very seriously and consider to be part of my feminist praxis, to think about in what ways I can make this situation better, and in what ways I can ensure that I, my team, and the work that we're doing aren't contributing additional harm. And I always make sure that when it's time for us to make decisions, they aren't made in isolation and conversations happen from the entry-level librarian working on the project, through our community partners, all the way up to the Chief Librarian.

ELVIA ARROYO-RAMIREZ: At the Center for the Study of Political Graphics (CSPG), I was hired to do a two-year federally funded grant project with National Historical Publications and Records Commission to arrange and describe their entire collection, which at the time was about eighty thousand political graphic posters. CSPG is an independent grassroots archive that collects social movement posters from all over the world with strong concentrations in the Vietnam War era and twentieth century Latin America. Their collecting policy stipulates that in order for posters to be collected by the archive they have to be overtly political and produced in multiples. The "produced in multiples" can be interpreted to mean that posters were originally produced for public display to call attention to social issues. In this case, I would say that the digitization of these posters aligns with, if not amplifies, their original intention to reach as many people as possible with their message. There are other cases, though, that the digitization of pre-Internet materials can be harmful and ethically unconscionable.

Tara Robertson has discussed ethical issues surrounding digitization of queer/pre-Internet resources in her talk "Not All Information Wants to Be Free: Ethical Considerations for Digitization." Digitization gets at one of the core values we have in the library and information science profession—to make information and content as accessible as possible. However, when materials were originally created for a specific community—for example, an underground queer community—the act of digitization can disrespect and overstep this intent. Tara talks about the "right to be forgotten," consent, and how to ethically go about doing this work.

MOLLY FAIR: Early on at Interference Archive, we were having conversations about the types of materials that we would collect, and thinking about that in regards to privacy. Things that would have been disseminated widely in the public, like flyers and posters, seemed like they would be all right. But we also wanted to think the identities of the creators of these materials, like whether they use an alias or not—do we want to make connections between a person's two different personas, if they have them?—and how we keep records of the names of people who donate materials. I think we're having honest conversations as a public archive and a DIY archive. The degree to which we could take protections, and not make false claims about what kinds of protections we can realistically provide, is really important to cultivating trust in our communities and protecting people.

There have been some contentious cases elsewhere. In particular I'm thinking of a collection of videorecorded interviews with members of the Irish Republican Army that were held by Boston College and then subpoenaed a few years back by a US court for a trial in the UK. Boston College tried to resist the subpoena, but ultimately one has to ask whether it would have been better if these interviews were not held in their repository where they might be discovered and seized as evidence. The issues of privacy and security came up for Interference when there was a question of whether or not to accept a collection of oral histories. The creators of this material wanted to ensure certain protections that we didn't feel comfortable promising. We wanted this collection to be as accessible as possible, and if there were caveats for taking in materials like, oh, this can't be made public for the next fifty years or something, that isn't necessarily something that we felt we could take on.

JEN HOYER: We talked a lot about those oral history collections, and it was a really good series of conversations. It forced us to think about our own policy on providing access to everything in our collection and whether or not we have the technology to lock things up or provide different levels of access, and whether or not that's something that we think is reasonable to accommodate in a volunteer-run space. As part of our collection policy we do say that we only take things that will be made accessible to the public; we don't take things like organizational records or personal papers that might be a little more personally sensitive. We just collect things that were produced in multiples for broad distribution, generally speaking.

Recently someone mailed us an album of photographs that this person took at Black Lives Matters protests, with no information except a Post-it that was basically like, "I thought you might want these." They're incredible, but there are some questions with respect to whether this photographer giving us the rights to these photos by giving them to us. We can never digitize those and put them in our online catalog, because these are people at protests that are just happening right now. People are getting in trouble. So I guess there is an access restriction there. We emailed the person back, just to say, "Hi, can you tell us more about this? Do you own the copyright to these? Are you giving us the copyright to these?" No reply. What do we do with this photo album? It's a tricky question.

HADASSAH DAMIEN: How do we talk about open access and wanting to find a way to strike the balance between making a findable digital record, and sort of respecting the fact that these materials were created at a time when people didn't know that there would be mass archiving and mass cataloging of items? Another conversation is about the right to be forgotten and the "do not digitize movement," which I know is really big in the world of creators of zines. That's something that I think will start to be larger for us as we work with makers of ephemera who realize that their ephemera might not be ephemeral after all.

MOLLY FAIR: I remember someone donating a zine, and I asked them, "What name do you want to be associated with this?" And they looked at me surprised and said they didn't want any attribution at all. I'm sure there's plenty of materials that we have in Interference Archive where someone does not want their identity to be associated with it and would prefer to remain anonymous. This could be for any number of reasons—whether you don't to be associated publicly with a movement as an individual, or you don't want people to know you wrote a zine when you were a young teen that includes a lot of intense personal information or conveys different political views than you currently hold. So how do we respect these needs to remain anonymous when we're cataloging or keeping records of donated materials?

Elvia Arroyo-Ramirez: The bulk of the content I process and make accessible is written in Spanish, and there's also some French and Portuguese. I've slowly come to the realization that, in some respects, it's a form of colonization to translate archival description to English when materials are written in other languages. It is a disservice to certain audiences—quite possibly your primary one—to translate folder titles simply because the collecting institution happens to be a majority English-speaking institution. It's an imposed and somewhat artificial signifier, and a disservice to the nature of the materials to describe them in languages they're not written in. When it comes to writing finding aids, I try to be as true to the native language that the materials were created in as I can be. For archival description, this can mean describing folders as how the creator titled them in whatever language the creator chose.

I'm currently processing the papers of Edgardo Cozarinsky, a filmmaker and polyglot who often weaves in and out of French, Spanish, and English in his archive. The draft of the contents list reflects this linguistic oscillation. I still write the front matter—biographical, arrangement, scope and content notes—in English, and if I had more time or had more colleagues working on non-English language collections I would explore the idea of writing bilingual finding aids. I believe Arizona State University developed a template to make this possible, and that's great. A running concern I have with regard to born-digital processing is the possible risks we introduce as archivists when automating certain analysis processes, in particular when it come to processing collections written in other languages. The digital preservation and curation field is relatively new, and archivists and software developers are just now developing processes and workflows with the long-term goal of keeping digital archives safe for as long as possible. A lot of the skills to conduct this type of work are picked up on the job, while managing other competing responsibilities. My worry is that this might pressure folks to automate a lot of these tasks for the sake of efficiency. In doing this, do we run the risk of losing cultural markers that get wiped off because they didn't fit the standards that the tools we use to automate are set to? With increasing automation there's the increasing risk of the unintentional whitewashing of inherent non-English cultural markers, like diacritics.

I've written about my experience working on the Juan Gelman Papers,[3] where I argued that it takes active intervention, a vigilance that might be hindered when automation is introduced in workflows, and a certain critical awareness to uphold the cultural and linguistic integrity of collections. I understand that we need certain types of automation to help with the circuitous and labor-intensive processes of born-digital preservation, but there's a need to find a balance between automating and iterative process. Breaking down automation into smaller interactive actions will help keep archivists accountable each step of the way.

JARRETT DRAKE: Even though my appointment is in the university archives, because I'm the only digital archivist at Princeton, I end up being asked to assist or advise on digital collections across the department. Elvia said she had a floppy disk, and she hadn't yet processed any born-digital material. I thought I would point her to the workflows that I've drawn up in BitCurator, and it was going to be a nice, straightforward experience. BitCurator is not a software; it's a customized Ubuntu operating system that packages a lot of software. So I always tell people BitCurator is just an operating system. Anything that you can install in any Ubuntu-Linux environment, you can install on BitCurator.

I can't remember which program we were using within BitCurator. I think it was Bagger, which was developed by the Library of Congress, and it was unable to execute because it said there were names of files that had invalid encoding. Now, the materials were created primarily in Spanish. It was a high quantity of files that this program said had invalid encoding, and that's the first time I'd ever encountered that. I've worked with hundreds of thousands of files, hundreds of gigabytes of materials, and I'd never come across that particular issue. The issue was that the environment in which these files had been created used encoding schemes that in the United States and other English-speaking nations, it just couldn't register. Literally, it was like, I don't know what these characters are, using these particular programs. It's not that the computer itself

---

3   Elvia Arroyo-Ramirez, "Invisible Defaults and Perceived Limitations: Processing the Juan Gelman Files" (presentation, Preservation and Archiving Special Interest Group meeting, New York, NY, October 26–28, 2016), https://medium.com/on-archivy/invisible-defaults-and-perceived-limitations-processing-the-juan-gelman-files-4187fdd36759.

couldn't recognize or read the files; it could. But this particular program couldn't operate because of the language difference.

We spent some time researching this issue, and the responses we got when we asked people, like, "What would you do if you got this issue?" or "Have you had this issue?"—there were some interesting responses. But we found, I think, an anti-oppressive way to enable the files to be recognized by this program and for Elvia to complete her processing of that collection. It wasn't my collection, but it probably taught me as much about the political and social context of digital records processing that anything ever has. It was a very illuminating experience, to say the very least.

ELVIA ARROYO-RAMIREZ: The bulk of responses we received from the digital curation and preservation community pointed to replacing or removing the accented characters with the use of scripts or tools that "cleaned" or "scrubbed" "illegal" characters by removing them entirely or replacing them with underscores. After I read some of those responses, I wondered, why do the diacritics of a file name have to be "scrubbed" or "cleaned"—these are words that people actually used—in order to be deemed "validated"? There might have been confusion about what an illegal character is. There are characters that everybody knows you can't create a file name with, like a question mark or an asterisk or a colon. But some people were confounding those characters with diacritics.

You'll always come across little snags while processing digital collections for preservation and access, and you have to step back and try to figure out the underlying implications to workarounds. I think what Jarrett and I recognized as the true lesson in this case study is the way we use language to identify and define issues and how this is informed by our perceptions of what is possible. We should try to figure out why we use certain words to describe certain processes, words like "detox," "scrub," "clean"—as if the file itself is dirty and needs to be cleansed in order to be saved. A filename that has diacritics shouldn't need to be "cleaned," because diacritics are part of the inherent understanding and structure of a language. When working with collections that come from other parts of the world or are from different cultures from ours, digital archivists need to practice an ethics of care that ensures we, as US practicing digital archivists, are not removing or taking something inherent to the meaning of our collections.

ANDREW WEISS: At CSUN, we did a couple studies. One was about Spanish language. We did a very small, random sample. I'm not quite sure how useful it is at scale; right now we're just dealing with very minuscule amounts. But we did find, within a typical collection, at least as HathiTrust was concerned, that Spanish language materials, for example, were represented far less than you would see in a Census record in the United States. The US has a very large Hispanic and Spanish-speaking population. According to the Census, it's about 12 percent of our population. But then when you look at what's in HathiTrust, it's about maybe 5 percent of their collection, so there's a bit of a skew there. I think that just shows the source of their materials is academic libraries in particular. For the longest time, Spanish was not necessarily seen as one of the primary languages of scholarly communication. That would be French, English, German—those are really the main ones over the past 150 years. And you can see that's reflected within the collections. That just shows the history, then, of those collections, but it doesn't necessarily reflect current needs.

I think that can get at some of the problems, too, of these massive digital libraries when you're doing a retrospective scanning. We also did some Japanese language investigation, and there were a lot of problems with metadata. I think some of that has to do with just the problems of OCR and non-Roman languages, those languages like Japanese or Chinese that are using characters, the kanji. Japanese also has katakana and hiragana as part of the writing system. The OCR for that is just not perfected, and you can see that in the metadata results—a lot of gibberish characters, a lot of characters that make no sense. Content that's been encoded into Roman letters instead of into kanji or the other writing systems. That also then impedes how people can find that information. So I think there are some issues that come out with issues of language representation within a culture or underrepresented groups, and then just the fact that these projects are based in English-speaking countries with people—the scanners working on those projects—who may not have any expertise with Japanese language or Chinese language, and so that perhaps reflects in some of the errors that come out in these projects.

HANA SLEIMAN: It's been kind of hellish. To make a bilingual digital archive has been very, very difficult, especially because Arabic language technology is still in its earlier phases of development. Whereas the software that we're using for the Palestinian Oral History Archive is automated for English, we have to manually put everything in Arabic. Actually, it was one of the very important challenges at the beginning of the project. We had material that was in Arabic that needed to be described in both languages. The tools we were going to develop in both languages—so the subject headings and the keywords—we did. But we could not use the Arabic tools directly in the software because it was developed for English language material. What the indexers were doing was listening, selecting the term in Arabic, translating it or looking up its English equivalent from our pre-controlled lists, inputting the English equivalent into the software, and then manually inputting the original Arabic term. It was ridiculous. And they still do this, because the other option would have been to develop our own software, which would have delayed the project by at least a year or two. So the decision was to make this compromise and go through the loop.

All this to say that if we weren't as committed to having a bilingual archive, it would have been very easy to just go for it only in English—which would have been a shame, especially since the very purpose of this archive is to make it accessible to the community that produced it. Because they own it, and not anyone else. The politics of having it in Arabic is super, super important; the technicalities are very challenging. I think that has been one of the main reasons why the project is taking so long. Otherwise it would have been up much sooner. Definitely I wish people were discussing the development of open source software that's Arabic-friendly, or that's friendly to transcripts.

JAYCIE VOS: For the New Roots oral history project, we were focused on reaching audiences beyond the academy. One of the primary goals of that project was making the interviews accessible to the interviewees and their families and their communities, and a lot of times that means English is not their first language, or maybe they don't speak English at all. We wanted the interviews to be available to them because they're the ones sharing their stories. But as far as describing the interviews, we didn't want to rely too heavily on things like Library of Congress Subject Headings. LCSH are truly useful, and they make a lot of sense in a lot of environments, but since this is so much more community-focused, the New Roots team felt like that would be another barrier to access for people who aren't necessarily researchers or really experienced using the subject headings.

So we came up with a new vocabulary to describe the interviews at a thematic or topical level. We used everyday language keywords where we drew the language from the interviews themselves and described things in a way that represents how it was discussed in the interview. I am actually not a Spanish speaker at all, and luckily we have some really great staff members who work specifically on New Roots—Maria Ramirez and Laura Villa-Torres. They're both at UNC for graduate school, and they're both native Spanish speakers. They've been incredible colleagues in this project. They've been really great about understanding how to translate things well and identifying breakdowns when the translation wasn't very clear or when a concept just doesn't really make sense in English or Spanish. I've deferred to them a ton when it comes to making those decisions.

All the interviews first go into CONTENTdm, but we're using Omeka as special additional space for New Roots to present the interviews in both English and Spanish. There's not a built-in "translate this" feature on Omeka, at least not one that works at the level that we want. So we did a lot on the back end, really figuring out what things need to be translated. We thought a lot about what information stays the same no matter what language it's in. Is it really more important for the archivist to know certain technical metadata, or do we need to actually translate that for our users? We decided we probably didn't need to, so we focused just on the descriptive metadata. It was really good to think about what's important to the broader audience versus what's important only for library staff, and for preservation and technical metadata. So we prioritized the description of the interviews. We made all the abstracts and the thematic browsing keywords available in both English and Spanish, as well as other descriptive information, like interviewee occupation. Along the way we had to add new fields in CONTENTdm to accommodate the Spanish pieces, because we were pulling that into the Spanish version of Omeka and there's not an automatic translation. So that was one little workaround that we came up with, to duplicate some of the fields and to have other dedicated Spanish-language fields.

We also have a lot of maps on the New Roots website. One map shows where every interviewee comes from, at the city or country level, and there's a map that shows where people moved in North Carolina at the county level. With these maps, users can observe the different migration patterns. I think it really helps to visualize the journeys. You can switch between having the countries labeled in English or Spanish, depending on what version of the website that you're in, because you can toggle the whole site from English to Spanish. Giving that sort of basic level of description in both English and Spanish was really, really meaningful.

BÉATRICE COLASTIN SKOKAN: In the Cuban Heritage Collection, interviews are conducted in Spanish. For the Caribbean Diaspora and Haitian Diaspora, we also offered multilingual options by hiring two interviewers that were bilingual in English-Spanish, and trilingual in French, Haitian Creole, and English. Interviewees were given the option of being interviewed in a foreign language that may have been their native language. In the case of the Caribbean Diaspora project, we have five interviews in Spanish. The other individuals felt comfortable in English and decided to have their interviews in English. I think part of the interviewees' preoccupation was that they didn't want there to be the linguistic barrier. If they felt comfortable enough, they wanted their stories told in English so that more people could understand and know the truth of their experiences.

At this point we are not able to offer translations, which are very costly. Of course, one can also make the argument that others may prefer to view content in their native language. These individuals have stories of trauma; they're coming from countries that have issues of democracy, freedom of the press, and freedom of expression. The interview was an opportunity for them to tell their stories without the narratives being filtered by media, or experts.

The interviews are posted right away in Kaltura with minimal metadata attached because we have a rubric at the point of delivery by the videographer. The digital department works with the videographer and conveys minimum requirements such as the intro card, the interviewer's name, the interviewee's name, the videographer, and the date of the interview. With that minimum descriptive information in place, the library can publish the interviews right away. This process allows time to do more metadata later, to post the content in CONTENTdm. I write up a finding aid that's connected to the video recordings; the finding aid includes a short bio and a synopsis of the interview, thus providing context that may not be immediately apparent if the video were published in isolation.

BONNIE GORDON: When I think about technology at Interference Archive in general and the catalog specifically, I think a lot about the importance of Interference as a physical space, and how technology interplays with that; at the same time I think about the fact that we're all volunteer and there's a lot of remote interaction that happens among volunteers and with the collection itself. But the catalog is really important, particularly in its relation to the physical space. It's very intentional that Interference's collection is primarily what's in the physical space, and it's not just a digital archive of cool radical stuff that's online and you can look at it from anywhere. And I think it's important how the catalog is organized and created, and how that interplays with how the physical collection is organized and interacted with by volunteers and visitors.

DANIEL KAHN GILLMOR: We had a bunch of discussions about what type of tooling we wanted to try to use for Interference Archive's online catalog. We were aware that decisions made early on were going to have long-lasting repercussions. At the same time, we were making those decisions in the dark because we didn't know specifically what workflows people were going to want to have from the toolchain that we chose. We didn't know how rapidly the collection would grow. We didn't know what kinds of human labor would be available to us for things like data entry or organization. And we also had to make decisions not about specifically what categories we were going to be cataloging, but even more meta than that—what *kinds* of categories would we be willing to work with?

In the decision-making about the tools, we were also faced with questions about whether we wanted control over the data ourselves. Do we want to have it be hosted in the cloud somewhere? Do we want it physically locally? Do we want it to be running free software? Do we want a subscription service? There's a bunch of open questions there, including questions about metadata structure—if you're cataloging, what kinds of metadata might you have about the objects, and how extensible do you want that to be? There's a huge range of options, and when you make some of them, you really can't revisit those options without a ton of work—not only in the work of making the change, but in the social work of acclimatizing everybody who was used to the old mechanism to the new mechanism.

We ended up deciding we wanted to use free and open source software. There was a general sense that we didn't know how sensitive the information we were going to be having, including patron and browsing information, would be, so we wanted to lean towards being in control of our data rather than having it out there in the cloud for somebody else to have access to. It's harder to claw back access than to give it out. We looked at a few different options for cataloging systems. There were basically three that came up—Koha, which is a traditional library system implemented in Perl; Omeka, which is in PHP; and CollectiveAccess. We ended up settling on CollectiveAccess after a lot of discussion, partially because we felt it would be the most flexible going forward. That flexibility has come at a cost for us, in terms of the complexity of the system making it unwieldy at times. But at the same time it means that we've had options that we maybe wouldn't have had if we'd gone with a simpler system like Omeka.

There was sort of a fourth option that was to build something from the ground up with some sort of more standard website toolkit, which would have given us probably the most flexibility and, in some senses, the easiest workflow steps. But then we wouldn't have had any additional support or community around the tooling. I think it was important for the group to know that there would be other people working on this tool, that the knowledge of how it worked wouldn't just be held in the heads of specific collective members. And it was important that the metadata formats we're working with have wide compatibility. If we wanted to do data interchange or produce documents that other folks could read easily, just making up your own data format is not the path to that.

MOLLY FAIR: I was involved since the initiation of Interference, and in the beginning there was more of a need to figure out how to transition a personal collection into a publicly accessible archive. This took a great deal of sensitivity to understand how much of the original collection's organization was necessary to preserve, versus understanding what the needs would be moving forward as the collection grew from other people's contributions. Our system of organization would have to make sense to a larger group of people, not just the founding members.

I initially suggested CollectiveAccess for our database because I had used it previously as a Fellow at the Queens Memory Project. I was aware of its capabilities as a cataloging platform that was highly configurable, and which could support a variety of media and file formats. It would give us the ability to really build off of a tool that could not just fulfill our technological needs but could also potentially reflect our shared politics. But once we settled on CollectiveAccess, there was a really big learning curve just to figure out how to use the tool itself—a lot of the back end isn't visible unless you're looking at the code—and so we were heavily reliant on our more tech-savvy collective members to investigate and problem-solve these issues. It was not a plug-and-play scenario by any means.

There also was a great degree of openness for people to be involved in the process on multiple levels—the librarians and archivists posed a lot of questions about metadata schemas, controlled vocabularies, organization, and copyright; the tech folks brought up a lot of issues of data security and storage, as well as the politics versus practicality of using open source software; and others were more involved in testing the cataloging interface and designing the look of the public-facing interface. Along the way, we kept asking a million questions in order to determine what our minimum requirements were versus what elements would be nice to include but not essential to be functional. For instance, was it essential to have media categorized hierarchically, like "Documents—books, magazines, pamphlets, etc."? What would it mean to create our own controlled vocabulary based on a crowdsourced vernacular that reflected a multitude of activist histories, and how labor-intensive would it be to input this vocabulary in CollectiveAccess so that the keywords weren't just searchable but could be created as linked data?

There were so many details like this to ponder, and so many rabbit holes to potentially fall down into. At a certain point, decisions needed to be made, and it was also hard to know when to pull the trigger to launch the catalog publicly. We were very lucky that we were able to assemble a group of people that was willing to donate their time and energy into setting up these tools and figuring out all the workflows, and who were also really invested in figuring out how to spread that knowledge and make sure that it wasn't just in a couple people's heads. But it was essential to acknowledge that this energy wasn't and isn't limitless. As in any volunteer-run organization, we knew that we couldn't just rely on one person to do the work. We relied on a lot of skillshares, volunteer user testing during cataloging parties, and a robust documentation wiki to pass along knowledge. That was very important. Additionally CollectiveAccess has a very active user community and a pretty responsive team of developers whom we occasionally contacted to report bugs and ask more complex questions.

HADASSAH DAMIEN: Something we did that I think was really helpful was spin up test instances of CollectiveAccess and Omeka and really look at both of them. That actually made it, in my recollection, a quick decision to go with CollectiveAccess, after looking at exactly how the two softwares allowed us to configure metadata and do some of the work and imagine how we might create workflows within the software. There was something really valuable about actually getting little test instances up for people to just touch and interact with. For all the discussion, and all the looking at specs and talking and writing, there was something irreplaceable about attempting to use the interface itself that really informed how we made our decisions.

Because *we* chose to host the software ourselves, using an open source software that was self-hosted, we were able to do this level of experimentation. We might not have been able to do it with a software as a service, a software in a cloud, or a software on a platform. So when you're thinking about the type of customizations or granular needs that you might have for a specific tool, being able to actually access the code makes a difference in terms of trying to poke at the thing to see if you can get it to do what you really want it to do.

JEN HOYER: One of the fascinating things is that in our public interface for the online catalog, you actually can't click on a subject keyword to jump to other things that have the same keyword. That's because of the field type that we chose for subjects. We had probably a year of meetings about creating a taxonomy that we could use in cataloging and then realized that even if we managed to figure one out, our interface wouldn't give it the functionality that we hoped for. It's not a bug; it's just the type of field that we chose. It's not impossible to change the field type, but it's a question of what type of field would be ideal, both for that front end capability as well as for ease of data entry on the cataloging interface. If we give it the front end functionality we want, it makes it more difficult for catalogers to add new subject keywords on the back end. So you're trying to lower barriers all around, but if you create the functionality you want on the front end, it makes things more complicated for newbie catalogers.

DANIEL KAHN GILLMOR: This is a classic case where I think the tool has given us bad constraints. We see a set of options for us, and one of the advantages of having a flexible tool—a tool that we can potentially modify or that has a larger community—is that we can say, "Look, we want this type of stuff on the back end for these fields, and we want this type of stuff on the front end, and I don't see how to get there." That's worth a bug report to the upstream, at least, to let them know that we felt stuck, right? Because they don't know that we felt stuck. It could be, "Oh, well, we can just add that thing to the front end and leave all of your data the same," or it could be, "You're going to have to change your fields, but we can make it so that you get an easy back end thing." So keeping those channels of communication open is critical to making sure that you ultimately get what you want. With software, everything is possible, with enough work. But when you feel like you're trapped, make sure that that's communicated to the folks who might know about it.

. . .

BONNIE GORDON: We ultimately decided not to use Library of Congress Subject Headings for the Interference Archive catalog and to enter our own subject headings, which is still having repercussions, because even now there are multiple lists of subjects that kind of hang out. Some overlap, and for some there are tensions between what people enter into the catalog and what people write on the box, when they create a box of anarchist pamphlets or posters that relate to whatever social movement. Initially we were like, "Oh, we'll come up with our own hierarchical taxonomy," and that just didn't work. For the physical collection, we're still figuring it out, but for the data in CollectiveAccess, it gives us more flexibility to do what we want.

JEN HOYER: There's a link between organization of the physical collection and the way you describe things in an online catalog. That's something that we constantly come up against because it feels like we need to figure out how to organize things on the shelf at the same time that we figure out how to describe them in the catalog. Often we're organizing them based on subject categories that we should probably then replicate in the catalog. I think a lot of this comes back to our main goal at Interference Archive of providing access. It's thinking about what makes things accessible for people who are browsing the shelves, but also what makes things accessible for people who are just entering keywords into an online catalog. How do we think of those keywords and subject terms that they might use? And how do we also let the material describe itself? Self-representation is something we believe really strongly in.

So that's a constant which-and-how kind of question. We also want to lower barriers not just for people who are accessing the catalog but also for people who are cataloging material. I've sat with first-time catalogers who have this look of pain and frustration because they can't think of subject terms for something. And I'm like, "Hey, it's cool. It's fine. Maybe look it up online and find some keywords that other people seem to have used for it in some context." Also we've had a lot of conversations about how this is a collaborative effort that's happening over time. You can build a catalog record, and if someone finds it later and says, "I would describe it with *these* three subject terms or keywords, or a descriptive paragraph that you haven't used," that second person can go in and add that work. It's being built as a community. It's not like metadata is created and that's the golden standard that no one else can touch. When someone creates metadata, they aren't keeping ownership of it. It's metadata that's owned in common and can be continually transformed in common.

MOLLY FAIR: I think there's this expectation that when you're cataloging something, people who are doing the work necessarily have all this knowledge. But even in the institutional library, that's not always the case. Usually if you're cataloging something, people are taking a record that was done by another institution. Many of us who are cataloging materials are not necessarily subject experts in the academic sense, or even have traditional library cataloging experience or training. We might be relying on our own knowledge or experience, we might do a little traditional research, or we might try to interview the creators of the materials if we have relationships to them.

This is what makes Interference positioned somewhat uniquely. We might interview creators of these materials as they are donated and get metadata that a regular collecting institution would not. So I feel like what we're doing is unique in the sense that we're continually evolving the information that's there. It's more in the style of Wikipedia. In terms of using a metadata schema, I wanted to include a lot of structural elements that would be useful in terms of cataloging a variety of materials. I looked at Getty's Categories for the Description of Works of Art, VRA Core, and the rules in *Cataloging Cultural Objects* for inspiration, but I didn't want to create something so rigid and prescriptive that someone without library, archives, or information science training couldn't follow it.

There were a lot of issues brought up with preserving and collecting born-digital objects, as well as digitizing physical objects, in terms of copyright, privacy, data storage, our preservation capabilities as an archive on a limited operating budget, data sensitivity, and more. At first we were more focused on the physical materials and getting them organized and accessible, which is kind of funny thinking back on it since so many of us are involved in creating art and cultural materials that live in digital realms. It just initially seemed like a lot more complexity than we had bandwidth to deal with until more people came along who wanted to wrestle with these questions full-on.

. . .

CECILY WALKER: Right now, what we've mostly been doing at Vancouver Public Library is not focusing so much on the metadata aspect of our digital collections, although that's a big part of it; we've mostly been focusing on building relationships with people in the community who might be interested in finding a semi-permanent home for artifacts that they either need digitized or that are already in digital format, so that they can share them with people around the world because it's available on the Internet. The biggest problem that we've had with a lot of library resources is that they're not indexed by search engines. But this is one library resource that wasn't built by a vendor, and it's something that for one of the first times is built with the intention of public library users being able to directly contribute their own materials to the collection.

Because it's now open and searchable and available on the Internet, when we're naming collections, or naming artifacts to go into our collections, we're very, very explicit and intentional about the names that we use. We don't just depend on our cataloging department—although we do depend on them, and we do use some standard subject descriptions—but we also depend on people from the communities that we work with who may have terms that they would use to refer to something that is a term that we may not be aware of. And we add that to the metadata for the artifacts. So instead of just going for the dominant, top-down description that we force on items that go into our repository, we're taking more of a community-led and community-directed approach, and a collaborative approach, and making sure that whatever term or name you might have for a specific event, person, place, or thing, that you can also find it that way as well.

Becky Yoose: The Fifth Law of Library Science is, "The library is a growing organism." So, metadata as the Fifth Law of Library Science—library technology is also a growing organism. Metadata is not static, partially due to standards that the library community and other organizations come up with in terms of their subject headings or description metadata.

A very good way that that Fifth Law applies to metadata is with subject headings. You have subject headings that were constructed for a particular time with a particular type of environment where you have folks saying, "We have a subject heading for this group," and they don't understand why that subject heading might be offensive to use for that group. Or it makes the assumption that it's just going to point out this particular underrepresented or minority group, while the base subject heading will be the default cis-hetero-white male. For example, you have "Authors" and "Women Authors," and other authors that are delineated by race and gender. And you have people out there who are actively trying to get these subject headings—which, again, firmly set standards—to reflect the reality. They should reflect that while these were done at this particular time, they're no longer appropriate for today's standards due to derogatory terminology, or they weren't inclusive, or just, "Hey, this is something that should be a subject now because there are people writing about this particular topic, and our patrons want to know about it, but there's really no good way that our system can accurately describe it because there's really no controlled subject heading that we can use on a consistent basis." If you're using a structure that was created in one particular culture and beliefs and norms and trying to apply it in a time where, honestly, those norms and beliefs are either outdated or offensive, then that standard needs to change.

Librarianship tends to slowly change throughout time. That can be a hindrance and also a blessing. But I would appreciate if we move a little bit faster or find ways that we can create more inclusive subject headings, or implement subject headings that meet the needs of users that otherwise would not be fully represented by existing organizational structures in our metadata standards.

ANITA COLEMAN: The Anti-Racism Digital Library came out of my reinvigorated faith perspective. I came into librarianship passionately believing that libraries are always inclusive and never exclusive, and that we represented information in all its forms. We made information available, and we never took sides. We presented all points of view; sure, we have our biases and prejudices—as anyone who has taught LCSH should know—but generally we tried to rise above them. What was discouraging for me was to realize that even as technology enables us to do that more and more, librarians still find ways to limit intellectual access. The other part of this is that information is very democratizing. I've come to believe now that librarians, despite their conservativeness, are critical in this process because of the sheer amount of information possible. But that means we have to have really high standards of integrity ourselves, to be fair and present that truth. Because we can't say, "This is the truth." Religion is a great example. Science is a great example. Almost any topic that you take, in these fields, there can be controversy.

The Anti-Racism Digital Library started because when all this racism stuff was happening, I couldn't believe that in the USA, where we have so much information for free and public libraries—no other country has this history of freedom of information and this history of intellectual access—that there was still something called systemic racism. I thought in our information institutions, at least, it won't be there. And I started to look. I thought, "This country has such a strong history in anti-racism, let me go and search in the library on Anti-racism." As I started to search in the library catalog and the indexes and the electronic databases on Anti-racism, I suddenly realized I was getting way more with "racism." I reported the results in my paper "Theology, Race, and Libraries," published in the Proceedings of the 2016 Annual Conference of the American Theological Librarians. There were more books on Racism and Race Relations and so on than on Anti-racism, and I also found that the Library of Congress Subject Headings entry for Anti-racism is very brief. Was the Library of Congress *not* using Anti-racism for some reason? In their Subject Cataloging Manual, do they have a policy of not using it? I've talked to the ATLA Religion Database indexers, and they said, yes, as a policy generally they don't put "anti-racism"; they prefer "race relations" and "race discrimination." And I asked, "Why?" If the solution to the race problem is anti-racism, why would you then hide it under "racism" and "racial discrimination" and all those other things? Why would you not highlight anti-racism?

The more I looked into this, I ran into intersectionality, where if a book is about class and gender and also ethnicity, then it gets lost. We tend to give just one subject heading even though we're allowed to give all these different ones. The more I saw that, I realized this is one example of how there is systemic privilege. There is structural racism built into our information institutions. I wanted to use the capabilities that web technologies have made available to highlight anti-racism. The technology to build a digital library is freely and openly available. All somebody needs to know is a little bit of these technologies. And so that's what I did. I started to build the Anti-Racism Digital Library just to give exposure to anti-racism. The groups that came alongside me initially were Christian faith groups that have been fighting racism for a long time, and now there are some interfaith groups. They are local, but some of them have national presence, and one of them is global. These are the people who are using it. The definition of anti-racism we're using is inclusive and much broader than the one LC provides. Theological librarians at ATLA 2017 were also very interested when I shared how the new ACRL Information Literacy Framework can be taught using the materials in the library; in reality, anti-racism is a great subject to use to teach the new threshold concepts of IL.

At this point the Anti-Racism Digital Library brings together resources on anti-racism, some created by us and others found on the Web. We're using Omeka, a content management platform, to catalog and describe the resources and then use those resources in small-group study, or in forums and talks that we organize around those different topics.

```
related_subjects = []
related_subjects.push("farm instruments")
related_subjects.push("search algorithms")
related_subjects.push("3D printing fails")
related_subjects.push("Amsterdam library computers")
related_subjects.push("short shorts")
related_subjects.push("Luddism")
related_subjects.push("scrum meetings")
related_subjects.push("garbage patriarchy")
related_subjects.push("Ally Skills Workshop")
related_subjects.push("Ada Initiative")
related_subjects.push("non-alcoholic options")
related_subjects.push("PatientsLikeMe")
related_subjects.push("New Orleans police")
related_subjects.push("Detroit schools")
related_subjects.push("the Women's Marches")
related_subjects.push("Gmail")
```

Being

This chapter opens with a reminder of the lack of neutrality of tech, and then gets deeper into the effects of structural oppressions. People talked about topics such as surveillance over bodies, racism, white supremacy, indigeneity, imposter syndrome, "the leaky pipeline," privacy and safety of marginalized people, and the ways that libraries are not in fact welcoming to all. Librarians and archivists are reflected on as laborers, too, in a discussion of trust and equity in the workplace.

I asked about anti-racism and critical race consciousness in the context of librarians' digital literacy, which brought up critical race information theory, data mining, and more. People also considered environmental issues—climate change, toxic waste—and their relative invisibility, at least among the more privileged among us. Reflections on gender and race led to a discussion of Code4Lib, LIS Microaggressions, Libraries4BlackLives, and other professional groups and efforts, especially conference codes of conduct.

. . .

MITA WILLIAMS: "What is technology" is an amazing question, and I've been thinking about it quite a bit. One of my favorite definitions comes from writer Paul Ford, which is "technology is what we share." I like that definition because it expresses that it's not just a tool; technology is not just something that allows us to do something in a different way or effect something, but it's also a practice. It changes how we do things, and it changes us.

I'm working on a project where I have to write an autoethnography, so I've been doing a lot of reflecting on my past. I believe that the time in which I really opened up to this larger holistic concept of technology came from library school. In my government documents class, we had a number of topics that we had the chance to explore and one of them was this idea that technology was neutral. For that assignment, I pulled Ursula Franklin's Massey Lectures, *The Real World of Technology*, from the library shelf. Ursula Franklin is an absolutely extraordinary person who I had not known of until then. She recently passed away. Her book talks about this real world of technology and about how it's not just a set of mechanics, but it's also a set of systems. So you can't say that technology is neutral in light of that context.

An example that she gives, which really stuck with me, is that you can see the non-neutrality of technology in the length of a handle of a farm hoe. She said that if you look back in our shameful history you learn that sharecroppers—the men and women working in the fields—would have very short handles for their farm instruments, even though if you had a very long handle you could work much more comfortably. She said, well, what were the reasons for this? And she pointed out that if you have a short handle, people have to work hunched over, which means that in order for them to rest they have to stand up. But if you are supervising the workers, the shortened tools are a benefit because you can quickly see from a distance whether people are working in the field or whether they're resting in the field. This sort of examination of the effects of technology lets us see what technologies restrict our freedoms and which ones enable them.

I had the pleasure of meeting Ursula Franklin through our faculty association. She has a remarkable history of social justice work, and she was being honored by the Canadian Association of University Teachers for her equity battle that she took on against the University of Toronto. I was able to have my copy of *The Real World of Technology* signed, and she gave me a hug. That was the best celebrity run-in that I've ever had in my life.

BÉATRICE COLASTIN SKOKAN: Use of technology is not value-neutral. The same issues of power and representation that continue to challenge cultural institutions and the authenticity of their discourse can be replicated with technological tools.

Bess Sadler: I worked in the start-up world for a while. At the start-up where I was working, it was fun in a lot of ways. It was a ridiculous amount of work. But I was also horrified by the ethics of the situation. We were working on healthcare software. We were developing a system for managing drug interactions in AIDS patients, so it was this expert system. I think it was 1997, there was this big AIDS conference, and they were going to make a big announcement. There were all these rumors flying about what the announcement was. And I remember all these people at work were terrified that someone might have found a cure for AIDS. They were *worried* about that. And I was like, "Boy, am I in the wrong line of work."

Cecily Walker: It's a notion that seems to be falling out of favor—which I'm really happy about, but a few people still cling to it—that technology is neutral. When you are deciding an interface, when you are designing a program—whether that's an application program or a library program—or when you are trying to show someone who may not have the same level of digital literacy as you have how to best make use of that tool, none of those things happen in a vacuum. None of those things operate or occur outside of the world that we live in, where we bring our own biases to the table.

If I could say anything about that, it would be for whomever might be reading this to challenge their assumptions about what they think about technology. Learn about the work of people like Safiya Noble, for example, who did some really amazing work where she discovered that Google's search algorithms are biased. At one point in the past, if you'd searched for, say, "girls" on the Internet, you might just get nonsexualized images of pretty, peppy white women who are fully clothed. But if you searched for "black girls" or "Asian girls" using Google, the images that were returned were by and large very sexualized. So technology is a tool that is used by people, and it's a tool that's created by people, and people are not neutral. It may not be malicious. It may not be intentional, but our biases creep into everything that we do.

Alison Macrina: Where to even start with structural oppression and power dynamics in libraries and through the lens of technology? Technology, like with all facets of life, is experienced much differently by marginalized people than it is by people in positions of privilege. In my trainings, people of color have related much more personal experiences with police surveillance than white people. I remember teaching a class in Philadelphia, where there were a lot of black Muslims. We had this whole conversation about people having anecdotal recollections of police taking their phones and returning them later, and the phone acting weird, or hearing about somebody who was under investigation for something and the kind of surveillance that was being used. One of the things that stood out to me most during that conversation was how many people in the room had a unique and personal experience of surveillance. This is part of the material reality for black and brown people in a way that is not for most white people.

Thinking about other identities and how surveillance affects them—older people are high-risk victims of identity theft and fraud. They use and are expected to use technology, and it seems like people in their families bring technology into their lives and don't really think about helping them learn how to use it. They get further marginalized as people who don't understand how any of this works, and so they get exploited very easily. Youth privacy can be exploited in many ways because they don't really have any rights, because their principals and their parents and their teachers and the police will just take devices away from them and look through their phones.

Thinking about people who have any kinds of health issues, be they mental or physical, that prevents them from using some kind of digital device in the way that it was built—when we think about who's making these devices and who's writing the software, it's usually able-bodied white men, and so the people who are not those people can't even use the device in a way that is safe for them. Privacy technology is no exception to this. People who are differently abled might not even be able to engage with the software. Something that I think of immediately is passwords. Passwords are a huge problem, and one of the problems is that if you have any difficulty remembering a long string of text, you're never going to have a good password. Even if you use a password manager, just trying to remember that master passphrase—if you have any memory difficulty, that is just outside of the realm of possibility for you.

Trans people, queer people in general, are under a lot more surveillance and that can affect their healthcare, their work, their families. These are things that are incredibly fraught. Whatever your identity might be, if you are a marginalized person for any reason, you can pretty much guarantee that technology is not working for you. It's working against you.

STACIE WILLIAMS: My husband is also a journalist as well as an editor at this point, and he's kind of a high-up editor. It is still the truth to this day that there are so few African Americans in journalism, but especially at the level that he's at. You could probably count on one hand the number of African American male editors at major news organizations in this country. Like, it's tiny.

We talk a lot about his job and the decisions that he makes in terms of how he communicates to other editors and reporters the stories that are important, because essentially people like him don't often get a seat at the table, and at the end of the day, editors are people, too. It's like we say about technology—technology's not neutral. Algorithms aren't neutral. Tech isn't neutral; it's very biased, because it's created by humans.

Well, editors are those same humans. Editors, you could consider, are kind of tech. If an editor is Google, an editor is sitting there deciding what's important, what's relevant, what the story of the day is to bump to the front page or page two of the Metro so that you see it right away and think, oh, this is important. Just the fact that my husband has the opportunity to sit at that table and offer pushback when people are insisting that stories concerning people who look like him, or who look me, or who look like people who are underrepresented or marginalized in our community—when editors are trying to tell him that those stories, or those people, aren't important, it's critical that somebody like him has the opportunity to be at the table to push back against that and say, "This is absolutely important. These are things that our readers need to know."

. . .

JESSA LINGEL: I think environmental issues around technology are huge and underdiscussed. The amount of energy our servers are using all of the time so that we can stream stuff and have access to entire libraries of content all of the time—there are real environmental consequences for that that are obscured when we talk about it as a "cloud," as if it's up in the air rather than underground in servers that require massive amounts of energy and water to keep cool. I think Robert Gehl is totally right that it's very hypocritical for someone to say that they care about the environment and then get a new smartphone every two years. I don't think we've even begun to square environmental consequences of how we're using technology in everyday life.

ELVIA ARROYO-RAMIREZ: People in the library and archives professions are not talking enough about the environmental impacts of an increasingly digital profession. See Eira Tansey's work with Project ARCC,[1] Archivists Responding to Climate Change, and others.

CHAD CLARK: We keep our 3D printing restricted to PLA. They say PLA is better than something like ABS. PLA I believe is biodegradable, but not without a process. We keep that in mind, and of course our community has asked, "What do you print with? And what is it? What exactly is this?" We'd had our 3D printer running for about a year out in the open and actually decided about six months ago to get a glass enclosure that has an air filtration system strapped to the back of it. So our printer is out in the open but it's technically enclosed, and it's got a little fan on the back that's supposedly catching the larger particles.

I still believe the research is not completely tight yet. We're trying to keep up with the technology. I think no matter how much we believe it or not, none of us really know what the implications are for newer technologies like this. We're burning plastic, right, at high temperatures. With our case and the filtration system and using the PLA, I feel like we're trying to respect the atmosphere. But also, with 3D printing, there are a lot of fails, obviously. Anybody who's used one knows that out of ten prints you're likely not to get ten perfect prints. You're going to have some failures. We've been keeping those failures in a big box. As a side project, we're thinking about asking the community to make a sculpture where we glue all the parts together and make some crazy figure. As far as we can tell, it's better than throwing it in a landfill. But we're learning and trying to adapt as we go.

MICHAEL CHERRY: In terms of the toxicity of 3D printing, that is something I haven't really addressed in the programs with students. Some of the controversy that came up surrounding 3D printing dealt more

---

1 Eira Tansey, "The Voice of One Crying Out in the Wilderness: Preservation in the Anthropocene" (presentation, Preservation and Archiving Special Interest Group meeting, New York, NY, October 26–28, 2016), http://eiratansey.com/2016/10/28/pasig-2016-talk-text/.

with the use of 3D printed firearms. I did a 3D printing demo for a teen book club, and a student mentioned 3D printed firearms. We were talking about science fiction books and the pros and cons of futuristic technologies. His remark generated a discussion about copyright, legality, and ethics, and instead of avoiding these topics, I engaged students in a discussion about them.

Elsewhere, in our robotics programs we've designed programs about environmental issues that examine how robots install solar panels and separate recyclables. In the past, we've taught a robotics club using Lego's Green City Challenge set. Students design and program robots that complete environmental challenges on the mats that accompany the set. I contributed a programming kit to the American Library Association's website[2] that details this program and provides a list of resources.

ELAINE HARGER: I wish library people were discussing where all of this hardware comes from, and what we can do to pressure the companies that make it and sell it to us to change to a humane mode of doing business and manufacturing, rather than the inhumane processes that they use right now.

I had an experience once. I visited the central library in Amsterdam, which was right next to the train station there. I had a train layover for a couple of hours. I wandered into the library and was just kind of looking around and thought, oh, I'll check my email. And I sat down at a computer and looked at the keyboard, and I was absolutely flabbergasted. You know those old pay telephones—Ma Bell had pay telephones in these little booths on every corner or down in the subways, and they had these keypads that were practically indestructible? You could take a baseball bat to one of those telephone keypads and couldn't hurt it. Well, these keyboards at the computer terminals at the library in Amsterdam were built like that. They looked and felt like they were indestructible.

I come from libraries in the States, like the high school library that I'd been working at, where the keyboards are these flimsy things. It doesn't take much to damage them, and kids, hundreds of them, every day, using them—there's a considerable amount of wear

---

2 Michael Cherry, "Program Model: Green City Robotics," *Programming Librarian*, February 2, 2016, http://www.programminglibrarian.org/programs/green-city-robotics.

and tear, and after a couple of years, sometimes you have to get new ones. And I thought, there must be something happening here. The city of Amsterdam, or maybe it's the country, requires that whoever sells computer equipment to public entities has to have a standard of indestructibility that the citizens are willing to pay for. I think that we librarians in the United States should start demanding that the manufacturers of the computer equipment that we buy make things durable and make things in a way that pays the workers a living wage and doesn't harm the environment and doesn't generate poison that gets dumped into the air and into the water. That's what I would like to see the profession talking about in relation to technology.

MITA WILLIAMS: I'm very concerned with the threat of global warming. It's something that I think terrifies most of us, which is why we don't talk about it as much as we should. The scale of it all is so enormous. That's the next stage of work that I'd like to bring into my professional practice. I've been doing more and more reading about how to reframe and rethink our relationships to technology, our relationships to our communities, our relationships to our high carbon-addicted lifestyles. In my latest reading and writing, I'm hoping to work through some sort of strategy to bring more of that work into our profession.

There's a number of people who I think have done a great job in trying to bring the conversation of global warming into librarianship. For example, there was a great book from Library Juice called *Greening Libraries*. And I keep coming back a forecasting report done years ago by an Australian library group called the "Bookends Scenarios." They named their four future scenarios after two works of science fiction and two works of non-fiction, and they used it as a way to showcase what the library could be in a world that was not unlike *Silent Spring, How Buildings Learn, Neuromancer,* or *Fahrenheit 451*.

I would also like to see myself as someone trying to bring a more positive future for libraries and our communities. And I hope that's not just my hope. I hope more of decide to meet these challenges and find ways to go forward and meet these challenges.

CARMEL CURTIS: Climate change is one of the most significant, unavoidable, universal issues of our time. And when we talk about digital preservation, it requires so much energy. I struggle with this often. I don't know what the compromise is. I don't know what the answer is for sustainable digital preservation. That's something that's really difficult to personally reconcile, that this is an extremely environmentally unsustainable practice. Yet I do it every day. I don't know exactly how to level that in my head and in my actions.

JARRETT DRAKE: Issues of the environment impact poorer people overwhelmingly. They impact black people overwhelmingly. Rural communities are impacted. I don't think it's any surprise that a lot of the server farms that we know about from these larger companies—Google, Amazon, Apple—where are they? They're not in super rich places; they're rural, poor places where you can just buy up a lot of land and sort of keep it dark.

Some of Amazon's offsite storage they offer is certified by the federal government. There are federal government agencies that store things in Amazon Glacier, I believe, or they may have a separate thing for the federal government; I don't know what it's actually called, but it might be Glacier. In any case, I think that there are huge implications in terms of where those actually live and whose physical space is impacted by the presence of those things.

My university is a Google university now. The University of Michigan is also a Google university. That means that so many of our business applications now are hosted on Google servers. One of the things I always try to push back on people is when they say, "Oh, digital archives, those aren't physical." Or they use "physical" and then they say "digital," as if they're incompatible. They say, "If it's digital, we do this, and if it's physical, we do that." I'm like, hey, it's all physical. This stuff doesn't exist in someone's mind. It's not like Facebook's servers are all in Mark Zuckerberg's head. These files and these applications, the data within those applications—they all live somewhere. You just don't see where they live. And that's how they kind of want it. That's partly a security measure, but it definitely is impacting people that I can't even see. Apple's probably the most well-known tech giant to have horrid work conditions abroad. I think about the issues of location in terms of, who does the work to make these things happen, where do they do the work, and whose lives are impacted when that work is being done? I think that there's such an invisible population there that we have to acknowledge.

It's similar to construction projects in the past. Recently it was some anniversary of the opening of the Panama Canal, and the US

National Archives or the Library of Congress tweeted a photograph and said, this is some anniversary of the Panama Canal, isn't this so great? And I was like, yeah, but what about the hundreds of people who died during that? What about the people whose lives were displaced? There are all of these things that take up a lot of space, and we don't grapple with the people who were there before, and what that displacement means for them and the people who are doing the labor to build those kinds of things. So I think of labor and the environment as going hand in hand. It's no different from other kinds of things that need space.

ZACHARY LOEB: When we talk about disparities in technology, it can be important to take a much larger view of the technology's life cycle. Who were the people who mined the coltan that's in the smartphone? Who were the people who assembled the smartphone, actually put it together? When we think about the labor that goes into Internet-connected technology, it's so easy to just think about the well-paid engineers working at the swanky Internet start-up campus, or working for Facebook in California, where the snack machines are free. But what about the people who actually assemble the devices? And what about the people who actually work in the stores selling the devices? And then, at the other end of the device's life cycle, what about the people who are recycling the devices, the people who are actually breaking them open in an attempt to recover a certain amount of reusable x, y, or the other thing? Or the people who then are living next to the places where all of this e-waste gets "recycled," which is really kind of a greenwashing term. E-waste is waste. It's garbage. It's just that when you call it "e-waste recycling," you make people think that it's going to a happy place in the sky, when in reality it's going to a landfill in China, where it's poisoning people there.

Of course, trying to take such an expansive view gets really, really complicated, especially from an attempt to live ethically. I'm not saying that I'm not also enmeshed in all of this messiness—but the first step to address this messiness is to at least acknowledge it. And some of these issues are of course much broader than the questions of access for your library.

JESSAMYN WEST: Because of the way capitalism works, and the way America is go-go capitalism even more than we see in Europe and other places, we're actually running through resources and discouraging sustainability in our technology even more than we might be able to. I have a smartphone and it's super helpful for me, but I think it's at this point two generations old. I would love to use it until it literally falls apart in my hands, but technologically, from a software perspective, I may not be able to, because the software is going to advance beyond my ability to have whatever's current run on my phone. And that becomes the interesting trap. We see a lot of it with legislation. People would be able to keep their cars longer if laws hadn't changed to mean that you can't use older cars. Some of that is safety, which makes sense. But some of it's just flat-out—we just kind of changed the way the world worked, and we want you to keep up.

For example, I have broadband at home, but it's slow broadband. According to the definitions, my broadband, which was fine five years ago, has been the same speed for several years. In rural Vermont, it's as fast as I can get without getting cable. It's not considered broadband anymore. That what's happening with the way the Web works; the amount of content that gets pulled down, the amount of autoplay videos I get on a page, is changing because the people on the Web would like to sell things or get eyeballs to the people with the disposable incomes who are the people buying the phones or whatever. I know this sounds kind of muddled because it's a couple things at once, but essentially the market determines that they would like us to keep buying new and more things, which means that we can't continue to use our old things, which would be a much more sustainable, responsible way of dealing with technology. This isn't true for everything, but it's definitely, complicatedly true for phones and certain technology. The resale market is complicated and difficult, and this is completely crazy for things like software and e-books. Like, try to resell an e-book. That money is just gone. You spent it on something digital, and you then don't have a thing. From an environmental perspective, that's great news, because you didn't cut down a tree in order to have this thing, which then has a value of kind of zero because it's digital, but from a personal "I own things" versus "I rent things" perspective, it's sort of not.

So balancing the ecology of these glowing boxes full of poison that we stare at all day long that we don't really have a plan for in a long range, with the kind of "hey, it actually is ecologically responsible to deal with more digital than hard physical content," you wind up in this weird unsteady situation where on the one hand you feel like you're responsible dealing more with bits and bytes and digital stuff, but on the other hand, the entire infrastructure to run that bits and bytes and digital stuff world is mostly just getting outsourced to other countries with cheap electricity, worse labor laws, and lower pollution requirements. We can pretend that our moving these digital bits and bytes around is actually a zero sum or a net good, because we don't see the hidden costs that are actually winding up on other parts of the planet, not our part of the planet.

. . .

Andromeda Yelton: There's a lot of history of people not feeling welcome in libraries for various reasons. It may be that they come from countries where civic institutions are not necessarily things you want to be interacting with. It may be that they remember not that long ago in American history when black people were not allowed in public libraries, or were not allowed to be part of our library associations. It may be that today you can't get into all these lovely Carnegie libraries in a wheelchair. You just can't do it. They're physically inaccessible. I think people underestimate the extent to which libraries fall short of our aspirations as a place that's welcoming to all, and I think that people who are doing well at this are going out of their way to make sure to include people from those communities with real voice and decision-making. People who are doing less well are assuming that they know what's going on and can speak for other people. People who are doing less well than that are just unaware that there are even issues there. Living up to your ideals is a process. We have this great ideal of being for everyone. Ideally we will get closer to it day by day.

Stacie Williams: I think that the public libraries are interesting. I love public libraries. I tend to think working in one should almost be mandatory for everyone in the field, mostly because I think it's the first point of contact for most people who are even interested in it. You're not, like, a six-year-old who knows what a systems librarian does. You go to the library, there's a person behind a desk—that's usually the first impact. I think that experience is fundamental to our understanding of what libraries are.

Public libraries are also in a very interesting situation. On the one hand, I think many of them are more or less on board with—like, protecting to the death—this idea of privacy of your record, privacy of your reading histories, your circ records, all of that. They all seem generally in agreement that you protect that information; you don't share that with anybody. But, surveillance over bodies and the privacy of your body in a public library is a very different idea. There's a library Facebook group that shall remain nameless. When that group first started, there were actually a lot of progressive librarians in there, and it sort of morphed over time into librarians who were complaining about patrons who smelled bad or looked "crazy." They would use this really insulting language to describe people whose bodies and persons didn't fit the ideal. For a lot of those librarians, because those people's bodies didn't fit this ideal, they were subject to additional surveillance or punitive security measures.

In some cases, people are doing not great things—I mean, I have worked at a public library, so I'm not shading that either. It's not good to let people do heroin in the stacks. I'm not saying that's good. I'm not saying that you shouldn't call a social worker or 911 to assist somebody who's actively using in your library, fifteen feet away from a kid. But what I am saying is that there does, in some cases, seem to be an expectation that if you don't look like the ideal user—and, again, that perspective isn't neutral, either, because we know that the field is like 88 percent white; it's mostly middle- to upper-class white women in this field. That perspective says, well, if you're not like me or similar to me, then I may have cause to consider you a threat or a concern. I think that's been my biggest worry, that there are people who are experiencing these extra layers of surveillance or policing because they don't fit whatever this expectation is of a perfect patron. Now, that's not everybody, but at this point I've seen enough anecdotally to suggest that there's still plenty of librarians out there who aren't necessarily about helping their communities. I had sort of come to that as well with a wary side-eye.

CECILY WALKER: There has to be a chance for us to address some of these inequities that exist within libraries, these seemingly benign but actually sort of malevolent oppressive structures, like that the people who work behind the information desks don't like or speak like the people from the communities that we're serving. That's really been a challenge that I know a lot of library professionals are interested in.

But just to start with the idea that libraries aren't always benign, that as a huge institution that has its foundation in the idea of "bettering people," and that that betterment is always positioned within a very narrow Eurocentric paradigm—that's a problem. Until we can seriously look at that problem and recognize that it exists, I think that—especially when it comes to re-envisioning libraries for the future, to getting our public to look at us as more than just storehouses for books and DVDs—if we don't begin to address some of those issues, our greater, more social-oriented programming and initiatives aren't going to be that successful. Because in a way we're being disingenuous, and I think the community picks up on that sort of lack of honesty, or that unwillingness to meet them on their level and be honest and vulnerable and convey that we have our shortcomings, but we're working very hard to try to address them.

I know that that doesn't necessarily have anything to do with technology, but the foundational structural issues that affect a lot of library service have to start with really looking at who makes up the profession, who ends up being in positions of leadership within the profession, and how we can interrogate and deconstruct that perception of whiteness that covers over pretty much everything that we do, even here in a city like Vancouver, where the minority population—particularly in the Asian community—is almost equal to the white population. So it's just being willing to take some of these issues to heart and make the commitment, no matter what your role might be in a library, to try to dismantle this inequity whenever you see it. I think it would be a huge step forward, whether that's a personal or an organizational step.

VIVIAN ALVAREZ: If there's any opportunity to introduce new technology, even if it's something that I purchase, like a new camera, a new Canon, and this thing is a beast, I will bring it to the library and show it to the kids and have them tinker with it. Because I want them to be exposed to it. A lot of the time the exposure part happens at the library, because of certain ways that the community is shaped and because of certain circumstances, mostly economic. If children don't have three dollars in their pocket, they're not necessarily traveling to a museum or to the Art Institute to check out artwork, or to places where they can look at new technology, because there's a cost to transportation. A lot of the time, the kids stay in the community because the parents are getting out of work and they want the library to be a hub where they can pick up their children, and they trust that they're in a safe environment.

With that said, the children are inadvertently constrained to just being in the community, and exposure to other parts of the world is mostly experienced either in books or computers. But in my eyes, it's very important to leak it out and to explore. For this reason, we offer field trips, again, because there's so much trust from the parents. In fact, if I happen to mention at the very last minute there's a field trip in the next hour, parents trust the staff so much that they'll say, "All right, I'm signing this this very moment. I'm going to go to the library, sign it, and you guys can go."

So the staff has to have, I guess, their heart in the right place, and the mindfulness about what it is that they're exposing the children to, what kind of information they're bringing in from the outside world into their communities, and then be mindful that these communities are also *their* domain. We can talk about meaningful topics, and we have to realize that at the end of the day, our shift ends at like five o'clock, but their lives keep evolving in these communities. So if I happen to say, "Oh, I don't know how I feel about girls wearing very short shorts that shouldn't be called 'shorts' at that point," we could have this conversation, and we can reflect on it. But there's another part to it, and that is that when I leave the place that is their home—in other words, they live in these nuances in their community where they're still being pressured to wear certain clothes, and then where do they go if they suddenly feel like they don't belong? That is why the library is very important, and we have to train our staff to understand it as well, because when children also develop voices that stand out from the rest of the community, they may suddenly feel like they don't belong in that community. But yet it is their community.

I support parents a lot. For instance, if a child and I have a meaningful conversation, if I leave this space, where does the conversation go? Is it just in the child's head? And where does it go from there? Because if it's not a shared culture, or a shared topic, then it doesn't really move from there. So when parents come in, I do share with them. We talk about certain topics, and parents chime in. It helps parents understand that there's more to just creating a portfolio. There is a sense more of emotional support, so when the child leaves the space, the child can now go home and go, "Hey, Mom, we talked about this." And Mom can go, "Oh, yeah, I heard about it," instead of, "I don't know how to support you," or "I don't know what you're talking about." And at least that conversation can exist at home; it doesn't just stay in the library.

In other words, we are borrowing the space at the library. What if the library doesn't exist? That particular branch—what if it just disappears, here in my fictional mindset? Where do the conversations that they were having go? The goal is to create that space in their own homes, so that they can bring those observations to that space, and we can continue dialoguing.

. . .

ZACHARY LOEB: I think that oftentimes librarians can be good about thinking about other people's labor but really bad about thinking about librarians and the other people who work in the library as workers, too. Especially in a time period where libraries are getting savaged by budget cuts right and left. In terms of gender and labor, librarianship is a field where there's a higher percentage of women working in libraries than men, although of course this is horribly and ridiculously reversed once you get to the upper echelons of management.

But I think that it's important for librarians to remember that they work in the libraries, that what they do is labor. And that there are lots of people who work in libraries who don't necessarily have the title "librarian" but who work there, too, and their labor also needs to be appreciated, recognized, and respected. When it comes to running a library, I really think that the person whose job involves sweeping the floors is as important as the person whose job involves keeping the computers running. So you need to keep that part of labor in mind, too. And to make a comment in terms of a straight-up Luddite position—when librarians think about what new technologies to bring into the library, it's worth considering, "Will switching to this result in me or my co-workers losing our jobs?"

CARMEL CURTIS: A number of the positions that I've had over the past several years have been these temporary grant-funded project-based positions. On the one hand, it's exciting that I've gotten to get a glimpse into so many of these different organizations. On the other hand, it's really challenging to work on a sustainable digital preservation project when I'm not there for more than nine months. A number of these projects have involved the beginning project-planning for digital preservation and, for example, a lot of the technological tools that I'm recommending are based off of initial observations from being there for only a couple of months. Often that involved intense in-depth interviews with people who had been working there for much longer, but, still, I have not been in a position where I've been able to follow through or make a recommendation for a workflow that involves many different uses of technology across it. I've not been in a situation yet where I've been able to then test a recommendation and revise it and see how it actually works in that environment.

I think that so many of these positions are grant-funded, temporary positions because audiovisual archives at large are underfunded, underresourced, and underprioritized. I don't know much about the world of libraries and archives outside of how it relates to audiovisual materials, so I would imagine that funding issues are a challenge across the board, but I'm really only speaking to my experiences with organizations and institutions that have audiovisual collections. It's not ever a priority, because there are sometimes, understandably, a lot of other things that need to happen. When the organization or the institution's main mission isn't to archive and preserve—even if the *archive* has a mission statement that is to archive and preserve—it is extremely challenging to get consistent, sustainable buy-in outside of the archive. And then the archives are reliant on this grant funding that's coming from an outside source that is very much needed but doesn't allow for consistency, which—in terms of implementing workflows that are heavily based in technology—could be really useful to have.

BÉATRICE COLASTIN SKOKAN: At the University of Miami, we have good relationships with our partners in digital, metadata, and preservation, and there are reliable workflows in place. Every year the distinctive collections submit their projects to the digital department. There's a committee that evaluates and ranks the projects and determines levels of access and the degree of preservation that is needed. There are templates developed to rank projects. The curators, the digital librarians, and the metadata librarians are part of that team that evaluates each project for accessibility. The priority is always to digitize projects, for preservation and accessibility. Resources can be limited, so there's always the desire to invest resources to digitize projects that are going to be available to a wider public for use. Copyright is also part of the discussion. The most desirable project is the one that doesn't have copyright restrictions and is easier to make widely available. The workflows have been developed, and it seems to work.

CECILY WALKER: A few years ago we underwent a massive reorganization here at Vancouver Public Library. The organization had been very siloed by subject divisions, and those silos were largely exploded. Instead of being organized around subjects, we're organized around what particular service are we providing. So now we have a Digital Services department, which is the department that I work in. Our Digital Services department is not only involved with digital collections like e-books, audiobooks, and electronic resources, and things like that, but we're also the site for all of the web development and the Community Digital Initiatives projects that happen in the library. It hasn't been a small thing, the fact that we now are freer to organize our work around projects instead of having to do a project on the side of your desk in addition to the public service work. We now have a department that is dedicated to public service, and that is what they do.

So now when we hit those points where we say, "Here's a new project" that's then handed down to us—"Here's a new direction that the library leadership would like us to take that supports the library's strategic initiatives"—it's made it easier for us to go to people in other work units. If the strategic initiative is about supporting the city of Vancouver's learning history, we might be able to go to, say, our programming and learning department and say, "This is our plan for building this particular tool, but we think that it would also be a really excellent opportunity for you to do some programming around this so that we not only build awareness of the tool, but we build interest in the tool. And by your building interest in the tool, we get more contributions."

I don't want to say it's completely flattened the hierarchy, but it's made it so we can say that not the only people who have to be, or who should be, involved in the project are people who have the degree. We can have technicians who may have a diploma from one of our local colleges here—in Canada, "colleges" are like junior colleges—or we may be able to go to someone who has absolutely no technological background or really hasn't expressed an interest in technology, but maybe they're connected to a specific community, or maybe they have a language skill that we need in order to bring a particular collection online. So it's made it easier for us to say that this isn't just a Digital Services project; this is a whole library project. One of the great things that I've seen as a result of this approach where we collaborate between and within departments is that people who have always assumed that Digital Services work is really technical, that's it's really above them, and they don't know anything about computers—it's helped them to understand that there are many, many different roles that come into play when you're working on these kinds of projects. Regardless of what your role or regular responsibility is, there's room for you to get involved in this kind of community work that we're trying to do. So that's been tremendous. We've been really supported by the organization, primarily just because our leadership here, our Chief Librarian and our directors at the time, took the chance at doing something a little bit different in how the library was organized. I think honestly if that had not happened, we would not be in the position that we're in right now.

In terms of the relationship that we have with our IT department, it has been a challenge. In talking to other librarians about this, I understand that this is not unusual, but for a time there was just the assumption on both sides—whether you were a librarian or a library worker, or whether you were someone in IT—that the other person doesn't know anything. The people from IT just assumed that they couldn't really talk about the nitty gritty down and dirty work that goes into building a web application because it would be completely over people's heads and librarians don't understand anything, and librarians may have assumed that we couldn't talk about the community building or the collection building that goes into working with these kinds of projects because it's not something that our systems people have any interest in. They're back of the house; they don't deal with people. We're front of the house; we deal with people. So that's been sort of a challenge.

A few years ago once the reorganization happened, when we were hiring people from within the library and from outside, we started paying closer attention to the kinds of skills that they were listing on their resumes. We rewrote several of our job descriptions to include not only just having experience with working with

WordPress or running a blog, but being able to have the kind of functional literacy to be able to go and talk to our web application developers. You may have a concept that's grounded in the traditional notion of librarianship, but maybe you don't know how to carry it out, and you need to understand what technology is involved to be able to carry this project out successfully. You have enough of a grounding and enough of an understanding of the language that people in IT speak so that you can work on building those relationships. I did have that foundation and that understanding of technological jargon and that sort of thing; it took a while to build those relationships with IT, and it took a while to build that trust with our IT department.

One of the things I've been able to do as Project Manager that's worked really really well for us is instead of our IT department staying two floors above the Digital Services department and our never seeing each other, we started having scrum meetings, one at the beginning of the week and one at the end. The meetings were never more than fifteen minutes long, and then we would have a longer meeting if we needed to hammer things out. But it was not only an opportunity for us to quickly go through and address what went right, what went wrong, what are we working on this week, what are our roadblocks, and try to hammer those out very quickly, but it was an opportunity for us to see each other face to face, which is not something that happened all that often. We even had an opportunity where one of the librarians who was working very closely at doing the front-end configuration of Drupal and one of our web graphics technicians were moved upstairs for about a month to the seventh floor where our web application developers were working. Being able to see that person every day and not having to wait to schedule a meeting, being able to turn around and say, "Hey, so-and-so, this is what I'm seeing, is this a problem? How can we fix it?"—just being able to put people in the same physical space has made a huge difference for us. In the past, a project that involved just getting a WordPress site up and running, for example, used to take anywhere from six to seven months or more. Now we usually have a much more rapid turnaround for these projects, and it's just because we took the time to build those relationships and to get people to learn to trust each other. Now we can usually turn these projects around in a couple of months or so, which is really unheard of for us.

Jonathan Harwell: When I began at Rollins College, we worked to combine two departments into one. There were formerly a technical services unit and a digital services and systems unit. We made it into the Department of Collections and Systems. We combined two departments that were already sharing an office space but not interacting much. It was sort of divided down the middle of a large space. The primary target of our project was respectful communication while also being adaptive to disruptive technologies. And so we wanted to be sure that everyone felt valued in the workplace, which was not always the case before I arrived. Even while I was there, we had some issues to work out. But we took this seriously as a department. We went out for a retreat. We took a whole day to talk about our issues together, talk about where we needed to go to get beyond our past issues as a department. We've had some turnover since then, but basically we've done this.

We've since gone through a system migration, which was very intense, very difficult, and we had some rocky periods through that. But we worked through those, very intentionally and very diligently, to make sure that people felt respected and valued in the workplace, because as soon as a technology changes, the daily work routine changes, and that's what stresses people out. If we can't treat each other as valued, respected human beings in the process, then all is lost. When I look over the past five years that I've been at Rollins, I've seen almost every technology that my department uses change. ILLiad is still the same, although it's moving toward a new technology, but everything else we use, from the library system to the time clock, has changed. I guess the only thing that hasn't really changed is Outlook. We're all still using the same email system. So these are times in which daily routines have constantly been shifting, and we've had to focus on being kind, patient, and respectful to each other in this process. That's why we've come out on the positive side through all this.

Becky Yoose: Going from Grinnell College to Seattle Public Library was an interesting jump in terms of going from systems administrator/developer/faculty member to a full-fledged middle management position in a large public library system. Using my particular background of data and systems, I'm able to better manage my staff. At the same time, I realize that my status within librarianship, with the job hops I've been doing—lowly technical services developer to someone who's more traditional systems librarian to a particular manager—it's revealing just seeing how people approach your work depending on how you describe yourself and what your work is. Of course, when you're a manager, you're an administrator, so there's that additional power dynamic you have between employers and employees, and people who are in lower positions than you and people who are in higher positions than you. But being in firm IT now, you have that tech privilege attached to that automatically. Even though you're a manager, there's still that tech privilege. And I have to be cognizant of that when I'm working with other departments, especially with departments and other areas of librarianship that might not have the same privilege or status that a particular position or duty or skill set gathers within librarianship as a whole.

. . .

JAIME TAYLOR: Technology and the Internet and coding is still one of those fields that you can join and do very well with and make a very good living without having a formal education. I don't know if you make it into the libraries doing it that way, but you could be a very successful coder and not have gone to college, still. Whereas in libraries, we need this master's degree, and that's a decision that we made eighty-plus years ago that was probably a bad decision. The profession made a collective decision in the '20s and '30s that we were going to be a profession rather than a trade, and so we were going to need this academic line of learning in order to become one of us. We did that at the time because librarianship had become this majority female thing, because they could pay us less. That's why we have so many female librarians, because they were like, "Oh, this is a job that the girls can do. And if we get the girls to do it, we can pay them less." Same with teaching at primary levels. This is obviously not exactly how it happened, but the profession got together and said, "Well, how do we want to conceive of ourselves? How do we want to make people give us a little bit of prestige?" And they decided to become a profession, that we're going to need these degrees and letters after our names and professional associations.

At the time it made sense, especially when higher education was not so expensive. In retrospect we probably made the long-term wrong choice. If we now had library school that looked more like the training for a trade, we'd be doing a lot better. If we, like many trades, were unionized—and professions for the most part aren't unionized in the same way trades are; we probably would have been better if we'd unionized as a trade rather than seeking professional education. So it made sense at the time, but in the long run we didn't do ourselves any favors. Whoops. Now we're sitting here decades later trying to undo it. So for tech at least, there is still this possibility of not going into tens of thousands of dollars of debt in order to become qualified to do what you do.

BESS SADLER: One thing that I've noticed is that for many of the technology jobs in libraries in particular—although I've found it to be true elsewhere as well—there's nowhere where you can go learn how to do it. I am not aware of any library school anywhere that can teach you how to be a systems librarian. And yet, every library I know has a systems librarian on staff. How did that person get their job and their training? They learned it on the job. Maybe they learned it because they came into the library profession with existing technology skills—which I think is rare. More often, they had a job in libraries, and someone identified them as a person who was likely to be able to pick up the skill set. And they worked through an apprenticeship model.

What I've noticed is that some people are more likely to be tapped for those things than others are. I think there's a lot of unconscious bias happening in that. What I've noticed in my career is that when some people who are, let's say, newer to the profession ask how something works, they get an explanation, but other people ask how something works and get told, "That's not part of your job description. You don't need to know that." The people who get an explanation will expand their understanding and probably get raises and career promotions. And the people who do not get an explanation will not get those things. In my experience, it's more often women who do not get explanations. They more often run into situations where someone says, "It's not your job to know that," or assumes that they couldn't understand the explanation if it were provided to them. I think that it's unconscious bias, but I also think that it's real and something that I've observed a lot.

JAIME TAYLOR: We have limited amounts of money, and so we have to be kind of smart about what we use it on. I think that we're already often neglecting some of our core services. Like, do you have a cataloging backlog? Maybe then instead of spending money on buying software if you have to or buying subscription programs if you have to or paying a social media blah blah, maybe you should fix your cataloging backlog. Or pay your librarians above starvation wages before you spend your time and money on this shiny thing that doesn't actually advance your mission very far, while you're neglecting all these really central things. Unfortunately, because we operate in a neoliberal capitalist garbage nightmare, it *is* a zero-sum game. You can do only so many things, and the things that you choose to do—and therefore choose not to do other things—are choices. And we could be making different ones.

The other thing about that, especially as it relates to money and tech in libraries, is you'll notice that libraries are still mostly female and tech is mostly male, so there's definitely this value that's put on this male thing in this female profession that then gets money and prestige when a reference desk in a poor neighborhood that is staffed maybe by women of color isn't getting the attention, even though they're doing what is ultimately way more valuable work. We definitely have this really gendered and raced and classed divide when you're talking about tech in libraries. We know. We have statistics that say that male librarians get paid more, male librarians get promoted more, male librarians work mostly in tech sides of things, as opposed to public service and cataloging. We know this. We have stats. But what are you going to do? We live in a garbage patriarchy.

. . .

CARMEL CURTIS: In terms of my personal identity and representation of identity within the world of archiving, it's of course extremely complicated. I have a very intersectional identity that's not represented in a middle-aged, white, middle-class man. For me personally, it means that when I go to an archives conference or professional development events, there aren't necessarily people who look like me or are coming from similar backgrounds as I am. It means that when I think about the decisions that are being made at large in my field and how that impacts communities—the people who are making these decisions, for the most part, probably aren't from the communities that I'm a part of. It's really hard. It is really hard.

CECILY WALKER: We need to do more around the idea of understanding that we are not the experts about everything, that there are people who don't have the degree or are from outside our hallowed halls who have expertise that is every bit as important as ours. And that we would be better served if we tried to create channels where we can bring some of that expertise in-house, or we can deputize people somehow so that they might be able to take that expertise to their own communities, using the library as a place of delivery. I would say that as the world continues to get browner—especially in the United States, less so here in Canada—if the complexion of the profession doesn't change, I think it's time for us to do some serious soul-searching and get beyond the idea that the pipeline is the problem, and that if the pipeline is the problem, what are some ways that we can either expand the pipeline, explode the pipeline, or just do without the pipeline entirely, or create a completely new pipeline? Because there has to be an opportunity and a change.

JOEL NICHOLS: Librarians have a lot to work on in terms of making sure that they are not enacting and reenacting white supremacy when dealing with people of color communities. Librarians have a lot of work to do around challenging and interrogating normative middle-class values when working in communities.

MYRNA MORALES: There's a lot of white defensiveness in libraries, so we need to do anti-racist work. As the founder of Community Change Inc.—the nonprofit organization focused on dismantling white supremacy in New England where I work—would say, "Being a racist is like being an alcoholic. Every morning you have to wake up and look in the mirror and say, 'Today I will work to not take a drink.'" Folks of color, we suffer from internalized racism. We're all victims and perpetrators of white supremacy. Every day we have to wake up and say, "Today I won't be racist." And for us to be able to say, "Today I won't be racist" means that first I have to say, "I am a racist." "Today I won't be an alcoholic" means I have to say, "I am an alcoholic." And I'd be hard-pressed to find folks in the library world that would take that perspective. Ask me that another five years from now.

JIM DELROSSO: On one level, the fact that our digital repositories deal with workplace issues, either in general or within the field of hospitality, means that we frequently deliver content that addresses issues of race, gender, age, and disability—though it's almost all within the context of the workplace. But on the meta level, I don't think I engage with those issues enough. There are some issues of accessibility with the software we use, and our user survey deliberately did not include demographic questions, even purely voluntary ones. In hindsight, that was a big mistake—by choosing to ignore many aspects of our users' identities, I effectively erased those identities. That's a failure on my part, and one I'd look to correct.

Beyond the repositories, though, I think a lot about these issues in terms of our hiring and retention of staff and librarians. Especially as our application processes have become more automated, I've been trying to educate myself as to how technology can be a boon to the establishment of a more diverse work force within our libraries, as opposed to a detriment.

MYRNA MORALES: I really wish that our discussions around social justice issues were more thoughtful. It takes time for folks to develop a critical lens. It takes time for folks to build relationships of trust. It should be like, "Listen, you fucking hurt me, and this is how your hurt translates in a broader sense. Let's figure out how to deal with that so that we can create our product once and not have to go back and redo this." I really do wish that we were talking about these issues in ways that I felt was beyond—and I'm not going to say "beyond the 101." What I remember in 2010, 2011, 2012, being on the ALA Think Tank and talking about whiteness and nobody talking to me, no one saying "Boo." And there were like twenty thousand librarians in the group. Whenever I would ask questions about race, people wouldn't say shit.

I think we've come a long way from then. But my internal goal is always to write myself out of a job. It's about no longer having to have that problem to solve because it is solved. I don't know if people are comfortable having that kind of conversation. But that's what I wish, that when we do talk about issues of the digital divide, when we talk about issues of race—I wish that in library school, I could look at the course requirements and be able to choose one class with a lens I do not have, like "Queering the Catalog," or "Libraries for Formerly Incarcerated Individuals," or "Libraries for

Folks with Disabilities." It should be one of the requirements to take a course with a lens I do not have, so that I'm honing that perspective. That would be awesome, and money well spent. And the profession would be better.

BECKY YOOSE: Allyship is a tricky thing, especially when you're dealing with intersectionality! A common suggestion given to allies is to educate themselves and their peers about marginalization, implicit bias, privilege, and other issues surrounding systematic discrimination of particular groups. You as an ally are ultimately responsible for your own education. Once you've learned what you need to learn, share that with your peers in privileged groups.

So, how does one learn? The next suggestion for allies is to listen. A seemingly simple suggestion, but in reality harder than it seems. The act of listening in this case does not only cover the initial hearing of one's words, but actively reflecting on what is being said, and responding when appropriate. Sometimes allies start to speak more than listen, which inhibits the dialog between ally and the group in question. Sometimes you need to step back. For example, as an ally, you need to learn why having exclusive safer spaces is necessary for some, and why you are not automatically welcome in said space. Signal boost writings, conversations, actions, and folks—with consent!—without appropriating their words, ideas, and actions. Be aware that an ally's privilege can easily lead to such appropriation, stripping that group's voice and in a greater sense, their agency. Since you're an ally, you have privilege that the group you wish to assist doesn't have.

While you work on the overall goal of creating a structure that creates equity and eliminates discrimination, use your position of privilege to start changing the existing structures from within. If your hiring pool at work is not diverse, find out why and fix it. Advocate for genuine inclusion in decision making processes, strategic planning, and in the general workplace culture.

BESS SADLER: I am really struggling with how to engage effectively with anti-racism work in technology and open source and libraries. I helped to lead a workshop at the Digital Library Federation called the Ally Skills Workshop that I think is really important. It's about how do we act as an ally to marginalized groups in our communities. I'm very interested in the research of people like Safiya Noble and Myrna Morales, who could say much better than I what course we should be taking around fighting racism in our profession and in our technology systems. I'm trying to learn. I realized a few years ago that I need to stop being complicit in sexism in our community. What I've realized even more recently was that I was probably engaging in a lot of "white woman feminism," and right now I'm trying to be a good ally by educating myself on what are the ways that my feminism might not include people of color the way it should. I'm still trying to figure that out. I'm very happy to say that the latest version of the Ally Skills Workshop engages much more effectively with questions of racism than it did previously. So I think there's work in the right direction.

I'm very happy with the latest mission statement and code of conduct of the Digital Library Federation, which is explicitly anti-colonial and anti-racist. It's just an excellent document. I'm really honored to be affiliated with an organization that's taking a stand like that. I think we need to be engaging much more critically with the kinds of collections that we are scanning and putting online. I think we need to be asking good questions about how to put those into context and have them be owned by the communities whose legacy they are. But I'm definitely not an expert on this subject. I'm a student.

JARRETT DRAKE: I have to emphasize that the Cleveland archive on police violence and the things that I've written have not just come from my head or heart alone. They've come from reading and talking with so, so many people. Virtually everything that I write or speak at, I name the people—especially the women, especially the black women—whose writings and whose work has informed so many of my views. There's a lot of privilege that comes when I speak. I'm a man. People tend to listen to men, even when the things that men have to say aren't particularly bright or intelligent. They just listen to them. So I have privilege in that regard, and I own it. I recognize it, and I reckon with it. I have privilege in my institution. So many people have reached out in regards to so many different things. If I were saying the same exact things and I worked at a community college, I don't think anybody would care. But because of my employer, people are like, "Oh, this person is saying it, it must be a thing." So I think that's very problematic. I constantly get emails from people, from other institutions—universities and not universities—who read a conversation I was a part of, and they're discussing it at their institution and trying to take steps to address it.

I do think that there are more conversations happening with more people in the field than were a few years ago. To me that's a credit to the community. It's not one person who's come in and changed anything; it's that people have been hungry for it and yearning for it. But I don't think it's enough. I think we need more people. I get happy sometimes, like, wow, people are really trying to come around. But then I still look up, and I'm like, yo, but I feel it's still super white, and we still collect a whole bunch of rich white men. What's the turnaround time for change? The fact of the matter is, just like with any kind of social change that people are pushing for, these oppressive structures took decades, generations, and centuries to erect, and they will take decades, generations, and centuries to undo. We're not going to get there tomorrow. We're not going to change everyone's mind tomorrow and get people to think of doing archives in a different way. But we just have to be persistent, and we have to be patient. There's a quote from Martin Luther King about how the arc of the moral universe always bends towards justice, and that's how I feel in this field. I think that we'll get there. We won't get there as quickly as I would like us to, but that's not going to stop me from pushing for it to get there as quickly as we can.

. . .

SARAH HOUGHTON: I think that because I started as a technology librarian—I was a woman, I was young, and it was the early days of web-based technology in libraries—it's very difficult for me to parse how much of the weird treatment I received was due to age, how much of it was due to gender, and how much of it was due to just misunderstanding technology in general. I will say that as a young librarian working in technology, I was often asked to be on a conference panel to be The Woman. They couldn't find anybody else, because everybody else was guys. All of my mentors and colleagues for probably at least the first five years of my career, other people doing the type of work that I was doing, were men.

Gradually you started to see more and more women filter into this part of the profession, which was fantastic. And you started to see more age diversity in the people who were doing the technology-type tasks in libraries as well. That continues, and I'm glad to see that kind of diversity trend continue in libraries. I think that more times than I can count, I was asked, "Are you sure you're a librarian?" I don't think that had to do with technology specifically, but it could be age, it could be appearance-based, I'm not sure. There were definitely many occasions working out with the public where I would get snippy or snide comments, or maybe even ones that weren't intended as such, about my age or my gender. "Wow, I'm just amazed you can understand this, you're such a little young lady!" Or things like that. Those kinds of comments still happen to staff that fit into various demographic groups, but I think they've lessened over time. The tech has become more integrated into everyone else's day-to-day lives, and also so much more integrated into the necessary tasks for everyone who works in a library, not just "the technology librarian" but every staff member from the people shelving the books up to the director level.

Within the last year, I have still been asked to be on a panel to be The Woman, and I have probably only in the last few years gained the confidence to start having conversations about that when the requests are phrased as such, to say that I have no interest in trying to represent an entire gender or to be a token participant on a panel. If I'm being asked for my expertise, I'm happy to participate, but if I'm being asked to give a stamp of approval or almost like a fake diversity pass to a group, I have no interest. I've definitely had to turn down or walk away from a lot of opportunities because I'm just not willing to fill that role anymore. It's not a role I'm comfortable in.

BESS SADLER: A few years ago, I went through sort of a—how do I put this—an awakening, I guess? This whole time, I've been working in open source software, and I've been doing a pretty good job. I'm not going to claim I'm a genius software developer, but I'm a decent one. I can hold my own on a team. And I've been making excuses for the sexism that I have been encountering. I was so desperate to be part of the open source software community that I put up with a lot of behavior that people shouldn't have to put up with. I often told myself that, well, *I* could make a successful career in this—because I was hearing all the time women complaining about sexism in the open source community, and I knew people who were leaving communities that I was part of because of the sexism in them. But

I told myself, well, if they really cared about the movement, they'd just deal with it, because that's what I'd done. If they cared enough, they'd just put up with it and they'd do it.

I changed my mind, a lot, a few years ago, and I started to realize that I had really been complicit in the behavior in those communities. I think I did some good work to change that behavior. In retrospect I'm not sure what I really would have done differently. But when I became a manager at Stanford, I decided that I just didn't have an excuse anymore. I had a permanent full-time job at a very well-funded institution. I had my successful open source projects. I had no more excuses for why was I continuing to turn a blind eye to this behavior that I knew was wrong, that I knew was preventing women from having the kind of career that I had had, but without putting up with some of the things that I had put up with.

So the last few years, that's been a much bigger part of my agenda. I still really believe in the promise of open source, and I think that the kinds of resistance to information surveillance and the kinds of collaboration that happens within the open source movement—there's no other way for that to have happened, and I want to be part of it. Also we've got to recognize the sexism and racism and marginalization that happens in those communities, because they're made of people. And they're products of the culture that we live in. So that's been really interesting. How do you make cultural change within an open source community? There's not an HR office you can call. There's no one you can sue for a hostile work environment. If you don't like it, they're just going to tell you to leave. So there's a lot of challenges there. I'm really inspired by the work that Valerie Aurora and the Ada Initiative have done. In the work that I'm doing, I'm trying to follow the lead of some of the precedents that they've set.

BONNIE GORDON: When I was hired, my department became four people, and the head of the department at the time was a woman. A few months later, she got another job, and now my department is three people. So it is a small department, but I am the only woman on the team, and our IT department is two guys. But in large part our organization is female. I would say that as a department, we're aware of it.

A big goal of mine, both more formally through my digital processing project and also through more informal means, is thinking critically about who has what attitude towards technology, how they're interacting with our IT department, and how to facilitate that. I'm always trying to find spaces where people are comfortable and can learn and interact with technology in a more productive way. And that gets to thinking about how eventually all archivists are going to be digital archivists, when now, with conferences I've gone to, regular archivist conferences tend to be more heavily female than when the word "digital" is in there. Which is changing. Like, I went to the National Digital Stewardship Residency; the New York program had a day-long symposium a few months ago, and everyone who spoke on stage was a woman. So I think, on the whole, it's changing. But I think that internally, as an organization, part of having other people in our organization work with technology in a productive way is being really aware of the gender dynamics of the D-Team, and trying to work with that.

Carol Bean: When I left library school, there was very little technology from that degree. By chance I took a class on programming in C, which was awesome. Then I went on and learned as much technology—systems, hardware, software, everything else—as I could, and my first job, I got it because of my knowledge of technology and systems, believe it or not. So I was, first of all, a female, and a librarian—which was acceptable in the law firm. "She's female, she's a librarian, that's fine, we like that, we're comfortable with that. And guess what, she knows all this stuff about technology, she's going to help us out." They were excited about that.

But they had outsourced their systems, their networking and everything. When I came up against some of their proposals—basically one of the partners came and said, "Carol, this is what they're suggesting. What do you think?" I looked at it, and, long story short, I wrote a long memo with an executive summary that said, "Don't do this, this is insane. *This* is what you need to do, because this is the direction technology's going." The outsourced people were all male. They acted very male technology, all of the GamerGate type of people that we hear about today. They weren't that bad, but they were of that ilk. And that was hard. I actually eventually got back on their good sides, which was nice. But it was still, "You know, I'm really not comfortable coming in the server room and seeing naked women on the screen of your computer. It's not something I'm really comfortable with, okay?" But they didn't see anything wrong with it, because that was their little domain; I rarely went in there anyway. Subsequent places that I worked, there was a lot of male domination in the technology. Institutionally, I didn't see so much racial things. But the gender thing was there, and I think it's still there.

BESS SADLER: We need to be talking about imposter syndrome and the reasons why librarianship is a profession dominated by women until it comes to the technology—which pays a lot better, and where it's a lot easier to get a job. Why aren't more women going into those positions? That's the growth area in libraries, and I think there's a lot of institutional systemic reasons why those positions are going to white men that I think we need to address.

MICHAEL GORMAN: I am acutely conscious of having worked in a highly female profession. Depending on what kind of library you're in, between 80 to 90 percent of the employees are going to be female. I am very aware of the problems that ALA is trying to address through, for example, the laudable Spectrum scholarship, of recruiting diverse workforces into librarianship. I think libraries have had a good record in employing diverse workforces at a nonprofessional level, but ensuring that more people from different ethnic backgrounds go to library school and become librarians is more of an issue. Technology is (white) male-dominated, of course.

One of the problems that I see in libraries is that we have an information technology ethos which is male-dominated, competitive, predatory—not in the sexual sense; I mean predatory in that it absorbs more resources than it is worth—up against a female cooperative culture. Most librarians are what Michael Frayn called herbivores, and most IT types are what he called carnivores. That clash of cultures has been largely deleterious to libraries.

I think it has been particularly damaging in the field of LIS education. If you look at the faculty hiring patterns, you find very often that library-oriented female faculty retire and are replaced by non-library-oriented male faculty. That has weakened library education substantially, to the point at which it's very difficult to get a real library education in many of the ALA-accredited master's programs. Look at the way in which information technology is dominated by the companies that have a quite strong laissez-faire capitalist ethos, dedicated to creating products to satisfy needs they themselves have created.

ANDROMEDA YELTON: The pipeline problem in technology—I think it's really a lot of pipelines, because the particular issues that may dissuade me as a straight white woman from being in tech are not necessarily the same as the issues that might dissuade someone from a different background being in technology. I think the classic work on this was and remains *Unlocking the Clubhouse*, which is an ethnography by Carnegie Mellon in the '60s. They had ethnographers and computer scientists work together to study why women did or did not choose to stay in computer science. They found a lot of really subtle things that affected people's willingness to participate and to see themselves as part of that discourse, and other people's ability to recognize their talent.

I think in society we start with this assumption that people in marginalized groups, their work isn't good, and they have to prove it. We don't necessarily start with that assumption for people in more privileged groups. I was just reading a study where just by removing demographic information, by blinding the review of a stack of resumes, they went from having a pool of qualified candidates that was 5 percent female to a pool that was 55 percent female. It was the same set of resumes, and the only thing they did was remove the identifying information from them. I think that the biggest problem is that we look at women or people of color or whatever and just assume that they aren't any good, even if the evidence is right in front of us that they are. That's a hard one.

I think representation matters, and celebrating work by lots of different people matters. Go beyond the first five people you think of off the top of your head in pretty much anything, if you're thinking about keynotes or potential people for a job or whatever—they are probably not people from marginalized groups. If you make yourself think for longer, you can come up with a much bigger and much more diverse list, where everyone on it is just as good; it's just they're not necessarily the first people you think of.

I think in library technology we have a further problem in that many of us pick up the tech skills along the way, but our workplaces don't necessarily support that. It's very hard to self-teach yourself tech skills unless you have lots of free time outside of work, which has implications. If you have significant caregiving responsibilities, if you are poor or from a poor background and you maybe have to work additional jobs or assist your family, there's a lot of things that will stop you from having the time and the mental energy to do that self-teaching if you're not getting assistance at work.

MITA WILLIAMS: Because I work both in the library profession and within academia, I have the opportunity to think and read about applying a lens of feminism to some of what's happening in the realms of technology. Some of that work is trying to state and make the case that "the problems of women and technology" aren't solely solved by what's known as improving "the pipeline problem," which is the idea that if only we just get more young women involved in their computer science, or just technology in general, that these increased numbers will somehow solve all the field's problems of gender inequity. It's sometimes necessary to enter these conversations about "getting more women and minorities into STEM" and remind people that "the pipeline is leaky" and that many women, as well as people of color, end up leaving technology fields because of systematic problems that are well-documented and well understood. *Unlocking the Clubhouse* outlines some of changes have been made in computer science departments that have resulted in programs that are more accessible to more people.

One of the things I'm really proud of the work at Hackforge is that instead of hosting twenty-four-hour hackathons, we choose to hold it over the course of a couple weeks because we recognize that there are people who have working lives and family lives and personal lives that need attending to. We try to make sure that we start off our hackathons with lessons so, at a minimum, people can join in and learn from the event. We also try to set up people with mentors you're able to check in with regularly. We don't try to encourage hackathons where you are rewarded to go it alone, fueled on Red Bull, and come out as some sort of coding victor. Instead, we encourage collaboration and learning, and that's something I'm really proud of Hackforge. I think we could still do much more as an organization. I think a lot of technology groups could do a lot more.

. . .

JASON GRIFFEY: I've been a director-at-large for the Library and Information Technology Association, the division of ALA that's primarily focused on technology. So I've had a national leadership role of some kind in library information technology, and one of things that I have spent quite a bit of time trying to look at are the systemic biases in our field. While librarianship itself, of course, is majority female, that is not the case in technology. The leadership roles in technology specifically but also just the general makeup of the technology world in libraries are much more heavily weighted male than female, which is not great, considering the makeup of our profession as a whole. I think there should be many more women involved in technology than there are. This is partially a systemic bias in technology itself that we have around the sexism of our educational system and STEM learning and women not feeling comfortable in STEM situations. Sexism because of inherent bias and problems with the technology field itself.

That's something that I feel really strongly about and that we've worked to try and make some little difference where we can. LITA is working very hard at being a safe space for women in technology and giving them support structures and such to make them more comfortable in the technology field and showing them pathways that help enable that sort of growth.

BESS SADLER: Code4Lib started as an IRC channel. When I got my first job in libraries in the early 2000s, at the University of Alberta, one of the first things my boss told me was, "Get on this IRC channel." And I just thought it was great. This was exactly where I wanted to be. It was basically an anarchist collective of people who were making technology in libraries. No one was in charge; there was no overarching organization. It was just people talking to each other, helping each other solve problems, chatting, being friends. I loved it. It quickly became just the most important thing in the world to me, to be an accepted member of this club.

There were some troubling events, though. There were very few women. I mean, there's already very few women in technology. There are many more women in Code4Lib today than there were in the early 2000s. At the time, I was one of maybe three or four who I can think of. One of them had a very negative interaction in the IRC channel and left the community. I felt terrible about that; this was someone who I really respected and whose work I thought was very important. She had been driven away by behavior that was absolutely unacceptable. And I didn't do anything. I didn't say anything. I really wanted to be part of the club. And if you wanted to do software development in libraries, you needed to be part of Code4Lib. They were the only place where anyone was doing anything effective.

There was a conference, Code4Lib got much bigger, there was a journal—it kept going. And then a few years ago, I was kind of going through this crisis of conscience. It had always been on my mind, these interactions that I'd had within Code4Lib. Like, on the one hand, Code4Lib is an outstanding organization. There was no effective group of people doing open source in libraries, writing the software that libraries needed, supporting each other in that. It just didn't exist before Code4Lib. And the fact that people made it themselves—I mean, I can't say enough about how important that was. Yet it also wasn't always very nice to women. Over the years I saw people I cared about driven out of the community. I was on the receiving end of unpleasant interactions. I was on the receiving end of unwanted propositions that didn't stop when I said, "No, thank you." And I didn't know what to do about it. I didn't want to do anything that was going to harm this community that I cared about very much.

Then the Ada Initiative started talking about having a community code of conduct, and they were making some very good arguments about why this was important. Let's say what our values are, as a community. Let's talk about the behavior that happens, because it's invisible to a lot of people. If someone harasses you or propositions you in the back room of a conference, the conference organizers don't necessarily know about it. So one day when I'd had a hard day at work and I was feeling at the end of my rope, I sort of naively wrote a message to the mailing list saying, "We should have a code of conduct in Code4Lib." The arc of that was what the Ada Initiative has on their website, a really good synopsis of what happens to a community when you propose a code of conduct. "Step One: Everyone says, 'We don't need one, there isn't a problem.'" People said that. All of the classic things happened. Demands for someone to "prove" that there had ever been an issue. Or a lot of concern that we were going to be creating some kind of heavy bureaucracy. Again, this is basically an anarchist collective. They're not big on rules. They're not big on having a boss. They're not big on having a parent organization. They don't want any of that.

There were also some unpleasant things directed straight to me, showing up in my inbox. Everything from just "Why are you doing this?" to some anonymous stupid horrible things that I wrote about on my blog. Oh my god, I got this one email that said something like, "I know there are people falling over themselves to please you because you have a vagina, but to the rest of us, don't play that game, you just look stupid." Not super eloquent.

But Code4Lib got a code of conduct. There was also, at that time, a group of people who formed LibTechWomen. It definitely kicked off a conversation, and I think it really moved the organization in the right direction. But I also want to say that I don't think that would have been possible at that time if there hadn't already been a decade of one-on-one conversations with people. Some of the folks who, in previous years, I had gotten into head-to-head arguments with about why open source needed to be an inclusive place at all, or some people who'd even been sources of problematic behavior in the past, became allies and people who were advocating for a code of conduct, and that's very encouraging to me. That's very heartening. Change is possible, especially in a community where people really do want to make the world a better place. No one's in Code4Lib because they're hoping to make a lot of money. They're there because they care about privacy and libraries and all the things that libraries stand for. And sometimes they also need some education about their own behavior.

But Code4Lib's a fantastic organization. I strongly, strongly recommend anyone who wants a career in library technology to be a part of it. It's really for people who are in the software development side of libraries; it's not so much like the LITA side of things, which also has a role to play, obviously.

CAROL BEAN: I'm very encouraged with what I see today in the group of library technology people that make up the Code4Lib group, which I've been part of almost since their inception. Not all of them are librarians, but they all work in libraries. They're very sensitive to gender, racial, diversity issues and are trying to make it right. There's some acknowledgement of, "Yeah, it doesn't always work and there's going to be people that are the wrong kind. But we are agreed now, we're going to deal with it." It's been a long, long haul.

I feel like the gender issue especially has lessened. Interestingly, at some point one male that had made me feel sort of out of place, and shouldn't have, subsequently had something like a public apology and said that he was not proud of what he'd done and how he'd been before. Which kind of felt nice, to actually have somebody acknowledge that, "Yeah, I acted like a jerk, and I wish I hadn't been that way." I see that happening more, and I see a lot of the men in the library technology side wanting to be more inclusive, wanting it to be a less dominating male type of environment. I don't think it's over, but I'm proud of the friends and colleagues I have that are working to get past that.

BECKY YOOSE: Code4Lib started out as a small group of library technologists who wanted to get together and share what they're doing and hang out with like-minded people. It's grown into this collective of library technologists, programmers, catalogers, design folks, managers—just anyone who's interested in the intersection of libraries and technology. It's been an evolving organism, obeying that Fifth Law of Library Science, where you've gone through various iterations and people are bringing to it a little bit more theory about how technologies in libraries intersect and how general technology culture has influenced libraries and vice versa.

For a lot of folks, getting into Code4Lib is more of the practical side, learning how people are using various tools for solving various problems, and you see a lot of that in presentations and in their journal and in local meetups. But a good amount of people are starting to get involved with Code4Lib and talking a little bit more about theory and how technology has affected our work, especially with the open source technology and the startup culture that you've seen the past few years. You have one culture that's very male-dominated, well-paid, very competitive, and then you're having another field that's more service-oriented, and it's been feminized and is lower-paying.

JIM DELROSSO: I have not yet had an opportunity to go to a Code4Lib conference. The New York State one was actually held on Cornell campus recently, and I didn't have the opportunity to catch any of the sessions, sadly. But from the people I talked to coming out of that, there seemed to be a pretty solid core of real practical implications. There was even a session on instruction, which is good, because you get worried sometimes when people are primarily focused on the development of specific technologies. There's always a question for me of how much those are the people who are actually out on the front lines trying to see how communities are interacting with those technologies. I'm just really glad that Code4Lib in New York at least seemed to be dedicating some sessions and breakout groups to that intersection of communities and technology. That was very heartening.

BECKY YOOSE: Code4Lib only covers a subsection of the population of women in library technology. What about women in LITA? ASIST? And what about those folks outside of those groups? If we get all the other organizations creating their own groups, then we end up with a hodge-podge of subgroups with varying effectiveness and few chances of collaboration between other organizations. With that in mind, I co-founded #libtechwomen as a way to provide an online place for self-identified women in library technology that was not tied specifically to one organization.

While the advocacy piece of #libtechwomen hasn't fully taken off, the group has grown into a support network for those looking to talk shop or ask for advice that they otherwise would feel uncomfortable asking in other places. Some of this talk includes salary negotiations and job responsibilities to your more sundry shop talk—APIs, troubleshooting code, and the like. In any case, #libtechwomen filled a hole in the library technology community at that particular time.

Speaking of holes in the library technology community, one of my earlier hopes with #libtechwomen was to expand the support network to other underrepresented populations in library technology. #libtechgender, #libtechwomen's counterpart, was born from the conversation surrounding gender and technology at a panel at Internet Librarian. #libtechgender has been used more to tag various resources, articles, and conversations relating to gender and library technology. #libtechwomen and #libtechgender have a good amount of overlap, even if they serve two more distinct purposes.

· · ·

BECKY YOOSE: Codes of conduct came on my radar when Code4Lib adopted their code of conduct. And from there, it started to branch out into ALA itself. Codes of conduct were one of the things that migrated over from the general technology field. How are women in library technology treated compared to other areas of librarianship? You have to deal with various things that women in general technology have to deal with. You have to deal with having to work harder to prove yourself, because the default for technologists is male, essentially, and not only male—a particular type of male. It's important to have a space where people feel comfortable enough, or they can at least have something to fall back to in case something happens, or have something to point towards saying, "Okay, this is the base level of expectations that we need people to abide by." It just creates a particular environment where it's not 100 percent a safe space, but it makes it safer. It's not a fool-proof way to ensure inclusiveness into a particular space, because a code of conduct is a good start, but it's not the end.

It's only a tool in a vast variety of other ways that you can create a space where you can have either underrepresented populations within the general technology field, or underrepresented populations within librarianship. Yeah, women are outnumbering everyone else in the field, but you also have representations by race, by sexuality, by religion, by ability, and by other particular traits that others might view as vulnerable or in the minority position in a particular field. Library technology codes of conduct, again, serve as one of those things that bled into librarianship by proxy of the general technology field, from my observations. Even though librarianship is a woman-dominated field, it doesn't mean that we're immune to all the problems that we're seeing in these other fields that are not as female-dominated. Codes of conduct are a mechanism to not only state the values of a particular organization, but also to give folks a baseline of what is appropriate behavior and also hopefully a reporting structure and a resource that people can go to in case something does happen.

MITA WILLIAMS: The first that I knew of an adoption of a Code of Conduct in the library community was through Code4Lib. I remember following its beginnings through the Code4Lib mailing list. One of the limitations with mailing list software is that it's difficult to gauge the weight of agreement on a new idea such as "should we have a code of conduct at the next conference." There were many, many threads. I have so much respect for the people who put the suggestion for an adoption of a Code4Lib Code of Conduct forward, who actively engaged in the concerns that were raised, and who brought the text forward through the discussions and turned it into a practice. Once that hard work was done it became a lot easier for other conferences to follow suit. So I think that work should be recognized.

A code of conduct is still not largely understood. I describe a Code of Conducts as making it crystal clear to everyone that if you are at a particular conference you are not "on vacation" and the rules of engagement of that conference should largely follow the conventions of a professional work environment. A code of conduct makes it clear that decent human behavior is expected even if there's alcohol being consumed. One of the things that I really respect the Code4Lib community for is its additional practice of hosting events that are alcohol-free or have entertainment options that can be enjoyable without consuming large amounts of alcohol. A code of conduct really means that the conference organizers are truly concerned for your safety. If you're a good host, you want to make sure your guests feel comfortable and safe. My local hackerspace has a code of conduct, and I think it's an essential practice.

ALISON MACRINA: Codes of conduct are necessary because patriarchy and racism and homophobia and ableism and all these things are very real, serious problems. What a code of conduct does is makes explicit the set of social rules that are implicit and can be difficult for people to articulate when they're not explicit, because they usually refer to difficult circumstances. If somebody says something sexist and there is no code of conduct that says, "Don't be sexist," bystanders often have a hard time knowing what they're supposed to do. But if you can point directly to something like a code of conduct that says, "Don't be like this," it gives people a tool that can help them know what to do next.

In the tech world, it's especially important because the tech world has a white dominance problem and a male dominance problem. If we want to—and I think we want to—change that, we need to make our spaces more welcoming and inclusive of people who have traditionally been excluded from them. In the library world, I think while it's still true about the white dominance problem, it's not so true about the male dominance problem. But even in a profession that is mostly women, there's a lot of sexism.

Sometimes there's this flip side of it where people think that because librarians tend to have kind of progressive politics and it's mostly women, we don't have these problems here. But I can recall a time at a New York Library Association conference where I witnessed this weird storytelling hour where two people from a very prominent New York-affiliated library professional organization got up and told these really bizarre racist stories. It was horrible. And I remember looking up immediately to see if they had a code of conduct at the conference and they didn't. I didn't know these people, they were in the front of the room, I didn't know what to tell the organizers. I eventually did go up and say something, but having a code of conduct is an easy way to be like, "Hey, this person is behaving in a way that is specifically identified on here that they shouldn't do. And I don't want to see them do it, and you've got a policy against it, so let's do something about it." I think it's a way to make sure that we're all acting in a way that is respectful of each other, and acknowledging that that doesn't always happen.

ANDROMEDA YELTON: The organization that probably did the most to advance codes of conduct at tech conferences was the Ada Initiative, which is a now-closed feminist non-profit advancing women in open technology and culture. I was actually on their advisory board for a while after I was part of getting the American Library Association to adopt a conference code of conduct. So libraries were a big community and constituency there. Code4Lib was quite early adopting a code of conduct, in large part thanks to Bess Sadler's vision on that one. LITA Forum adopted ALA's code of conduct after ALA did. I'm pretty sure Access has a code of conduct, DLF has a code of conduct—lots of library tech conferences have codes of conduct.

I think they serve two important functions. One is that, particularly in the broader technology world, but sometimes also in libraries, there have been real issues with harassment and assault and just bad behavior. Having a plan and a procedure for handling that—and having one that you've thought of in advance and don't have to make up on the spot as a conference organizer—is just a good thing. You don't want to be caught flat-footed if there is some kind of problem of that nature at your conference. But then the other thing is that a code of conduct is a signaling mechanism to people that this is a community that is aware that conferences may not be equally welcoming to everybody, and this is a community that's thought about it. Ideally it does in fact mean that they've thought about it; it's not just words on paper.

The Code4Lib process is really admirable to me here, because that's a code of conduct that's been developed in the open via a discussion process that has involved a lot of people from the community and that we revisit periodically. People talk about it—is this something that needs to be changed in light of some situation?— and then it's part of a broader conversation about hospitality. How do you examine the conference to see who might be excluded? Are you making sure that your venues are handicapped-accessible? Are you making sure there are events that are hospitable to people who don't drink alcohol, and that there are good non-alcoholic options available? Are there color-coded lanyards that indicate from a distance whether people are okay with being photographed, because not everyone is?

So codes of conduct are ideally a jumping-off point for thinking about all the different ways that people might feel uncomfortable or excluded in your community, and what you can do to be intentionally hospitable and reach out and mitigate that. That's part of making sure that a wide variety of people can comfortably participate, not just people who happen to fit your community's defaults.

. . .

CELESTE Â-RE: Anthony W. Dunbar introduced the concept of critical race information theory (CRIT), connecting critical race theory with information and archival science, as a means of analysis from microaggressions in the work place to systemized racialization projects that Christine Pawley, Todd Honma, and others have discussed. Culture, heritage, and information professionals have been deemed gatekeepers and stewards of Western culture and collective memory. The voices of Indigenous and colonized peoples of the past five centuries have been silenced or hidden in Western cultural collections. There's much work needed to counter the myths that culture heritage institutions have, quite frankly, played a role in disseminating. At the same time, we're tasked with the responsibility of making digital portals and repositories accessible and creating, maintaining, and funding them.

This calls for a collaborative, restorative effort that bridges information silos and incorporates communities whose stories have been left out or distorted. I envision CRIT highlighting the contributions and heritages of communities of color, as well as the experiences of culture, heritage, and information practitioners of color. We need to be examining not only library, archive, and museum policy and praxis but the ways marginalized communities experience culture and heritage organizations, and assessing the institutional trust in communities of color where culture-led redevelopment projects are underway.

JARRETT DRAKE: One of the points that I've tried to make is that archives and archivists are complicit in racial oppression. Archives and archivists are complicit in racism. They're complicit in sexism, they're complicit in ableism. There are all these structural inequalities that archivists and archives are complicit in. I try to use my publications to raise awareness so that people can see the ways in which our jobs can be used for oppressive ends. The technology of it is only, I think, amplifying that reality. I think as we get into a more digital world, and a more digital archival world, the opportunities to oppress increase. I think the surveillance of marginalized people, and of oppressed people, increases, and that increase will have implications for archives and archivists. So I just try to use my publications to bring awareness to that. I try to get very detailed and tell stories, and not just sort of throw out cold quantitative data. I try to use as much qualitative data as possible to put names and faces to some of these lived experiences.

MYRNA MORALES: One of the ways that I'm looking at my dissertation is through data curation and health disparities. Initially that was my avenue in going into my dissertation—looking at data curation, data mining, and the ways that it can alleviate or facilitate health disparities, but looking at it in the context of patient portals. There's things like Association of Cancer Online Resources (ACOR) and PatientsLikeMe—places where people with specific conditions aggregate you and talk to one another. There's patient logs and medical logs and pharmaceutical logs. If I as a patient have, let's say, lupus, and I'm taking a steroid to decrease the attacking of my tissues, I can go to that and be like, "I took it today, I'm feeling bad, I'm feeling good, nausea"—list all the side effects—or "I'm feeling great." At least at that point I've figured out the titration of the amount of the dosage that I need to actually feel better and at the same time not have the side effects.

So you have these portals that are a bastion of data and information from patients. What was really hitting me was, one, up until a couple of years ago, PatientsLikeMe did not have the option of putting "race" or "ethnicity." They just had gender, and your name and age. But we all know—it's written in the literature—that education correlates to good health living because of the health literacy piece. They didn't have "education," they didn't have "income," they didn't have "race." So that data, I felt, was incomplete. I've got issues with

PatientsLikeMe, because the way they keep their portal free is they strip all the HIPAA violators off the data and then sell it to pharmaceutical companies. In looking at the data competencies and data mining, I was trying to look at whether or not librarians had the wherewithal to actually sit there and talk to researchers to assert to them the ethical implications of data mining, of aggregating and organizing data and placing it in a repository.

That's where I was coming from. I was looking at PatientsLikeMe and ACOR because those are more specific, and I think that generally, in a context of a white supremacist culture, you actually need a concrete product to wrap your head around it. People aren't necessarily very comfortable with living within a theoretical paradigm. We know the implications of white supremacy, we know we live within a white supremacist world, and "So, let's try to solve for that"—that makes people feel really uncomfortable because they can't grasp it. We can't solve for white supremacy, but we can help alleviate health disparities. That's something people can put their hands on.

So in looking at surveillance and data mining in the context of communities of color, this is what pisses me off about technology and librarians and archivists. Folks of color have always been a part of this conversation, whether or not you guys—and when I say "you guys" I'm talking about the universal library world—recognize the role that librarians of color have played in these positions. It's almost as if they're erased. I have a hard time trying to figure out whether it's because we as librarians—cutting across race and class but personified by gender—have a problem putting ourselves at the forefront.

In the end, where I really hope to make the impact is around data curation and the role that librarians and technologists will have to play. Right now, it's fucking Babylon in the data mining world. Everyone's doing whatever they want to do, and no one's holding these companies or the government accountable. Our technology laws walk really slow, and they don't protect our interests. Look at the Library Freedom Project, doing a lot of education with privacy and technology. Look at Documenting the Now, which is trying to develop an ethical perspective and honor the ways we can mine social media. Whether or not they want to, librarians have a role in being the conscience of the data mining world and asking questions—just because you *can* don't mean you *should*—and coming up with guerrilla tactics to prevent the misuses of the data mining.

JARRETT DRAKE: My article about police in New Orleans during Hurricane Katrina was really trying to describe and problematize the creation of records. There's been an interest in the archival literature around silence and erasure, and I think the act of silencing and erasing people—whether that means completely obliterating them or manipulating the story—happens at the moment the record is created. So one of the things I tried to highlight in the paper I wrote about police in New Orleans was that that the archive cannot be a truth forum if the records we obtain have been otherwise sanitized or manipulated. One could make the case that police records are an exception, and I think there's a little bit of a truth to that. But I think it exemplifies the logic of what the state does, and what government archives do.

For better and for worse, the way that government records and government archives operate impacts the archival tradition and the archival trajectory in the United States. Even though most archivists are not employed by a government or state agency—I think SAA figures show that most people are employed by colleges and universities—still the impact and the power that the state has in archives is unparalleled. That article on New Orleans police officers hopefully raised the attention and the consciousness that the records that we see, especially pertaining to acts of violence from the state—that we have more reasons not to believe them than we have to believe them. And if that is the case, what's the technological intervention? Is it having a way to create records more authentically, more organically? What are the ways we could use technology to address those problems critically and ethically and not further exacerbate the inequality, the violence that the state enacts on marginalized groups of people?

MANDY HENK: Having moved to what is a bicultural society, the question of indigeneity and technology—there's not been a lot on it that I've read, and I think that it's actually incredibly important. If you're a librarian who's working with indigenous populations, then I think it's something you need to consider as a baseline part of librarianship. It is in fact listed at LIANZA, which is New Zealand's ALA equivalent, as one of the things that you need to know and understand. I believe it's very reasonable to pay attention to the way in which technology differently might be impacting indigenous folks.

It's also worthwhile to pull in class here, because I think class is something that doesn't get talked about as much as it should. Part of the issue with the digital divide is that people don't understand how severe it is and the extent to which it exists. If you're working with students and in fact the only real access to your library catalog is through mobile—because that's all they can afford; they can't afford a laptop and they probably don't have wireless or any Internet at home so they're relying on mobile data—it says a lot about what we need to do to maintain our mobile interfaces. The same thing with ability. I think that with ability issues, making sure that our interfaces are friendly both for staff but also for our users is part of our obligation.

I think for me it actually comes back to the environment. Part of dealing with technology is looking at its overall impact, and it's very easy for us to focus, when we're doing this, on the interfaces, on the sort of lived impact that you can see. But if you start looking at technology and environment, you get very quickly into environmental justice. If what you're doing is creating a technology, no matter how good it is, no matter how fabulous you've made your interface for all different kinds of people, chances are that one particular community, namely poor people, people who might be in a specific geographic region, are being greatly harmed by it. It could be Pacific Islanders, whose water supply is in danger from rising sea levels. We could be looking at African miners who are trying to mine the minerals that are used in building servers. I think that when you're thinking about the impact of technology, you really have to go much more broad than interfaces, which I think just contradicts what I said before, sorry.

. . .

KAREN LEMMONS: Our young African American males are feeling the racism harder. They're definitely feeling it more than, I would say, our African American females. Young African American males are more likely to be either shot or killed—not just by police; by others. They feel the impact even more. So they've become cautious. Some say they become defensive. One young man just said to me recently, "You know, I'm just kind of numb on this right now, because I've experienced it so much. I'm just not sure how to respond to it on a daily basis." In terms of trying to connect that with digital literacy and digital citizenship, I believe most of them are aware that being African American, they are going to be targeted. I think some of them do know how to respond intelligently, but I think others do not. And so they lash out in different ways.

There's another part of this. Because of the arts school that I'm in, we also have a LGBTQ population as well. There's some concerns, not only in terms of their sexual orientation, but of course being African American with their sexual orientation. Our school is small and it's like a family, so we accept them within our school. This is who they are, and we're okay with that. Outside the school, I can't really speak about how their life is and whether or not they get bullied, but I will say, the students who know themselves, who are confident, who have strong self-esteem—they can handle any type of racism that will come at them. They just need to be aware, in my estimation, more broadly of how racism sometimes shows, not just in terms of violence, just in terms of the whole perception. Because I tell them, "You know, you come in wearing the shirts and the ties—regardless, somebody still may perceive you in a different or negative way, just because you happen to be a young African American man in a shirt and a tie. They still may think that you are this type of person."

In Computer Apps class, we've had some very interesting discussions about race and education in particular, because of the way our school system has changed drastically within the past few months. Our school system has experienced declining enrollment; serious mismanagement of funds by some former superintendents and administrators; state-appointed emergency financial managers to "help" manage the school district funds—only to put the school district in more debt because of their expenses, salaries and people they hired; and state-run Education Achievement Authority schools, which took funds away from Detroit Public Schools. The final change was the state legislature creating a new Detroit Public School District, now called Detroit Public Schools Community District, and dissolving the "old" Detroit Public Schools and its debt. The state will never admit its role in exacerbating the debt.

The students have some very strong thoughts and opinions about the lack of resources and the quality of education they receive. Some of them are very concerned about themselves and their future. And I assure them and I encourage them and I say, "Those of you who know who you are and have some goals and plans, you're going to be successful. You're going to work hard. You're going to have to work twice as hard, sometimes, than your competitors who may not work twice as hard. You're just going to have to do that, just because of the perception, racism and other factors."

CELESTE Â-RE: Personally, I loved learning and school as a child, but as an African American child I was bombarded with a narrative propagated by commercial media that countered my lived experience—"Black folks fail in school, black folks aren't well educated…" I questioned my authenticity in spite of my parents' efforts. I shrank to make other people feel comfortable; I think that's what many young girls do to not to draw attention to themselves. Around my friends and family, within my circle on my block, people thought I was smart, but when I would enter institutional settings, I was quiet in class and didn't talk much. It wasn't until later that I began to embrace who I was.

One day in high school, while in Biology class, the instructor—a white male—said, "I'm going to try something different here." I think he was having a moment of racialized cognitive dissonance. "You can do extra credit projects for points to improve your grade. Currently, the person with the most points is—" and he said my name! I had no idea. But there were a couple of things that struck me about what he did in the classroom that day.

First, I was seated towards the back of the class when he said my name. I was sitting there, with my friends around me, and they were like, "Hey! High five! Good for you! You got the most points!" Second, when I looked toward the teacher, I noticed that the white students in the class who were sitting in front didn't know who I was. I didn't talk a lot, though I definitely did my work, and the teacher knew who I was. The white students were looking amongst themselves trying to figure out, who is Celeste? Clearly she must be sitting up front. And the black students were high-fiving in the back. When the white students saw who I am, the expressions on their faces—I can still feel it to this day. Their eyes like daggers, they were incredulous. When I saw the looks on their faces, I was determined to stay the student with the most points.

That experience made me realize that I shouldn't feel uncomfortable about my intelligence. In undergrad, I had a wonderful math tutor named Rodney Barber that I worked with in the Charles Drew Laboratory for Science Enrichment at Michigan State University.

He would always say, "You can do anything you want, as long as you have someone who can break it down so you can understand and practice." So, I started taking science classes, and I learned a side of myself that I had submerged. I finished undergraduate with two bachelor degrees, one in physiology and the other in psychology.

ANITA COLEMAN: One of the biggest forces we are dealing with today as a society is identity politics and the binary divide. I grew up in a society that does not have the concept of race. So I would not acknowledge the important of race here in the US until, I would say, in the last few years when I started my anti-racism research. The white/black binary divide is a *huge* factor here in America. Besides the binary categories of race, the recent language of "person of color," which puts all people who are not white or black into another ambiguous, nebulous group—by the way, this is completely stupid—really affects how people interact. Equally importantly, sex, sexual orientation, gender, age, profession, religion, and class all matter. When I look back on my experiences, I see my own process of racialization and how I was racialized.

One of my first experiences came when I was in my twenties, shortly after I had implemented the online system NOTIS (North-Western Online Total Integrated System) that my university had paid half a million dollars for and had faced significant challenges in implementing. I was able to get the university's online library catalog launched by the end of the three months after I came in simply by cooperating with the computing staff and with the reference librarians. So after that, they put me in charge of training all the staff and training the different faculty. Well, I remember there was this Mexican-American woman, a library technician, who refused to report to me, and my boss, who was the library director, telling her that, well, if she didn't want to report to me, then she would be happy to accept her resignation. The woman actually resigned rather than report to me!

I was too young, and too naive, to really understand what that meant. But now, looking back more than twenty years later, with hindsight, I realize race was a huge factor there. To her, I was somebody to whom she just could not report; I remember the many instances prior to that when she'd spoken derogatorily to me, both in terms of me as a native of India, and as an immigrant. I'd disregarded it because that's what I was taught growing up in India, as a Christian—"Turn the other cheek." And so I think globalization, with all its attendant fears, along with racial hierarchy, cultural and national hegemony, and competition between minority people groups (internalized racism and white supremacy), were being played out in libraries. That's what I see now, looking back.

When I worked at another institution, this time after my PhD, I was again in charge of the library systems, and, again, I faced hostility, this time from professional librarian colleagues. And, again, I ignored it as racism and rationalized it as something else. After all, there is a lot in the literature about fears of automation, and I knew that many librarians were really afraid they were going to lose their jobs. Every time I implemented library systems, though, I've always seen it as an opportunity to expand intellectual access to our clients and also to empower and connect all the different groups, including the library staff and administration, in our mission and shared purpose. So there's really no job loss. Instead, I saw it as opening up more job opportunities, better job opportunities, more growth, a better way of doing old things, and a flourishing for everybody involved. But the sad part of it is, then people also see somebody like me differently.

At this institution, a community college library to which I'd gone so idealistically believing that my education and expertise could make a real and concrete difference, one of my colleagues, a librarian who'd been hired at the same time as me, would ask me, not once, but several times, "You are from a Third World country. How can you be so smart? Is our government telling us lies?" These and other similar quotes from librarians—whom now I see as people of Western European ancestry—who were caught up in racial notions of white versus black and hegemonies. These are factors that we don't ever acknowledge openly in the library as existing among professionals. And this plays a part in how librarians can be trained, because many students can't really learn from somebody who isn't "white" and, in their mind, incapable of teaching.

I experienced this over and over again as a library school teacher—not all students, but definitely the majority—and this does not seem to have changed either with the passing of years or the generations. I don't know the right term for this because it's not just discrimination or lack of respect or stereotyping; for example, two of my male colleagues, of whom one was African American and the other Chinese American, reported similar experiences, too. We all experienced this not just from students but, sadly, also from our own faculty colleagues and leadership. It's an inability to listen when different others speak, which then results in the other being unheard. How can you learn then?

CELESTE Â-RE: There's a part of me that still resists the world of academia. I take issue with a lot of its hierarchies—who is an expert, who is knowledgeable. There are ways of knowing that pre-date Western science. People have been taught to discount or devalue the things they know and that their communities know. It's important for us to preserve these ways of knowing digitally and make them available for generations to come. Oral transmission and communion are ways to transmit knowledge being merged with information and communication technologies.

I studied the social and natural sciences because of my interest in the spirit-mind-body connection. We see examples of transdisciplinarity and the bridging of mind-body space with technology through the use of augmented reality technologies in interactive heritage spaces, virtual reality therapy, and immersive research facilities like the AlloSphere at the University of California, Santa Barbara. I believe Indigenous knowledge systems and decolonizing methodologies temper the modularity of Western science.

ELVIA ARROYO-RAMIREZ: LIS Microaggressions is a labor of love. The project was initiated by Cynthia Mari Orozco and a group of friends confiding in each other, and confiding in their experiences of feeling marginalized in their work life. This group of people are all women of color working in some capacity in the LIS field. Some of us have known each other even before we decided to be in the profession. So because we've known each other as friends and for a long time, that created this space of comfort and realness that, I think, when you meet people in the profession, you don't really know if you can go there or not.

I think the safety of the group was the reason why LIS Microaggressions started. It began in the form of a Tumblr blog where we left the platform open to anyone who decided to share their microaggressions experience in the workplace. All submissions are anonymous. It's pretty low-budget—no-budget, actually. Outside of the Tumblr, we also started presenting at different conferences, giving the in-person platform to anyone who wished to come up and share or write their microaggressions onto Post-its. That was also really positive because—and I think this is the best part of the project—as someone who has experienced microaggressions in the workplace, it's validating to hear people's stories, and it also helps you understand that it's not a personal issue. It's an inherent part of bias in the workplace, because it's inherent in the way people categorize or locate people of color or anyone who is not white, not male, not cisgender, not straight. But just because we all have inherent biases, it doesn't make it okay.

I think that's where the activism part comes in, that not only should we be critical of it, we should also try to actively respond to it through creative and empowering ways. We brought in more friends of ours, in particular those who do zine work in the profession, like Simone Fujita and Erika Montenegro. They had really great ideas to expand the concept of LIS Microaggressions into zine form. With the zine, we've been able to tap into the profession in more tangible and creative ways, and the response has been generally positive and supportive.

I try to be careful when trying to define or safeguard LIS Microaggressions, because my inclination is to be as inclusive as possible to all who have felt microaggressed and feel comfortable in sharing their microaggressions. But because the spirit of the project grew out of conversations initiated by women of color, there is a recognition there to protect the space and make sure the people of color feel like it is a place they can have. We've also had several online submissions that are obviously jokes from online trolls, so the collective vetoes those submissions.

JESSICA ANNE BRATT: I've always had a strong sense of who I am, and pride. I feel like I was more doing things in an organic way, like, this is what I do for my institution, this is what I do for my population, this is what I do as a black librarian. Amita Lonial was listening to me, and she said, "You're doing all this stuff that has certain librarians labeled as 'radical' or 'progressive' librarians; you're just doing that same work in a more natural way."

The pushbacks I felt were not rooted in racial sinisterness; it was more money or staff capacity. It seemed a little different than what I felt other librarians have had to battle at their institutions. I think it's due to our library director setting the tone that she expects us as an institution to use our professional expertise to reach into our communities of color. We should be avidly programming for inclusion and equity. If there's a program and we're getting pushback because it was not diverse enough, then we need a way to judge our programming. The higher-level managers developed an equity and inclusion toolkit to judge programming, book display, etc. That all helps foster a culture that's not afraid to help promote equity and inclusion in the library.

I knew I wanted to do something more to help other institutions that may not have the same organizational culture, especially when Trayvon Martin's mom came to speak at our local community college, which is right across from our main location. I went there, and it was packed. It was so full of everyone from the community. It was intergenerational; people were bringing their kids. There were a few white people, but it was mostly black. Any time there was a police shooting, there's a few black managers at different locations who were like, "My community comes in and they want all these materials, books, and they want more, they want to talk about it." So we listened to them vent and rant, but no one was really taking the reins of doing more than that.

When the Alton Sterling thing happened, I think that was when I was like, I'm done with just the book lists. Partially it was that other things were happening and the Chamber of the Commerce had reached out to my library real quick and said, "We need to set something up, something that anyone in the community can attend, because we need to provide a safe space for people to talk and get our feelings. We're getting a line-up of speakers so people can hear and process and begin to start asking these really hard questions." My director asked if I would be willing to switch my schedule around and do this, and I said, "Yeah, I'm on it." And then in back of that, Amita was finally like, "I really want to make this statement, and I want to push this issue that might not get pushed in national committees and places like that." I told her that I completely understood and wanted to support.

The first iteration was a draft, and I asked, "So what are we going to do with this draft?" She told me that they were just going to pass it off and have people sign it. And I felt that people would, but they wouldn't take it seriously. It wouldn't have the impact, just seeing a document. So I suggested, "We have to create a website." Everyone replied, "A website?" And I said, "Yes, we have to do this. We don't have any time. We have to do this in, like, two days." I felt like that would make a very strong impact on people. With that technology piece, I feel like websites have so much importance; it sort of legitimizes it—no matter how terrible the website could be, it just helps. So we did a website in a couple days, and then we released it into the world. And that's how Libraries4BlackLives was born.

We've been working to figure out how we can support our colleagues that may not know how to navigate institutional neutrality or community conversations around the Movement for Black Lives. We've added a few core members to help us strategize harnessing the collective energies of the members who signed up for the pledge and provide a space and support for them. We have a few projects being developed, such as a toolkit to help librarians facilitate community conversations surrounding the Movement for Black Lives platform. We're hoping that our digital platform serves as a way to facilitate necessary, albeit at times discomforting, dialogue in our profession.

. . .

JESSAMYN WEST: I'm one of those boring dorks who doesn't really care what people know about me, but that's a position of privilege. I'm lucky that I don't have to care. I'm lucky I don't have a creepy ex, a bad family, a shitty boss who wants to surveil me and figure out everything about me, a creepy stalker neighbor, somebody I owe money to who wants to track me down, somebody who owes me money who wants to track me down. Just being a woman on the Internet, I'm actually really, really lucky that these things do not happen to me more often.

But as we see the world of the Internet getting less and less civil, especially towards people of color and women and other marginalized people, the more I think we have to be incredibly careful about the more things we allow in our lives which theoretically would allow us to be tracked, because we're now in a situation online where women on the Internet expect to get rape threats if they take controversial positions. That's an embarrassing, shameful thing about the world, but given that it is true, we then need to be double, triple, quadruple careful that we don't inadvertently tell the Internet where those women live. This is true for all groups of people who are challenged, but women on the Internet is the group of which I am a part, so I feel like I can talk about that specifically.

So it's a combination of the ubiquity of technology with the storability of the data, with the amount that people kind of maybe don't give a shit, and figuring out how much maybe they should. Part of tech literacy is trying to explain that situation to people, without its scaring them off the Internet entirely, but also making them really understand the risks so that they can make their own decisions. That's super challenging, because you have to explain the whole landscape before you even get to the point where you tell people what they need to think about their own personal safety and risk mitigation.

MITA WILLIAMS: There are definite concerns about how more and more data is collected on all of us directly and indirectly. A lot that data surveillance tends to disproportionately hurt people who are poor, who are less fortunate in our societies. They tend to be surveilled more and subjected more to restrictions just based on where they live or who they are. I live across the river from Detroit, which still suffers from the legacy of redlining, a practice by which banks would draw red lines around maps to exclude largely African American communities from proper mortgages. There's been some great work done that demonstrates that if you take those old redlining maps and overlay income levels and poverty levels of Detroit right now, you can see that the correlation between the redlining maps and areas of current high poverty levels are quite striking. It's largely because middle-class black families weren't able to keep hold of their financial equity in regular mortgages, and they became quite vulnerable to predatory financial instruments. We're still living with that legacy. With so much more data now readily available about ourselves, it's all very disconcerting.

STACIE WILLIAMS: I'm the co-chair of the Women Archivists Section for the Society of American Archivists. Many of the members of our section were very interested in not only going to but participating in archiving the Women's March. I remember as the membership started buzzing about it, there was this sort of quick, "Oh yeah! We'll just document all the things and get all the stories and take all the pictures!" It was almost like water out of a fire hydrant. A lot of people seemed to feel this way, and I felt like I was sort of trying to tamp that down with a bottle cap, just in terms of saying, "Hey. Wait. I know that you're really, really excited, but there are communities who might be a part of this who don't want to be documented, who are already part of vulnerable communities." Like, you guys can't just go snatching up tweets and taking pictures and saving avatars. There are people who have very, very good reason to want to maintain an underground or a hidden presence here.

So we need to be sensitive about that. Consent needs to be a thing. It can't just be, "Well, we're just taking all the stories, and bye." Because essentially this had already happened. There were the women who started that Pantsuit Nation Facebook group, which seemed like a place where people were being encouraged to share their stories with sexism or leadership, or just stories in general about being a woman. Well, the women who started that then decided, "Oh, we're going to write a book." Now, there were women who shared in that group who probably didn't feel like their stories were going to go live. I don't know the manner in which they're going to proceed with writing that book or getting consent with people to talk about their stories, but it was sort of like, all of a sudden this space was being mined for money, and that wasn't the understanding that anybody had going in. There were people sharing their personal stories about abortions and things of that nature.

I think in our field there are a lot of people with the desire to help, but it can get so slippery. Everybody doesn't want to be documented, and for those who do, there needs to be, I think, a bit more engagement between those communities. I've seen a lot of collecting efforts that had no respect for the actual community that they're in. They're just sort of like, "Yeah, give us your stuff." Random messages thrown out that haven't even explained what's so great about your repository that somebody would want to give it to you. Just this expectation that you're the repository, so everybody should give you their stuff. "Hey, come give it to us." No, that's not how we go about this. That's not how we engage people.

And I think, with regards to digital privacy, we should actually be looking to bridge that digital divide and move across and meet people in person. The People's Archive of Police Violence in Cleveland project is up online right now, but it would have never happened had the archivists not been out in the street, physically meeting people face to face, one on one, and allowing them the opportunity to say, "Yes, I want to be documented," or "Yes, I would, but don't use my name," or "No, I don't at all. I just wanted to be able to share my story and get it off my chest." Allowing people the ability to do that is really important. That's where something like Documenting the Now did a great job. I look at the work that Yvonne Ng has done over at WITNESS.org. It's a human rights archive, and she has these great best practices[3] for how you might want to document human rights abuses, for instance, and how to go about documenting protests—basically, how to document wrongdoing in such a way that preserves the record for legitimacy and authenticity but that also maintains people's privacy.

STEPHANIE IRVIN: A lot of what I'm looking at tends to go from a different angle, because my focus is on creating and advocating for media that people with disabilities can use themselves. And if you have autonomy, a lot of times you have privacy. If you have a fillable form for something rather than one you have to print and fill out, or get someone to fill out for you, you have privacy. You can fill out that form and apply for whatever it is without having to worry about getting someone trusted to put your Social Security Number on the document. Technology always has its various privacy quirks, but from my point of view and for those that I serve, since it provides autonomy it provides you more privacy because there's less reliance on others in order to navigate your role and apply for jobs, get books, whatever it is. So I see technology as having great promise for providing more privacy for my patrons.

CECILY WALKER: When I first got into public libraries, I had come from the private sector, where you could use whatever tool you wanted, and you didn't really have to consider—not that you didn't *have* to consider, but you just didn't really consider things about privacy. The assumption is, if you're providing somebody with a service, especially a service that's free, that people were willing to give up part of their privacy. They're willing to make that trade in exchange for getting something that makes their life easier. So when I first started working at the library, I felt really stymied and hampered by the fact

---

3 WITNESS, "Human Rights Video Documentation," https://github.com/witness/Human-Rights-Video-Documentation.

that we had this privacy legislation in place, which meant that we couldn't do things like use Google Docs for collaboration.

But what eventually changed my mind is just coming to an understanding over time that with services like Google, you aren't a person; you've become a product. It's less of an effect in the United States, but also there are some technology companies who have said that they will cooperate with any sort of investigations that are involved in the US PATRIOT Act, and Google was one of those corporations that said that. And just understanding that in exchange for this free service, all of my personal information, all the data that I've created by using these tools—whether it's sending an email, a very, very heartfelt and personal email to somebody through Gmail, or working on a sensitive project in something like Google Doc—becomes part of the machine, so to speak. It was just a gradual awakening to understand that this is not something I want for myself. I don't want to be a product anymore. Now that there are alternatives out there that are available to me, either because there are other free tools that provide services that are just as good, or because I'm at a point in my life now where I can pay for services that don't sell my data, I can make that choice.

I decided to just walk away from using Google services. I still have a Gmail address. Nobody uses it for me really anymore. Most of my address goes through another service that's based in Australia. It's not something that I feel particularly smug about, but if I'm working on a project with someone and I have the opportunity, I'll suggest an alternative service, like using Skype, for example, instead of using, say, Google Talk or Google Hangouts, or using Zoom, which is another platform that's very similar. I'll make that choice, just because it's personal to me. It's something that I care very much about.

After

At my job, I consider what people regard as the markers of tech prowess. "You type so fast," patrons sometimes say admiringly at the reference desk as we attack the catalog via keyboard. "How did you *learn* all that?" one regular will ask me when I perform an especially dexterous copy-paste maneuver. A few of my colleagues consider me to be a bit of a techie librarian because, to use Jessamyn West's phrase, I'm "up for it" when someone comes in with, say, a question about borrowing e-books. Not to brag, though—I have plenty of gaps in my knowledge. For example, having avoided ever being a subscriber to cable or streaming services, I have no idea how one watches television in 2017.

But I try to keep up in other ways. In addition to a number of people mentioned above, not to mention several of the interviewees themselves, I follow Zeynep Tufekci, Audrey Watters, danah boyd, Zara Rahman, Surya Mattu, Matt Mitchell, Julia Angwin, and others working and thinking around "big data," learning, privacy, and the human elements of this ecosystem. The areas of digital technology that seem most urgent to me are the encroaching surveillance nightmare of the so-called Internet of Things and the centralization of platforms—Apple, Facebook, Alphabet, Amazon. As a librarian, much less as a regular human, I feel as disempowered as anyone. I suppose I'm too hopeful, or naive, to really be full-on apocalyptic, but I don't share the optimism of some of the people I interviewed regarding our shared future of technology. I'm not as worried about humans' ability to adapt to the new tech to come; we will still use it to articulate our beliefs, complain about things, and love each other. What I am scared of are things like the monopolistic online platforms we use (willingly and not), the untamed machine learning algorithms all of our data is being poured into, and, as ever, the still-widespread belief that human bias never influences "neutral" digital technologies. I'm worried about the sexism, the racism, the issues with representation, the material inequities, the environmental destruction from what we're building.

I'd like to think that the digital literacy and inclusion work I do at my public library is part of empowering people to combat acceptance of the black box of the Internet and its surveillance economy, of the potential loss of net neutrality, of the over-reliance on the big platforms. Every time I schedule a cryptoparty or audio production workshop at my library, or go to a meeting about creating "digital sanctuary" in New York City, or simply try to make someone who doesn't even do email but needs to renew their state barber's license online feel as if they haven't been left behind, I have to hope that these acts represent a bit of good in the technological universe. It's what I can do at work.

In any event, I hope that readers have been inspired by some of the ideas you've encountered in this volume for your own workplace or life. Perhaps you've got a fresh approach to staff training, a tool you want to try, resistance tactics to carry out, or at least some new people to follow on Twitter. As individuals, as professionals, and as collectives of humans, we have to use the powers at our disposal to keep ourselves and our communities engaged, healthy, and safe in all of the dimensions that technology touches. Onward.

People

Celeste Â-Re is a doctoral candidate in cultural heritage informatics and a Laura Bush 21st Century Librarian Fellow at the School of Library and Information Science at the University of South Carolina. Her interests revolve around transdisciplinary approaches to urban informatics and placekeeping in communities at risk to gentrification-induced displacement. Prior to receiving her MS in library information science, Â-Re did freelance work in stagecraft as a technical director, production manager, and sound designer. She currently works as an audio archivist at a research library and serves as a coordinator of the Radical Libraries, Archives & Museum track (RadLAM) at the nineteenth annual Allied Media Conference.

Vivian G. Alvarez is a teen mentor at Chicago Public Library, developing programs supporting the maker movement and teaching STEM-based programs, coding, and digital media workshops. She works collaboratively with students to interpret, critique, and reimagine the physical, social, and cultural environments. With thirteen years of professional experience in the nonprofit field, she has implemented an innovative curriculum based on student agency and has worked within a variety of school and community contexts. She is a current graduate student at the School of Information Sciences at University of Illinois at Urbana-Champaign, concentrating in Youth Services. She is a member of AASL and was an ALA Spectrum Scholar.

Elvia Arroyo-Ramirez holds an MLIS from the University of Pittsburgh and a BA in Art History from UCLA. Her professional interests are digital archives, digital preservation, and inclusive community building.

Carol Bean has worked in medical libraries, law libraries, public libraries, and the US Department of State. Her experience with technology includes development of the Mousing Around Tutorial and the Getting Started series of computer classes for novice older adults, developing software tools, and setting up and migrating web sites to Drupal. Carol has been a member of the Code4Lib community since its beginning and is one of the founding editors of the Code4Lib Journal. Carol calls Chicago home now, where she splits her time between technology, photography, and grandparenting.

Jessica Anne Bratt is the Youth Services Manager of The Grand Rapids Public Library. She began a partnership (DigiBridge) between Grand Rapids Public Schools and the Grand Rapids Public Libraries, which received her a 2016 Library Journal Mover & Shaker Award. She has presented nationally on collaborations between schools and libraries, engaging teens in literacy through technology, and reader's advisory gap for tweens and young adults. She is also serving on the 2018 Coretta Scott King Book Award Jury Committee. Her other whimsical adventures include playing piano, writing professional book reviews, and playing Fantasy War Tactics.

Michael Cherry is the Teen and Youth Librarian at the Evansville Vanderburgh Public Library (EVPL) in Evansville, IN. He received a Master of Library and Information Science from the University of Pittsburgh. Prior to working for the EVPL, Michael worked for the Andy Warhol Museum and Crafton Public Library in Pittsburgh, PA. He is the author of "Animation Programs at the Evansville Vanderburgh Public Library" in *How to STEM: Science, Technology, Engineering, and Math Education in Libraries* (Rowman & Littlefield, 2013) and "A Picture is Worth a Thousand Words: Teaching Media Literacy" in *Critical Literacy for Information Professionals* (Facet Publishing, 2016).

Chad Clark received his master's degree from the Dominican School of Library and Information Studies in 2011. He currently leads the New Media Services Department at Highland Park Public Library in Highland Park, IL. Chad is committed to empowering people outside the technology industry to participate meaningfully in a networked world. Chad has presented at numerous conferences, including Creative Libraries Utah and Colorado and the Public Library Association. Most recently he authored a chapter about hackerspaces in *The Makerspace Librarian's Sourcebook*, published in 2017 by ALA Editions.

A native of Madras (now Chennai), India, **Anita Coleman** is an independent scholar who has now lived and worked more years in the USA than anywhere else. A former University Professor, Digital Library Researcher, Cataloging and Systems Librarian, and Manager, Anita is the recipient of a 2006 award from the Library of Congress for her pioneering work with metadata education and a 2007 Library Journal Movers & Shakers award, given to those shaping the future of libraries. In 2002 she established DLIST, the first open access inter-disciplinary repository for the Information Sciences.

Carmel Curtis is a moving image archivist who has experience working with a range of institutions and individuals including the United Nations, Brooklyn Academy of Music, NYU Libraries, Planned Parenthood, Human Rights Watch, and Deluxe. Carmel is a proud member of XFR Collective (pronounced "transfer collective"), a volunteer-run group that works to increase community access to at-risk audiovisual media by providing low-cost digitization services and fostering a community of support for archiving/access through education, research, and cultural engagement. Carmel is a 2015 graduate of NYU's Moving Image Archiving and Preservation master's program.

Hadassah Damien develops digital and analog technologies that are human-centered and accessible, and that grow communities. Currently with the Participatory Budgeting Project, previously a worker-owner at Openflows Community Technology and a touring performing artist with the Heels on Wheels Roadshow, Damien worked with Interference Archive from 2012–2014. As a technologist focused on strengthening grassroots movements, she intersects functionality with agility, practicality, and the transparent, democratic politics of open-source cultures in her work. She holds an MA in American Studies from the CUNY Graduate Center and an HBA from the University of Toronto.

Jim DelRosso is the Digital Projects Coordinator for Cornell University's Hospitality, Labor, and Management Library. He manages two open access digital repositories: DigitalCommons@ILR, which supports the New York State School of Industrial and Labor Relations; and the Scholarly Commons, which supports the School of Hotel Administration. Jim also serves as a scholarly communication, research, and instruction support librarian. He has presented and written on topics surrounding open access, scholarly communication, and community building, and has served on the boards of both the Upstate New York Chapter and the Academic Division of the Special Libraries Association.

Jarrett M. Drake is a PhD student in Social Anthropology at Harvard University and an advisory archivist for A People's Archives of Police Violence in Cleveland. His lines of inquiry converge on issues of justice, state violence, accountability, and memory work. Prior to Harvard, Jarrett spent four years as the Digital Archivist at Princeton University. While there, he volunteered as an instructor in the Princeton Prison Teaching Initiative, teaching preparatory and introductory college composition. Jarrett earned a BA in history from Yale College and an MSI from the University of Michigan School of Information.

Molly Fair is a librarian and artist, interested in exploring the intersections of social justice and information work. Through co-founding Interference Archive she has explored the radical potential of alternative and community-based archival practices—deepening her understanding of how they emerge from the context of personal collections and local history projects. She has also been involved with projects including Librarians and Archivists with Palestine and the Queens Memory Project, and has archived the collections of independent media-makers. As an artist, she believes in the power of art to contribute to radical social transformation, and is a member of Justseeds Artists' Cooperative.

Daniel Kahn Gillmor is a civil rights and civil liberties activist with a technological focus. His day job takes advantage of those interests as a policy-oriented technologist for the ACLU, and he tries to make Internet protocols to safer for everyone. As a software developer, he contributes to Debian (a foundational free operating system) and other F/LOSS projects, with a particular focus on secure communication tools and infrastructure. He's a bike rider, a reader, a vegan, a dabbler in cryptography, and a curmudgeonly gadfly. More people probably know him by his Internet handle "dkg" than "Daniel," but he answers to both.

Bonnie Gordon is a digital archivist, working in the Digital Program at the Rockefeller Archive Center and volunteering in the Admin, Born Digital, and Cataloging Working Groups at Interference Archive. She cares about sustainable digital preservation and equitable access to archives of all formats. Bonnie received her Master's in Archives and Public History from New York University.

Drew Gordon has spent the past three years helping researchers and students organize, store, share, and access research data at New York University. In a previous role Drew was Systems Librarian at the New York Academy of Medicine. He has been volunteering at the Interference Archive to support their catalog technology and cataloging efforts since June 2015 and holds a Master of Science in Information from the University of Michigan.

Born in 1941, **Michael Gorman** began work in a London public library in 1957, retired in 2007. University Librarian, California State University in Fresno, California (1988–2007). Senior administrator, the library of the University of Illinois at Urbana-Champaign (1977–1988), British Library (1971–1977), British National Bibliography (1966–1971). Taught courses in many different library schools. Editor of the *Anglo-American Cataloguing Rules, Second Edition* and its revision; author and/or editor of twelve books; author of many articles in journals in Europe and in the United States. Former president of the American Library Association. Longtime member of the [British] Labour party, social democrat, atheist, pacifist.

Jason Griffey is a librarian and technologist. He is the founder of Evenly Distributed, a technology consulting firm for libraries and education, and a Fellow at the Berkman Center for Internet & Society at Harvard University. He consults and speaks internationally on the intersection of technology and society. Griffey directs the Knight Foundation funded Measure the Future project, a privacy-focused space analytics tool. He is also the creator and director of The LibraryBox Project, an open source portable digital file distribution system.

Elaine Harger has worked in libraries for forty years as a clerical worker, para-professional, and librarian, and is currently teacher-librarian at Washington Middle School in Seattle. She is the author of *Which Side Are You On? Seven Social Responsibility Debates in American Librarianship, 1990–2015* (McFarland, 2016), an editor of *Progressive Librarian*, and one of the co-founders of the Progressive Librarians Guild. She's taught workshops in book arts and zine publication to people ages ten to a hundred, and loves being outside.

Jonathan H. Harwell is Head of Collections & Systems at Rollins College and was previously a librarian at Georgia Southern University, the University of Alabama at Birmingham, and Berry College. He holds an MLIS from The University of Alabama, an MA in Social Science (emphasis in anthropology) from Georgia Southern University, and a BA in English (minor in Spanish) from the University of Southern Mississippi. In his former life, he was a teacher in Albania for two years. His passions include collection development, finding international cuisines, and researching the cultural history of Quakers in the US South.

John Helling is the Director of Public Services at the Indianapolis Public Library. He has previously worked at libraries in Kansas City, New York, and southwest Indiana. He is a Fulbright Scholar and author of *Public Libraries and Their National Policies: International Case Studies*. He once had a pig butchered in his library.

Mandy Henk is the Public Lead for Creative Commons Aotearoa New Zealand. She's a librarian, writer, and advocate for a healthy and vibrant scholarly communications system. In 2012 she was named a Library Journal Mover and Shaker for her work as a founding member of the People's Library at Occupy Wall Street, and she is the author of *Economy, Ecology, Equity: The Path to a Carbon Neutral Library* (ALA Editions 2014).

Sarah Houghton is the Director of the San Rafael Public Library in Northern California and has been the author of LibrarianInBlack.net since 2003.

Jen Hoyer helps make things go at Interference Archive and teaches about local history at Brooklyn Public Library. She loves working through how archives can help people understand themselves and their place in the world around them.

Stephanie Irvin is Outreach Librarian for the Georgia Libraries for Accessible Statewide Services (GLASS). She's also its webmaster, newsletter editor, and go-to source for information on document and web accessibility. Prior to that she worked six years in public libraries. She continues to support universal access in libraries as an active member of the Association of Specialized and Cooperative Library Agencies (ASCLA) and the Georgia Library Association (GLA).

Karen Lemmons is a high school librarian/teacher at the Detroit School of Arts. She is Chair of BCALA Services to Children and Families of African Descent. She is a member of ALSC, AASL, and YALSA. She serves as Treasurer of the Coretta Scott King Book Award Committee. She has served on several book award committees including Newbery, CSK Book Award, Caldecott, and the Black Caucus Literary Awards. She recently served on the 2017 We Need Diverse Books (WNDB) Walter Award. Karen received a BA, MAT, and MLIS, all from Wayne State University.

Jessa Lingel is an assistant professor at the Annenberg School of Communication at the University of Pennsylvania. Prior to that, she was a postdoctoral research fellow at Microsoft Research New England, working with the Social Media Collective. She received her PhD in communication and information from Rutgers University. She has an MLIS from Pratt Institute and an MA from New York University. Her research interests include information inequalities and technological distributions of power.

Zachary Loeb is an aspiring academic, writer, activist, librarian, and terrible accordion player. He earned his MSIS from the University of Texas at Austin, an MA from the Media, Culture and Communication department at NYU, and is currently working towards a PhD in the History and Sociology of Science department at the University of Pennsylvania. He has worked as a librarian at the Center for Jewish History and the New York Public Library and in Zuccotti Park. His research focuses on technological pessimism, utopian spaces, and impending doom. He has been known to make terrible puns.

Alison Macrina is a librarian, Internet activist, director of Library Freedom Project, and a core contributor to The Tor Project.

Mark A. Matienzo is the Collaboration & Interoperability Architect at the Stanford University Libraries, serving as a technologist, advocate, and facilitator for cross-institutional projects. Prior to joining Stanford, Mark worked as an archivist, technologist, and strategist specializing in born-digital materials and metadata management, at institutions including the Digital Public Library of America, Yale University Library, The New York Public Library, and the American Institute of Physics. Mark received a MSI from the University of Michigan and a BA in Philosophy from the College of Wooster, and was a recipient of the Society of American Archivists' Emerging Leader Award.

Myrna Elsa Morales is a doctoral student in Library Information Sciences at the University of Illinois, Champaign-Urbana. Her research focuses on the intersection of library sciences and racial justice, a passion that has led to Myrna's participation in Radical Reference, which brings reference services to movement work. She currently works at Community Change Inc., a racial justice organization. As the Program & Communications Director, she founded and supports the Boston Knapsack Anti-Racism Group and the Boston chapter of Standing Up For Racial Justice (SURJ). In her past lives, Myrna was a middle school teacher and completed three years of medical school in Havana, Cuba.

Melissa Morrone (editor) is Supervising Librarian in the Shelby White and Leon Levy Information Commons at Brooklyn Public Library in New York City. She has written about and helped develop training curricula around libraries, privacy, and surveillance. Melissa is also the editor of *Informed Agitation: Library and Information Skills in Social Justice Movements and Beyond* (Library Juice Press, 2014).

Joel A. Nichols is a library administrator for Data Strategy & Evaluation at the Free Library of Philadelphia, and the author of *Out of this World Library Programs: Using Speculative Fiction to Promote Reading and Launch Learning* (2017) and *iPads in the Library* (2013). He writes and speaks about library impact evaluation and measuring outcomes in a public library setting, as well as library programming for children and teens and queer library services. He has previously worked as a branch manager and children's librarian.

Bess Sadler has been building digital repositories for over fifteen years. She is a co-founder of both the Blacklight and Hydra (now called Samvera) software projects, and is a passionate advocate for open source software. Bess has worked as the Manager for Application Development at Stanford University Library, as the Chief Architect for the Online Library Environment at the University of Virginia Library, and as a software developer and systems administrator in many other places. Currently, she is a developer and consultant for Data Curation Experts, building digital repositories for institutions around the world. In her spare time, Bess enjoys gardening, cooking, contributing to social justice movements, and reading comic books.

Béatrice Colastin Skokan has been the Manuscripts Librarian in the University of Miami's Special Collections and the Otto G. Richter Library's subject liaison for Africana Studies, Caribbean Studies, and French for the past ten years and is currently serving as the Interim Esperanza de Verona Chair of the Cuban Heritage Collection. Much of her work has been focused on documenting oral and immigrant cultures of South Florida often left unheard by the "mainstream." She has contributed: "From Haiti to Miami: Security, Serendipity, and Social Justice," published in *Informed Agitation, Library and Information Skills in Social Justice Movements and Beyond* (Library Juice Press, 2014) and "The Collaborative Archive from the African Diaspora: Access and Outreach," published in *Identity Palimpsests: Ethnic Archiving in the U.S. and Canada* (Litwin Books, 2014).

Hana Sleiman is an archivist and a graduate student in history. Her work on archive creation and appropriation in modern Palestinian history has been published in *Arab Studies Journal* (Spring 2016), and exhibited in the context of Qalandia International, Beirut (October 2016). After receiving her MA in Middle Eastern Studies from Columbia University (2013), she worked as a Special Collections Librarian at the American University of Beirut Archives (2014–2016), focusing on Palestinian oral history and contemporary Arab visual culture. She is currently a PhD student in History at Cambridge University, working on curricula formation in early twentieth century colleges in Beirut and Damascus.

Jaime Taylor is a dirty punk masquerading as a responsible adult. By day she is the systems librarian at the Center for Jewish History, in New York City. Off the clock, she works with Radical Reference; is a street medic; and rides with FWOD, a trans-inclusive women's bicycle group. She holds a BA from Smith College and an MLS from Simmons College, and lives in Brooklyn with a one-eyed cat and two bicycles.

Jaycie Vos is the University Archivist and Special Collections Coordinator at the University of Northern Iowa. Prior to that, she worked as the Coordinator of Collections for the Southern Oral History Program at the University of North Carolina at Chapel Hill. She earned her master's in library science from UNC.

Cecily Walker is a librarian at Vancouver Public Library, where she focuses on user experience; community digital projects; digital collections; and the intersection of social justice, technology, and public librarianship.

Andrew Weiss is a digital services librarian at California State University, Northridge, with over ten years of experience working in an academic library. He focuses primarily on issues of scholarly communication, especially open access, copyright policy in academia, institutional repositories, and developing better strategies for data curation. His current and prior research examines the impact of massive digital libraries such as Google Books and the HathiTrust on libraries and library users, the future directions of open access publishing, information overload, and the intersection of big data and assessment in libraries.

Jessamyn West is a librarian and community technologist and writes a column for *Computers in Libraries* magazine. She was a recent research fellow at Harvard University Library Innovation Lab and wrote the book *Without a Net: Librarians Bridging the Digital Divide*. She works with small libraries and businesses in Central Vermont to help them use technology to solve problems.

Mita Williams is a science librarian at the Leddy Library of the University of Windsor in Windsor, Ontario, Canada. She is on the Board of Directors of Hackforge, a community-focused hackerspace based in

Windsor. She blogs about librarianship at "Librarian of Things" and technology matters at "The Magnetic North." She can be found on several social networks going by the username of copystar.

Stacie Williams is the head of Digital Learning and Scholarship, which involves oversight of the Freedman Center for Digital Scholarship, at Case Western Reserve University in Cleveland, Ohio. She has worked in archives at the University of Kentucky, Tufts University, and Harvard Medical Library. She currently serves on the archivist advisory board for a People's Archive of Police Violence in Cleveland and is the co-chair of the Women Archivists Section for the Society of American Archivists. Additionally, Williams is an essayist and has been published in LitHub, The Rumpus, Catapult, and The Toast.

Andromeda Yelton is a senior software engineer at the MIT Libraries and president of the Library and Information Technology Association. In the past, she's been a freelance software developer working on library space usage analytics, bespoke knitting patterns, and the Wikipedia Library Card Project; a jack-of-all-trades working on open access ebooks at Unglue.it; a middle school Latin teacher; and member of the advisory board of the Ada Initiative, which advocated for women in open technology and culture. She's a past listener contestant on *Wait, Wait, Don't Tell Me*.

Becky Yoose is the Library Applications and Systems Manager at the Seattle Public Library. She was previously Assistant Professor and Discovery and Integrated Systems Librarian at Grinnell College and Bibliographic Systems Librarian at Miami University of Ohio. Becky received her MA-LIS at the University of Wisconsin–Madison in 2008. Her library community work includes Code4Lib, LibTechWomen, Mashcat, and Troublesome Catalogers and Magical Metadata Fairies, as well as connecting other communities, such as Write The Docs, to the library world. Becky works for tea, and prefers to use lard for her pie crust.

Works

Interviews

Celeste Â-Re, interview by Melissa Morrone, October 14, 2016.
Vivian G. Alvarez, interview by Melissa Morrone, October 14, 2016.
Elvia Arroyo-Ramirez, interview by Melissa Morrone, September 27, 2016.
Carol Bean, interview by Melissa Morrone, August 18, 2016.
Jessica Anne Bratt, interview by Melissa Morrone, September 12, 2016.
Michael Cherry, interview by Melissa Morrone, August 4, 2016.
Chad Clark, interview by Melissa Morrone, August 29, 2016.
Anita Coleman, interview by Melissa Morrone, October 2, 2016.
Carmel Curtis, interview by Melissa Morrone, October 12, 2016.
Hadassah Damien, interview by Melissa Morrone, October 4, 2016.
Jim DelRosso, interview by Melissa Morrone, August 18, 2016.
Jarrett M. Drake, interview by Melissa Morrone, August 10, 2016.
Molly Fair, interview by Melissa Morrone, October 4, 2016.
Daniel Kahn Gillmor, interview by Melissa Morrone, October 4, 2016.
Bonnie Gordon, interview by Melissa Morrone, August 30, 2016.
Bonnie Gordon, interview by Melissa Morrone, October 4, 2016.
Drew Gordon, interview by Melissa Morrone, October 4, 2016.
Michael Gorman, interview by Melissa Morrone, September 1, 2016.
Michael Gorman, interview by Melissa Morrone, September 8, 2016.
Jason Griffey, interview by Melissa Morrone, July 28, 2016.
Elaine Harger, interview by Melissa Morrone, August 17, 2016.
Jonathan H. Harwell, interview by Melissa Morrone, August 24, 2016.

John Helling, email message to Melissa Morrone, October 17, 2016.
Mandy Henk, interview by Melissa Morrone, August 2, 2016.
Sarah Houghton, interview by Melissa Morrone, September 1, 2016.
Jen Hoyer, interview by Melissa Morrone, October 4, 2016.
Stephanie Irvin, interview by Melissa Morrone, August 31, 2016.
Karen Lemmons, interview by Melissa Morrone, October 11, 2016.
Jessa Lingel, interview by Melissa Morrone, July 20, 2016.
Zachary Loeb, interview by Melissa Morrone, August 22, 2016.
Alison Macrina, interview by Melissa Morrone, September 22, 2016.
Mark A. Matienzo, interview by Melissa Morrone, September 26, 2016.
Myrna Morales, interview by Melissa Morrone, October 1, 2016.
Joel Nichols, interview by Melissa Morrone, September 14, 2016.
Bess Sadler, interview by Melissa Morrone, November 11, 2016.
Béatrice Colastin Skokan, interview by Melissa Morrone, October 24, 2016.
Hana Sleiman, interview by Melissa Morrone, November 4, 2016.
Jaime Taylor, interview by Melissa Morrone, September 13, 2016.
Jaycie Vos, interview by Melissa Morrone, August 23, 2016.
Cecily Walker, interview by Melissa Morrone, December 15, 2016.
Andrew P. Weiss, interview by Melissa Morrone, September 16, 2016.
Jessamyn West, interview by Melissa Morrone, September 25, 2016.
Mita Williams, interview by Melissa Morrone, August 31, 2016.
Stacie Williams, interview by Melissa Morrone, March 8, 2017.
Andromeda Yelton, interview by Melissa Morrone, September 16, 2016.
Becky Yoose, interview by Melissa Morrone, August 24, 2016.

Books

Alexander, Michelle. *The New Jim Crow: Mass Incarceration in the Age of Colorblindness.* New York: New Press, 2012.

Antonelli, Monika, and Mark McCullough. *Greening Libraries.* Los Angeles: Library Juice Press, 2012.

Brunton, Finn. *Spam: A Shadow History of the Internet.* Cambridge, MA: MIT Press, 2013.

Doctorow, Cory, and Jen Wang. *In Real Life.* New York: First Second, 2014.

Esquith, Stephen L. *The Political Responsibilities of Everyday Bystanders.* University Park, PA: Pennsylvania State University Press, 2010.

Farge, Arlette. *The Allure of the Archives.* New Haven, CT: Yale University Press, 2013.

Franklin, Ursula. *The Real World of Technology.* Montréal: CBC Enterprises, 1990.

Gehl, Robert W. *Reverse Engineering Social Media: Software, Culture, and Political Economy in New Media Capitalism.* Philadelphia: Temple University Press, 2014.

Harger, Elaine. *Which Side Are You On?: Seven Social Responsibility Debates in American Librarianship, 1990–2015.* Jefferson, NC: McFarland & Co., 2016.

Henk, Mandy. *Ecology, Economy, Equity: The Path to a Carbon-Neutral Library.* Chicago: ALA Editions, 2014.

Howard, Philip. *Pax Technica: How the Internet of Things May Set Us Free or Lock Us Up.* New Haven, CT: Yale University Press, 2015.

Kepple, Sarah. *Library Robotics: Technology and English Language Arts Activities for Ages 8–24.* Santa Barbara, CA: Libraries Unlimited, 2015.

Koerber, Jennifer, and Michael Sauers. *Emerging Technologies: A Primer for Librarians.* Lanham, MD: Rowman & Littlefield, 2015.

Margolis, Jane, and Allan Fisher. *Unlocking the Clubhouse: Women in Computing.* Cambridge, MA: MIT Press, 2003.

Martinez, Sylvia Libow, and Gary Stager. *Invent to Learn: Making, Tinkering, and Engineering in the Classroom.* Torrance, CA: Constructing Modern Knowledge Press, 2013.

McNicol, Sarah. *Critical Literacy for Information Professionals.* London: Facet Publishing, 2016.

Nichols, Joel A. *Teaching Internet Basics: The Can-Do Guide.* Santa Barbara, CA: Libraries Unlimited, 2014.

Thompson, Clive. *Smarter Than You Think: How Technology Is Changing Our Minds for the Better.* New York: The Penguin Press, 2013.

Vaidhyanathan, Siva. *The Googlization of Everything: (And Why We Should Worry).* Berkeley: University of California Press, 2010.

West, Jessamyn. *Without a Net: Librarians Bridging the Digital Divide*. Santa Barbara, CA: Libraries Unlimited, 2011.

Yelton, Andromeda. *Coding for Librarians: Learning by Example*. Chicago: ALA TechSource, 2015.

Articles and talks

Arroyo-Ramirez, Elvia. "Invisible Defaults and Perceived Limitations: Processing the Juan Gelman Files." Presentation at the Preservation and Archiving Special Interest Group meeting, New York, NY, October 26–28, 2016. https://medium.com/on-archivy/invisible-defaults-and-perceived-limitations-processing-the-juan-gelman-files-4187fdd36759.

Arroyo-Ramirez, Elvia, Kelly Bolding, and Faith Charlton. "Moving Beyond the Lone Digital Archivist Model through Collaboration and Living Documentation." Presentation at Code4Lib, Los Angeles, CA, March 6–9, 2017.

Coleman, Anita. "Theology, Race, and Libraries." Presentation at the Conference of the American Theological Librarians Association, Long Beach, CA, June 15–18, 2016.

Dash, Anil. "The Web We Lost." December 13, 2012. http://anildash.com/2012/12/the-web-we-lost.html.

Drake, Jarrett. "Insurgent Citizens: The Manufacture of Police Records in Post-Katrina New Orleans and Its Implications for Human Rights." *Archival Science* 14 (2014): 365–380. doi: 10.1007/s10502-014-9224-2.

Geraci, Aliqae, and Jim DelRosso. "To Collect and Preserve: The State of State-Level CBA Collections in the U.S." Labor Studies Journal (2017). doi: 10.1177/0160449X17703485.

Ketelaar, Eric. "Archival Temples, Archival Prisons: Modes of Power and Protection." *Archival Science* 2 (2002): 221–238. doi: 10.1007/BF02435623.

Robertson, Tara. "Not All Information Wants to Be Free: Ethical Considerations for Digitization." Presentation at Code4Lib, New York, NY, August 5, 2016.

Sadler, Elizabeth (Bess). "Project Blacklight: A Next Generation Library Catalog at a First Generation University." *Library Hi Tech* 27, no. 1 (2009): 57–67. doi: 10.1108/07378830910942919.

Tansey, Eira. "The Voice of One Crying Out in the Wilderness: Preservation in the Anthropocene." Presentation at the Preservation and Archiving Special Interest Group meeting, New York, NY, October 26–28, 2016. http://eiratansey.com/2016/10/28/pasig-2016-talk-text/.

Web resources

Breeding, Marshall. "Library Technology Guides: Mergers and Acquisitions." https://librarytechnology.org/mergers/.

Cherry, Michael. "Program Model: Green City Robotics." *Programming Librarian.* February 2, 2016. http://www.programminglibrarian.org/programs/green-city-robotics.

Koester, Amy. *The Show Me Librarian.* https://showmelibrarian.blogspot.com/.

"Library Privacy Guidelines." *American Library Association.* http://www.ala.org/advocacy/privacy/guidelines.

Little eLit. https://littleelit.com/.

Oral History in the Digital Age. http://ohda.matrix.msu.edu/.

A People's Archive of Police Violence in Cleveland. http://archivingpoliceviolence.org/.

Preserve the Baltimore Uprising. http://baltimoreuprising2015.org.

WITNESS. "Human Rights Video Documentation." https://github.com/witness/Human-Rights-Video-Documentation.

Media

Goodman, Amy. *Democracy Now!* Radio/online broadcast.

Leonard, Annie. *The Story of Electronics.* 2010. https://www.youtube.com/watch?v=sW_7i6T_H78.

MIT Comparative Media Studies. *Podcast: Kevin Driscoll, Re-Calling The Modem World: The Dial-Up History Of Social Media.* http://cmsw.mit.edu/podcast-kevin-driscoll-re-calling-the-modem-world-the-dial-up-history-of-social-media/.

Robinson, Phoebe. *Sooo Many White Guys.* Podcast.

Robinson, Phoebe, and Jessica Williams. *2 Dope Queens.* Podcast.

People, communities, and institutions

Rabab Abdulhadi
Amelia Abreu
American Civil Liberties Union
Julia Angwin
Kelsey Atherton
Frank W. Baker
Matt Blaze
danah boyd
Doug Boyd
Stewart Brand
Mandy Brown
Gary Burnett
Ingrid Burrington
Maciej Cegłowski
Center for Documentary Studies (Duke University)
Center for Oral and Public History (California State University, Fullerton)
Deb Chachra
#critlib
malkia cyril
Angela Davis
Anthony Dunbar
Electronic Frontier Foundation
Jacques Ellul
April Glaser
Sherna Gluck
Matt Green
Renee Hobbs
Bayan al-Hout
Ivan Illich
Institute for Oral History (Baylor University)
Paul Jaeger
Jessica Johnson
Kevin Kelly
Naomi Klein
Sarah Jamie Lewis
Mashcat
Shannon Mattern
Surya Mattu
Kathleen de la Peña McCook
Matt Mitchell
Evgeny Morozov
Lewis Mumford
Yvonne Ng
Helen Nissenbaum
Safiya Noble
Tig Notaro
Naomi Oreskes
Cynthia Mari Orozco
Trevor Paglen
Christine Pawley
Radical Librarians Collective
Zara Rahman
Samuel Proctor Oral History Program (University of Florida)
Rosemary Sayigh
Assata Shakur
Clay Shirky
Rebecca Solnit
Eira Tansey
Zeynep Tufekci
Tiffany Veinot
Addie Wagenknecht
Audrey Watters

Index

3D printing, 33-34, 42, 64, 169, 171, 308-309. *See also* digital media labs; makerspaces
Abdulhadi, Rabab, 93
Abreu, Amelia, 92
accessibility, 120-127, 134-135, 197-198, 346
  standards, 90, 120, 126
Acker, Amelia, 56, 176
Ada Initiative, 333, 339, 345
al-Hout, Bayan, 92-93
Ally Skills Workshop, 329-330
Alvarez, Vivian, *34-35, 86, 89-90, 138-139, 173-174, 218-219, 259, 316-318*
Amazon, 254, 311
American Civil Liberties Union (ACLU), 95
Angwin, Julia, 364
Anti-Racism Digital Library, 300-301
Archivematica, 156, 158
Â-Re, Celeste, *95-96, 115-116, 144, 208, 232, 237, 255, 272-273, 346, 352-353, 355-356*
Arroyo-Ramirez, Elvia, *54-55, 56, 57-58, 156-157, 274, 282, 285-286, 286, 287, 287, 308*
Atherton, Kelsey, 95

Baker, Frank W., *43-44, 91*
Bean, Carol, *14-16, 17-18, 20-22, 23-24, 25-26, 31, 69-70, 128, 129-130, 334-335, 340-341, 355-356*
Bettivia, Rhiannon, 56
BitCurator project, 56, 156, 271-272, 286
Blacklight, 152, 183, 189-190, 246,
Black Lives Matter, 94, 284
Blaze, Matt, 95
boyd, danah, 363
Boyd, Doug, 92
Brand, Stewart, 91
Bratt, Jessica Anne, *35-36, 39-40, 71-72, 109-111, 137-138, 155, 166-167, 255, 356-358*

broadband Internet, 132-133, 313
Brown, Mandy, 93
Burnett, Gary, 95
Burrington, Ingrid, 75

Canada, 30, 115, 160, 320, 327
catalogs, *see* Integrated Library Systems (ILS)
Cegłowski, Maciej, 95
censorship, 8, 76, 139-140, 143
Center for Documentary Studies (Duke University), 92
Center for Oral and Public History (California State University, Fullerton), 92
Chachra, Deb, 93
Cherry, Michael, *33, 40, 42-43, 43-45, 91, 169-170, 172, 173, 308-309*
Clark, Chad, *23, 28-29, 34, 86, 90-91, 170-171, 171-172, 172-173, 308*
Code4Lib, 65, 108, 338-345
codes of conduct, 330, 339-340, 342-346
Coleman, Anita, *50-51, 83-84, 107, 107-108, 196, 200-201, 206-207, 210-211, 211-213, 300-301, 353-355*
CollectiveAccess, 117, 118, 293-296
Computers in Libraries conference, 83
CONTENTdm, 235, 290-291
copyright, 37, 63, 196, 199, 209, 214-216, 218-220, 237, 242, 250, 284, 294, 298, 309, 320
  fair use, 195, 218
  in Canada, 160
critical librarianship (#critlib), 95, 107
critical race theory, 75, 95, 346
Curtis, Carmel, *94, 104, 156, 229-231, 234-235, 236-237, 237-238, 241-242, 265-266, 280, 310-311, 318-319, 326-327*
cyril, malkia, 95

Damien, Hadassah, *123, 284, 295*

Davis, Angela, 94
demand-driven acquisition (DDA), 192, 202
DelRosso, Jim, *83, 84, 101-102, 131-132, 205-206, 213-214, 215-217, 242-244, 244-245, 269-270, 328, 341*
DigiBridge program, 109-111, 137-138
digital citizenship, 36-38, 41, 43, 137, 260, 351
digital divide, 36, 71, 119, 129-133, 195, 328, 350, 360
digital forensics, 56, 88, 271-272
Digital Library of Information Science and Technology (DLIST), 206-207, 211-212
digital media labs, 28, 34, 86, 91, 170-172.
 See also makerspaces
Digital Public Library of America (DPLA), 58-60, 159, 247, 250-251, 268-269
digital repositories, 53, 92, 196, 206-213, 215-217, 226, 242-246, 265, 269-270, 328, 348
digital rights management (DRM), 191-192, 194-195, 197, 199-200, 203
digitization, 104, 112, 170-171, 180, 223, 229-230, 234-235, 242, 247-249, 264, 277, 281-282, 284, 298, 320
Domain of One's Own project, 150
Drake, Jarrett, 57-58, *87-88*, 92, 96, *96, 231-232, 232-233*, 233, *264-265, 271-272, 274-276, 286-287*, 287, *311-312, 330-331, 347, 349*
DuckDuckGo, 77-78
Dunbar, Anthony, 95, 346

Electronic Frontier Foundation (EFF), 95
Ellul, Jacques, 80
e-books, 36, 88-89, 139, 154-155, 191-200, 203, 313
 demand-driven acquisition (DDA), 192, 202
 OverDrive, 36, 108, 111, 194, 197, 200
 privacy, 256-257
environmental issues, 37, 80, 175-176, 196-197, 209-210, 307-314, 350
 climate change, 81, 92, 94, 164, 174, 310-311
e-readers, 88, 135, 137-138, 197, 200
 Amazon Kindle, 136, 192, 194

Facebook, 38, 48, 105, 106, 125, 132-133, 140, 145, 150-151, 219, 240, 311-312, 315
 and information literacy, 78
 digital preservation, 143
 and privacy, 29, 31, 360
Fair, Molly, *283, 284, 293-295, 297-298*
filters
 email, 157
 Web, 76-77, 111, 140-142
Franklin, Ursula, 304
Freedom of Information Act (FOIA), 76-77

geographic information systems (GIS)/geospatial data, 74, 160-165, 267, 290-291, 359
Gillmor, Daniel Kahn, *118, 143, 151, 292-293, 296*
Glaser, April, 95
Gluck, Sherna, 92
Google, 20, 127, 144, 163, 244, 247, 311
 and accessibility 127, 135
 Gmail, 28, 362

Google Analytics, 254, 269-270, 305, 311
Google Books, 247-250
Google Drive/Google Docs, 116, 148, 155, 362
Google Glass, 4
Google Hangouts, 103, 362
Google Scholar, 213, 245
Google Search, 29-30, 40-41, 46, 77, 182-183, 264, 305
 and privacy, 28-29, 254, 269-270
 YouTube, 28, 36, 42, 113, 125, 140, 171, 176, 198, 218
Gordon, Bonnie, *56-57, 58-59, 117-118, 158, 159, 271, 276-277, 292, 296, 333-334*
Gordon, Drew, *151, 219*
Gorman, Michael, *5-6, 49, 107, 180, 181, 186-187, 247, 249, 253-254, 335*
Green, Matt, 95
Griffey, Jason, *6-7, 46-47, 53-54, 61-62, 139-140, 152, 163, 254-255, 337-338*

hackerspaces, see makerspaces
Harger, Elaine, *33, 36-38, 40-42, 43, 93-94, 136-137, 165-166, 174, 180-181, 203-205, 259-260, 309-310*
Harwell, Jonathan, *182-183, 192, 196-197, 201-202, 202-203, 208, 211, 217-218, 260, 323*
HathiTrust, 248, 250, 288
Helling, John, *25, 63-64, 101, 127-128, 134, 154-155, 171, 190*
Henk, Mandy, *32, 82-83, 85, 143-144, 181-182, 205, 209-210, 261, 349-350*
hiring practices, 52-54, 58, 67-68, 153-154, 321, 328-329
Hobbs, Renee, 43, 91
Honma, Todd, 346
Houghton, Sarah, *5, 7-8, 16-17, 24-25, 68-69, 87, 91-92, 106-107, 128, 133-134, 140-142, 162, 195-196, 255-256, 331-332*
Hoyer, Jen, *112, 220, 283-284, 295, 296-297*
Hydra, 163, 246,

Illich, Ivan, 8
immigrants, 27, 32, 130, 220-221, 225-226, 353.
 See also refugees
Integrated Library Systems (ILS), 60-61, 87, 114, 117, 143, 151, 159, 182-188, 205, 292, 295, 296-297
 versus card catalogs, 180-181
 discovery layers, 65, 152-153, 182-184, 189, 192, 202-203, 246
 open source, 152-155, 188-191, 292-295
 teaching about, 43, 51
Interference Archive, 112, 117, 118, 151, 219, 220, 253, 283, 284, 292, 293, 296, 297
Internet Archive, 198-200, 215, 229, 247-248, 250, 265-266
Internet of things, 149, 263, 363
Irvin, Stephanie, *90, 121-122, 122-123, 124, 125, 126, 127, 134-136, 149-150, 197-198, 361*

Jaeger, Paul, 95

Index

Johnson, Jessica, 92
journalism, 45-47, 79, 233, 307

Kelly, Kevin, 91
Klein, Naomi, 93

Lebanon, 50, 112, 222-223
Lemmons, Karen, *38, 77-78, 137, 140, 167-169, 175, 187-188, 350-352*
Lewis, Sarah Jamie, 95
Libraries4BlackLives, 358
LibraryBox, 151
Library Freedom Project (LFP), 75, 95, 118, 257, 268, 348
Library Information Technology Association (LITA), 5-6, 337-338, 340, 342
    LITA Forum, 345
Library of Congress Subject Headings (LCSH), 50, 224, 289, 296, 299-300, 301
library school, 15-16, 48, 50-53, 72-75, 79, 82, 127, 207, 304, 325, 328, 334-335, 354
    learning to code in, 62-63, 66, 68-70, 75
LibTechWomen community, 340, 342
Lingel, Jessa, *26, 87, 99-100, 114-115, 144-145, 175-176, 208, 263-264, 307-308*
LIS Microaggressions, 355-356
literacy, computer/digital/technology, 12-26, 35-36, 39-41, 129-130, 132-133, 149-150, 273, 305, 359, 364
    of librarians 63, 68-76, 112, 321-322
    for people with disabilities, 125
literacy, data, 160
literacy, information, 28-29, 35-38, 45-46, 78-80
literacy, media, 43-45, 78-79, 91
Loeb, Zachary, *4, 5, 7, 8-9, 12, 29-30, 31-32, 80-81, 312, 318*

Macrina, Alison, *14, 24, 26-28, 30-31, 74-75, 76-77, 94-95, 102-103, 118-119, 183-184, 257, 305-306, 344-345*
makerspaces, 6, 33-34, 39-40, 108-109, 165-166, 171, 173-177, 344. *See also* 3D printing; digital media labs
Mashcat, 60, 89
Matienzo, Mark A., *55, 59-60, 103, 124-125, 250-251, 268-269, 277*
Mattern, Shannon, 93
Mattu, Surya, 363
McCook, Kathleen de la Peña, 95
metadata, 60-62, 65, 158, 182, 220, 244-245, 248-249, 266, 269, 287-301
    and privacy, 151
    racism in, 50
Microsoft, 15, 20
    Access, 114, 159
    Office, 24
    Excel, 14, 87, 114
    Word, 14, 26, 155
Mitchell, Matt, 364
Morales, Myrna, *75-76, 104-105, 327, 328-329, 330, 347-348*

Morozov, Evgeny, 95
Mousing Around tutorial, 20-22
Mumford, Lewis, 9, 80
municipal government data, 160-165

netbooks, 137
New Zealand, 261, 349
Nichols, Joel, *18-20, 22-23, 28, 36, 70-71, 72-73, 88-89, 125, 161-162, 193-194, 218, 327*
Ng, Yvonne, 361
Nissenbaum, Helen, 31
Noble, Safiya, 305, 329-330

Occupy Wall Street, 116, 144
open access, 101, 118, 193, 204-218, 245, 270, 284
Open Library, 13, 121, 198-200
open source
    browsers, 148, 188
    software, 26, 58-59, 119, 148, 152-158, 185, 188-191, 201, 246, 254, 271, 289, 293-294, 329, 332-333, 339-340
Oreskes, Naomi, 81
Orozco, Cynthia Mari, 355
oral history, 92, 220-221, 226, 227-229, 234, 235, 236, 238-241, 266, 267-268, 279-280, 283, 291
    Haitian Diaspora Oral History Project, 225-226
    Institute for Oral History (Baylor University), 92
    New Roots, 224, 289-291
    Palestinian Oral History Archive, 157, 222-224, 225, 267
    Samuel Proctor Oral History Program (University of Florida), 92
    Southern Oral History Program (SOHP), 221-222, 228-229, 278
Oral History Metadata Synchronizer, 157, 224, 235-236

Paglen, Trevor, 95, 346
Pawley, Christine, 96
podcasts, 94, 170, 171, 232
    Southern Oral History Program (SOHP), 238-241
police
    and privacy, 30, 113, 256, 275, 306
    violence 94, 112, 231, 232, 233-234, 330, 349, 350, 357, 360
Postman, Neil, 81
prison
    libraries, 238
    support, 113-115
privacy
    in archives, 273-277, 281-284
    and disabled people, 27, 121, 361
    as ethical principle, 8, 47, 253, 361-362
    and immigrants, 32-33
    and marginalized people, 305-306, 315, 347-349, 359-361
    organizations, 95

385

protecting patron data, 151, 182, 188, 253-258, 260-273, 315
in schools, 33, 42-43, 259-260
surveillance state, 80, 364
teaching librarians about, 73, 75
teaching patrons about, 16, 26-33, 36, 38, 43, 348
See also filters; surveillance cameras
professional development, 54, 70, 139, 326
in schools 43, 259
public programs in libraries
critical approaches to, 33-34
makerspaces, 34-35, 39-40
privacy instruction, 26-33
technology instruction, 3-26, 35-36, 40-42

racism, *see* whiteness/white supremacy
Radical Librarians Collective, 95
Rahman, Zara, 363
refugees, 223-225, 267, 273. *See also* immigrants
Robertson, Tara, 281, 282
robotics, 39, 166-170, 172-173, 309
Rockefeller Archive Center, 56, 58, 117, 158, 271

Sadler, Bess, *52-53, 73-74, 147-148, 152, 152-153, 163-164, 183, 188-190, 246, 305, 325, 329-330, 332-333, 335, 338-340,* 345
Salo, Dorothea, 269-270
Sayigh, Rosemary, 92-93
schools, 22, 33-38, 40-43, 77-78, 136-138, 165-168, 175, 187-188, 259-260, 351-352.
See also library school
search algorithms, 40-41, 46, 77, 183, 244-245, 305, 307, 364
Second Life, 82
sexism, 145, 326, 330-345, 347, 358-359, 364
Shakur, Assata, 94
Shirky, Clay, 91
Skokan, Béatrice Colastin, *32-33, 100-101, 142-143, 143, 220-221, 225-226, 227-228, 235, 239-240, 266-267, 279-280, 291, 304, 319-320*
Sleiman, Hana, *50, 66, 92-93, 111-112, 112-113, 157, 222-224, 225, 235-236, 267, 273, 288-289*
Solnit, Rebecca, 93
special collections
and privacy, 273, 274-276
surveillance cameras, 33, 254-255, 273-274, 276

talking books, 126, 134-135, 197
Tansey, Eira, 92, 308
Taylor, Jaime, *4-5, 51-52, 82, 87, 89, 113, 116-117, 153-154, 184-186, 273, 324-325, 325-326*
Tor, 103, 118, 140
Browser, 30-31, 257
Tufekci, Zeynep, 363
Twitter, 13, 48, 61, 67, 84, 89, 91, 93, 96, 105, 106, 107, 117, 132, 133, 140, 144-145, 151, 232-233, 240, 265, 270

Universal Bibliographic Control, 181, 186
Universal design, 121, 124

Veinot, Tiffany, 95
Vos, Jaycie, *92, 221-222, 224-225, 227, 228-229, 235, 236, 238-239, 240-241, 267-268, 278-279, 289-291*

Wagenknecht, Addie, 95
Walker, Cecily, *4, 68, 81-82, 103-104, 176-177, 260-261, 281-282, 298-299, 305, 315-316, 320-322, 327, 361-362*
Watters, Audrey, 363
Weinraub, Evviva, 56
Weiss, Andrew P., *96, 126-127, 209, 218, 244, 245-246, 247-249, 250, 264, 288*
West, Jessamyn, *12-14, 48-49, 66-68, 72-73, 101, 105-106, 119-121, 122, 130-131, 132-133, 148-149, 191, 192-193, 198-200, 261-263, 312-314, 358-359,* 363
whiteness/white supremacy, 75-76, 94, 306, 316, 330, 348, 352, 353
in libraries, 315-316, 327, 328, 331, 353-354
in technology, 335, 344
Williams, Mita, *64, 88, 93, 108-109, 150-151, 160, 164-165, 191-192, 202, 213, 303-304, 310, 337, 343-344, 359*
Williams, Stacie, *45-46, 47-48, 78-80, 92, 105, 129, 210, 233, 273-274, 307, 314-315, 359-361*
World Wide Web Consortium (W3C), 90, 124, 126

XFR Collective, 94, 229-231, 234, 265

Yelton, Andromeda, *56, 62-63, 158-159, 194-195, 214-215, 256-257, 314, 336, 345-346*
Yoose, Becky, *60-61, 64-66, 182, 257-258, 299-300, 323-324, 329, 341, 342, 342-343*

zines, 219, 284, 294

www.ingramcontent.com/pod-product-compliance
Lightning Source LLC
Chambersburg PA
CBHW051347290426
44108CB00015B/1921